❧ The ❧
NORTON TRILOGY

❋ Three Bestselling Volumes in One ❋

Peter Gethers

With an all new foreword by the author

BARNES & NOBLE
NEW YORK

❧ FOREWORD ❧

Love between human beings is a strange thing. I guess what makes it odd and all too fragile is the fact that it's so inconsistent and unpredictable. I'd even go so far as to use the word unfair. I mean, let's face it. Love will often fade or change to something else (usually hate but, if we're lucky, mere annoyance, or, if we're *really* lucky, friendship). It will way too often turn out to be false or it won't be reciprocated or, worst of all, sometimes it's just plain taken away from us. Love is the only thing I can think of that we all actually crave that also does so many horrible things. It makes our stomachs hurt, keeps us awake at night, drives us to drink, and allows people like Danielle Steele, Dr. Phil, and Celine Dion to make a good living.

Love between humans and animals is a little less fragile. It rarely fades or changes, I can't think of one instance I've ever heard of where it turned to hate on either side, and there are no afternoon TV talk shows on which dogs or cats sit in chairs and talk about having affairs with their three-hundred-pound cousins.

But inevitably, as with humans, the love we share with an animal is also taken away from us. It is not only the nature of love, it is, for better or worse, the nature of life.

That's one of the reasons I'm delighted that this three-in-one volume has been published: it gives me (and, knock wood, many tens of thousands of Norton groupies) an opportunity to take a look at the love I shared with my extraordinary Scottish Fold pal over a more than sixteen-year span. On a somewhat shallower level, it also gives me one final opportunity to get these books into the hands of Anna Kournikova so she can see what a witty, charming guy I am and take all those letters I keep sending with marriage proposals seriously.

I don't have a huge amount left to say about my wonderful cat. I think the books pretty much speak for themselves (especially with the inclusion of the Afterword that I wrote for the paperback version of *The Cat Who'll Live Forever*, which details the period of my life immediately post-Norton). But I do have an update and, as with everything else in my life, so many things that happen to me are still Norton-related.

The letters and emails keep on pouring in (well, perhaps trickling is more like it) after all this time. Norton still touches people on a deep emotional level and many of them like to share that bond with me. The occasional gift still arrives, too. One very talented artist sent me an oval rock—maybe eight inches long and weighing about eight pounds—on which she painted an extremely good likeness of Norton, front and back. One man wrote to me asking if he could sculpt Norton. I responded that he was welcome to do whatever he wanted. A few months later a package arrived at my office. It was a clay sculpture of Norton's head (it, too, was quite good, although the presentation was a bit unnerving: it was mounted on a block of wood with a small spike coming up from that, and atop the spike was Norton's head; it was a little bit like seeing Norton displayed at the Tower of London after a quick visit to the guillotine).

Let's see . . . what else? Well, believe it or not, after all these years, there is real and serious film interest in *The Cat Who Went to Paris*. Tribeca Productions has optioned the book, I've written a sure-fire Oscar-winning screenplay, reminiscent of Pinter at his best—oh, okay, not Harold Pinter, maybe Ralph Pinter—and as of this writing the script is circulating out there on the West Coast in search of a director. So by the time you read these pages, one of three things will have occurred with the movie: 1) It will be going forward and I'll be preparing my speech for the Academy Awards; 2) I'll have been fired and the new writer will have made Norton a dog and the whole thing will now be set on a World War II submarine; 3) Absolutely nothing will have happened and for the fiftieth anniversary of the book's publication, I'll write a new Foreword saying that we're still hoping to get the wheelchair-bound Adam Sandler to play me.

The biggest change in my life—at least as far as anyone reading this volume is concerned—is that I'm no longer catless. I went over two years after Norton died before taking the plunge. It happened because of an email that came in, from a woman I didn't know (although I've since met her). Her name is Judi Traynor and her email said that she was sitting around, talking about Norton—as she was clearly wont to do—and she was concerned that I hadn't gotten a new cat yet (don't ask me how she knew, but cat people seem to know these things). So Judi sent me, via the email, web site addresses for what she said were the ten best Fold breeders in the country (and Canada). A bit disdainfully, I went on a couple of web sites and suddenly was bombarded with hundreds of pictures of insanely cute Scottish Fold kittens. They were impossible to resist and suddenly I realized I was ready to be owned by a cat again. More than ready. I had the craving. Within a very short period of time, I found myself flying out to Phoenix, Arizona and the home of Patrick and Dawn Sartz, superb Fold breeders (and owners of approximately fifty Scottish Fold cats; going to their house is a little like going to the Louvre Museum if, instead of Rembrandts, the Louvre only had Scottish Folds and many litter boxes). I went out there deciding I wanted a male cat with folded ears. Naturally, I immediately fell for a four-week-old girl— every inch of her solid, dark gray—whose ears didn't fold. As I pondered what to do, her brother scrambled over to play with us. He was red and white and had perfectly folded ears. Much to my shock, I heard myself saying the words, "I'll take both of them." Four weeks later, I was back in Arizona, taking my new kittens home to New York in a brand new Sherpa bag.

Harper is the girl and Hud is the boy (named after two Paul Newman movies) and not only are they wonderful and adorable and sweet as can be, I'm absolutely nuts about them. Is it the same feeling and relationship I had for and with Norton? No, of course not. For one thing, neither of these two guys is a genius—they won't be supporting me in the style Norton got me accustomed to. But I get so much pleasure from them that I almost can't believe it. Hud is the ultimate boy—he eats like a pig and he's rowdy and needy and jumps about as well as I do. Harper's as ladylike as it gets—graceful, regal, elegant and lovely. They're good travelers (they, too, are now welcome visitors at the Los Angeles Four Seasons Hotel, and they've been to Dallas, Washington D.C., and Cleveland [don't ask]). They hang out with me all day long—one on the floor by my feet, one sprawled next to the computer—while I'm working (Harper also likes to relax on top of my fax machine/ printer; when it rings and goes off and starts shaking, for her it's a bit like a kid riding a roller coaster at an amusement park). When I wake up every morning, Hud is asleep on my chest and Harper's nestled comfortably on my legs—I am enveloped in cats, and it still surprises me how comforting and soothing that is. It makes me smile just to be finally writing this paragraph about them.

I can hear my publisher telling me that this intro is getting too long and it's time to wrap things up. So let me just say this about love and cats and, I guess, about life . . .

Sure love hurts. And all the bad things I said about it when I started this piece still apply. It sucks. But unfortunately it also happens to be the greatest thing there is. The fact is, no one's come up with anything even close to being better. I loved Norton and nothing will ever replace that or top it. I'll never lose that feeling and the joy it gave me. But things fade and change and, yes, die. So now I've got Harper and Hud. And, since they're only two years old, I'm going to have them for a long, long time. How bad can things be when you've got a lifetime ahead of you of being enveloped in cats?

–PETER GETHERS

New York, 2005

THE CAT WHO
WENT TO PARIS

To Dad. You're missed.

To Mom. You're appreciated.

To Janis. I can't believe you let me do this.

To Norton. What can I say? You'll be hand-fed Pounce as long as I'm around.

contents

Acknowledgments   ix

Foreword   1

1   Before the Cat Who Went to Paris   3

2   The Cat Who Came to New York   11

3   The Cat Who Went to Fire Island   27

4   The Cat Who Commuted   45

5   The Cat Who Went to California   71

6   The Cat Who Went on Dates   107

7   The Cat Who Went to Paris   143

8   The Cat Who Fell in Love   163

9   The Cat Who Went to Los Angeles   185

Afterword   193

Acknowledgments

First and foremost, thanks to Leona Nevler. All she did was come up with the idea for the book, think of the title, have confidence that I could write it, then come up with all the right suggestions to fix it. That's a good definition of a great editor.

Esther Newberg deserves a line or two (or a hundred) for convincing me that this was a good idea and, just generally, being the perfect agent.

Kathleen Moloney went through the manuscript word by word, as a favor. That was invaluable.

I wouldn't have Norton if it weren't for my brother, Eric. There's no way to even *try* to thank him for that.

Also thanks to everyone who let me write about them (whether they knew it or not).

Foreword

A few weeks ago, I made out my first-ever will. At thirty-six, it left me feeling slightly melancholy, more than slightly middle-aged, and somewhat sentimental. Looking to share my sentiment, I mentioned to my mother that I had—quite magnanimously, I thought—left my New York City apartment to my brother Eric's one-year-old son, Morgan. Instead of the expected motherly glow of affection and pride, she looked at me as if I were an insane person.

"Can you do that?!" she asked.

I didn't understand her wide-eyed confusion, especially since, on the scale of human accomplishment, my mother ranks her small grandchild somewhere between Mahatma Gandhi, Thomas Jefferson, and Bo Jackson.

"Why not?" I said, just a tad confused. "I mean, I hope he doesn't get to use it for another forty or fifty years, but if he does, it'll go to Eric first and he can—"

"Did you say Morgan?" she interrupted.

"Yeah. Who else?"

1

"I thought you said Norton," *dear old Mom told me.*
"My cat? *You thought I left my apartment to my* cat?"
"Well," she said, in a particularly wise moment, and
shrugged, "with Norton, you never know."

Before the cat who went to paris

This is a book about an extraordinary cat. However, the extraordinary thing about *any* cat is the effect it has on its owner. Owning a cat, especially from kittenhood, is a lot like having a child. You feed him, do your best to educate him, talk to him as if he understands you—and, in exchange, you want him to love you. He can drive you mad with his independence. He can, just as surely as a child, create a tremendous desire to protect him from anything bad. He is small, vulnerable, wonderful to hold—when he lets you. And he throws up on just about the same regular schedule.

Like children, cats exist on a separate and probably higher plane than we do, and like children, they must be at least partially defined by their relationship with their parents. And though they can do all sorts of amazing things such as hiding in the tiniest room imaginable and refusing to be found no matter *how* late you are for wherever it is you have to take them, they cannot write their autobiographies. That is left to humans. So this, as it must be, is also a book about people. And thus about relationships. And all sorts of other things cats have no business being involved with but can't seem to help themselves.

My involvement with a cat was strictly accidental. In fact, I had to be dragged into it kicking and screaming.

By way of example, a little over seven years ago, someone asked me to name ten things that I believed were truly self-revealing, deeply heartfelt, and absolutely irrevocable. This person, a woman I was going out with, asked me to do this, I believe, because she thought I was a person without much emotion, without a lot of passion. She had, I also believe, been through way too many years of Upper East Side New York therapy in which she had made way too many lists like this. The fact of the matter was that I had plenty of emotion and plenty of passion. I just didn't have much for her. People often seem to fall into this trap in their relationships. They seem to feel that if someone doesn't do what he is expected to do, then there must be something *wrong* with him. This is a much easier way of getting through life, I suppose, than having to think there might be something wrong with the expectations or oneself or the world. Or life.

I did, finally and over my better instincts, make a list of ten things I believed were true about myself. This is another trap that people fall into in their relationships (which cats *never* fall into): we do a lot of stupid things just so we don't have to be alone.

Anyway, this is the list that appeared:

1. I will never vote Republican.
2. Love does not usually hold up to close inspection . . .
3. . . . except for baseball. I *love* baseball—watching it, listening to it on the radio, talking about it, reading box scores. I am a baseball junkie.
4. Life is basically a sad thing, with an even sadder ending, so anything that brightens up a moment along the way is okay. Especially if it's funny.
5. I don't like being a part of anything—a religion, a regular softball game, a corporation, a government, you name it. As soon as some*one* becomes some*thing,* I tend to think he or she is lost.
6. Friendship must be earned. It is too important to fritter away on someone who doesn't want it, won't reciprocate it, or isn't worthy of it. As near as I can tell, people don't have all that much inherent value, but friends sure do.
7. There's very little cause for cruelty.
8. On the other hand, I'll pick entertaining and intelligent over nice any day of the week.
9. I don't care what anyone says: I think Meryl Streep's a lousy actress.
10. I hate cats.

In the years that have passed, a few of these irrevocable items have actually remained steadfast. Several have been altered somewhat, some bordering on the brink of unrecognizability. And there is one of the above that is so ludicrous it now seems inconceivable that it ever crossed my mind, much less made it through my mouth or found its way onto paper.

Numbers 1, 3, 6, and 7 remain absolutely unchanged.

Number 4 is basically sound, although I cannot be nearly so definite about the word "anything." There are terrifying things I did not conceive of when I made my initial list: oat bran, crack, *People* magazine cover stories on recovering alcoholic celebrities, wilding, sequels, and Abe Rosenthal's "On My Mind" column in the *New York Times.*

Numbers 8 and 9 are a little tricky. 8 now depends more and more on my mood and how hard my day was. And Meryl Streep's Australian accent really is astonishing.

Number 5 has changed somewhat. I have found something I am willing to join.

Number 2 clearly relates to Number 5, which will become much clearer as this book continues, and they both, amazingly enough, have changed because of Number 10.

Ah yes, Number 10 . . .

Well, now we've come to the youthful folly, a statement made in such ignorance it boggles the mind . . .

I, of course, have a cat now. Norton.

I treat this cat as very few animals—or people, for that matter—have ever been treated.

If he is asleep in the middle of the bed when it's time for my day to end, I sleep curled up in a corner of the mattress, happily braving stiff necks and bad backs so he remains undisturbed.

I take Norton everywhere I go. He's been skiing in Vermont, to a writers conference in San Diego, to the best restaurant in Amsterdam, back and forth on a regular basis to Paris. At one of that city's premier hotels, the Tremoille, when my assistant calls to make a reservation for Mr. Geth-

ers, the desk clerk knows to ask: *"Avec son chat?"*

I bought a house in Sag Harbor, a real-life Bedford Falls of a town near the tip of Long Island, and though there were many other mitigating circumstances, the secret and overriding reason for the purchase was because my cat *loves* to run around in a yard.

I've had one girlfriend break up with me because she believed I liked Norton better than I liked her (which I did). And I once didn't go on a vacation with another girlfriend to my favorite resort hotel in America because they wouldn't accept small, very well-behaved felines.

I worry about him, I talk about him (and *to* him, I have to add) to the point of idiocy, and if he doesn't sleep within a crooked arm's reach of my pillow—which he doesn't about one day a week—then I don't sleep very well. I actually worry that I've done something to offend him.

I sometimes—and this is a particularly tough one to admit publicly—let him eat off my spoon. Usually ice cream or yogurt. Chocolate's his favorite flavor, and it's a pretty funny thing to watch when he decides it's time to lick that sucker clean.

It is hardly a one-way street, however. He does all sorts of things for me that are pretty wonderful for a cat.

He goes for walks with me. No leash. On a beach with no cars around to disturb him, he's gone up to two miles, walking anywhere and everywhere from ten feet behind me to three feet in front of me. His record in traffic is three blocks, which he does most Sunday mornings when I stroll to Sean's Murray Hill market in Sag Harbor.

Norton will wait for me anywhere, no matter where I

leave him. If I'm at a hotel, I can dump him outside by the pool or in the garden, and let him play there all day or night long. When I go to get him, he will be nowhere in sight, but when I call or whistle for him, he'll meow exactly once, then leap out of his hiding place to rush to join me. I honestly believe I could drop him in the heart of an African jungle, leave him for a year, reappear, and as long as I could find the bush he was last seen scurrying under, he'd be there waiting for me.

He likes to roughhouse. His favorite game is to pounce on my hand when it's moving tauntingly under a sheet, wrestle it, and try to eat it—but he will *never* bite or scratch any part of me that he recognizes as mine. If sometimes he gets carried away in the heat of battle and a claw accidentally isn't pulled in in time when my hand comes out from the linen, he will freeze at the sound of my yelp, put his paws over his eyes, and bury his nose under the pillow in shame until I pat him on the head and assure him I'm okay.

He sits on the side of the tub when I take a bath.

If I, as I sometimes forgetfully do, close the door to a room, leaving Norton on the other side, he will howl and meow as if possessed until I open the door. He does not like to be left outside of anything I am inside.

He trusts me.

He is quite a comfort when I'm sad and makes being happy much more fun.

He has seen me through broken hearts and illness and death.

I love my cat, if you haven't gotten the drift yet.

He actually forced me to change my list of irrevocable self-realizations.

In doing so, he changed my life.

When a small gray animal does a little thing like that for you, how can you *not* let him sleep in the middle of the bed when he's tired?

The cat who came to New York

Have you ever seen a Scottish Fold?

One cat book I read dared refer to the breed as a "mutation." What they are, in fact, are incredibly handsome cats whose ears fold over in half, forward and then down, giving them a vaguely owl-like look. Their heads tend to be rounder than regular cat heads, and their bodies, at least all the ones I've seen, seem to be short, firm, and trim. Officially they are a shorthaired cat, but I would unofficially place them somewhere in-between a long- and a shorthair. They feel particularly soft and nice. Their temperaments range from sweet to sweeter. All of the ones I've met and spent time with are intelligent, though of course none have risen to the heights of brilliance that mine has.

They actually do come from Scotland. Apparently, the first one was discovered in 1961 at a farm near Dundee, by

some people named William and Mary Ross. All of the
fold-ear cats running around today can trace their pedigree
back to Susie, which is what the Rosses named the first one
they discovered.

The first time I ever heard of a Scottish Fold was when
I got a phone call from my brother, Eric, who lives in Los
Angeles. We talked about life (it seemed fine), work (since
he's a screenwriter, it was hard, nasty, and full of deceitful
intrigue), women (they were getting younger), and our
health (we were getting older). The conversation seemed
to have run its course when he dropped the bombshell.

"Oh, yeah," he said. "Did I tell you I got a cat?"

If this were a screenplay, the words *Long Pause* would
now appear in parentheses, because there was a long one.
A real long one. In that long pause my eyes rolled back in
my head, my mouth dropped open as far as it could stretch,
and I was certain the world had gone mad.

"You hate cats," I reminded him when I was finally able
to speak.

"I know," was his response. "But this one's different."

I then heard the description of my first Scottish Fold,
whom he'd named Henry. I have to say, I wasn't convinced.

"But you hate cats," I repeated. "We both hate cats. We
loathe and despise them. We always have and we always
will." By this time I think I was starting to whine. "We like
dogs."

I could tell, even from three thousand miles away, that
my brother was smiling that annoying superior smile he has
when he thinks I'm saying something idiotic.

"You'll see," he said again. "This one's different."

I have to sidetrack here.

At the time, my girlfriend's name was Cindy Wayburn. We'd been going together for three years or so, having quite a nice time. At one point, about six months earlier, Cindy had casually mentioned to me that she was thinking of getting a cat. I, just as casually, mentioned that if she did she might think about spending her nights in someone's apartment other than mine.

We argued, we discussed, we argued some more. She cajoled. I brought up my "cats don't fetch" premise and we argued even more. She even took the tack that it would be good for *me* to have a pet. I'd made the mistake of mentioning to her once that I missed having an animal around the house, that it felt lonely without one.

"A pet, yes," I said. "A cat, no."

"But you travel so much," was her comeback. "You couldn't have a dog. It would die in about two weeks."

"I know," I said. "That's why I *don't* have a dog. But that still isn't convincing me that a cat is a good idea. A cat would die in about two weeks, too—because I'd kill it."

"You've never even been around cats. You'd like them once you got to know one. And it would be good for you. You spend a lot of time at the beach house—you could have company. You wouldn't have to spend so much time talking to the old ladies who hang out at the grocery store."

"How do *you* know I spend so much time talking to the old ladies? Who told you?" I thought this had been a well-kept secret. Every summer I spent a solid month writing at a beach house I rented in Fair Harbor, Fire Island. Cindy, during the years it was Cindy, would come out on weekends, and I'd toil alone during the week, insisting that I loved the solitude. But after three days of slaving away over the typewriter (this was before I dared to punch away at a laptop), I'd begin to miss human companionship. I'd start to make a few more phone calls than usual, beginning around ten-thirty in the morning. After six days, my friends would start to keep their phone machines on since most of them didn't have the time to spend helping me avoid doing my work. At the ten-day point, I'd finally break down and start making three trips a day to the Fair Harbor market. It was only two blocks from my house, and there was usually a group of elderly housewives hanging out there, gossiping with the butcher and with each other. By my third season at the beach, I'd become a regular at the market. I knew everything there was to know about hundreds of people I'd never met. And best of all, I wasn't at the typewriter for half-hour stretches, three times a day.

"Have you ever lived with a kitten?" Cindy demanded, ignoring my pleas to reveal the Fire Island squealer.

"I've never lived with a snake, either. And I don't want to. I don't like them. Was it Frank, the butcher? Was he the one who told you?"

We went around in this adultlike manner for a reasonable amount of time—about seven hours—until eventually she decided that getting a cat for herself or for me wasn't going to be a plus in our relationship. To my great relief, our arguing ended and things went back on an even keel.

Until Cindy went to Los Angeles to visit her mother.

She wasn't particularly looking forward to the trip, since

she didn't much care for her mother. Once a year, however, filial guilt won out over common sense and Cindy would go west and pay a visit. Mrs. Wayburn—and I'll try to be as fair and objective as I can here—was an absolutely horrid woman who lived in some part of the outskirts of L.A. I'd never actually heard of, in a delightful little community called La Mobile Home Cité. If they'd had a slogan, it would have been "Come Spend a Few Depressing Years with Us Before Your Internal Organs Start to Fail." All in all, it was a great place to spend time if you didn't care about air, space, or ever looking at anything attractive.

This visit was worse than usual. After the second day, they had a huge fight. Cindy wanted to take her mother out to a fancy dinner, simply to be nice. Mom, in her typical upbeat way, said that all food tasted the same to her—like a lump of decaying, cold, gray clay—so there was no point in throwing money away on something as unpleasant as eating well. Cindy thought this was an unhealthy attitude, mentioned this to her mom, and the battle ensued. An hour after that, she was in my brother's house, crying and eating a delicious *tarte tatin* (my brother happens to be an excellent cook).

Eric was extremely nice to her, really cheered her up, and by the time she called me to say good night, she was in a terrific mood. Much better than could have been expected. So good, in fact, I should have been suspicious. She told me she was going to spend the next morning shopping with my brother, then would be on a mid-afternoon plane home. She'd decided she didn't want to see her mother anymore, and with no mother responsibilities, she didn't want to stay in L.A. The last thing she said before she hung up was,

"You won't believe how cute Eric's cat is. Wait till you see him."

I hung up, deciding I could wait a pretty long time.

At eleven-ten the next night, my phone rang.

"I'm at the baggage claim," Cindy announced. "Are you awake?" Her voice had that special singsong quality it had when she was feeling particularly affectionate toward me.

"I'm awake," I said, in much the same tone.

"I'll be there in thirty minutes."

"I can't wait," I told her. And, in truth, I couldn't.

Cindy had a key to my apartment and could bypass the various security buzzers and phones and TV cameras most people had to go through to get into my building. So thirty minutes later, I heard my front door open. When I came out of the bedroom, Cindy was standing by the door, grinning happily.

I went to kiss her.

"No," she ordered. "Stop."

I stopped.

"I have something to show you."

"You do?"

She nodded.

"Do I have to go to the hallway to see it?"

"No," she said, still with the biggest grin I'd ever seen on her face. "Stay there. Close your eyes. I'll tell you when."

I stayed, I closed my eyes. I heard her "when" and opened them.

Cindy was holding a little ball of fur in her hand. One

hand. It was so small, for a moment I thought she'd brought an extremely well-behaved mouse back from California.

But it wasn't a mouse.

It was a tiny, tiny gray kitten with a round head and funny-looking ears that folded forward and down. The kitten was sitting up in her palm, boldly swiveling his head around, gazing at all the sights in my loft apartment.

"You got yourself a cat?" I stammered weakly.

The kitten stopped swiveling his head, now stared directly into my eyes, and mewed. A quiet little mew right at me. And to this day I swear that he smiled.

"No," Cindy said. "He's not for me."

"Who's he for?" I asked quietly.

When she didn't answer, I said, again quite softly, "Cindy? Who's the cat for?"

When she burst out crying, I had a vague suspicion I knew the answer to my question.

I'd known for years that if I ever had a pet—I assumed a dog—I'd name him Norton. There wasn't even a close second choice.

My favorite name for an animal—and my favorite animal up to that point—was Yossarian, my brother's dog. Yossarian was, in my opinion, not just an incredibly cute cockapoo, which, for those of you who are strictly cat lovers, is half cocker spaniel and half poodle. He was also a genius.

He was never on a leash, not even in New York City. He would walk with you to the corner, stop, wait for you to cross the street, then trot along beside you. He would wait outside of stores for you while you shopped. He was also

extremely friendly and just generally had a kind of existential, world-weary air to him that made you believe he was capable of carrying on a very interesting drawing room conversation. In French.

I got to take care of Yossarian once, for a stretch of about six months, when Eric was living in Spain. I was living in a fifth-floor walk-up in the West Village, a divey little apartment, and Yossarian moved in with me. It didn't take long for me to realize that Yos wasn't wild about climbing up and down the five flights of stairs whenever he had to go for a walk. He especially wasn't wild about it in winter, when the snow and ice were already tough enough on his L.A.-tenderized paws.

I'd had him perhaps all of a week when, to my horror, the little guy started limping. I noticed it as we were strolling down Greenwich Street. His right front paw was definitely curled up in front of him, and he was favoring it. I went over to him, picked him up, and checked him out. I couldn't find anything wrong, but he was looking at me in such a pathetic way, clearly the dog was in great pain. I set him down just long enough for him to do his thing, then scooped him back up, carried him back to my building and up the five flights to my apartment.

I decided not to panic. I figured I'd give it a few days, then if the limping continued, I'd take him to the vet.

Yos seemed fine in the apartment, perhaps moving around just a bit slower than usual. Once he'd get outside, though, the limping would start up. I'd have to carry him around, set him down when he had to relieve himself, then pick him back up and return to my apartment with the dog cradled in my arms.

On the third day of this routine—he was now limping slightly even in the apartment and I was caringly carrying him up and down the stairs three times a day—we went for our afternoon stroll. I set Yosie down on the snow, and since I was with a woman friend, she and I walked on ahead to give him some privacy. After about half a block, I turned back to see how my ward was doing. He was doing just fine. In fact, he was doing so well, he was racing around the sidewalk in front of my building, playing with another dog. I couldn't believe it. I mean, this dog was *moving*. Full weight on that right front paw.

"Yossarian!" I called.

The dog froze. Didn't move an inch. Then he looked down at the snow on the ground, looked at me, looked back down at his paw, which was resting on the snow, one more look at me, and his paw shot up in the air in a desperate attempt to replicate the pathetic position he kept it in when he was feigning his limp.

"Forget it," I said. "The free ride is over."

If dogs can shrug, Yossarian shrugged, put his paw back down, and resumed his frolic with his playmate. That was the end of the limp.

I wasn't the only one who felt that Yossarian was far more human than the normal quadruped, by the way. A few years ago, when he was thirteen years old and getting sickly, my brother had a "roast" for him. About twenty people showed up with presents for the dog, Eric served food and drink, and everyone proceeded to tell their favorite Yossarian stories. I called from New York just to make sure that someone told my "limping" story, which was by then part of the Yossarian legend.

When, about a year after that, Yos died, I promise you, everyone who was there that day was truly happy that they'd gotten to tell him how much he'd meant to them over the years.

Ever since Eric had taken the *Catch-22* name for this brilliant little dog, I'd been trying to come up with a comparable name for my future pet, which I always assumed would also be a dog. Dunbar was a consideration, but it came from the same book, so I discarded it. McMurphy was a possibility, but then the movie version of *Cuckoo's Nest* came out and I hated it, so that was the end of McMurphy. I went further back in the annals of literature and quickly rejected everything from Falstaff to Tristram to Verloc, then moved on and rejected Malloy, Zorba, and finally even Snoopy.

I considered Steed (or Emma, if it was a female) from "The Avengers," but somehow those just didn't stay with me. Travis stuck around for about six months—that being the name of the character played by Malcolm McDowell in *If . . .* and *O Lucky Man!*—but then a friend of mine got a dog and named him Travis as in Travis McGee.

I switched to the sports field in a move of anti-intellectual desperation.

I couldn't name a pet Willie. What if some poor oaf thought I was naming it after Willie Davis or Willie Wilson or some other inferior imitation of the godlike Mays? I couldn't risk it. None of my other idols' names really lent themselves to being repeated over and over again while trying to coax a four-legged animal out from under the bed. Muhammad? Julius? Roger "the Dodger" Staubach? No.

Jim Brown? Forget it. I'd wind up with a pet who'd periodically throw me off a balcony. I was just about to settle for Clyde, figuring I would have a very cool pet who would never panic under pressure and would play great D, when, about two years before Cindy walked into my apartment with a cat, the name came to me.

I'm a television baby. I always watched it, I always liked it, when I grew up I even wrote for it. Sitcoms were always my fave (once "Bronco Lane" and "Sugarfoot" went off the air). From an aficionado's lofty view, there are only a handful of sitcoms that deserve the label "great." I'm not talking about campy "Gilligan's Island"–type garbage. I'm talking great writing, great acting, great characters. "Bilko" has to be near the top. Same with "The Mary Tyler Moore Show" and "The Dick Van Dyke Show" and, later, "Barney Miller" and "Taxi." But there's one that's in a class by itself. The others aren't even close. Best characters, best fat jokes, best sets, best straight man (or woman, actually), best Grand High Exalted Wizard, and the two best performances in TV sitcom history. Obviously, I'm talking about "The Honeymooners," and like a flash, I had visions of one day—and then every day for years and years—being able to come home from a hard day's work, call out, "Norton, pal o' mine, I'm home!" and see a little furry guy come leaping toward me, licking my face in a frenzy of joy.

As soon as this little cat mewed up at me from Cindy's hand, I knew that Norton had finally arrived.

I knew one other thing, too. And this came in just as much of a flash as the name.

It was love at first sight.

It doesn't make sense. There's no explanation. It's never happened to me before or since with man, woman, or beast, and I don't know if it ever will again.

I started to get angry at Cindy. I wanted to yell. I began to sputter and to say things like "How could you do this!" I was all set to pace and wave my arms around in the air like a lunatic. But I wasn't able to do any of those things. I didn't have the opportunity. Cindy was busy doing her impersonation of Lucy when Ricky comes home after finding out she disguised herself as a painter to get an audition at the club. "I thought you'd like him . . . *sniff* . . . Eric said you'd like him . . . *sniff* . . . I'm sorry . . . I thought . . . *sniff* . . . *Unaughhhhwaaaaaaaaa* . . ." I knew I wasn't going to get anywhere in that direction, so I turned to you-know-who. With my mouth still open, I looked into the little cat's eyes and I melted. Just dead away, gone, total mush.

Cindy, now switching to her Laura Petrie mode, trying not to cry but letting me know she might start again any moment, held out her hand, and I took the kitten from her. Having absolutely no experience with babies of any species—human or four-legged—I held him kind of awkwardly. Cupping him in my right palm, which I supported with my left, I brought him closer to me, raising him up to my face until we were nose to nose. I don't think he could have been more than six inches long or weighed more than two pounds. He was a light, soft gray with irregular patches of dark gray circling his body. Bits of white spread across the top of his paws and ringed around his little black-and-orange nose. Three startling lines of black began right between his eyes and streaked all the way down his back, broadening by his tail so that his back half was darker than

his front. His tail, even then, was very bushy, with black rings around it. It looked like a tail that could have belonged to a raccoon. His eyes were huge, twice too big for his head, oval and green. I had absolutely never in my life seen anything that was so cute, so independent, so smart, or anything that had ever looked quite so much as if it belonged to me. He never flinched or shifted his gaze away from me. He simply mewed once more and licked me more or less on my right eyelid with a sandpaperlike tongue the size of a small bristle on a paintbrush.

"He's six weeks old," Cindy said in a little bit of a hushed tone, drying her eyes. "And there's something very special about him. I don't think he's just a normal cat."

I switched him to my left hand and ran my right hand lightly over him, from his head to his tail, the first time I'd ever petted a feline.

"Of course he's not just a normal cat," I said. "How could he be? He's mine."

The shopping Cindy had done with my brother, of course, was to go out and buy this little cat, Norton. When she had seen what a Scottish Fold looked like, she flipped. She told Eric all about how she wanted to get a cat and how I wanted a pet but refused to consider a cat, and he, having known me for a much longer time than she had and knowing how I'd react when I saw a Fold, told her they'd go looking the next morning.

They drove out to the Valley, to the breeder where Eric had gotten Henry. The breed was, at the time, relatively unknown but already on the expensive side. Eric had paid

three hundred dollars for his. (Now, believe it or not, a good Scottish Fold will cost you up to fifteen hundred smackers.) He was a big believer in the theory that if you're going out to buy something, it's much better to spend as much money as possible and be as impractical as you can.

As luck would have it, the breeder had recently ushered in a new litter of Folds. She had too many Folds. Because they were so expensive, she didn't think she could sell them all before they got so big that they'd get underfoot. She knew Eric, she took a liking to Cindy, so she gave them one for seventy-five dollars, with the simple promise that they'd give the kitten the best possible home.

"Here, I'll give you my favorite," she told them.

She picked a six-week-old cat out of a cardboard box and handed him over. Along with his breeding papers, she gave them an article that had appeared the week before in the *San Fernando Valley Register.* The story was on exotic breeds of cats, and as an example of the exotic Scottish Fold, there was a photograph of the cat Cindy was holding. For the use of the article, the kitten had been named Baby, and the caption under his photo said, "Unlike some deceptively named feline families—Himalayans, for example, have no tie to the mountains—Scottish Folds like this kitten, 'Baby,' actually originated in Scotland."

"He's a star," the breeder said.

"I sure hope so," Cindy told her.

He certainly acted like a star on the trip home. Cindy was a bit nervous taking such a young animal on the airplane. She wasn't sure how he'd react, what he'd do to go to the

bathroom, whether such a long flight would make him neurotic the rest of his nine lives. She quickly found out he wasn't the neurotic type. She had him in a little box, but minutes into the flight, she lifted him onto her tray table just to check him out. He yawned, lay down, and immediately went to sleep. She figured she'd leave him there until either the cat or the stewardesses started to freak out. Neither happened. The cat sat or slept on the tray, happy as could be, for the entire trip. The dread bathroom problem never came up. (As Norton has proved on many a flight since, he either has an abnormally strong bladder or an equally dominant sense of decorum. On this initial trip and on hundreds to come, he simply waited until proper facilities presented themselves.) Occasionally he would stretch, look around, then sit back down. He meowed only twice. Both times Cindy cooed at him and stroked him—and he made it very clear that that was exactly why he'd bothered to speak. The stewardesses fussed over him delightedly, brought him milk, even picked him up to show him off to various passengers. Through it all, the little kitten acted as if he'd logged as many miles as Chuck Yeager.

In the taxi from the airport to my apartment, he scrambled on the backseat over to the door handle, which he stood on, stretching up to peer out the window as the car drove him into Manhattan.

"It was weird," Cindy said, as I held him in my hand. "Not only did he have absolutely no fear, he acted like he knew where he was going—*and was looking forward to getting there.*"

The cat now wiggled a little bit in my palm, so I gingerly set him down on the floor.

"He'll be scared now," Cindy told me. "Kittens are always scared of new surroundings. This place'll seem huge to him and that's frightening to a cat."

Uh-huh.

My frightened kitten meandered over to a couch in my living room. Then he strolled over to the couch opposite it. Then he went back, halfway between the two, plopped down on the rag rug, and went to sleep.

I watched his little chest moving up and down while he slept. I'd never seen anything conk out quite so quickly. I knew I had an imbecilic grin on my face, but I couldn't help it.

"Norton," I called to him softly. "Norton . . ."

The kitten's eyes opened slowly. First they were just a slit, then they held at half-open, then his head tilted and he was looking up at me.

I smiled at Cindy.

"Look," I said. "He already knows his name."

The cat who went to Fire Island

3

Most people think that owning a cat is a lot less of a responsibility than owning a dog.

They're wrong.

They're especially wrong if a particular owner happens to decide that a particular cat is so sensitive, intelligent, and aware of what's happening that he has to be treated on a higher level than the owner's fellow human beings.

There actually is a certain logic to this. After all, people have *choices.* They do not have to be friends with someone they don't like or who mistreats them. They do not have to be alone if they choose not to be. (This is a general classification, remember: it does not necessarily apply to those people who don't use deodorant in the summer, think Sandra Bernhard is funny, or who idolize the Robert De Niro character in *Taxi Driver.*) They do not have to eat only when someone remembers to feed them. And, most of all, if the person they live with comes home late, most people do not have to worry that that person has been eaten by a predator.

Cindy thought I was going a little overboard with this last comparison, but *she* was the one who gave me a book called *The Natural Cat.*

She gave it to me because it was rather immediately apparent that Norton was not only breaking down my resistance to *him,* he was breaking down a lifetime resistance to his entire species.

First of all, it's very difficult to resist anything that is so vulnerable. And there are very few things more vulnerable than a six-week-old kitten. Second of all, he didn't *act* vulnerable, which is even harder to resist. He scrambled, he clawed, he nudged; he took over my apartment is what he did. Third of all, he took over *me.*

His first sneak attack in this regard came in the middle of the night.

Cindy and I had a very particular sleeping order. I always slept on the left side of my bed, she on the right. I slept on my side; she curled around my back with her arms wrapped around me.

We weren't sure whether Norton should sleep on the bed. We didn't know if he'd wriggle around all night, keeping us awake, a prospect which didn't much excite me. We also didn't know if he'd even *want* to sleep with us. Maybe we were too huge and frightening. So we decided to leave it up to him.

His first night, we heard him sliding around the living room floor as we were falling off to sleep. It seemed as if

he'd made his choice—he'd find his own bed. Fine with me. No problem. Everyone knew cats weren't as affectionate as dogs, anyway. He could sleep wherever he damn pleased.

I awoke in the morning, as usual a few minutes before Cindy. With my eyes half open, I listened for the sounds of a small cat at play. Nothing. A bit worried, I strained to listen more carefully. It seemed natural that a newborn kitten should be awake causing trouble. Still nothing.

Then I felt a very light stirring from my pillow, and I rolled my eyes down to get a look.

What I saw was a small, gray ball of fluff, comfortably resting under my cheek and neck. He was awake, his eyes wide open, but he wasn't moving. Not an inch. He was staring straight at me, waiting for me to make the first move.

Without lifting my head, I slowly twisted my left arm, bringing it up so I could pet him. With two fingers, I stroked the top of his head, rubbing between his eyes down to his nose. He shifted, ever so slightly, stretching his neck so I could scratch under his chin. We stayed like that for several minutes, the cat stretched out luxuriously, the owner scratching away.

I felt pretty good.

He'd chosen me to sleep with. Not just the bed. Me. Not Cindy. *Me.*

It was *embarrassing* how good it felt.

I swiveled around to glance at Cindy. She was awake now, too, watching us and smiling.

Thus began a whole *new* sleeping arrangement. When Cindy spent the night, Norton would stay in the living room until we fell asleep. But every morning, when I awoke he'd be scrunched against my neck, partly under my cheek, absolutely wide awake, waiting for me to scratch under his chin.

If it was just the two of us—me and the cat, not me and Cindy—Norton would take Cindy's place before the lights went out. He'd lie in her spot on the bed, head on her pillow, body stretched out like a person, usually under the covers. I'd turn my back to him, and he'd snuggle up there, exactly as Cindy did. In the morning he'd still be on her pillow, wide awake, staring straight at me, waiting for me to rise and shine. When I'd open my eyes, he'd move a few inches to me, lick my eyes or my forehead, then move to his under-the-cheek-and-neck position for five minutes of petting and scratching.

He never, ever woke me up. Never, ever meowed for breakfast. *A deux* or *ménage à trois,* he would stay quietly in bed until I was awake, wait until his morning petting, then he'd get up and join me for breakfast in the kitchen—one black coffee, one chicken and kidney in cream sauce deluxe.

His next sneaky little way of worming himself into my life was my own fault.

I wanted to show him off. (I knew that was a bad sign, but there you have it; there was nothing I could do about it.) So I started taking him places. Not far away. Just to friends' apartments. He was, needless to point out, quite a hit, proving to be as fearless in these apartments as he was in mine, prowling and hopping around from room to room. Some of these friends had cats of their own and were a bit worried about possible confrontations. I couldn't imagine how anything—even a rival cat—could object to Norton, and as it turned out, I was right. Most of the time, the cat whose turf we were invading would immediately hiss and

circle Norton, whom I'd have plopped down in the middle
of the living room. Norton would peer over at the tough
king of the castle, give him a look as if to say, "Who are you
kidding?"; then he'd roll over on the ground and look as
cute as an animal could look. The grown cat would, more
or less, have no choice but to come over and be friendly.
Otherwise he'd look like a warmongering idiot in front of
his owner.

It seemed like too much of a bother, on these goodwill
tours, to lug his carrier around the city, especially when he
was so tiny, so I'd simply put on a windbreaker or a raincoat
and stick Norton in the pocket. Walking a few blocks was
no problem. He'd sit calmly, occasionally sticking his head
out over the pocket's rim to peer around, then retreat back
inside. He actually got pretty good at this form of transportation. Even on long subway rides to the Upper West Side.
The noise didn't seem to frighten him; rather it intrigued
him. The sudden jarring stops and starts struck him as something of a fun game. The only drawbacks were (1) the bums
who, thinking they might be hallucinating, would want to
touch him to make sure he wasn't the step before the pink
elephants, and (2) the garrulous strangers who were positive that a cat in one's pocket was an open invitation to tell
life stories, tales of woe, or worst of all, adorable pet anecdotes of their own.

On Saturdays, I started to get into the habit of taking him
with me on my errands. He never squawked about this; in
fact, I think he liked it. Most shops were happy to see his
little head pop out and swivel around. In my local bakery
he came away with quite a few scraps of cookies and sweet
rolls and he developed a serious taste for jelly doughnuts;

in the local grocery store he often lucked into pieces of cheese and the occasional chicken part. He'd even stay quiet—in an oversized pocket—for a relaxing brunch in a Village restaurant on a Sunday afternoon. A few waiters and waitresses wondered why I always ordered a glass of milk—a short, round glass if at all possible; if not, a tall glass and an empty saucer on the side—to go with my Mimosa or Bloody Mary, but no one ever said anything. To this day, I'm sure there are several maître d's and busboys who talk about the bearded fellow who always left little puddles of milk under his seat. You'll just have to take my word for it that I was actually quite neat. Norton, however, is one of the sloppiest lappers I've ever seen. When he's thirsty, his tongue reminds me of nothing so much as one of those machines that swirls paint around, nearly at the speed of light, on small canvases so kindergartners can create instant works of abstract art.

I got used to keeping my hand inside my coat on my travels about town, and constantly stroking this soft little cat. He got used to these hour- or two-hour-long adventures. When I'd leave the house without him—as I was forced to do far more often than I liked—he would look way too sad. As a result, it was taking me longer and longer to get out the door. (Have you ever spent five minutes explaining to a cat about your day's agenda and how it just wouldn't work if he came on your important meetings with you? Have you ever tried it when you have company? A word of advice: Don't.) Norton clearly didn't like being left behind. He much preferred being carried around in a pocket to spending the day dozing on the windowsill.

My only problem other than my five- and ten-minute

out-the-door soliloquies, was that summer was coming up. Even for Norton I didn't think I could wear an overcoat in the New York summer.

Meanwhile, since it was immediately apparent that Norton and I were joined at the hip (or the pocket, as the case may be), Cindy did two things. First, she got a cat of her own, a normal full-eared cat for whom she paid Bide-a-Wee five dollars. She named him Marlowe, as in Chandler and *The Big Sleep,* not the sixteenth century and *Tamburlaine.* I couldn't really object. I mean, here I was with my own cat who was sleeping on my head and for whom, twice in the first two weeks of our relationship, I'd stayed home from work so I could get to know him better. I no longer had a leg to stand on as far as cat-prevention was concerned. Besides, I liked Marlowe quite a bit. He was just as sweet as Norton. (In fact, in some ways, sweeter; it was clear from the beginning that Norton had a touch of the rebel in him. He liked to test me. Little things like scratching at the couch. To be perfectly honest, my attitude was that if scratching the couch gave him so much pleasure, let him scratch. It wasn't that big a deal to get a new couch every so often. But a horrified Cindy insisted that was no way to raise a kitten, so whenever Norton scratched, I would tell him "no!" just the way Cindy told me I was supposed to. He was definitely smart enough to realize he was doing something wrong and would immediately respond to my warning. He would stop scratching at once and move about three feet away from the leg of the couch. Then, watching me all the way, he would, inch by inch, slink back to the leg, stick his paw out, and give the thing one or two good rakes. I would clap my hands, say "no!" again, and he would

scamper those three feet away. I'd turn my back and, two minutes later, hear the familiar scritching of claws on canvas. I must admit I was proud of this James Dean–like adventurous streak and secretly encouraged it, whereas Cindy loved the fact that *her* cat wouldn't *dream* of doing anything to upset her.) Marlowe was quite handsome in his own way, too, a beautiful dark coat streaked through with black and brown, though even Cindy had to admit he wasn't in my guy's league. He was also a much better jumper than Norton. Marlowe could do something that never failed to amaze me. He could jump from the floor to the top of an open door and balance himself there. Norton used to eye this physical agility with some envy, I believe, though he soon realized his own limitations and comfortably settled for intellect over brawn. Overall, though, as truly nice as Marlowe was, he was *normal.* He was a cat. Norton was something more.

The second thing Cindy did was buy me the aforementioned book, *The Natural Cat,* so I could actually learn something about my animal. It's a wonderful little book, and I quickly studied up on such things as how cats clean themselves and how they adjust to litter boxes and all the things cat owners around the world already know and don't need to read about here. To me, it was all fascinating, much like discovering a whole new culture. I had never heard anything purr before, and I thought it was very possibly the most wonderful, soothing noise I'd ever listened to. I liked nothing better than having Norton stretch out on the bed or couch with me lying on top of him, the full weight of my head plunked down right in the middle of his body. He would purr and purr and purr in delight. I soon realized I

was passing up reruns of "The Rockford Files" in order to spend an hour listening to this motorboat sound.

I had also never seen fur on anything's back stand straight up or claws that retracted. I was particularly fascinated by his claws because, as much as he loved to scratch, his claws *never* came out when we were roughhousing. He made it quite clear that such a thing was unthinkable, and I found myself touched and moved by his instinctive gentleness. In general, I was extremely interested in reading about the whys and wherefores and history of all such behavior and physical reactions.

In the last chapter of *The Natural Cat,* the psychology of the feline is discussed. At some point in the chapter, it says to watch and notice: if you come home from work every day at six o'clock, when you arrive at the regular hour, your cat will be dozing contentedly in some comfortable spot. He will be relaxed and calm when he lifts his head up to welcome you home. HOWEVER: if you usually come home at six o'clock, and then you don't come home until eleven or so, when you walk in the door your cat will be pacing up and down, nervously wondering if you've deserted and abandoned him. This is because his fifty million years of jungle instinct will have taken over, and the cat is sure that you've been eaten by a predator. He has no idea you went for a drink with a co-worker, then hit a ballgame with a pal. The only thing he can conceive of is that you were minding your own business, lapping up some water from a lagoon, and some tusked animal weighing over two tons came along and bit you in half.

I started worrying about this. Not obsessively, not day in and day out. I wasn't that far gone. But if Cindy and I were

out to dinner and it got past nine o'clock, I would start to get a little edgy.

"What's the matter?" she'd say.

"Nothing," I'd respond. Then I'd glance at my watch nervously.

"What *is* it?" she'd want to know. "You're wriggling. You only wriggle when there's something wrong."

"It's nothing. Really. I'm just a little tired."

"Do you want to go?"

"No, no," I'd say. "Absolutely not. I'm fine. Let's stay."

Five minutes would pass and I'd nudge her under the table. "Maybe we should go *now,*" I'd whisper. And we would, much to Cindy's confusion and annoyance.

When we got to my place, Norton would be standing by the front door, looking, I was sure, incredibly stressed out. I'd pick him up, pet him for a while, reassure him that his dad had survived another day in the nasty jungle, tell him what a great dinner he was in store for, then sigh with relief and exhaustion that a crisis had been averted.

After a couple of weeks of this, Cindy figured out what was going on. She took *The Natural Cat* off my bookshelf and threw it away. She also forbid me to read anything or learn anything more about cats. She decided it was too dangerous.

The germ had already been forming, but this whole predator business put it over the top. I was beginning to think that, whenever and wherever possible, I should just take Norton with me. I would be a lot more relaxed, and I was pretty sure he'd enjoy tagging along with his dad rather

than sitting around my apartment all day. The short pocket trips worked okay. Why not the more major excursions?

Cindy wasn't as supportive as I'd hoped. She told me I was crazy.

"You can't just take your cat on trips all over the place," she informed me.

I didn't understand why not. "He likes me. He's pretty calm. He goes to your house okay. What's the big deal?"

"The big deal is he's a *cat*. Cats don't like things like that."

"*He* does."

"He's a kitten. He'll go along with anything. When he gets bigger, he's going to hate it."

"I don't think so," I said. "I think he'll go for it."

"It just doesn't work that way," she said, shaking her head.

"Well, I'm gonna try it," I told her. "I like him. I like being with him. I don't see why he won't like being with me."

In fact, I had a place in mind I knew he would love to visit.

Fire Island is about an hour's drive or train ride from Manhattan. As mentioned, I rented a house there every summer, in the town of Fair Harbor. It was a wonderful little guest house, painted a deep sky blue; one room, comfortably furnished, with a Pullman kitchen and a sleeping loft. It had a cozy deck, which, even though the beach was only fifty feet away, I could rarely bring myself to leave. The entire island is approximately twenty-six miles long and about two blocks wide from bay to beach. There are many different little communities, each with distinctly separate

rules and equally separate lifestyles. The rules range from *No Eating in Public* in one particularly crowded community to *No Campfires on the Beach* in a particularly cautious community to *No Rich People's Seaplanes Landing Here or We'll Blow Your Head Off* in one particularly blue-collar community. The lifestyles range from *Wild-Divorced-Heterosexual-Manhattanites-Discoing-the-Night-Away-in-Desperate-Search-of-a-New-Year's-Eve-Date* to *Boring-Please-Don't-Give-My-House-a-Funny-Name-I'm-Here-to-Relax-Not-Talk-to-Strangers* to *If-You're-Not-Gay-and-Haven't-Rented-*Can't-Stop-the-Music*-at-Least-Three-Times-Don't-Even-Bother-to-Step-Off-the-Boat.* I was in one of the Boring-Please-etc.-etc. communities and I liked it fine. In fact, I thought it was pretty close to heaven. There was one restaurant, which I dined in once a summer, a little grocery store, which, as mentioned, I went to a little too often, and a five-and-dime run by a woman who used to be a Rockette. (She was kicking when *The Men,* Brando's first film, played there.) There were a lot of nice families around me with a lot of nice kids. Best of all, cars aren't allowed on Fire Island. If you don't want to walk, you take a bike. If you don't want to do either of those, your only other choice is to sit in the sun and listen to the waves lap up to the shore. It seems like a place, with its wooden boardwalks and water taxis and everybody-knows-everybody-else feel, that time has forgotten. Above all, it is safe. Fire Island makes you feel that nothing bad can happen there, certainly nothing worse than, if you're a kid, falling down and skinning your knee, or if you're an adult, having too much to drink at a cocktail party and winding up in bed with a fat woman named Naomi. Which is why I thought

it was the perfect place for Norton to make his first excursion.

Once Cindy understood I was quite serious and that there was no way I was leaving my cat home alone for a whole weekend, she decided to give it a try with Marlowe. She didn't want him to grow up feeling like the neglected stepchild.

For our first trip *en famille,* we took Tommy's Taxi, a van service that picks you (and a lot of other yuppified weekenders anxious—and loud about it—to leave the city) up in Manhattan and drops you off at the Fire Island ferry. We bought a regular pet carrying case, a plastic one with metal bars on the top. Since both cats were so little, we figured one case would be plenty big enough.

We met the van at Fifty-third and First Avenue, loaded our bags on, then climbed aboard and made ourselves as comfortable as we could amidst the jewelry and designer clothes and exposed body parts. The cat case sat on my lap.

About fifteen minutes into the trip, I decided that it couldn't possibly be very comfortable curled up inside a portable pet prison, so I opened it an inch and stuck my hand in to reassuringly pet both guys. Marlowe didn't respond. His nose was buried in a corner, and he was trying his best to pretend he had been in a coma for about three weeks. Norton, however, scurried over to my fingers and began shoving his nose up against them. I stroked him for a minute, then when Cindy was looking away, staring rather horrifiedly at a pair of dangling gold earrings that spelled out a phone number—three numbers hanging from the left ear, four hanging from the right; I assume the woman wear-

ing them had the area code tattooed someplace I didn't want to know about—I lifted Norton out of the box and quickly shut it back up.

He looked up at me gratefully and meowed. At the sound, Cindy glanced over. When she saw the kitten on my lap, she rolled her eyes.

"I know, I know," I told her and tried to pretend that I sympathized with her hard-hearted approach to pet travel. "But he looked so unhappy in there."

"He wasn't unhappy," she told me. "He's a cat. *You* were unhappy because you weren't holding him."

I glanced down at Norton, who was curled up in a ball on my lap, his head resting on the back of my hand. I nodded at Cindy, acknowledging that her assessment was correct.

"At least move your hand," she told me. "You can't be comfortable sitting like that."

"I'm all right," I told her.

"You're comfortable?"

"Well . . . not exactly. But . . ."

"But what?"

"But *he* looks so comfortable."

"I think," Cindy said, "I may have made a mistake."

The rest of the trip went according to form. Marlowe cowered in the box, doing his best Helen Keller impersonation; Norton wound up inching his way up my arm and perching on my shoulder, watching the countryside slide by as we sped along the L.I.E.

One of the things I liked best about his position on my

shoulder was that it didn't ever seem to occur to him that he couldn't just push me out of the way or take up whatever space he wanted to take up. That's where he wanted to be, so that's where he belonged. And I had to agree. It only seemed fair. He was little; he was being lugged around not by his own choosing; he had no idea where he was going or why. If he wanted to sit somewhere and at least get a good view, how could I complain? I felt—and I think this is one of those clever things that cats somehow manage to do—*honored* by the fact that he chose me to be his piece of comfortable furniture.

In fact, not only wasn't I complaining, I was mesmerized watching Norton on his first trip in the van. He spent almost the entire hour staring out the window, hunched forward, his neck craning, his nose pressed against the glass. Something fascinated him out there, though I sure couldn't tell what. Every so often he'd turn to look at me and his eyes were full of questions. He'd stare at me until I felt ridiculously ignorant, and I'd whisper, "What? What do you want to know? *What?* Tell me!" When it became plain that I couldn't help him, he'd turn back to the window and continue his vigilant watch.

The thing is, it's not as if he were watching a flickering fire in a fireplace, unfocused and glazed by simple noise and movement. For Norton, this was hardly a vacuous way to pass the time. He wasn't *just* staring. His eyes were alert, constantly moving, his head shifting back and forth as if he were keeping track of a baseline-to-baseline rally at an exciting tennis game.

He was so *interested.* And it made me incredibly curious. I acted like a proud father whose son was about to win a

sixth-grade spelling bee. I kept nudging Cindy, not saying anything, just flicking my eyes toward Norton as if to say, "Will you look at him? Is he smart or what?"

Several people on the van actually stopped talking about themselves long enough to notice that there was a kitten perched on my shoulder, a kitten with folded ears who seemed to be unduly interested in the landscape of Long Island.

A couple of them reached over to pet him. Norton took the attention with what I would come to know as his typical laissez-faire reaction to adoring crowds. He didn't shrink away or scurry back into his carrier. Nor did he rub his nose affectionately against unknown palms or offer encouragement in any way. He simply sat there and took the cooing and petting and compliments as stoically as he could. At some point he turned to me, since we were basically at eye level to each other, and the expression on his face said, "It's all right. This is just the price I have to pay for being me."

I nodded at him knowingly, and when the petting stopped, he snuggled a few inches closer, turned away from the strangers, buried his face against my neck, closed his eyes, and went to sleep.

Marlowe, who in the van had certainly been, if not happy, quiescent, did not take well to the twenty-minute ferry ride from mainland Bay Shore to Fair Harbor on the island. He wouldn't move an inch in the carrier, and when Cindy went to pet him reassuringly, he drew away from her touch. I think, if he hadn't been as truly sweet as he was, he might

have hissed at her. But things hadn't quite reached that tragic level.

Norton, of course, only made matters worse because he took to the open sea (or, at least, the open bay) as if he were related in some way to the Popeye family.

As in the van, his nose went right to (and through) the metal bars at the top of his carrier, and he made it plain as day he wanted out. So, once again, I reached in, scooped him up, and set him on my lap.

Within a few experimental minutes, we found the position we both liked best: me with my left leg crossed over my right knee at a ninety-degree angle, Norton with his body on my right thigh and his head resting on my left foot. (For him, that's still his favorite traveling position, although as he's gotten older and bigger, his body and head now go from right thigh to left knee. For me, as *I've* gotten older and my joints creakier and creakier, it's less and less comfortable. Of course, I'm too well trained to change. I much prefer creaky joints to a disgruntled traveling companion.)

He also, about ten minutes into the crossing, decided the water was practically as interesting as the highway. With me holding the middle of his body as firmly as I could, he perched himself back on my shoulder, with his front paws resting on the ferry's railing.

Cindy was a little nervous seeing him in such a precarious position, and I must admit so was I. Believe me, I had visions of myself diving overboard in search of a floundering kitten. But I did have hold of him. And even more of a but, I simply had a very strong sense that this particular cat would not do anything as rashly crazy as jump off my

shoulder into the freezing bay. I don't know why I had such
faith in him, except to say that he more than justified it. I
expected him to behave in a certain way right from the
beginning, and he almost always did. I've left Norton in
cars with the doors open, in airport waiting rooms while I
went off to confirm tickets, in restaurant chairs while I went
to use their toilets. Not once do I ever remember him
running or jumping or hiding.

We got some awfully strange looks on that boat: a boy
and his seafaring kitten. Then in twenty minutes we were
back on land. We'd been on a taxi, a van, and a ferry. We'd
braved rush-hour traffic, the spray of sea salt, and crazed
sun-worshippers. The premier leg of Norton's first real
journey was complete.

The cat who commuted

4

Norton took to outdoor life immediately. It was a little frightening how easy it was to begin thinking of him as a country squire.

We took both cats into the little beach house and flipped open the carrier. Marlowe—poor guy; I hope no one ever reads this to him because he's going to get one hell of a serious inferiority complex—wouldn't come out. If I hadn't spent many more months in his company and *seen* him out and around, I'd venture to say he might *still* be in that box. Norton, on the other hand, had his new pad all checked out in a matter of minutes. He was the second coming of Tony Bill in *Come Blow Your Horn.*

He sniffed the miniature house out thoroughly—around the couch, over to the Pullman kitchen, up the ladder stairs to the sleeping loft. After exploring the upstairs, he stuck his head over the edge of the loft to look down at us, and I knew exactly what he had in mind. When we made eye contact I shook my head only once, but firmly—and I'm convinced that's why he took the stairs back down to the living room floor, one little jump at a time instead of one great twelve-foot leap. I knew (and he knew) he could have done it. But I knew (and I'm sure he knew it, too) I probably would have had a heart attack.

Back downstairs, he checked out the bathroom, hopped onto the rim of the tub, slid down inside it. It was vinyl and very smooth, far too slippery for a kitten his size to easily leap back out, so when he began meowing impatiently I had to go fetch him. This became a fairly regular ritual until he grew to a more adult size and could get out of his own scrapes. At least once a day I'd hear a plaintive meowing echoing from the bathroom and have to go to the rescue. I must admit, partly to pay him back for dragging me away from work or fun or bed, partly because it was extremely funny to watch, I'd usually give him three or four tries on his own. He'd see me, try to scamper up the wall of the tub, not make it, and slide back down toward the drain. After a few unsuccessful attempts, he'd meow sharply, just once, to let me know the game was over and he wanted my help—*now*. He was not humiliating himself for my enjoyment any longer.

Norton particularly liked the walls of the beach house, which were covered with a burlap cloth. Quite attractive, no doubt, but also very handy for climbing.

While Cindy and I were doing our best to coax Marlowe out of the carrier, we heard a very quick ripping noise— actually five or six quick ripping noises—and turned around

to find Norton up near the ceiling, his claws clinging to the wall fabric.

I, of course, thought this was the greatest thing I'd ever seen. I was ready to rank Norton with Columbus, Tom Sawyer, John Glenn, and the first guy who ever ordered mail-order meat on my list of great adventurers. Cindy, luckily for my bank account, quickly pointed out how expensive it would be to completely refurbish every wall in the house. So we quickly pulled Norton down and tried to discourage this particular excitement, although it, too, became something of a regular occurence.

We next went out of our way to orient our adventurous cat. A litter box was set up in the bathroom, and we carried him to it so he'd be unable to use ignorance as an excuse for any accidents. (It turned out that in three years on Fire Island, he never *once* used a litter box. Outside, one giant sandbox was at his disposal, and I think he took great satisfaction in relieving himself in the freeing manner of his ancestors.) We also put food and water down for him and Marlowe—separate bowls, of course—but we figured Marlowe was *weeks* away from eating. Norton acknowledged the food with a quick bite or two of kibble, but his mind was elsewhere. He wanted the great outdoors.

Although he went straight for the screen door, he was still such a small kitten—not yet three months old—Cindy thought that, for health reasons, we shouldn't really let him loose outside. He was too young to be exposed to all those unknown germs and ticks and other strange things that abound in nature and that I couldn't even bring myself to think about. But he seemed so anxious to take off for parts unknown . . .

I had a solution. It was a perfect summer day, so we quickly changed into our formal Fire Island wear—shorts, no shoes, no shirt for me, tank top for Cindy—made ourselves some iced tea, and began Step One of turning Norton into an outdoor cat. We put a blue collar on him—quite distinguished-looking nestled in his gray fur—and got a long, long string, maybe thirty feet long, from the Rockette lady. We used the string to make an impromptu leash, carried Norton onto the porch, and tied him to the handle of the door.

Minus Marlowe, who still hadn't budged from his portable prison, Cindy and I took our iced teas—by the way, these were nonalcoholic iced teas; this is worth explaining because we'd learned that, for some unknown reason, in bars and restaurants anywhere on Long Island, if you just order iced tea, they give you something with enough alcohol in it to topple an elephant—sprawled into our madras beach chairs, and waited to see what would happen.

We didn't have to wait long.

Norton needed a few seconds to get his bearing. This was a little different from being transplanted into a strange living room. This was like being picked up by Brian Dennehy in *Cocoon* and going for a stroll on a strange planet.

First he went into a crouch. He glanced around nervously, as if waiting for something to pounce on him. Then he relaxed a bit. He took a step forward, still staying fairly alert to the potential for danger. His nose twitched, taking in the hundreds of brand new odors, and his folded ears switched from side to side, hearing all sorts of things, like birds and crickets and bees, that he had had no idea ever existed. Then a great thing happened.

Norton suddenly sprang into the air in a joyous leap. Baryshnikov would have been jealous of his form. He landed on his padded feet and went right back up, this time swatting at the string, which lay stretched out before him. A meow came out of him, but not a normal meow. This one sounded suspiciously like "whooooppeeeee!"

It took maybe thirty seconds for my cat to race exhilarat-edly all around the deck. It took me maybe thirty *minutes* to unwind the string—which was now tangled up under a chair, around a square outdoor table, around another chair, twice around Cindy's ankles, over and then back under a third chair, somehow wrapping around the table again before coming to a sudden stop somewhere in the middle of the deck as the leash ran out of slack.

Norton couldn't move an inch. By the time I'd managed to straighten things out, he was raring to go again. And go he did. Another thirty seconds later, I was doing my best to unwrap him from his string straightjacket. Cindy couldn't stop laughing, Norton couldn't stop running, and I couldn't stop unwinding. All three of us were as close to happy as it's possible to get.

Within a couple of weeks, we had the routine down cold.

Thursday evenings, pack one bag each, load each kitten into his own carrier—we'd splurged for comfort's sake; *their* comfort—catch the five-thirty Tommy's Taxi and the seven P.M. ferry to Fair Harbor. Marlowe would hunker down in his carrier, emerging only when he was safely inside our house. Norton would spend the van ride on my shoulder, staring out the window, and the ferry ride on my lap, lean-

ing up against the railing. Once we hit land, he was beginning to squirm and think seriously about jumping out of his
carrier. I knew it wouldn't be long before he'd be prowling
the island on his own.

I'd bought a new travel case, perfect for him, easy for me.
It was really meant for dogs, but he was quite comfortable
in it and seemed to like it better than the old one. It was
a soft cloth shoulder bag with a hard strip underneath it for
support. There was a mesh patch in front so the animal
could breathe and see out. Norton didn't need the mesh to
see or breathe, because I never zipped the thing closed. I
just stuck him in and hung the bag on my left shoulder while
he sat there, head swiveling in every direction, taking in
every single sight, sound, and smell. It wasn't long before
I didn't even have to pick him up and put him inside. When
it was time for us to take a trip, I'd simply lay the bag on
the floor and he'd step right in and settle himself there.

After a month of weekends spent mostly trying to untie
string from every available item on our deck, we decided
it was time to turn the cat loose. My landlord, whose family
shared the front deck with us, was complaining. Their bicycles were so tightly wrapped in string by this point, they
looked as if they were bike mummies excavated from Tut's
Tomb.

On the chosen weekend, Cindy and Marlowe had to stay
in the city. One of Cindy's best friends was in from out of
town, and they decided to have an official GNO (Girls'
Night Out). The whole wild works—non-diet Cokes, oil on
their salads, loud public discussions of bladder infections.
Norton and I were on our own, bacheloring it up.

Friday night, on Tommy's Taxi, I happened upon a star-

tling and, in years to come, useful revelation. It had always struck me as quite odd that none of the reveling weekenders in the van or on the ferry ever paid much attention to the fact that there was an incredibly cute cat on my shoulder, doing incredibly cute things. I didn't expect banners or original songs about "A Cat Named Norton"—

> *Who's the cat with the floppy ears?*
> *Who's the cat who ain't got no fears?*
> *Who's the cat doin' all the cavortin'?*
> *That ain't no cat—that's Norton!*

—or anything like that, but I did expect the occasional "What a cute cat!" or "Is he always this good?" or "What happened to his ears?" No. Usually I got nothing.

Well, this Friday I was riding along as usual, immersed in the *Post* sports section, cat on my shoulder studying the L.I.E. landmarks, when a woman behind me, wearing a sweatshirt that read "Life's a Beach," said, "What kind of cat is that?"

"A Scottish Fold," I explained. "His ears fold in half. See?"

"He's amazing."

Smiling, I went back to the sports section.

"Excuse me," the woman sitting next to me said. She had on a T-shirt that said, "Life's a Beach." "What kind of a cat did you say he was?"

"Scottish Fold," I repeated. "See? His ears fold like this."

"He's beautiful."

"Thank you."

"Is he always this well behaved?"

"Always," I said proudly.

Back to the sports pages.

"Is that a Scottish Fold?" the woman in front of me asked, turning around to smile at me. She *didn't* have on a T-shirt that read "Life's a Beach." But the guy sitting next to her did.

"Uh-huh." I nodded.

" 'Cause his ears fold like this."

"Uh-huh."

"He's so *cute.*"

"I know."

"Is he always this good?"

As a person who's always prided himself on being an acutely sharp observer of human behavior, naturally enough I had absolutely *no* idea why, all of a sudden, Norton's ears were the main topic of the car ride. I had zero concept of what was different from past rides.

It wasn't until I was on the ferry that it hit me.

We were on the upper deck. Norton was peering fixedly at the gulls swooping around the waves. I was munching on a take-out order of fried clams, a specialty of Porky's, the wonderfully divey pub by the ferry.

I was single this trip.

That was the difference.

No one wanted to bother admiring my cat when I was sitting next to an attractive woman I was obviously attached to. But this night there was no Cindy. So all of a sudden, Norton was the perfect conversation starter.

I was mildly stunned. I'd never really seen myself as the object of a van-ful of women's lust and desires. And I'd certainly never viewed Norton as bait to be trolled. Were

times so bad that people wouldn't even *talk* to someone unless they wanted something? Like a mate for life? It was amazing. It was . . .

As if on cue, a hand swooped down in front of me and plucked a clam—*my* clam—from the styrofoam plate.

I looked up to see a reasonably attractive woman, late twenties, holding the clam in her fingers. She was wearing—remember, this goes back a few years now—a *Flashdance*-type T-shirt. Over the course of the summer, I was going to become far too familiar with this look. (One of the amazing things about a sleepy little place like Fire Island being so close to Manhattan is the way fads sweep in and take over the entire island. My own personal favorite fad is a game called Kadima. It might also be called The Stupidest Game Ever Invented. It consists of one wooden paddle per player—of which there are usually two or three—and a hard black rubber ball. The object of the game is to stand ape-like on the beach, preferably in the middle of a particularly crowded section, where you can annoy people who are trying to mind their own business and have a good time. One player hits the ball to another person, not letting it touch the sand. There's no net, no out of bounds, no points, no rules other than what I've reported. What there *is* is a really loud, annoying noise that echoes every time ball hits paddle. Sounds like a lot of fun, doesn't it? Believe me, that summer Kadima was good for *hours* of entertainment on the ocean's edge.)

Anyway, back to the clam thief.

Her T-shirt was intentionally torn at the neck, revealing a darkly tanned shoulder (with a lot of flesh to tan) that had a tiny tattoo on it. I had an irrational fear that if I got too

close to the tattoo, it would say, in micro letters, "Life's a Beach." So I averted my eyes, or at least refocused them on the clam.

"I knew that anyone with such a cute cat," she began, "wouldn't mind sharing his food. I'm *starving.*"

She showed me all her teeth in the friendliest smile I'd ever been on the receiving end of. It would have been more effective if her gums hadn't gone from her forehead nearly to her knees.

"May I have my clam back, please?" I asked her politely.

Her teeth sparkled again, only this time she popped the little fried sucker right in between the uppers and lowers.

"What kind of cat is that?"

I didn't answer. I was too busy watching her chew.

"How come his ears are down? Is he afraid?"

I shook my head. She swallowed. I watched the little bulge in her throat slide down out of view.

"Did you sedate him? How can he just sit there like that?"

Then she moved. Her bejeweled, tan fingers reached toward my plate again. This time my hand went up to meet hers. To her surprise, our fingers locked for a moment. But she managed that dazzling smile again. The smile faded somewhat when I said the words "Touch another clam and die."

I'm pretty sure she thought I was kidding, because she tried to disentangle her hand and make another go at my dinner.

"I don't want to be rude," I said, in my best quiet Clint Eastwood impersonation, "but I'm extremely hungry. I bought these clams so I could eat every single one of them,

except for the ones I give to my cat. I don't mind if he reaches down and takes one because I know him. But I don't know *you*. So if you try to get to them, I'm afraid I'm going to have to find out where you live, sneak over in the middle of the night, and break your thumbs."

I did everything but say, "Are you feeling lucky, punk?" It seemed to do the trick.

She backed away slowly—clearly she'd been flirting with the Ted Bundy of the ferry set—and disappeared into the crowd.

I looked down at the cat draped over my shoulder. He looked back at me and meowed.

"I know what you mean, pal," I told him. "I don't think we're ready for the singles scene."

The next morning was D-Day. Norton was about to hit the shore.

He knew it, too. Don't ask me *how* he knew, but he did. I've come to expect this from him. He always seems to know when a big event is upon us: if I'm going on a trip, if *he's* going on a trip, if something particularly sad has happened, if something particularly festive is about to happen. If I didn't know better, I'd swear he keeps a calendar hidden somewhere in the apartment. Because as he got more and more used to going away to the beach for the weekends, his morning routine even changed. Mondays through Thursdays, we'd go through our wake-up cuddling, and then, as I dragged myself out of bed, Norton would race to the kitchen, jump up on the counter, and wait impatiently for me to feed him. On Fridays, he'd race along the same path—off the bed, through the bedroom door, around the corner, sharp right, cut through the living room, past the front door, into the kitchen—only he'd skid to a sudden stop at the front door and wait there eagerly. On Fridays he didn't even care about breakfast. He just wanted to hit the open road.

On the day of his first outdoor solo expedition, the moment my eyes popped open in the morning, my guy was out of bed, waiting at the front door of the Fire Island house, glancing back repeatedly to see what was keeping me.

Still rubbing sleep out of my eyes, I pulled on a pair of shorts, climbed down the stairs of the loft, and met him at the door. I hesitated. For one brief melancholy moment I had a vision of Norton on the side of an endless road, thumb out, heading far away in search of fame and glory. I composed myself, remembered that he didn't *have* a thumb, then I swung the screen open. Norton *didn't* hesitate. He scooted outside. In the blink of an eye, he was gone, racing across the yard, racing right back, disappearing in a flash under the deck.

I realized I had two choices. I could act like a total lunatic and tail him outside, try to follow him around wherever he went and keep an eye on him. Or I could be a rational, sane man: relax, make myself a pot of strong French Roast coffee with just a dash of cinnamon, get the newspapers, read about the fascinating events of the day, then go for a healthy, invigorating morning swim. It seemed like an obvious choice.

I decided to follow Norton.

He was having the absolute time of his life. Frolicking, chasing birds and squirrels—not catching, just chasing—

crawling through the grass on his belly, chomping on flowers, and generally enjoying his new role of jungle beast on the prowl.

After half an hour or so, I decided he was safe and sound, more than able to cope on his own with the great outdoors, so I went back inside to attend to some people-related chores such as trying to write a book and earn enough money to pay for Norton's summer house.

I never *really* worried. I knew he'd stay fairly close to home or, at least, wouldn't go so far away that he couldn't find his way back. Periodically, I'd step to the front door or back window and call his name, just checking up. I'd hear one crisp meow in response, letting me know all was well, then I'd go back to work.

At lunchtime I decided to head to the market (I'd forgiven them for ratting on me to Cindy). Going for the surprisingly mature route, I didn't even check up on Norton. I figured he wouldn't miss me for the twenty minutes I'd be gone, so why bother him? I didn't want him to think I was an overprotective dad. Feeling as proud as a father whose son has just gotten his driver's license and is driving away on his first date, I made a list of what I needed to buy and took off.

I was three quarters of a block toward the market when I first heard it. A faint growling of a meow, a little whiney in fact. I took another two steps, heard it again. *Brrrrrrmeowwwww.*

I stopped, turned my head. Norton was in the middle of the sidewalk, twenty feet behind me. He was trying to follow, but I was walking too fast.

"What are you doing?" I asked. "Go back to the house."

Again I headed for the store, managing to take all of two steps before hearing a much more insistent meow. When I turned, Norton had scampered a few feet closer.

"Then come on," I called. "Let's go."

And much to my astonishment, he ran up until he was about five feet behind me. Then he stopped. "Come on," I told him. "I'll walk slow." But he wouldn't budge any farther.

I took a few more steps, glanced behind me. He was following—but he stopped when I stopped. I went a few more steps, glanced. He'd kept pace.

I walked the rest of the three blocks to the market, and Norton followed, always staying five feet behind, every few feet meowing to let me know he was still there. Several Fair Harborites passed by and stopped to stare in amazement. I acted as if there were nothing at all unusual about the world's cutest kitten going for a lunchtime promenade with his favorite person.

Twice, people on bikes zoomed past and Norton froze. But he never panicked. Once they were gone, I just had to reassure him that everything was okay, that bikes were only an occasional hazard here in the real world; then he'd resume his faithful trot, taking my word that I was watching out for his best interests.

In a few minutes we were at the entrance to the market, where there were about ten times the number of people Norton had ever seen in his entire life. Kids were racing around playing tag, bikes and skateboards were skidding to and fro, several people with "Life's a Beach" T-shirts were trying to impress several other people with *Flashdance* T-shirts. Even for Norton it was a bit much.

As we approached, I wasn't sure what to do with him. See if he'd stroll inside and peruse the aisles with me? Pick him up and carry him? Ask someone to keep an eye on him while I shopped—a ten-minute cat sitter?

Norton ended my pondering and took matters into his own paws. After sizing up the situation, he darted past the door to the market, sprinted ten feet or so toward the dock, then disappeared into a thick row of bushes.

I had a feeling that most of my afternoon was going to be spent coaxing him out from under the greenery. After twenty minutes of trying, I figured there was nothing to be done about it. I could see him and he clearly wasn't going anywhere, so I decided it was safe to leave him while I shopped. I went into the market, bought the makings for a delicious lunch—two juicy knockwurst, some German potato salad, a dark Heineken, a can of Nine Lives Turkey Giblets—then trooped back outside to assess the cat situation.

The situation was this: the cat was gone.

Standing in front of the bush he'd been hiding in, I called his name. Nothing. Not a sound, not a stirring. I got down on my hands and knees and peered through the thicket, but there was no sign of gray fur anywhere. My throat felt as if I had a two-ton chunk of granite stuck in it; my stomach was flip-flopping to beat the Seven Santini Brothers. I couldn't believe it. How could I have left him alone outside? What was I thinking of? As smart as he was, he wasn't human. He wasn't even a dog. He was just a cat! A cat who'd never been outside on his own before, and I'd deserted him, left him stranded! And now he was either hiding somewhere, shivering in total terror, was hopelessly

lost, never to be found again, or had been kidnapped by two brothers named Rick and Mick who had already tied the first firecracker to his tail.

Forcing myself to be calm, I took a deep breath and called Norton's name a second time. There was only a terrible silence. For one long second. Then two seconds . . . then . . . *brrrrrmeowww.*

A gray head with folded ears poked its way out of the bush—exactly where I'd last seen it. The rest of the body followed. Norton stood on the sidewalk, looking up at me with one of his "What's the problem?" looks.

I didn't want him to see that I'd completely lost faith in him and panicked, so I only allowed myself a minute sigh of relief. Then I turned and walked past the market, not stopping until I was on my own front deck. There was no need to look behind me: Norton, of course, had kept pace, trotting briskly five feet behind the entire way.

Over the course of the summer, Norton's little jaunts turned into a wonderfully pleasurable routine. Cindy was having to work more and more on the weekends, so Norton was, every two or three weeks, my only beach companion. He always walked me to the market in the morning, he usually walked me there at lunchtime, and he sometimes deigned to come along at dinnertime. Rarely did he walk by my side. He was most comfortable lagging those five feet behind. He would meow periodically just to let me know he was still tagging along. Once I got used to this, I stopped even bothering to turn around to check on him. I'd simply walk merrily on my way, hear him alert me that all was well,

and I'd call back, "Okay, okay, let's try to keep up." I got quite used to, as people passed us by, someone turning to a friend, whose eyes would be bugging out, and saying, "See, I told you."

As we both got comfortable with our walking patterns, he (and I, I suppose) got more adventurous.

My writing partner is named David Handler. We do most of our television and film scripts together; the business is so filled with sharklike monsters whose greatest pleasure is chomping their sharp teeth down on helpless writers that we feel, erroneously no doubt, there's safety in numbers. David and his girlfriend, Diana, had a house four or five blocks north of mine. On the days we worked there, Norton took to accompanying me. He got to know the route well: straight for several blocks, left, then go all the way to the bay. He got to know it so well he began making the excursion on his own. Not infrequently, Cindy and I would be cooking dinner and David would call, saying Norton had been visiting for a couple of hours but he'd just trotted away, so I should expect him home soon. Sure enough, twenty minutes later there'd be a meow at the door, and a certain wandering feline would make it very clear he wouldn't mind eating a can of Cheese and Chicken Chunks and eating it *right now*.

One thing I learned early on is that I never had to worry about losing Norton along the way, no matter how far we traveled. Taking Central Walk—the erratically paved path that went for several miles along the center of the island— to David's, Norton would periodically get distracted or frightened or simply playful. If a squirrel happened to cross his path, Norton would scamper after him, sometimes into

the bushes, sometimes under someone's house, sometimes up a tree. If a dog decided to act doglike and bark or growl, Norton was outta there. Same if a bike came clanging along and cruised too close. At first I would simply wait impatiently until he'd reappear, which sometimes took as long as fifteen minutes, or I'd spend the same amount of time crawling around trying to find and catch him. Once, I was in a particular hurry. David and I were to be on the receiving end of a conference call from a producer in L.A. who felt he could just as easily humiliate us over the phone as in person. So I just left Norton where he'd sprinted away to, hidden under someone's deck. I went to my conference call, spent forty-five minutes trying to iron out the intricate plot elements of a super-realistic sitcom episode (involving a college student who broke out in a rash whenever the girl of his dreams kissed him), then convinced David to come and try to look for my kitten. We went to the spot where I'd last seen him, I called his name, and presto, there was Norton, popping out into the sunlight, happy to follow us back to David's, where he could spend the rest of the afternoon playing in the tall reeds by the bay.

It became obvious I could leave Norton anywhere, and for any length of time. Even if we didn't want him, he'd often follow me and Cindy when we left the house. If we were walking over to someone's place for dinner, he'd stay with us until he got bored, meow loud enough so I'd be sure to turn and see where he was, then dash off to have fun on his own. Hours later, after dessert and coffee, I'd make my way back to the spot, call his name, and with one of his *brrrrmeowwwws,* he'd be ready to head back home.

Norton clearly liked the combination of his freedom and

my company as much as I did. It got to the point where it was rarely necessary to stick him into his shoulder bag/carrying case. He wanted to walk everywhere instead. Leaving for Fire Island from my apartment, he always hopped right into the bag because, even for Norton, asking him to walk on a crowded Manhattan sidewalk was a bit much. Then, when Tommy's Taxi hit the ferry dock, he'd also willingly slip off my lap or shoulder back into the bag—there was too much foot and car traffic, not to mention the general sense of hysteria from the hordes of city dwellers overly anxious to drink frozen daiquiris, get skin cancer, and exchange phone numbers with members of the opposite sex who either owned or looked as if they would soon be able to own a two-bedroom co-op in a doorman building.

But once the ferry was headed across the bay, forget it. Norton was on his own.

As soon as were seated, he was out of the bag and either on my lap or propped up against the railing, checking out the fascinating movement of the waves. He would race to the door the moment we were tied up to shore and hop onto the dock's wooden planks himself. He'd wait impatiently for me and Cindy to make our way through the crowd (Why New Yorkers line up for five minutes—on a boat! Which you can't get off because it's still in the water!—then push and shove so they can get somewhere to *relax,* I'll never know), then race ahead of us toward the house, stopping every ten or twelve feet to make sure we were following. If he was hungry, he'd deign to come inside long enough to chow down, then he'd meow or scratch the screen door until we let him out. I didn't like the idea of

his staying out all night—okay, okay, so I had a *touch* of Jim Backus in *Rebel Without a Cause* in me, get off my back—and, to his credit, he always came inside when it was time for me to go to bed. Even having glimpsed the world beyond, he didn't alter our regular sleeping arrangements.

Sunday night or Monday morning, when it was time to head back to the concrete jungle, he would walk with us to the ferry, stopping right before we reached the dock, where he'd hop into the bag and allow me to carry him until we were seated on the boat.

The more comfortable I got traveling with him, the more I realized how much I could trust him.

At the ferry stop was a great divey restaurant/pub, Porky's, whose desirable fried clams were mentioned earlier. Porky's had a take-out window, and I soon got into the habit of leaving Norton's bag—with Norton in it—on one of the benches by the boat while I went to get food before boarding. (I highly recommend their toasted homemade blueberry muffins, washed down with a long-necked bottle of ice-cold Bud.) I wouldn't be gone long, maybe ten minutes, but it would usually be long enough for a small crowd to have gathered round the gray cat with folded ears who was lying nonchalantly on top of his bag, taking a snooze or checking out any interesting fellow passengers.

He was quite relaxed and extraordinarily obedient when told to stay put. Eventually, as his modes of transportation and range of travels broadened, I was able to leave him in airport lounges for as long as twenty minutes while I went magazine or upgrade shopping, and in restaurants, sitting in his own chair while I ate peacefully in mine.

One of my proudest accomplishments, leading to one of

Norton's shining moments, was getting him to walk on the beach. For some reason, cats don't like the sand. Maybe it's too hot for their padded paws; maybe the water scares them; maybe they're put off by all the "Life's a Beach" shirts, umbrellas, and towels. Anyway, Norton was no exception.

Here was Norton walking along the boardwalk *toward* the beach: cocky swagger, confident gleam in the eye, the look of someone who'd been parading around town pointing his finger at a neighbor, saying things like "Howdy, Bill, we missed you at the town hall meeting last night."

Here he was when I'd plop him *in the middle of the beach:* cowering, shaking, racing as far away from the waves as he could get to huddle terrified against the dunes. Picture Jimmy Cagney on his way to the chair in *Angels with Dirty Faces. Norton Dies Yellow!*

I decided this simply wouldn't do.

When a kid takes horseback riding lessons and tumbles off, what's the very first thing he's told? *Get right back on.* I knew I'd never get Norton to go for a horseback ride— well, there's no point in saying *never*—but I couldn't see any reason for him to stay off the sand.

In my own defense, let me say right here and now that I'm not one of those pushy stage parents. I mean, if Ethel Merman were alive, she wouldn't play me in a musical. Although Norton is a show-quality cat, I'd never even *think* of displaying him or training him to do tricks. Those things are for *other* people. This was for me and him. He'd *enjoy* having new areas to roam and explore. Why should he limit himself when he could be frolicking with some beach bunnies down by the water's edge? To end my own defense, let me say that I felt then, and I feel now, a little too much

like the parent of a nine-year-old boy who's making the poor lad take piano lessons and says, "Believe me, he'll thank me for this when he's older."

The first few times I let Norton loose in the sand, he was gone the moment I set him down, running for the protective safety of dirt and boardwalk. The next few times, I put him down and held him, letting him get used to the feel. He didn't struggle and he didn't appear too miserable. When I let go, he'd hesitate, realizing that perhaps this whole beach thing wasn't as terrible as he'd assumed—as I'd been telling him repeatedly—but then he'd hunker down and skulk back to real land. Not sprinting exactly but not stopping to admire the view either.

After that it got easier. His instinct was to follow me. I'd never led him astray before; there was no reason for him to believe I was starting now.

Within a week, Norton was walking comfortably on the beach, his usual five steps behind me, meowing a lot more and a lot louder than usual, but he was there. He wouldn't go all the way to the water, but he *would* walk about halfway there, wait while Cindy or I shook loose a towel to lie on, and stick around for half an hour or so, especially if he got to share any of our picnic lunch. I still believe he would have spent more time relaxing there if it wasn't for the constant *thwapp-thwapp-thwapp* of the Kadima balls.

One day, toward the end of August, Cindy and I were invited to a cookout in Seaview, one of the other beach communities. Cindy had a girlfriend who was in a "share" there, a share being when six people share the cost of a

three-bedroom house, figuring out such complicated schemes as alternate weekend visits, splitting food costs, and prorating the fee for the largest bedroom or the one with the ocean view or the one closest to the refrigerator.

On this particular weekend, all the sharers were stuffed into the house because it was the weekend of the annual Seaview Clam Bake. Every year, everyone in the small community brought food and drink to the beach—clams, lobsters, burgers, hot dogs, kegs of beer, pitchers of margaritas—dug pits for barbecuing and steaming, and cooked out, drank, and generally made merry. This went on all day and a goodly portion of the night. There was usually music and volleyball games and three-legged races and other Andy Hardyish events; all in all, it was awfully hard to think of a much better way to spend a ninety-degree day in the heart of a New York summer.

Cindy went early to help prepare. She thought it would be fun to be in on the beginning of the festivities. As much as I always enjoyed the Seaview bash, my antisocial theory about large gatherings of human beings always was and is "less is more."

I puttered around until the late morning, did a little work, and, since Cindy wasn't around, caught up on my Rotisserie League stats. Rotisserie League, for those of you in the baseball dark ages, is sometimes called Fantasy Baseball. The game has swept the nation—*USA Today* estimates that 750,000 people now play it—and I'm proud to say I'm one of the cofounders of the original league. The premise is a simple yet immensely gratifying one. You put together a team at an auction, bidding against nine or eleven other "owners," depending on whether you're in the National

League or the American League. The structure of the team is specified: two catchers, three cornermen, five outfielders, nine pitchers, and so on. If you buy Darryl Strawberry—God forbid!—and he hits a home run for the Dodgers, he also hits one for your team. Being a total maniac about the game, I have *two* teams, which makes it nearly impossible to get any real work done during the summer months. My American League team is called the Gethers YeRosebuds, my National League team is the Smoked Fish. (I am respectfully referred to by my National League *compadres* as the Sturgeon General. And believe me, I'd way overpay if there was any way to get Steve Trout on my pitching staff.) I liked to do my stats when Cindy wasn't with me because she thought it was rather scary that a reasonably intelligent person would actually *want* to spend two hours a day totaling up the Hits and Walks Per Inning Pitched ratio for people who toiled in such places as Memorial Stadium and Chavez Ravine.

Satisfied that the Rosebuds were sprouting up for a big stretch run and a little depressed that I saw no end to the Fish's floundering, I decided it was time to head off to the Seaview bash.

Norton was lazily sunning himself on the porch as I stepped outside. His half-ears twitched in idle curiosity when I passed him by. I think he was wondering why anyone would bother leaving such a perfect spot.

"Whaddya say," I asked him. "You up for a stroll?"

Now, Seaview was two miles from where we were in Fair Harbor. The only way to get there in a reasonably straight line was by walking on the beach. Norton had never gone more than about thirty feet on sand. This had the potential

for disaster. But I thought Norton would like the cookout once he got there. It seemed worth a shot.

My pal was ready to give it a go. He lifted himself up from his sprawled position and began trotting after me. When it came time, half a block later, to descend to the beach, he meowed loudly.

"Come on," I coaxed gently. "What have you got to lose?"

If I'd been by myself, I probably would have made it to the party in twenty-five minutes. With Norton, I got there in thirty-five. He was perfect—never slowing down, never letting himself be distracted, always keeping pace right behind me, except for when he got frisky and raced ahead of me. He meowed a little more than usual, but he didn't seem to be complaining. He was just feeling gabby.

The way Seaview is set up along the beach, you have to climb up a small incline to get there. When you've climbed, you're standing on a dune overlooking the town's entire stretch of beach. It's not the Grand Canyon or anything, but it's quite nice, especially on a day when there are a couple of hundred people happily cooking and serving and playing.

I climbed, stood there for a moment enjoying the view, and spotted Cindy. She waved; I waved back. I swiveled my head back behind me to check on the walking wonder and said, "Let's do it."

Norton meowed once and followed. Up the incline, down into the laughing hordes. Within moments, the noisiest event of the season was eerily quiet. One by one, heads turned, eating stopped, music ceased. These sophisticated Fire Islanders had seen Frisbee-playing dogs in their midst.

They'd seen a spider monkey with a pail and shovel digging holes in the beach. They'd even once seen a female member of the singles-oriented Kismet community who *wasn't* wearing an ankle bracelet. But they were all staring at the kitten who'd traversed the sandy shores to help them party hearty—Norton of Arabia.

"Where did you come from?" the first person I passed asked.

"Fair Harbor," I told him.

"Your cat walked *two miles* like that?!"

I nodded. By the time I reached Cindy and her friends, I was nodding like a madman, my head bobbing up and down, and I was repeating all the familiar phrases: "Yup, does it all the time . . . Scottish Fold. See the ears? . . . Norton . . . Two miles . . . Fair Harbor . . . Yup . . . See the ears?"

Gradually the cookout went back to normal. The band started up again, backgammon games resumed, shrimps were skewered. Norton, after sampling some grilled tuna, went to play in the grass, away from the sand. I went with him to the steps leading away from the beach, told him I'd come get him in a few hours. I picked him up, kissed the top of his head, then I watched him disappear, knowing he'd be waiting when it was time to go home.

The cat who went to california

My Fire Island landlord was nice enough to extend our summer season until the end of September. But over the Labor Day weekend it hit me: What was I going to do with Norton when I didn't have a summer home where he could frolic the day away? How was he going to adjust to being an indoor cat? Especially—since I had recently learned that the biggest cause of fatalities in New York City cats was their leaping to their deaths out of apartment windows—an indoor cat whose father wouldn't ever again open a window so much as a crack.

By October 1, I hadn't come up with any intelligent solutions. Norton's travels were relegated to going back and forth between Cindy's and my apartment. When she spent the night at mine, Marlowe would come along. He was perfectly comfortable at my place, so it seemed only

right that Norton should be their houseguest when the
sleeping arrangements were reversed.

I was starting to do a fair amount of business-related
traveling. (I should probably explain that the traveling was
complicated because my business was complicated. I should
say businesses—and perhaps "confusing" is a better description than "complicated" since I don't actually have one job,
I have several, none of which makes all that much sense.
One part of me runs a publishing company. That part allows
me to make honest-to-goodness grown-up financial decisions, meet anyone interesting I can think of who might like
to write a book, and work with very talented and very
temperamental authors and personalities. Another part of
me writes and produces television and movie scripts. That
part allows me to wear sunglasses and hate actors and get
really aggravated when producers say things to me like, "I
love it! It's perfect! And don't worry, I know exactly how
to fix it!"—which actually *was* said by the executive producer of a TV series I worked on. The third and final part of
me—probably my favorite part—writes books. This is the
part that allows me to sit alone in a room and torture myself
trying to invent characters and plots that most people will
never read or hear of. It also gives me a chance to create
some meaning out of all sorts of otherwise meaningless
things. None of these jobs particularly fits together, and I
never actually meant to turn into a compulsive workaholic—but somehow it's happened and I kind of like it.) My
publishing job—at this point I was helping to start a new
imprint within the large and still growing Random House
complex—would take me away for a sales conference here
and there, a trip to San Francisco to see agents, a quick

sojourn with an author to make sure he or she felt loved and appreciated. My writing career was also keeping me busy and on the road. When you live in New York and write for Hollywood, you've constantly got to prove to the networks and studios that living three thousand miles away from the people paying you—and usually paying far too much money to write things that never get made—isn't anything they should worry about. The only proof is visibility, which meant my partner, David, and I had to hop on a plane on a fairly regular basis and show our faces around town.

Norton and Marlowe were great pals; thus it was never a problem figuring out what to do when I went away: Cindy would take him. She was nearly as crazy about my guy as she was about hers, and she truly enjoyed watching the two cats play and stay together for three or four days in a row. All three of them had fun when I was gone.

Everything seemed perfect until this pleasant and easy routine was forced to change. Cindy broke it to me that she was having a little *too* much fun when I was gone.

We had a strange relationship, Cindy and I. I had been smitten the moment I saw her; she had hated me on sight. She thought I was smug, egotistical, and watched too much baseball. But I was persistent—writing, sending flowers, calling, doing everything but watching less baseball—and eventually won her over. We couldn't have been more opposite. She was wary of relationships and hesitant to get involved, positive that she'd be wounded irreparably just at the moment she relaxed enough to decide our particular relationship was a permanent one. Although I didn't believe in or even consider the possibility of permanence, I was an incurable romantic and was more than happy to rush

in with my chin jutting and get knocked out with the first straight right hand that came my way. She didn't believe in spending money unwisely and thought it was almost sinful to spend it on one's immediate pleasure and comfort. I believed in spending any money I received as soon as possible—and *only* on things that would bring me pleasure and comfort. She thought she was a terrible human being—which she most certainly was not—while I, on the other hand, couldn't imagine anyone being a better, nicer guy than I. She got depressed all the time; I was almost always happy. She was always cold; I was always hot. She thought it was important to be serious—that times were bad and only serious thought and behavior might improve them. I was of the *Sullivan's Travels* school of behavioral thinking—times *were* bad, so let's laugh it up and try to find amusement in everything. She was searching for meaning. I hoped I'd *never* find meaning in *anything*—or I was in big trouble.

What really brought us together was the fact that we had *one* thing in common—we both wanted to stay independent.

The only thing we could agree on was that we didn't believe in a standard, old-fashioned, monogamous relationship. We didn't believe in marriage. People should stay together because they *want* to stay together—not because a piece of paper tells them they've made a legal commitment. We wanted to be free, unrestricted. If we felt like spending Saturday night together, fine. If we didn't, fine again. No problem. And no ties.

We never actually came out and said the words "I love you." We danced around it with clever phrases like "I

really love being with you" and "I love the way we don't
have to say 'I love you' and we still know how we feel about
each other," but once we realized we liked each other a
whole bunch and that we didn't *have* to be in an old-
fashioned relationship where we saw each other every Saturday night, we fell into a very comfortable old-fashioned
relationship where we saw each other every Saturday night
and generally took good care of each other. Neither one of
us ever really thought about making more of a commitment
than we had to make. In retrospect, it seems obvious that
neither Cindy nor I truly understood the nature of commitment. Although, I realize now, I was in the process of
learning. It just wasn't with Cindy.

Toward the end of the previous summer, Cindy and I had
spent more time apart than usual, but I had attributed that
to Cindy's new job and the fact that she was working long
and hard hours. It turns out I should have attributed it to
the fact that she'd fallen in love with her doctor.

She'd switched to him sometime in the spring. I remembered that she'd mentioned how great he was—and how
cute. I also remembered that sometime around the Fourth
of July, she'd started saying things like "You know, you
really shouldn't eat popcorn. It tends to clog up your intestines" and "Did you know that by the year 2020, the average doctor will spend nearly a million dollars to go to
medical school? Doesn't it steam you that people think of
doctors as selfish and unfeeling when they have to risk so
much to do what they do?"

I'd usually say things like "Oh yeah?" or *"What?"* and
then not give it any thought. But I gave it a lot of thought
when she told me I was getting dumped for the doc. Espe-

cially because it came right after I had invited her to England—the week's vacation was to be a present for her birthday.

"I just can't live a lie anymore," Cindy told me.

I readily agreed that she shouldn't have to live a lie, although I wished she could have lived it until after we'd been to a couple of farmhouse bed-and-breakfasts in Devon. She also wanted me to agree that it was a sad thing that it hadn't worked out between us. I managed to say that I thought it *had* been working out between us.

"No," Cindy said. "I don't know if you're capable of the kind of feelings that I need."

"You mean the kind of feeling where it's okay to dump someone who tries to do incredibly nice things for you like taking you to England?"

"No, I mean abandoning yourself to love. You're an observer," she told me. "I don't know if you're a participant in life."

This stopped me short. I'd always thought I was a good participator. Granted, my idea of a good time was watching *On the Waterfront* for the sixty-second time and then calling Sports Line to find out how the Mets had done, but I'd stack my life experiences with anyone's.

"Oh, you do participate," Cindy now said, "but you hold back. It's as if you're waiting for something."

"For what?"

"I don't know. For something better. Something *different.* Something you don't have. And you're holding back your true self until you find it."

"This *is* my true self," I tried to tell her. "You may not

like it as much as Dr. Polaro's true self, but it's mine."

"You don't understand," she said. And with that I had to agree. I had thought Cindy and I were on the same wavelength. I'd thought we were giving each other what we both needed. I'd thought there was a bond of honesty and trust between us. I'd thought we were finally at the comfortable stage, something men and women have an awfully difficult time reaching together without being in a rest home. Obviously I'd thought wrong.

I didn't stick around for too much longer. For one thing, I was getting awfully sad. For another, I was fairly certain Dr. Polaro's true self would be coming over soon, and I didn't particularly want to be there when it did.

It wasn't easy saying good-bye to Cindy. In a weird way, it was even harder to say good-bye to Marlowe. I'd really gotten to like the little guy. And with Cindy, at least I could hate her a little bit. I knew that wouldn't last, but it was some comfort at the moment. I had no reason to hate Marlowe. He'd never done anything to me but make me laugh and make me feel good. I'd even gotten him finally, on our next-to-last weekend on Fire Island, to go for a short walk with me and Norton. He made it almost all the way to the market. Now I picked him up and scratched his full, standing-up-straight ears. "You can come over anytime," I told him.

Norton was surprised we were leaving so soon. Once I'd lugged him over there, he was prepared to spend the night. He meowed, a tad annoyed, when I put him back into his bag. Cindy didn't pet him or say good-bye to him. In fact, she wouldn't even look at him. I think she felt too guilty.

Or else she thought that *his* true self might ask her what the hell she was doing dropping us for a guy who wouldn't eat popcorn.

The last thing Cindy said to me was, "You won't be sad for long. You don't really love me. You don't know what love is."

The next few weeks were a little rough. I felt funny watching *On the Waterfront* by myself on Saturday night, and Norton didn't understand why (1) he hadn't been out of the apartment at *all,* not even across town to Cindy's, and (2) if he wasn't going to be able to leave, where was his friend Marlowe to keep him company?

Most of my time was taken up working and feeling sorry for myself. I found comfort in little things: I remembered that Cindy once actually told me she thought the ending to *On the Waterfront* was *stupid*—that Brando shouldn't have had to stand up at the end for the men to go back to work; he was risking serious injury (and this was *before* the doctor). I remembered that she liked to sing the theme song to "The Brady Bunch" when she cooked. And I realized, at last, I could now take taxis everywhere without someone trying to make me feel as if I were personally responsible for famine in Pakistan. In fact, within a day, I'd managed to make a list of things about her that so infuriated me, I had almost forgotten about going back to her to beg and plead for a second chance.

Luckily for my sanity (and the sanity of those around me), I was distracted by the need to prepare for a week-long trip to California. I kept busy making appointments, figuring

out what I was going to do and say . . . It was only three days before I had to leave that it occurred to me I had to do something with Norton.

I considered calling Cindy to see if she'd still take him. I was fairly certain she would, but I didn't feel it was quite the appropriate thing to do. I didn't like the idea of her knowing I couldn't manage without her. I also had visions of Dr. Polaro, whom I could no longer separate from Son of Sam when trying to imagine what he was really like, performing some strange surgical procedures on Norton's fragile and vulnerable body. So Cindy was out. I called almost everyone else I knew—and not one of them could cat-sit for the week. Either they had a cat of their own and felt it wouldn't work, or their apartment building had a strict no-pet rule, or they were allergic to cats, or they were too nervous because they knew what I'd do to them if anything happened to Norton while he was in their care. By the time I'd run through my phone book, I had two days left to come up with a plan.

The reason I was going to California was that I'd agreed to speak at a writers conference in San Diego. I was going to spend three days there, then go to L.A. for the rest of the week to work, see a few people, have a few meetings, and spend some time with my family. Nothing too hectic, nothing too formal, nothing too intimidating—in other words, absolutely nothing that would preclude taking an extraordinarily well-behaved and well-adjusted cat.

I got on the phone immediately. San Diego was a breeze. The conference had booked all the speakers and would-be writers into a large motel near the UCSD campus. The motel was delighted to have a cat spend a few nights in their

care. I had a sudden and brand new appreciation for the laid-back, Southern California lifestyle.

Los Angeles was more difficult, however. My regular hotel wouldn't hear of it. Out of the question. The next five hotels also wouldn't consider having Norton as a customer. But then I struck pay dirt.

The Four Seasons had just built a new hotel in L.A. It was in a very convenient location, was the right price, and was supposed to be terrific. This was their first week open for business.

"How big is he?" they wanted to know.

"Little," I said. "He's very little for a cat."

"Over forty pounds?"

"No. I said he's a *cat,* not a *lion.* I think he weighs *six* pounds.

"Claws?"

"Yes," I said, then realized I should have lied my head off. "But he never scratches anything!" I added immediately. "And if he does, I'll happily pay for any damage." At those last words, I rolled my eyes to the heavens and prayed if there were a god that he hadn't given the Four Seasons a decorator who had a fetish for burlap wallpaper.

"Let me check with the manager. Hold on."

I held on, a wreck, preparing all sorts of arguments for the manager in favor of allowing cats in their rooms. I decided I was even prepared to audition him. "How's this for a deal," I was thinking of saying. "I'll pay for a separate room for Norton for one night, put him in there for an hour. Then you can check him out . . ."

"Hello?"

"I'm still here," I said quietly.

"We'd be pleased to have your cat stay with us," the reservation clerk told me. "What's his name, so I can add him to the guest list?"

That was the first moment I realized I might be able to survive without Cindy. If I was going to marry this wonderful woman on the other end of the phone, I *had* to survive.

The day of the flight, I was totally unprepared. I had no idea how to make a cross-continental airplane trip with a cat, so I was forced to improvise. I assumed that if I were doing anything wrong, some right-thinking airline employee would set me straight.

I was flying with my agent, Esther Newberg, who was also speaking at the conference. Esther happened to have two fears—flying and cats—so when I picked her up at her apartment and she saw Norton, she was ready to call the whole trip off. But Fear Number Two was eradicated by the time we reached the airport. Within thirty minutes, Esther, whose mind is about as easy to change as Attila the Hun's, decided Norton was the greatest animal she'd ever seen. She couldn't get over the way he sat on my lap and peered out the window for the entire drive.

"I'm hoping he does that on the plane, too," I told her.

"What's he done on other flights with you?" she asked.

I decided I wouldn't break it to her. Esther's the nervous type.

When we got to the airport, I put Norton in his bag, slung it over my shoulder, and went to check our bags. At the ticket counter, the woman gave me a boarding pass, tagged my suitcase and sent it slithering along the conveyor

belt, then looked Norton right in the eye. She smiled at him, said nothing, and returned my ticket to me.

Next we went to the security checkpoint. Esther went through with no problem. When Norton and I stepped through, I expected alarms to go off to beat the band. But no. I guess those things are a lot more sensitive to steel and explosives than to fur. All that happened was that one of the female guards patted Norton's head when he stuck it out of the bag to check out his surroundings.

When we got to the gate, I began to have serious doubts that anyone was ever going to say anything about my flying with a cat. Perhaps it was a lot more common than I thought.

Boarding, Norton snuggled down into his carrier when I showed my ticket to the stewardess. All she said was "Seat 8C." Not a word about you-know-who.

Esther and I took our seats, and Norton hopped out of his bag and settled onto my lap in his favorite position—lying straight along my crossed legs, head resting on my left foot. I got a blanket and laid it over him, figuring it would make it easier to hold on to him when we took off.

We saw a short film, instructing us how to correctly fasten our seat belts. (I must say, my theory is that if you're a grown-up human being who can't figure out how to fasten your seat belt, the odds are that you wouldn't have been able to make a plane reservation and actually get to the airport, which means you wouldn't be in a position to enjoy this superb cinematic experience.) Then a stewardess passed by, checking to make sure everyone had managed to understand the film and do the fastening correctly. She looked straight at my lap—upon which sat the cat—smiled,

said nothing, and passed by to look at the next lap. Still no one had said a word about Norton.

For two hours, Norton sat there, the perfect gentleman, staring out the window, fascinated by his first adult close-up glimpse of clouds. He didn't stir; he didn't make a peep. I began to relax.

Two hours and one minute into the flight, someone finally said the very first thing about the fact that there was a cat on board. It was the head stewardess, a woman of about fifty, who had the delicate good looks of Marie Dressler and the charming personality of Nurse Ratched.

"You've got a cat!" were her exact screaming words.

I looked up from my book. Norton turned away from the window to see who was making so much commotion.

"Get him *out* of here!" she hissed.

I looked over at Esther, glanced back to the stewardess.

"Where would you like him to go?" I asked.

"I don't care!" the woman said. "Just get him out of here!"

"Why don't you open the door," I suggested, "and I'll toss him out over Cleveland."

I didn't have a moment to even admire my own calm and wit, because at this point, things accelerated. The man behind me stood up and said, "Oh, my god! There's a cat! I'm allergic to cats! Get him out of here!" The guy started sneezing like a lunatic.

"The cat's been right here for two hours," I said, trying to be a sane voice in the wilderness. "What the hell are you sneezing *now* for?"

The guy couldn't answer me, unfortunately, because he was too busy sneezing, wheezing, coughing, and struggling

to get out of his seat belt so he could escape from the dread cat hair. I thought of suggesting to the stewardess that they should show a short film about how to *un*fasten your seat belt but decided against it.

"Get that cat under the seat!" the woman snapped at me.

"I don't think you want me to do that," I told her.

"Did you hear what I said?!"

"I did. But if you'll just listen for a second—"

"Put him under the seat!!"

I picked Norton—who was responding to the crisis by acting particularly docile and cute—up off my lap and put him on the floor under my seat. When I told him to "stay," the stewardess flew into an absolute rage.

"In his box! Put him in his box!"

Now, I'm not big on public scenes. I'd place them somewhere right below walking on hot coals and sitting through Bette Midler movies on my list of least favorite experiences. But I was starting to get annoyed.

"I *can't* put him in his box. He doesn't *have* a box. That's why I told you you didn't want me to put him under the seat."

This charming woman could not have had a stronger response if I'd said, "I'm carrying a bomb. Give me all your money or this plane's confetti." As far as she was concerned, I was the Salman Rushdie of passengers and she was the Ayatollah.

"What do you *mean* you don't have a box?!" she demanded. At this point I realized there was no way to stop this whole thing from getting completely out of hand, so I figured what the hell and decided to go for it.

"You know those little cages that cats go into? The ones

that fit under the seat? I don't *have* one of those. *That's* what I mean!"

By now, I didn't think it could get any worse. I was wrong. Esther decided to get involved.

"Look," she said—and when Esther says "Look" at the beginning of a sentence, the only thing that comes to mind that *might* be as scary is the moment in *The Godfather II* when Al Pacino hears that Diane Keaton got an abortion—"one of the other stewardesses saw the cat on his lap earlier. She didn't seem to think it was a problem."

"Stewardess?!" The woman was now in an apoplectic fury. *"Stewardess?!!"*

Esther and I looked at each other, not sure what the problem was now. Esther, ever the forceful agent, took a stab at it. "That's right. The other stewardess walked right by and—"

"We are not stewardesses! We are *flight attendants!"*

The next five or ten minutes is a blur. I remember giggling. Then I remember the stewardess . . . er . . . attendant accusing me of smuggling Norton aboard. I have a vague memory of trying to explain that she was mistaken, of her telling me I was breaking the law, of me telling her to go ahead and throw me in airplane jail. I definitely remember Esther rising to Norton's defense and unleashing a string of expletives that would have made John Gotti blush. They didn't seem to have much effect on the Dragon Lady, though.

Other than the fact that there was a wild, untamed jungle beast running free, able at any moment to terrorize the passengers—if you believed what our attendant was saying, the flight was quickly turning into one of those disaster

movies starring Helen Hayes and George Kennedy—the biggest problem seemed to be that they were about to serve us some of their scrumptious airplane food. Apparently, health regulations make it illegal on American planes for a pet to be out of his cage during mealtime. Is this a great country or what? We can't lick the homeless problem, but the FAA has made damn sure that we're able to sit in really cramped little chairs and eat microwaved teriyaki chicken in peace and quiet.

We did eventually work out a compromise, which unfortunately didn't involve my being able to staple our attendant's lips together. I simply agreed to forgo the delicious meal, as did my loyal agent. In exchange, I didn't have to toss my cat out and let him parachute his way to safety. He could stay on my lap. The guy behind me could switch seats with another passenger sympathetic to my plight. And our plane could continue on to San Diego without any more hysteria.

Which is exactly what we did. Norton stared out the window, perfectly content, until we landed. Mr. Allergy moved to the back of the plane and spent the rest of the trip breathing clean, cat-free air. Esther was so furious about Nurse Ratched's behavior that she forgot to be afraid of crashing and dying; she even allowed Norton to sit on her lap for a while. The evil stewardess—on principle alone I refuse to call her an attendant—steered clear of us for the rest of the trip, even refusing to bring us coffee or little Wash 'n' Dries.

The final three hours of the trip were calm.

The hysteria didn't begin again until we landed.

By the time we got our bags, rounded up two other publishing people who needed a ride, waited on line at the rental car desk, found our car, and got directions to the conference, we'd been traveling for nine hours. This is the second lesson I learned (after the one about buying a carrier that will fit under one's seat) about transporting a cat across state lines: nine hours is too long to go without a litter box.

Four people and one cat crowded into a shiny Oldsmobile. The people immediately started grumbling about being hungry and hating Southern California. The cat uncharacteristically started meowing like a lunatic. Norton perched himself on the shelf under the rear window and howled. He kept this up for fifteen minutes or so. I think it took that long for him to realize we still had a ways to go to hit the motel. But once the realization set in, he decided to do something about it.

He urinated all over the backseat.

Needless to say, this didn't go over all that well with my traveling companions. Especially because we couldn't get him to stop. I'd never seen an animal—two- or four-legged—pee for quite so long.

I didn't get angry. I couldn't. It was awfully hard to blame Norton. And from the miserable way he looked, he clearly didn't like it any more than we did. He just didn't know what else to do.

As we stopped at a gas station, in a desperate attempt to clean things up, I realized that I was totally unprepared to have a cat with me for the next week. Not only didn't I have a litter box, I didn't have any litter. I also didn't have any cat food, any cat food dishes, or any little cat treats. Basically, I realized that because of my selfishness in wanting him to travel with me, I'd just put my beloved cat through a crash course of Cat Torture 101.

Norton was clearly mortified and humiliated about his public . . . ummm . . . accident. He didn't seem to understand that it wasn't his fault. He hid under the driver's seat until we pulled into the motel. And once I had let my disgruntled passengers out of the car, I took immediate action to rectify my thoughtless ways.

The first thing I did was drive to a market, where I got a large cardboard box. (I've since gotten *much* more sophisticated about this potentially awkward problem. I now stock up on portable, folding litter boxes, twenty at a time. Any pet store sells them; they're sturdy enough to last a week or two, and they easily slip into my briefcase or traveling bag. I can't recommend them highly enough.) I bought some litter. (Again, years later, I've now gotten this all down to a science: two small five-pound bags of litter easily fit into my suitcase. The moment we hit the rental car, I open up the folding litter box, rip open one of the bags, and *voilà,* Norton's got everything he needs, *immediately* laid out on the floor of the backseat. There's no need to torture him for the entire drive to our final destination, and it makes it a lot easier for me to drive him around town for the rest of my stay. Once I get to my room, I take out a second box and tear open the second bag of litter. Not only does Norton appreciate the extra facilities, I'm sure the rental car company and the hotel are a lot happier. I know the bellboys are. The first time I thought to put a litter box in the car,

I didn't have a second one. So when I checked into the hotel, a not-very-happy guy in a uniform had to lug a used cat box up to my room.) I also bought a scooper at the market so I could clean the box out, a week's worth of food, and a container of cat treats.

Back at the motel, I checked in and set Norton up in fine style. Two ashtrays made perfect food and water bowls. I fed him, showed him that I was setting up his litter box next to the sink, then set him on the bed and started petting him, telling him with the utmost sincerity that he was, very possibly, the greatest animal who'd ever lived. It wasn't too long before he was purring. After half an hour, I decided it was safe to unpack. I was pretty sure I'd been forgiven.

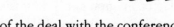

Part of the deal with the conference was that I would spend a portion of each day critiquing manuscripts. Any student who wanted my opinion could leave fifteen to twenty-five pages for me to read; then I was to spend several hours sitting by the pool, and each of the students could spend fifteen minutes with me discussing his or her writing ability (or, at least, my educated opinion of his or her writing ability). I always like this part of every writers conference I go to. It's always interesting to see what people are trying to write and to hear what they *think* they're trying to write. Sometimes, however, these sessions can get a bit hostile. Many editors go right for the throat and actually tell the truth. This is not a recommended course of action. Many of the student writers don't take kindly to even the remotest criticism of their precious words. One has to delicately balance truth with encouragement. It's not always easy.

(Imagine trying to critique, without offending the writer, an Oklahoma dentist's true account of the hilarious world of tartar control, called *Open Wide.*) I try to be gentle since, for the most part, I'm not dealing with professionals. With a pro, an editor can actually come out and say, "This paragraph stinks. Cut it." The pro will usually reexamine the paragraph with an open mind and, if it does indeed stink, get rid of it, or at least rewrite it. With an amateur, such a blunt response can produce anything from tears to guns. So I try to look for positives as well as negatives. Basically, I try to give the would-be writers their money's worth.

Along the same lines, I thought I should try to give Norton *his* money's worth. As long as he'd made the trek across country, it seemed foolish to keep him cooped up in the motel room. So the day of my first poolside sessions, I carried Norton with me, set him down by my chair, and told him to have fun for the next few hours.

As soon as he was free to go where he wanted, he took off for the far side of the motel, where there was a lawn and bushes to prowl through. Before he rounded the corner and disappeared from sight, he meowed once, loudly. I looked up, our eyes met (I'm not making this up, I swear), he made sure I took notice of where he was, then he was gone.

A New York editor who was also teaching at the conference came over to me and asked if I knew there was a freeway on the other side of the motel. I told her I wasn't in any hurry to go anywhere, and she then told me she wasn't all that concerned with my travel plans, she was concerned that my cat was going to end up as road kill. I assured her that he was all right, that he did this kind of thing back on Fire Island all the time, and forgot about it.

I began my first session, a critique of what was supposed to be a novel but what was obviously a thinly disguised true story, about a tumultuous love affair between a young Jewish girl and an older Italian man in the 1930s. The book was poetically titled *Matzos and Spaghetti,* and the author was a seventy-year-old woman named Naomi Weinblatt. My helpful comments ("The dialogue is strong, but are you really sure it has a contemporary feel to it?") were interrupted by the worried editor, who stopped by to tell me she'd just been looking for my cat and he had clearly jumped ship. She'd tried calling his name, but he was nowhere to be found. Once again, I told her to relax and went back to my student, who was defending her novel by saying, "But this really happened!"

While I was commenting on the next manuscript, a Civil War novel about a beautiful, tempestuous woman named Scarlett who was in love with a handsome, brutish rogue ("You have a good feel for the era, but it seems a bit derivative"), I heard the editor's voice calling "Norton . . . Norton . . ." I glanced over, and sure enough, she was thrashing through the bushes near where he'd disappeared, trying to coax him out. I shook my head and went on to my next eager writer.

An hour and several manuscripts later (one science fiction novel in which computers that are really human beings create human beings who are really computers; one series of uplifting essays meant to convey the simple pleasures of life, called *Hey, It Doesn't Matter If You're Fat;* one short story by an extremely clean-cut woman named Joy about an extremely clean-cut woman named Jill who's raped by the side of a muddy road, then crawls for miles until she reaches

a garbage heap, which she staggers into, buries herself in
filth, then dies, wanting only to know the name of her rapist
so she can forgive him—my extremely helpful insight:
"Write what you know."), my editor friend had organized
a little search party. There were now four or five students
crawling around the lawn screaming Norton's name, begging him to come home.

By the end of the next hour (a screenplay in which screen
time mirrored *real* time—in other words, *nothing* happened; a dozen poems about everyday life, of which the
only thing I remember is that the author actually rhymed
"June" with "spoon"; and a thriller that had this for an
opening line: "The bullet creased his forehead and he felt
faint, barely having the energy to remove the pin from the
grenade which was hidden in his coat, which he threw at the
onrushing Krauts, knocking them to hell and gone, which
they deserved." My only comment on this one was "Did he
throw the grenade or the coat at the Krauts?"), I couldn't
stand watching what had now become a dragnet for Norton. It seemed that most of the San Diego community was
searching the grounds for my lost cat. I have to say that
although outwardly I was cool, calm, and collected, in-
wardly I was beginning to get pretty worried. What if
Southern California *wasn't* like Fire Island? What if Norton
decided to *find* Fire Island and decided the freeway was his
best and quickest bet? What if . . .

I decided these musings were getting me nowhere, although I was quite sure one of my students could turn the
situation into a bad prose poem. I decided to find out for
myself if my faith in Norton had been misplaced.

Never showing my fear, I strode over to where I'd last

seen him meow and called his name once. Without even a moment's hesitation, my little gray cat leaped from the bushes and meowed excitedly, happy I'd come to rescue him from all this noise. I petted him proudly, then turned on my heels and headed up the stairs toward our second-floor room. There was nothing but silence from around the pool as Norton trotted after me, ready for his pre-cocktail nap. When I opened the door to usher him inside the building, there was a spontaneous burst of applause.

As Norton scampered inside, I wondered if it would be possible to teach him how to bow. I decided it was probably worth spending a few minutes working on it.

The rest of the conference went smoothly. Norton, depending on his mood, spent part of each day in the room snoozing and part of each day by the pool prowling. He did attend one of my seminars, spending most of it asleep on the podium, directly on top of my notes.

When the readings and seminars and lectures and poolside sessions were over, reaction to my participation was decidedly mixed. Some people thought I was too harsh; some thought I was a welcome dose of publishing reality. I judged my chances of being invited back the following year at about fifty-fifty. The response to Norton was far more one-sided. It was quite clear he was welcome back whenever he wanted to come.

Before he could return to San Diego, however, Norton had to be introduced to the unique town of Los Angeles.

He, Esther, and I got back into our rental car and headed up the coast. Our only stop was at the first market we came

to before we hit the freeway. I explained to the manager why I needed two empty boxes, and he was nice enough to oblige without charging me. The trip went quickly, memorable only because Norton decided to spend half of it perched on my shoulder with his head sticking out the open front window and because Esther decided to spend *all* of it complaining about the fact that the car still smelled decidedly from our last trip with Norton.

I dropped Esther off at the Beverly Hills Hotel, and I went on to the Four Seasons. The Beverly Hills is just a little too show-bizzy for my taste. It's extremely difficult to walk through the lobby or make it through a meal without hearing such charming words and phrases as "fuck *them* if they think I'll go for a step deal" and "the idea is great, but the concept is way off" and "sure, I can get it to Dusty, but is he right for it?" All these things are usually uttered by people who would, in fact, kill for a step deal, have no idea what a great idea actually is and would be terrified if they actually heard one because then they'd have to make a decision, and could only get something to Dusty if they bumped into him on the street and began the conversation with the words, "Excuse me, Mr. Hoffman, you don't know me but . . ."

I dropped Esther off at Show Biz Central and went on over to my hotel. Still a little wary from my encounter with our flight attendant, I was much relieved to hear the desk clerk say to me, with a huge smile on her face, "And this must be Norton."

While he sat on the registration counter, we got checked in quickly and easily, and then we were shown to our room.

I was happy and, as soon as I'd set up the litter box and ashtrays for food and water, so was my cat.

Norton quickly took a liking to L.A. His only problem was at my parents' house. I should say his only problem*s*.

The first problem was an unsolvable one. My parents' house was up in the hills above Coldwater Canyon, and they had coyotes roaming the countryside. Once, when the folks came home from a dinner party around midnight, two coyotes were actually standing in the driveway right in front of the garage. Luckily, the beasts were as frightened of my parents as my parents were of the beasts, and nobody was eaten. But a lot of little animals in the area *had* been eaten. The people who lived next door to my folks had an adorable little poodle. They wouldn't let the dog out at night, fearful that the coyotes would attack under the cover of darkness. But they figured it was all right to let the dog romp around during the day. One morning they let the pooch outside at ten A.M. At noon, they went to find him— and all that was left was the head and the four paws. It was pretty gruesome.

It's difficult to feel sorry for coyotes, as they're unattractive and unappealing animals, but one has to, just a bit. There's so much construction and upheaval around Los Angeles that the coyotes have basically been displaced. Their land is gone and they have nowhere to live or hunt. They are left with little choice but to hang out around rich people's homes and go after their garbage and their pets. I tried explaining all this to Norton, but it didn't go over too well. He didn't care much about the plight of the coyotes. He only cared that he wasn't allowed to venture into the backyard, which looked incredibly inviting to him. But I decided better he be frustrated indoors than coyote food outside.

The second problem was that my parents had two golden retrievers who had the size and intelligence of dinosaurs. Dolly and Rewrite are as sweet as dogs can be. But being around them is like being around two of the Three Stooges. They wag their tails, and expensive crystal goes crashing to the floor. They jump up to greet you, and white linen suits are covered with muddy paw prints. Go to pet them and you spend the next ten minutes trying to wash several gallons of dog slobber from your hands, arms, and even your neck. My parents were wild about these dogs. My father had taken to calling them his "children," and when I called from New York to say hello, if I didn't ask about them, I was severely chastised. I was fairly sure that, by this point, Dolly and Rewrite stood to come out a little ahead of me and my brother in the will.

While I will admit to liking my four-legged "brother" and "sister," it was difficult for Norton to warm up to them—mostly because their favorite activity was chasing him at full speed up the steps, cornering him under my bed, and barking as loud as they could possibly bark, which is about as loud as anything I've ever heard outside of a Who concert I went to in 1972.

Norton got along with the few dogs he encountered on Fire Island. He was usually cautious around them but would give them the benefit of the doubt. I wouldn't say he had any dogs as his best friends, but I had seen him on more than one occasion in my backyard, lying peacefully right next to one of my Fire Island neighbor's dogs. Dolly and

Rewrite, however, were another matter. There was no peace at all when the three of them were in the same house.

The matter settled itself fairly easily. When Dolly and Rewrite were outside (the coyotes willingly stayed away when these two lummoxes were running and jumping about), Norton would come downstairs and poke around the kitchen, the den, and the living room. When the dogs were let in, a gate went up, blocking them off from the upstairs part of the house. Norton would lie on the steps just above the gate, secure in the knowledge that they couldn't get to him and enjoying the fact that his presence there nearly drove them mad.

The third problem was a little more delicate.

My father absolutely loathed, hated, and despised cats.

I tried everything I could think of for his first meeting with Norton. "Don't bring him to the house," he said. I went through my explanation that my guy was different from normal cats, that he was incredibly smart, that he wouldn't bother my father, that at some point in my life, I, too, thought that I didn't like cats, but when I met Norton that all changed. This had about as much effect on my dad as it would have had on a slab of marble. He was unmoved and simply repeated his instructions: "Don't bring him to the house."

I have to say a few words about my father here. He was as perfect a dad as he could have been. We were terrific pals, and I don't think I could have had more respect for him. For years he was one of the top television writers in L.A., and then he became, in his late fifties, one of the top television directors as well. He was a bear of a person, dominating a room with both his looks and his personality.

His shtick was to be gruff and cynical, and on the surface he sure was, but in fact he was the most caring and generous man I ever met in my life. He solved problems and gave advice and was usually just strict enough and unbending enough to provide the right kind of fatherly support. He certainly made plenty of mistakes in his life and his career, but his correct choices more than made up for them. Cindy, who for the first two years she knew him was totally intimidated by him, once said he was the first person she ever met who was larger than life. I always thought he was funny and smart and talented and exceedingly moral, and I enjoyed being with him and my mother as much as I enjoyed being with my closest friends. But he was still my dad and I was still his son—and as such we could, without much provocation, drive each other completely crazy.

As I was taking Norton up to the house for the first time, I had a funny feeling he was going to be another one of those crazy-driving provocations.

The only thing I can really add to the picture, as Norton is about to be introduced to the family, is a brief description of my mother, who happens to be the perfect mom. While my dad tended to bluster, my mom would stay quiet and, behind the scenes, make certain everything was really all right. She has always been the quiet strength behind the family, although she always made sure that everyone else always got all the credit.

My mother, by the time she reached the age of fifty-five, had never officially worked a day in her life. One afternoon, she was in a very "in" restaurant—at the time—Ma Maison. She had decided that she wanted to learn how to be an expert French cook, so she asked the owner, Patrick, how

she should go about it. I think she had something dilettant-
ish in mind, such as going to France for a few weeks and
taking cooking classes. Instead, Patrick told her she should
go to work in the restaurant three times a week—without
pay—and that in six months she'd be a great cook. That's
exactly what she did. She started going in three times a
week as an unpaid apprentice, and within a year, not only
was she a terrific chef, she had started and was running a Ma
Maison cooking school. In the twelve or so years since, she's
become a queen of the L.A. cooking mafia, writing several
respected cookbooks, working intimately with people like
Wolfgang Puck, and befriending people like Julia Child and
Maida Heatter. The only drawback to this is that my mother
is now slightly obsessed with food. I can call up and say,
"Mom, I'm a little down—I got fired from my job and my
girlfriend left me and I was just run over by a truck." The
odds are Mom will sympathize for a minute or so and then
say, "Did I tell you about the crème brûlée I made last
night? It was wonderful. I added some lemon and . . ." And
she'll be off giving me instructions on how to make the
perfect custard.

My mom is fairly unflappable. Nothing much seems to
bother her, and especially as she's gotten more secure over
the years, she always seems to take the long view and the
sane view of things. A good way to illustrate the difference
between the two parents is their reaction when they saw my
first New York City apartment.

I suppose everyone who ever had pretentions of being an
artist and who moved to New York has at one time lived
in an apartment similar to mine. But, to be honest, that
seems almost impossible. I think it's safe to assume that my

apartment was the worst apartment ever built in New York City. It was on Perry Street near Seventh Avenue, right in the heart of Greenwich Village. It was a basement. I don't mean a basement apartment—I mean a basement. A good chunk of what was supposed to be the living room had no floor. It was just dirt and, without working too hard, you could poke around in it and peek down to the subway. When I took the place, there was no kitchen, no bathroom, not even a shower. There was also no light. The only two windows faced the street but were blocked by the building's enormous garbage cans. It also wasn't too well constructed. On particularly rainy or snowy nights, there was usually a pretty good chance that the elements would blow through the cracks in the walls. There is no feeling quite like coming home from a Greenwich Village bar at two A.M. on a snowy, icy, winter morn, crawling into bed—and finding that your sheets have been soaked through and through by snow that has been drifting into your apartment all night.

In my apartment's defense, however, it did have a great painted tin ceiling and a brick wall and a great wooden floor (the parts of it that *had* a floor). Also, it was right in the heart of the Village. *And* it was only $105 a month. Even I knew, however, that it wasn't the kind of apartment that parents love to see their child living in.

I had tried, at the time, to prepare my folks for what they were going to see when they visited New York. I found out later that for weeks beforehand, my mother had driven my father nearly mad saying things like, "Now, remember, when you see Pete's apartment, no matter what you think about it, tell him you love it." Nearly every minute of the day, according to my father, was taken up with her lectures

about how important it was to me for them to support my lifestyle and my taste. Finally my father promised he would be on his best behavior and tell me he approved of where I was living—no matter what it was really like.

When it came time for them to actually see it for themselves, my mother spent the entire taxi ride downtown repeating the rules to my dad. "Tell him it's great . . . Tell him you love it . . . Try to remember what it was like when you were young . . ." She'd been psyching herself up for so long that when I finally heard their knock at the door and opened it to let them in, before I could say a word my mother gushed, "Oh my god! It's lovely! It's perfect! Isn't it perfect? What a great apartment!" I had the presence of mind to say, "Mom, don't you want to come in and *see* it first before you decide if you like it?" Embarrassed, she stepped inside. My father followed. After a two-second pause, my father, looking around in wonder, blew his promise to my mother and said, "Holy shit. What a craphouse!"

The best description of my parents—and the difference between them—came from a director named Bill Persky, who, in a toast at one of their anniversary parties, said it was like "Adolf Hitler being married to Julie Andrews."

Adolf, Julie . . . meet Norton.

I came up to the house for dinner, Norton contentedly hanging from my shoulder in his usual bag. I knew my father had told me not to bring him, but I was sure he didn't really mean it.

My mother made an appropriate fuss when she saw him. Not a cat lover herself, she appreciated the two things that were immediately apparent—he was great looking and so

sweet natured. She petted him delicately, not used to being around a feline. She relaxed when Norton nuzzled her hand with his nose. As he was nuzzling, my dad called down from upstairs, "Is that *cat* with you?" When I called up that yes, indeed, he was, the next roar was, "Well, make sure I don't see him when I come downstairs!"

After a little bit of confusion and a bit more arguing, we all finally agreed that it was impossible for me to arrange for my father never even to *see* Norton, but I did agree to try to keep him out of the way. First I tried to get my dad to understand how special this particular cat was, but he seemed to be the very first person able to resist Norton's charms.

Norton stared at him with his cutest look. He rolled over on his back, paws up in the air, inviting my father to scratch his belly. He tried rubbing up against my dad's leg. He tried snuggling up to him. Forget it. The man was ice. He truly didn't like cats, and Norton was a cat. There was no way this was ever going to be anything but an uneven truce between man and animal.

I dealt with this as best I could, although I was extremely disappointed. I felt bad that my dad couldn't open himself up to the special pleasures that Norton brought me. But clearly he couldn't.

After dinner, I took Norton back to the hotel, making sure he knew that it wasn't his fault my father didn't appreciate him. The next few days, I made my L.A. rounds, seeing agents, writers, film and TV people—a lot of people who called me "babe," told me they loved me like family, and let me know I was "hot." Luckily, one agent kept me from getting a swelled head by explaining to me

that it was "easy to *get* hot. The hard part is *staying* hot."

Sometimes Norton came in the car with me, sometimes he hung out at the hotel. When he was in the car, his new idea of fun, begun on the ride from San Diego, was to perch himself on my shoulder while I was driving and hang his head out my open window. By this time I had no fear that he might jump out. That just wasn't something Norton would do. Even in L.A., where people are used to just about everything, I got a few interesting double takes as we were cruising around.

All in all, I decided that taking Norton from coast to coast was a simple thing to do, bound to get simpler as we both got more experienced. And just as I decided I could see no drawbacks to it, a major drawback occurred.

I got a call from my office. We were publishing a celebrity's autobiography. As is so often the case, the celebrity didn't really write the book; he just talked into a tape recorder and with a writer who was supposed to turn out a book that seemed as if it could only have been written by the celebrity himself. This is fairly common practice, as most celebrities, at least most actors and athletes, have a lot of trouble writing anything other than the words "I," "me," "mine," or "more." I had thought that this particular celebrity's book was under control. The ghost writer had done a terrific job, the book was entertaining, and the timing was right—this lucky celebrity had managed to *stay* hot. But as so often happens, this famous man had gotten cold feet. When he read over his book one last time before we were to go to the printer, he decided that, even though he'd assured us every step of the way that he loved the book that bore his name, he couldn't *really* say all those things for the

record. We'd have to cut and rewrite and drastically change things—or he wouldn't let us publish. If we tried to publish anyway, he wouldn't do any publicity, which would effectively kill any chance of selling the damn thing.

This charmer lived in Santa Barbara, just a couple of hours' drive from L.A. Since I was already close by, the powers that be had decided I should get in my car, head immediately up the coast, and get to work. I had five whole days to completely rewrite the book so we could meet our promised publication date.

No problem.

Scratch that . . . one problem.

Since our celebrity was already bordering on hysteria, and since I was going to be staying in his home—another minor problem was that since this guy drank so much, it was thought I should be next to him twenty-four hours a day or we'd *never* get finished—I didn't know what the hell to do with Norton. My author was so deranged he could claim he was allergic to cats and throw me out of his house, killing any chance for my mission to be a success.

I could think of only one thing to do.

My mother gulped but agreed to let Norton stay in their house for the five days I was to be in Santa Barbara.

"Do you want to . . . ummm . . . check with Dad?" I asked weakly. "Just to be sure?"

"No," my courageous mother said. "I think it's better if we surprise him."

I had to agree. So, since my dad was off at a meeting, I drove Norton over to the house as quickly as possible, left even quicker, and went out to spend what I was sure would be the worst five days of my life—but which would *still* be

better than being around my father when he found out he had to live with Norton for a week.

I was right. When I checked in that night, Mom told me it hadn't gone as well as she'd hoped. For my mother to make an admission like that meant that their house on Hazen Drive must have been something like Nagasaki the day of the bomb. She assured me, however, that Norton was still there—and was still welcome to stay.

When I called in the second night, the report was that Norton had spent some time on the couch in my parents' bedroom and that my father hadn't thrown him out.

The third night, I had been mentally beaten into a near stupor by the aggrieved author, so I was sure I hadn't understood correctly when I heard my mother say the words "Your father told me he thought Norton was quite handsome—for a cat."

The fourth night, I figured I must be getting delirious trying to rewrite fifty pages a day, because I was positive my mother told me, "Norton slept with us last night."

The fifth night, I was too exhausted to even call home. I finished my rewrites somewhere around five in the morning, loaded the manuscript into my suitcase, and ran straight for my car. I arrived back in L.A. at seven A.M.

My mother, who usually is out of bed by six every day, was already up. I kissed her hello and nervously asked after my cat. She smiled, motioned for me to be quiet, and led me up the stairs to her and my father's bedroom. There I saw one of the greatest sights I had ever been privy to.

On the bed, sound asleep under the covers, was my father. On his chest, on top of the covers, was Norton, also sound asleep. My father's arm was curled around the top of the blanket, his hand resting gently on Norton's back.

We tiptoed out of the room, and my mother told me that, during the course of each day, Norton kept trying to get closer and closer to my dad. At first my dad shooed him away. Then, as Norton refused to give up, he began to be intrigued. As soon as the poor guy weakened, Norton went in for the kill. By their fifth night together, he had my dad petting him for hours while he sat directly on his chest. They fell asleep like that. My mom told me that my dad actually kissed Norton good night.

I had a cup of coffee and waited for the two pals to wake up. Norton was glad to see me, although not nearly as glad as he should have been. All my dad talked about was what an amazing thing it was to listen to Norton purr. "He must be happy here," he kept saying. "He purred the whole time."

"I do think he likes it here," my mother acknowledged.

The last words my dad said to me, before I drove to the airport, were, "When are you coming out here again?"

"I guess in a month or so," I told him. "Why?"

He caressed Norton. "Are you sure you don't want to leave him here until you get back?"

The cat who went on dates

When I returned from California, two significant—and not unrelated—events occurred: Norton discovered Pounce. And I rediscovered the nearly forgotten, rather distasteful yet undeniably exciting ritual of modern dating.

Pounce, for those of you who are ignorant of this nectar of the cat gods, is bite-sized morsels, perhaps the size of a Cheerio. It is serious junk food, the Reeses Peanut Butter Cup for the discerning feline. Pounce comes in small cardboard cans, each can a different color depending on the chicken, liver, shrimp, or beef flavor. I saw them sitting on a supermarket shelf one afternoon and, always on the lookout for a pleasurable experience for my gray companion, decided to bring one can home and try it out.

That night, before I went to bed, I gave two Pounce (Pounces? Pince??) to Norton, then put the can inside a kitchen cupboard. I got undressed and did some reading for work. After half an hour or so, I was ready to turn out the light. Norton wasn't in his usual position on the pillow next to me, so I called his name. As usual, he came running and jumped onto the bed. But he didn't, as usual, settle right down to go to sleep. Instead he scurried and prowled and nuzzled his nose into my face until I realized he was trying to tell me something. I felt as if I were in the middle of a "Lassie" segment, except when I finally got up and agreed to follow Norton, he wasn't trying to tell me that Timmy was in trouble. He was trying to tell me he wanted another Pounce.

I obligingly opened the cupboard, gave him one, told him that this would not be acceptable behavior on a regular basis, then went back to bed. In the morning, I woke up, stretched, felt for a familiar chin to scratch—but there was nothing there. Somehow—I'm sure I should be a tad nervous about how closely Norton and I are attuned to the same wavelength—I knew where he was. My instinct was confirmed when I got out of bed: Norton was sitting on my kitchen counter, staring hungrily up at the cupboard that held the Pounce, scratching pathetically at the cabinet door.

I gave him two more of the biscuits and thus began a daily ritual that goes on to this day. Every morning, before I head off to work, my last deed before I go out the door is to give Norton two or three Pounce. Every night, right before I go to bed, he gets two or three more. I have no idea what makes this stuff so appealing to him, unless it's the scrumptious-sounding pregelatinized wheat feed flour or the equally delicious ferrous sulfate. But I do know that the thought of eating them drives my cat wild

with desire. In between his morning and late-night snacks, Norton seems to spend an awful lot of time attempting to tunnel his way through my kitchen cabinet, trying to get to the Pounce on his own. Judging by the scratch marks on the pine, he's just about ready to give the Count of Monte Cristo a run for his money. I expect a major break-through in another few months, when he should either reach the cans of Pounce or the apartment on the other side of the hall.

In case you haven't yet come up with the connection between Norton's snacking habits and the title of this chap-ter, just start thinking of women, during this period of my life, as my Pounce.

For the first time in several years, I was unattached. It was a very strange feeling. As much as Cindy and I had fought against the concept of coupledom, there was no denying that we had been a full-fledged couple—and had been for a long time. As such, we'd fallen into our own routines and been included in the routines of others.

Our deal was that although we were not required to include the other in every little social occasion, there *were* situations that qualified as command performances. If any-thing particularly good or interesting came up that I knew she would enjoy (or, of course, vice versa), she (or I) had first dibs. The same if anything important, horrendously boring, or terrible popped onto our social calendars, a situa-tion where one of us needed the other's support. On the other hand, if either one of us had a normal, everyday, run-of-the-mill occasion to attend, we were not stuck—ei-ther doing the inviting or being the invitee. If I had tickets to the opening of the new Sondheim musical, Cindy *had* to be my date. If I was invited by an actor friend who was appearing in a summer stock revival of *Six Rms Rv View,* I was free to take anyone I wanted. If Cindy had a dreadful wedding to go to that involved driving two-and-a-half hours into New Jersey, I was there. If she had her semi-boring monthly dinner with her uncle who always insisted—loudly—that people were constantly coming up to him on the street and mistaking him for Rouben Mamoulian, she was appreciative if I went, but I didn't *have* to go. It made sense at the time, and it seemed to work for us, for a while at least. (I actually went to dinner a surprising number of times with Uncle Max, but no one, while I was there anyway, ever came up to him and called him Mr. Mamoulian. He liked me because I was the only person he'd ever met, other than all these alleged strangers on the street, who actually knew what Rouben Mamoulian looked like. In case you're wondering, yes, he was the spitting image.) When it *stopped* working, one of the first things to get used to, if I didn't want to go alone, was finding a partner for special occasions. As much as Norton would have appreciated the opening night of *Cats,* I don't think he could have handled most theatrical events or very many charity dinners.

I think I handled the breakup with Cindy fairly well. The night that it happened, I went back to my apartment and had a decent cry. Norton hung out on the bed and let me pet him and hug him to my heart's content. He kept looking up at me, concerned, trying to figure out what could possibly be wrong. I guess I can't say that he ever truly figured it out, but he did purr particularly loudly for a stretch, an open invitation for me to collapse, put my head on his

stomach, and use him for a pillow, which I did gratefully for quite a long while.

When I finally felt like talking to a human, I called my oldest friend, Paul Eagle, in Los Angeles. Paul wasn't there, however, so I had to settle for his phone machine. I left a message, something subtle along the lines of "Hi, it's me. Just checking in. How 'bout those Giants, huh? Rams stink. Oh, by the way, Cindy dumped me and I'm suicidal. Give me a call."

Next on my list was my brother, Eric, also in L.A. The message I left on *his* phone machine was a bit more rational: "Hey. Just calling to say I hate women. Talk to you later."

Between the crying, the soothing purring, and the emotional trauma of the day's events, I was now ready to go to sleep. In fact, I was looking forward to a night of lying in the dark for several hours, gazing ahead with a ghostly stare, contemplating the meaninglessness of life, followed by a fitful period of tortured dreams. That was actually starting to seem like fun. So I turned off the lights, gave Norton one last hug and kiss, and began my suffering.

I had suffered for about a minute and a half when the phone rang. I turned on the light and picked up the receiver. It was Eric, my brother, who had cleverly detected the hysteria in my message and wanted to know what was wrong. I told him. The whole story. Repeating the thing out loud, rather than just inside my head, brought a few more tears. When I was done, Eric began to be supportive.

Now . . . understand this: My brother is a great guy and we've been close all our lives. But he lives in L.A. And he's a screenwriter. *And* he's been through therapy (and, worse,

acting classes). Add it all up and you get someone who *loves* to be supportive. He likes to hug and share his feelings and tell people he loves them.

Which is all very nice, I must say, except that I am *not* like this. I don't particularly like to hug anyone unless there's a chance we're going to exchange bodily fluids. I don't actually think my feelings are particularly interesting; sharing them usually is about as appealing to me as the idea of sharing Leon Spinks's dentures. Another reason I'm not wild about all this feeling sharing is that I've found most people don't really want you to share your feelings. They want to share *their* feelings and then have you tell them you feel exactly the same way. In general, when it comes to feelings, I much prefer showing to telling.

Nonetheless, I was in no position to complain about my brother's support. I'd just poured my heart out to him. I could clearly take a little genuine emotional contact in return. So Eric told me he was there for me. He told me he loved me. He told me he was sorry the whole thing with Cindy had happened, but at the same time, he was glad because it gave him the opportunity to tell me he loved me, which he didn't get to do often enough. I, in turn, appreciated all the sentiments, except perhaps the last one, which I thought was going a bit far, and told him I loved him, too, which I certainly did.

After half an hour of such talk, we hung up.

I was now exhausted. All that sharing had taken a lot out of me.

The light went off, my head hit the pillow, my eyes closed. Sleep was very near.

But not near enough. The phone rang again.

It was Eric. He asked if I wanted him to come east. For support. I was genuinely touched by the offer, but I told him it wasn't necessary. I had plenty of people to share feelings with in New York if I really felt the need.

"I love you," he said.

"I know," I said before hanging up. "Thanks again."

I think I actually dozed off for a good thirty or forty seconds before the phone began ringing. It was now after two A.M.

"What?" I sighed into the phone.

"Pete," Eric said, "I just hope you understand that I'm here for you, totally and absolutely."

"I understand," I said. "Totally and absolutely."

"I'm just so concerned. You don't sound good."

"Well, I'm pretty tired right now. I'll sound a lot better in the morning. After I get some sleep."

"Are you sure?"

"Pretty sure. Sleep is what's important now."

"I love you," Eric said. "I really do."

"Good night," I said.

This time I didn't even bother to try to fake it. I sat up in bed, lights on, stiff as a board, waiting. I didn't have long to wait.

"Yup," I said into the phone.

It was Paul this time. He'd just gotten my message. He was surprised how awful I sounded and wanted to know exactly what had happened. Well, by this time, I was too exhausted and too cranky to go into much detail. Also, I'd already poured my heart out once; twice in one day was near impossible. So I told him he'd have to settle for the abbreviated version and then get the full rundown the next

morning. He understood, and I gave him a short take on the breakup with Cindy: unsuspecting me, trip-to-England birthday present, evil doctor, crying, crying, purring and crying, phone call, phone call, phone call, I love you, I'm there for you, I love you, tired, the end.

Paul sympathized exactly the right amount—about fifteen seconds' worth—then said good-bye. Before I could hang up the phone, though, he managed to get in one quick "I love you."

I sat in bed for a minute, light still on, waiting. I knew my friend Paul. This would be a hard situation for him to resist. After all, this was a person who, when I once called him from New York, long distance, to see if he had the number of an L.A. florist so I could send some Mother's Day flowers to my mother, made a big deal out of finding the right number, keeping me on hold for several minutes, then gave me the number of a pet store. When I called him back, demanding the real number and yelling at him for making me look like an idiot trying to order roses from Phil of Phil's Pet Parlor, he apologized for his sophomoric sense of humor, thumbed through the yellow pages, and gave me another number—which turned out to be a bowling alley. Running up a huge phone bill now, I called him a third time, screamed, and he swore he'd do it right—and gave me the number of a Korean massage parlor. So I was fairly certain he'd be unable to resist a follow-up call now in my moment of despair. It was too good an opportunity to waste.

I was right. In two minutes, the phone rang. Wearily, I answered it.

"Are you calling to tell me you love me?" I asked.

"How'd you know?" a woman's voice answered.

"Who is this?" I asked.

"Laurie."

Paul's wife. She loved me as much as Eric did, she said.

But not as much as the next person, an old college friend Paul had called the moment he'd hung up on me. And that old friend didn't love me nearly as much as the next three old friends who called. When Paul finally called back to tell me that the more he thought about it, he *liked* me but *loved* Cindy, I decided that my period of mourning for Cindy was pretty much over.

I realize it seems fairly brief—one night of mourning after several years of love—but I have to say that despite the emotional upheaval, there was a certain sense of relief when the relationship ended. It was a little like being reborn, although, granted, it was like being born with an enveloping sense of sadness. To fight off that sadness, I immediately began to indulge all my single-man fantasies: I bought several boxes of Sugar Pops and Cocoa Puffs and ate bowls of the stuff for dinner—with *no* vegetables on the side. I never went *near* the public television channel on my TV dial and watched sports practically every waking minute. (I realized I had gone slightly over the edge when I was starting to care—deeply—about which woman was going to win the Dinah Shore Open golf tournament.) I didn't make my bed. And I left all the little post-shaving hair particles on the sink—for days on end.

Of course, eventually, other fantasies and yearnings came into play. It wasn't too long before I began scratching at the cabinet door for women.

I wasn't really looking for anything serious or substantial at this point. I was much more interested in shallow, superficial, and, preferably, sweaty.

I wasn't much of a dater. People of my generation never really dated. We hung out, we did stuff, we burned banks, we took psychedelic drugs and rolled around on water beds together, but we didn't really date. This was a whole new experience, and I was determined to make the most of it.

The first thing I learned was that attractive women (and here I'm going with the following somewhat limited definition: models, actresses, and any woman who drives her own jeep who isn't named Gutty, Rocky, or Gertie) like to go out with writers. Not all of them, mind you. A lot of them like to go out with investment bankers or very ugly rock stars or photographers who only have first or last names, not both, but on the whole, they think writers are smart and they're attracted to smarts. This works out well because I've also observed that most writers like to go out with attractive women. In fact, going out on a limb, my own theory is that, deep down, male writers, with the possible exception of Vaclav Havel and Oscar Wilde, write *only* so they can impress women. Otherwise, why go through the sheer agony of lonely, torturous days trying to create, not to mention entire lifetimes of poverty and often ridicule? It's all done in the hope of an Ophelia, an Emma, a Daisy coming up to you in a bar and saying, "Excuse me, aren't you Fyodor Dostoyevski? I just *loved The Brothers Karamazov.* That Alyo-

sha was the *sexiest* man. Is it true that writers create characters based on their true selves?"

Models go for smarts, I believe, because they don't respect their own beauty. How could they? They're around women all day who are even *more* beautiful than they are. Where I see perfection, they see hair that's not as thick as Paulina's. I see sculpted grace, they see skin that's not as tight as Christie's. Their beauty has no mystery for them, no allure, because they see it as something they have no control over. It's an external, artificial attribute. Writers, on the other hand, worship beauty above all. This is partly because most of us are ugly little rodents with bad posture and ailing gums whose sole sense of worth comes from what we can produce from within. And it's partly because we spend most of our lives stooped over a word processor trying desperately to *create* beauty—and we know how difficult, how near-impossible and absolutely hellish that is to do.

So . . . it's established that writers go for attractive women and that attractive women go for writers. But there's one other thing that women tend to go for and fuss over and melt at the sight of.

Riiigghhhttt.

Cute gray cats with round heads and folded ears.

Hallelujah.

~~~

The first step in restructuring my social life was to decide what to do about a place for the summer. The little blue house in Fair Harbor had never been *my* house as much as it had been *our* house. Cindy and I had found it together and enjoyed it together. It didn't seem right for Norton and me to go back without her and Marlowe.

Enter Norm Stiles, a man destined to go down in the Fire Island Hall of Fame.

A friend for several years, Norm had been out to the house to visit us a few times over the various summers. Now he'd decided it was time to take the plunge and begin regular weekend visits. He asked if I wanted to share a house.

The more I thought about this, the better it seemed. It would be fun to have a big place instead of the blue dollhouse. It would be great to have a regular tennis partner. We could have parties—actual people coming over to Pete and Norm's for fun and recreation. Plus, I liked to cook and Norm said he liked to clean up.

Done.

We not only took a bigger house, we took over a familiar one. David, my writing partner, and Diana had decided it was time to settle in Connecticut, so we moved into their place. Norton certainly appreciated the convenience of this resettling, since he already knew how to get to the house from all points. His only reservation about the spot was one particular bluejay who lived around there. This bird had a thing for my cat and would fly around him, mocking him loudly, occasionally swooping down and pecking at Norton's head. Norton *hated* this bird. I used to try to explain to him that *he* was the cat, he was supposed to be able to take a bird one on one, but my pep talks never took hold. Until the day we left Fire Island, Norton was totally intimidated by the bluejay.

My initial instincts about the move had been correct. Having a bigger house was a nice luxury. Norm and I played

combative tennis. I learned to make a mean grilled chicken and Norm turned out to be the best dishwasher stacker I ever saw. (I swear, it seemed that he could cram most of the house, including the living room couch, into that thing.) But the one thing I had to get used to was people.

I'd been a summer resident of Fair Harbor for four years. In that time, I hadn't met one single person other than the two guys who ran the market, the Rockette Lady, and my excuse for not writing—the coffee klatch. A good part of this is due, as I'm sure you've realized by now, to the fact that I welcome new, close relationships into my life about as warmly as the eighteenth century welcomed lepers. Norm, on the other hand, had been a weekender for about a minute and a half before he knew every single person who had a home in the community, most of their regular guests, and all of their personal habits. Walking down the street with Norm was an amazing experience. His level of popularity was such that I nicknamed him "the Mayor," as in "the Mayor of Fair Harbor." Thinking of Norm as the Ed Koch of the beach set was not so farfetched.

"Hey, Norm! How's it hangin'?"

I couldn't get over the fact that near total strangers would just stop and pat him on the back. Women flocked around him. Norm happens to be the head writer for "Sesame Street," which, in addition to being the best job in the world, means that women automatically think he's intelligent, sensitive, and funny. He actually is all of those things—although if you ever meet him, ask him what he was doing with those binoculars on the porch that night.

"Norman, you were a wild man last night! Are you discoing tonight?"

I had to stop at this one and ask him where the hell one discoed in Fair Harbor. Norm told me they turned the restaurant into a club at eleven P.M. Shocked, I wondered when they'd started doing that, a week or two ago? No, Norm told me—four years ago.

Oh, well. So I wasn't big on staying up past ten o'clock during the summer.

One little guy who obviously *had* been out and around, however, was a certain debonair Scottish Fold.

Norton usually tagged along on my strolls with Norm to the tennis court or the market or the bay. It was unbelievable how many Fair Harborites knew him. It seemed that every other person we passed would first say hello to Norm, then give Norton a warm greeting—by name—then look at me and stare quizzically, as if to say, "Hmmm, this guy looks vaguely familiar. Oh, well, maybe not."

Sometimes I'd initiate the conversation and ask how they knew my cat. A common response was "Oh, he comes over and visits with us all the time."

When people would speak to me directly, I'd usually get "Oh, you're the guy Norm told us about. Is it true you refuse to ever leave your porch?" or, my favorite, "Ohhh, you're Norton's dad!" It wasn't until *many* people had greeted Norton on our strolls that it occurred to me he never wore a name tag. Which meant that unless he *spoke* to my neighbors when he went visiting, they couldn't possibly know his name.

I decided not to pursue this line of thinking any further. It didn't seem healthy.

"Normie, meet you at the sixish ce soir?*"*

Now this is something that deserves to be discussed.

There was a strange and eerie Stephen Kingish ritual that took place in Fair Harbor every Friday and Saturday evening. As I'd sit on my porch sipping a beer, shoes off, relaxing, I'd see scores of people, dressed as if for the ballet—or, at worst, a "Miami Vice" audition—parading by, heading toward the dock. Most of the women had on enough makeup to make the National Kabuki Theater of Japan proud. Most of the men had on shirts that revealed enough hair on their chests, shoulders, and backs to re-sod a good-sized minor league baseball stadium. They all had drinks in one hand, and their arms were all cocked at forty-five-degree angles, I suppose the best possible angle to prevent spillage.

It wasn't until Norm was there to explain the mysteries of Fire Island that I truly understood what I was witnessing.

The dock was the best place in town from which to watch the beautiful sunsets. So all the townspeople would gather there under the pretense of enjoying nature's spectacle but, in reality, they would be desperately trying to pick up any member of the opposite sex who didn't have sun poisoning and spend the night with him or her. These gatherings regularly started around six in the evening, thus the endearing word "sixish" was born into our vocabulary.

There were regular sixishes and special sixishes (like July Fourth, when there were not only fireworks but local artisans peddling their photographs, jewelry, T-shirts, and personalized Kadima paddles), and there were theme sixishes. There was something awe-inspiring when, come the annual *Animal House* sixish, fairly successful lawyers, publishers, realtors, what have you, would stand around in togas, sipping their drinks, swiveling their heads in search of amiable

companionship, and chanting, "Par-*ty* . . . par-*ty.*"

Norm took me to a sixish, against my better judgment. I didn't really like mingling with people who dressed up in togas (even if they weren't dressed in togas then, it was enough to know that they *would* do so at some point in the summer), but he decided it was something I had to do. This was supposed to be a new life.

I brought Norton along, figuring he'd like to see it. Why not—he already knew most of the people who were there.

I have to say, I didn't quite get it. The whole concept slid right by me. Why would people come from New York City—the stress and dress capital of the world—to the most beautiful, quiet, relaxing beach imaginable and *re-create New York?* Why would anyone wear stockings on an eighty-five-degree Saturday night when they didn't have to? Or silk sport jackets? Why wouldn't people wear shorts and a T-shirt? And what was this fear of spending an evening alone? After five days of pushing and shoving your way through several million people crammed into a few square miles, why would anyone want to cram into a few square feet with several hundred of the same people?

Norton was a big hit at his first sixish—he got many compliments, from old friends as well as new, on his ears as well as his personality. I was less of a hit. No one complimented either my ears or my personality. I think I found it a little too hard to conceal my despair at the amount of exposed cellulite. It was as if I'd been suddenly transported into Jack La Lanne's personal hell. (For those of you who have already been captivated by Norm's charm and think he's a much more sensitive guy than I am, please note that after this first dockside experience of mine and ensuing state

of shock, he devised the perfect sixish lure for a member of the opposite sex: First, tie a piece of danish to a string. Any flavor will do, though cherry, prune, or cheese are preferable. Casually drop said danish on the ground. When your unsuspecting prey bends over, thinking he or she can surreptitiously shovel away some free dessert, yank the string, pulling the delectable pastry several feet closer to your house. Your prey will pursue. Repeat as long as necessary, which is until you've got the poor sucker trapped in your living room. This simple trick should be good for up to a solid three blocks. For best results, have lit candles, a batch of frozen daiquiris, and some peanut M&M's all set up, waiting at home.)

Norton, to his credit, seemed to share my lack of interest in the sixish. There were certainly no other cats to befriend. The only other quadruped was a small sheepdog whose idea of fun was barking loudly and chasing Norton into the bushes by the market. We left after I overheard a conversation Norm was having with a woman psychologist. Her specialty was people with ego problems. "Sometimes," she was saying, "I want to shake these people and say, 'Don't you understand? I'm the best damn psychologist in New York! Why don't you just get better?'"

Norton let me carry him after that one. We both wanted to get home as quickly as possible.

~~~

Norm, Norton, and I shared a summer house for three years. Norm set new records for popularity on the island and—I like to think that rooming with me was some help here—wrote some of his best sketches for Oscar the

Grouch. Norton had a very happy transition from kittenhood to adolescence, acquiring all of the traits that go with
the teenage and early twenties years. He became an incredible know-it-all. It was impossible to tell him anything. If it
was raining and he wanted to go out, all my explanations
of how he was going to be very wet and miserable if I
opened the door went for naught. He insisted on learning
everything for himself. He also became much more independent, taking to staying out all night when we were at the
beach (or *almost* all night—he'd usually meow very loudly
for me to let him in at five A.M.). I never questioned his
whereabouts; I did give him the benefit of the doubt that
he was staying away from the all-night disco. Probably the
most traumatic event of this period was the removal of
Norton's . . . uh . . . manhood. Although I would have loved
to have a kitten fathered by him (I'll try to stay away from
any grandparent comparison), everyone and anyone who
ever had a cat impressed me with their vehemence about
avoiding all the things that went with breeding. It was the
thought of a cat (and Norton, during this thought process,
became *"a* cat," not *"my* cat" or "that cute little guy" or
anything like that) spraying all over my apartment, my
clothes, my work, my life that finally swayed me. I couldn't
face it. So I made an appointment and took him to the vet.

Norton's vet, who has his practice down in the Village,
looks exactly like Santa Claus. He's large, jolly, and has
long white hair and a white beard. He's a terrific doctor
with a great bedside manner. When I took Norton in for
this dreaded operation, I was in desperate need of that
manner.

"Really," he told me. "It's painless. He won't feel a thing."

"Maybe I should stay," I said. "I could get a cot, set it up in his room . . ."

"He doesn't have to spend the night," Santa told me. "You can pick him up at five."

"Should I do anything special for him? Buy him a soft bed? Should I get the cable guy to disconnect Channel J?"

"He'll be *fine*," the vet said. "This is not going to be traumatic for him."

The vet was right. Norton handled it like a champ. I, however, was a wreck. I spent most of the day doubled over with cramps in the groin area. I was also sure that Norton would hate me when I came to pick him up. I was positive there'd be lots of resentment. I was already dreading his shrink bills.

At five sharp, I returned to the vet's, and there was Norton, slightly groggy but looking none the worse for wear. Santa showed me the incision, and when the room stopped spinning around, I had to admit that it didn't look bad. He told me to make sure Norton took it easy for one night— and then the whole thing would be forgotten and he'd be completely back to normal.

He was certainly right about that. Norton showed no ill effects from the operation, neither psychological nor physical. It certainly didn't keep him from catting around all night on Fire Island. He didn't even gain weight, which I'm sure was due to his outdoor life climbing trees and prowling the Fair Harbor undergrowth.

As for me, during these house-sharing years, my tennis

game improved tremendously, I progressed from grilled chicken to a superb (if I may say so myself) cold poached salmon with an aioli sauce, and we had an incredible amount of fun. But I never managed to become an habitué of the sixishes. I also never dated any egotistical psychologists; nor did I have to resort to The Mayor of Fair Harbor's Original Danish Lure.

But I did enter the full-fledged world of hemming and hawing, awkward embraces, and tentative intimacy. In fact, I did more than enter. I plunged in headfirst.

My first real post-Cindy involvement was with a woman named Sarah. Sarah and I, it would eventually turn out, had about as much in common as Madonna and the Pope. But for the first three months we went out I thought she was perfect.

To begin with the superficialities, she was absolutely stunning. She had dark hair and skin that tanned a deep, deep brown. She had long, perfectly tapered legs and—remember, I warned you this was during my Shallow Period—she wore the shortest skirts I'd ever seen this side of the Twiggy era. She was sensuous and sensual, and to top it all off, as I got to discover when she decided she could trust me, she didn't mind doing a certain amount of her clothes shopping at Victoria's Secret.

Unfortunately, after beginning with the superficialities, I couldn't come up with anything else. And what kept poking through and causing serious trouble was that there were two areas in which we could never resolve our differences. One was *sense of humor.* Sarah's philosophy—which she hap-

pened to mention fairly often—was that "A sense of humor is fine, but there are certain times in life that are inappropriate for humor." She would get rather upset when I would unleash *my* philosophy of life, which was that she was probably right but that "I just haven't ever found any of those times yet."

The other great area for our fights was none other than Norton. Sarah was terribly jealous of him, most specifically because I often used him as an excuse not to spend the night at her apartment. She used to insist that Norton was my means of avoiding commitment. I suppose, if forced to analyze it, she was right, though I prefer to think he was just my means of not having to actually *tell* Sarah I was avoiding commitment. My excuse for not spending the whole night in her apartment was that I didn't like leaving Norton alone.

"He'll survive a night alone," she'd say.

"I know," I'd say back. "But he won't *like* it."

As far as excuses went, this one was mostly true. I *didn't* like leaving him alone. But there were other reasons, too. I also didn't like Sarah's apartment. It was one of those new, white brick buildings that have the same sense of warmth as Stalin's Russia. She had filled the apartment up with little knickknacks and kinetic sculptures and modern art prints. It looked like the kind of place I always figured Andy Warhol would go to die.

We once had a huge fight when, at two in the morning, I slipped out of bed and told her I was going home. She was furious. I told her about my Norton and the Predator Theory. She became even more furious. As I kept trying to explain away my leaving, Sarah finally burst into tears and

told me she absolutely couldn't see me anymore. She was ending the relationship. A little surprised at the extent of her reaction, I wanted to know exactly why she felt this way.

"Because Norton is just a cat," she sniffled. "And he only has cat feelings. I'm a person. I have *people* feelings. But you don't care about my feelings. You really don't." By this time she was crying. "I think you like your cat better than you like me," she said through her tears.

"Sarah, that's just not true," I said.

"What isn't?" she asked hopefully.

"I don't think Norton only has cat feelings."

Needless to say, this turned out to be one of those inappropriate times for humor. Sarah wouldn't see me for two months after that.

Sarah was constantly refusing to see me for two months or announcing that our relationship was over. Somehow, though, we'd always get back together. Our reunions usually came about when we'd run into each other at a restaurant and realize we liked each other better than the person we were with, or when she'd be depressed about her job and need someone to talk to, or when I'd get the new Victoria's Secret catalogue in the mail and happen to be browsing through it at bedtime. We couldn't seem to stay together and we couldn't seem to stay apart.

One Valentine's Day, on the spur of the moment, I decided to take her up to Vermont for a weekend of skiing and romance. Sarah was so appreciative of gestures like this it was a little scary. We rarely took vacations or trips together. Again, chalk this up to that lack of a commitment.

Once, we almost went to Arizona for a few days at the Phoenix Biltmore, just about my favorite place in America outside of the Liberace Museum in Vegas. But the Biltmore refused to accept cats so, outraged, I canceled the reservation. As soon as I did that, Sarah canceled me for three weeks. Now, with the promise of a long, snowy weekend ahead of us, I don't think I'd ever seen her so pleased and affectionate. Even I felt a little guilty when I realized that all I had to do was, on two days' notice, find a romantic Vermont inn that took cats.

By my twentieth phone call, Sarah was a lot less pleased and substantially less affectionate. As I made my twenty-first call, I was a desperate man. When the innkeeper answered, I went through my by-now rehearsed Norton pitch. I sensed a hesitation on her part—which was far better than the immediate turndowns I'd received already—so I really poured it on. I was almost ready to go the whole route—and tell her about the time Norton rescued my poor lost grandmother in that horrible snowstorm—when the innkeeper cracked.

Which is how my Scottish Fold came to go cross-country skiing.

The day after we arrived at the inn, Sarah told me she was pretty good at downhill but had never gone cross country. We set out to remedy this. First, however, we thought we'd experiment with Norton and snow. He'd never been outside in snow before; most of his outdoor experience up to this point was in the summertime. But in Vermont, summertime was a distant memory. There was a foot-high blanket of soft powder, so we gently tossed Norton out the front door of the inn and waited with bated breath.

The first thing that happened was that he sank without a trace. He was so light and the snow was so high and so soft, Norton was simply enveloped. In the next moment, however, he went flying up into the air, so caked with white flakes he easily could have fit in with Siegfried and Roy's act.

Much to my surprise, he loved the snow. He ran to the nearest tree, raced up halfway, and dove back to the ground. He burrowed, gopherlike, forging a tunnel with his nose and face. He rolled over on his back, now-white paws clawing at the blue sky. I don't think I'd ever seen an animal having so much fun.

After half an hour of this, I think it got too cold for him. He showed up at the inn, snowflakes and tiny icicles dripping off his coat. I wrapped him up in a towel, dried him off, which he seemed to appreciate, and then he lay down in front of the living room fire for a nap. By this time, of course, the owner of the inn was ready to adopt Norton as one of her own.

After lunch, Sarah and I put on cross-country skis and headed out. Norton, as usual when I went for a walk in the country, followed. I tried to talk him out of this one, but he insisted. Snow or no snow, cold or no cold, he was ready to explore.

When we hit the nearby woods, Norton didn't exactly stay on the trail with us. He zigzagged around like a lunatic, jumping onto trees, bounding into snowbanks, then suddenly stopping and meowing like crazy until I'd come and carry him for a while.

All in all, he was happy. And he was even happier when, two hours later, we repeated the toweling and fireplace

routine. Even Sarah was happy and had to admit—over a late-night cognac and backgammon—that Norton was a worthwhile addition to the Valentine's Day weekend. She sighed contentedly and told me she thought she was falling in love.

Two days later, however, when I refused to spend the night at her apartment, she decided she never wanted to see me again.

In between the various romantic interludes with Sarah, there were other romantic (and not so romantic) interludes. Norton managed to involve himself in almost all of them.

For about six weeks, I fell head over heels for a woman sportswriter who lived in Boston. This meant some serious weekend commuting, either to Boston or to some college basketball game in some southern town where lox and bagels were only a disturbing myth.

The first time I went to Boston to see her, I showed up with two steaks, a bottle of red wine, and a cat.

Norton liked Boston (the Pan Am Shuttle stewardesses, er, flight attendants, are *very* nice to small, friendly animals), but the sportswriter couldn't envision interviewing Dean Smith with a cat on her shoulder, so that cooled off fairly quickly.

I went out with an editor at a rival publishing company who used the word "Dickensian" more than anyone I'd ever met. When she was introduced to Norton, she admired his looks but made the mistake of asking if I'd named him after Norton Simon. The idea that someone thought I could actually name my cat after the world's dullest billionaire was a staggering concept to me. If she'd said Kenny Norton even, she might have stuck around for a reasonable period of time. As it was, we lasted two weeks.

One week was spent in the company of a fashion designer. She probably wouldn't have made it through the whole week except that we met a few days before Halloween and she confessed to me over our first lunch that the previous Halloween she'd gone to a costume party completely naked—except for one coat of body paint. The reason she didn't last longer than a week was that she had a tattoo of a snake on her shoulder, and Norton kept leaping at it in the middle of the night, doing his best to remove it from her skin. For some reason, she felt this a sufficient reason to end our brief fling.

One of the best things about dating was watching Norton's reactions to the women I brought home (or, in the case of the sportswriter, brought him to). Most of them he liked. The normal routine was as follows: I'd come home after dinner, usher the woman into my apartment. Norton would get a late-night Pounce; I'd introduce them. We'd go through the "Oh, what funny ears" exchange, while Norton sized her up. If he liked her, he'd nuzzle up to her with the side of his head, pushing it against her quite seductively. This was a considerable help in encouraging my date to think more seriously about my charms.

As she and I sat on the sofa, listening to music, talking, trying to figure out what the rest of the evening had in store for us, Norton—again, only if he approved—would sit a few feet away, turn over on his back, and peer up at us. This was so startlingly cute that once eye contact was made be-

tween date and cat, almost all female reservations could be overcome.

Of course, if Norton *didn't* like someone, forget it. No cute nuzzling or adorable backward glances. Oh no. In these cases we got a lot of running around, scratching at the legs of the couch (and sometimes of the woman), possibly even a little throwing up. We usually had the same taste in women, Norton and I, so when his behavior turned, it was hard for me to get annoyed. In fact, except for the couch scratching, I often felt like joining him.

Cindy and Norton had adjusted expertly to a mutually agreeable sleeping arrangement. None of her successors was ever able to work things out quite as smoothly (particularly one named Michelle, who would wake up every hour on the hour, sputtering, gasping for breath, and waving her arms wildly because Norton kept putting his tail in her mouth). Norton, unlike his dad, was extremely fussy about whom he'd let scritch him under the chin in the morning.

I tended to trust Norton's judgment when it came to women, and for the most part, he gave me the benefit of the doubt. The only time we ever had a serious disagreement was over Karyn.

Karyn was a Danish model whom we met in Paris (on one of Norton's first trips). She was twenty-two years old, six feet tall, and the most gorgeous woman I'd ever talked to without actually drooling. She also spoke and read many languages, was overwhelmingly sophisticated, had a sharp and nasty sense of humor, and . . . I suppose you're getting the picture that I was smitten upon first meeting. Miraculously, she was smitten, too. Life seemed perfect.

Except for one problem.

A certain member of my family decided that he absolutely couldn't stand this tall blond woman who occasionally took up his side of the bed. Norton hated her.

My cat doesn't hiss—but he hissed at Karyn. My cat doesn't bite—but he bit her. He liked to wait until she was sound asleep, and then he'd jump on her pillow and meow as loudly as he could, scaring her to death. He once urinated in her shoe—just as she was rushing off on a modeling assignment.

I tried to convince him he was wrong. I also tried to convince Karyn that I couldn't leave him in New York when I came over for a brief Parisian stint. I had no luck convincing either one of them.

Happily I never had to choose between them. It is probably a sickness, I know, but in a choice between someone who could have won the Miss Universe contest (and probably performed some sort of simple brain surgery as her talent) and a temperamental Scottish Fold, my little cat would have won hands down. I might have killed him—but he would have won. Before it came to that, however, I learned once and for all to abide by Norton's judgment when it comes to women.

On my first date with Karyn—which lasted a week—we had a spectacular time. We ate at little, out-of-the-way Parisian restaurants, we drank great wine, I sampled my first peach champagne, we danced cheek to cheek, we held hands in underground *caveaus des jazz.* Then I came back to New York. We wrote letters, we ran up phone bills that

rivaled the national debt, we made plans to meet in all kinds
of exotic places.

The second stretch of time we spent together was also
fantastic. It lasted only five days, which was how long I was
able to get away for. That trip, two friends, Nancy and
Ziggy Alderman, happened to be in Paris. Nancy, who is
extremely attractive but five-feet-four with dark, curly hair,
was a little thrown when she strolled into my room at the
Tremoille for a glass of champagne, only to find a blond
goddess—wearing something not much bigger than Captain Hook's eye patch for an outfit—busy pouring the bub-
bly for us all. Zig, in one of his suaver moments, panicked
completely at the sight of Karyn and told us he just had to
step into the bathroom for a moment. His only error was
that he stepped into the closet—and was so embarrassed, he
stayed there for a good five minutes, hoping somehow that
we might not notice.

The next trip to Paris, Karyn and I went out to dinner to
celebrate my first night back and our love-starved reunion.
I hadn't seen her in several months. She looked as lovely
and inviting as ever—and Norton hissed just as loudly as
ever when she came to the hotel.

When dinner was over, we strolled back along the streets
of Les Halles, holding hands, kissing adoringly every few
steps. We arrived back at the Tremoille and went upstairs.
I prepared for an evening of extraordinary passion. Then
she mentioned, "Oh, by the way, my boyfriend is a little bit
upset that I've been seeing you."

It's amazing how that kind of line puts a damper on
extraordinary passion.

"Wh-what do you mean, your boyfriend?" I asked. "You

told me you'd broken up with him a long time ago."

She looked at me, confused. "Broken up?"

"Yeah. That first time we went out . . . when we spent a week together . . . you told me you'd just ended your relationship and . . ."

"Oh, *that,*" she said. "I just had to wait until he went out of town. He was gone that whole week. I didn't really break it off with him."

"What about the last time I was here?"

"He was gone, too."

"Well, why didn't you *tell* me?!"

"Because I thought you wouldn't see me."

I started pacing around the room. I wouldn't look at Norton because I was sure he'd be smirking.

"What's his name?" I asked. "Your boyfriend."

"Robert."

"What does he do?"

"He's a podiatrist."

If he'd been a race car driver or perhaps an international clothing designer, I probably could have settled for some kind of sophisticated if painful sharing arrangement. At least I could have salvaged some pride. But a podiatrist?!

"How . . . um . . . how does Robert know that we've been seeing each other?" I asked.

"Oh, I had to tell him this time, since he's in town."

"And what did he say?"

"Robert has a very bad temper," Karyn said with a shrug.

"What did he *say?*"

"Something about killing you."

"Does Robert also have a very good sense of humor?" I wanted to know.

"Robert has *no* sense of humor," Karyn told me.

That was the end of Karyn. It turned out that Robert really *didn't* have a sense of humor and really *did* want to kill me. He had some Arab blood in him, and it seemed that killing was an acceptable solution in whatever country that blood came from. Even if he wasn't actually going to murder me, I must say some very unpleasant images—my being strapped in a chair, shoes off, podiatric instruments of torture being put to good use—did flash through my mind. I had no intention of spending my life with no feet, even for a beautiful Danish model.

Norton, to his credit, never gloated. I have deliberately never taken him to Denmark, however, and I doubt I ever will. The last I heard of Karyn, she'd moved to Rome and was living with some count. I can only hope it's Dracula.

One of Norton's regular trips was a yearly jaunt down to baseball's spring training in Florida. I went every year in March with the nine other guys from the Rotisserie League. Originally it was men only and some serious baseball was watched. Gradually, wives and girlfriends were added; then, as we all got a little older, golf somehow became part of the trip. Over the years, as we wrote about our outing in our annual Rotisserie League book, players from other leagues would show up. Now it's turned into something of a big deal—a Rotisserie League convention with a few hundred stat-crazed fans coming from all over the country to watch and talk baseball with us.

The Rotiss weekend isn't for the casual girlfriend. Sarah made it one year (and managed to sell more Rotisserie

League T-shirts than anyone ever imagined possible; she looked a *lot* better in one of them than any of us did), but this weekend usually fell during a period when she wasn't talking to me. So for a couple of years, Norton was my only companion. He loved the hotel we all stayed at, the Belleview Biltmore, an absolutely spectacular turn-of-the-century sprawling monster with all the old Southern charm one could want. Part of that charm was that the people who worked at the hotel loved Norton as well.

The second year that Norton went with me, I also took two married friends, the same ones who met Karyn in Paris, Nancy and Ziggy Alderman. (Ziggy is not his real name. His real name is John, but because he works at a rather straitlaced investment brokerage, he doesn't want them to know that to most people he's something out of a David Bowie album—which makes it somewhat complicated being friends with him. When he's with his officemates, we're supposed to call him John, even though they call him Aldy. As if that's not confusing enough, there's another hotshot named John at the firm, a hotshot with more seniority than Ziggy, so Zig's bosses told him they were going to refer to him as Jack to avoid confusion when people in the office yelled out for John. As a result, some people now know him as Ziggy, some as Aldy, some as John, and some as Jack. It's a lot like being friends with Sybil.)

On the way down to St. Petersburg with the Aldermans (or, if you prefer, Alderpeople), Ziggy/John/Aldy/Jack was giving me a very hard time about my bringing Norton. He couldn't understand how I could lug a cat along to such a macho affair as a spring training trip. I was made an object of ridicule for the entire flight—something my pal Zig is an

expert at. Several years ago, the three of us went out to the Arizona Biltmore for five days of tennis and golf (right— Sarah wasn't speaking to me that week). The second day we were there, three friends of mine came down from Tuscon for a meal. We all ate a lot and drank a lot at the fairly expensive hotel dining room. When we were all done, Ziggy insisted on picking up the check. I argued with him— these were my friends after all; he'd never even met them before—but to no avail. He signed the bill with a flourish and basked in our profuse thank-yous the rest of the night. For the next two days, overcome by guilt, I did my best to pay for everything—Nancy and Zig's breakfast before we played golf, the round of golf itself, drinks at the nineteenth hole, you name it. When it came time to check out, as I was handed my bill, Nancy said to her hubby, "Don't you think it's time to tell him?" It was—and Zig broke it to me that he had indeed signed for the big dinner check—only he'd signed *my name.*

Anyway, the expression on his face as we stood in our Florida hotel's lobby didn't make up for the near-millions he'd stuck me with in Arizona, but almost. After hours of tormenting me for bringing my cat, Zig had to stand at the check-in desk and watch every attractive woman who worked in the hotel (no more than ten or fifteen of them) screech, "Norton? Is that *Norton?*" Then he had to watch them come over, play with you-know-who, smile at me, and say, "Remember—if you need anything, just call."

Now that I think about it, it *did* make up for the check.

The annual Rotisserie convention was also the site of perhaps Norton's greatest adventure.

A couple of years ago, I went down as usual to do my

Rotisserie scouting. Also as usual, Norton came along. My plane was quite late, so we didn't arrive at the hotel till after eight P.M. After the celebratory greeting of Norton at the desk, I put him in our room on the second floor, set up his food and litter box, then went downstairs for dinner. After a couple of hours of decent food, good beer, and excellent baseball chatter, I was exhausted, so I went back up to the room. The rest of the gang went to the outdoor patio restaurant for more of the big three.

This year, I had a balcony off the bedroom. When I entered, Norton was standing by the balcony door, anxious to be let out. He was used to having the run of the Belleview Biltmore. They have a huge pool area with lots of grass and many bushes for him to skulk around in. His favorite part of the hotel, for some reason, is the basement. He has spent many a day wandering its nooks and crannies. He particularly likes one dusty, concrete corner; it seems to be the perfect napping spot. But he'd never, at least to my knowledge, played up on the various steeples and levels of the roof.

After a moment's deliberation, I figured I'd give it a try. What could go wrong? So I opened the door. Norton scooted onto the balcony, hopped up on the railing, and then went over, exploring the peaked roofs that seemed to stretch for miles. I waited ten or fifteen minutes, called out for him as a test, and sure enough, he came running. That let me know it was safe, so I told him he was free to roam.

Forty-five minutes later, I was ready for sleep. As I stepped over toward the balcony to call Norton in for the night, my phone rang. I picked it up to hear the voice of

Glen Waggoner, an original Rotisserian and one of my best friends.

"I think you'd better come down here."

"What's going on?"

"Norton just fell through the roof of the dining room."

You know the cartoon of the Road Runner, zipping along the road, covering many miles in mere seconds? That was me racing down the stairs to find my cat.

When I got to the patio, the Rotiss group was hysterical with laughter. Glen led me over to the middle of the dining area and pointed up. Ten feet above my head was a gaping hole in the green-and-white striped awning. Apparently, Norton, bored with the roof, had crawled out onto the awning. Midway, he reached a weak spot and the thing gave out. He plummeted sixteen feet down, landing inches from a table where two seventy-year-old women were finishing their dinner. Needless to say, they screamed—you'd scream, too, if you were calmly eating in a restaurant and a cat came flying through the air, landing three inches from your head—and one of them came very close to needing CPR. They were very nice about it, however, as I began apologizing (over the background din of an entire Rotisserie League crying with laughter), and they suggested I find my cat, as doubtless he was far more terrified than they were.

Glen, whom Norton knew well, had tried to catch him after the great fall, but Norton wouldn't be caught. He'd gone racing around in the dark until Glen lost sight of him.

Having no idea where he'd run off to, I stumbled around the giant lawn, calling out his name. No response. I kept

stumbling for fifteen or twenty minutes with no sign of
Norton, until I suddenly realized where he had to have
disappeared to. I went over to the creaky, wooden basement door, opened it, and stepped inside. My eyes took a
few minutes to adjust to the pitch dark; then, when they
had, I inched my way toward a familiar, dusty corner.
There, sound asleep, was Norton.

"Pssst," I said.

Norton's eyes opened; he *brrrmeowed* and came into my
open arms.

For the rest of the weekend, people fussed and clucked
over him. But he stayed close to me for the remainder of
our stay. He'd had enough adventure. I saw him nuzzling
up to only one person who worked at the hotel—a very
attractive blond woman who worked at the desk. When I
went over to get the little troublemaker, the woman smiled
at him, then at me.

"Is he yours?" she asked, practically batting her eyes.
"He's so *sweet.*"

If I didn't know better, I'd swear that Norton winked at
both of us.

The cat who went to paris

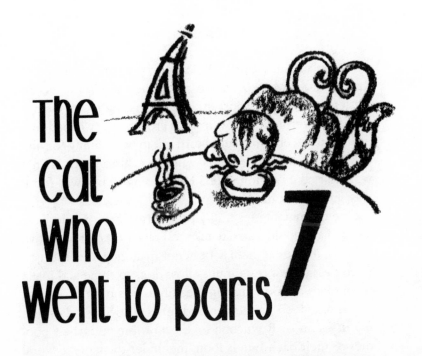

7

Over the course of Norton's first few years on earth and in my care, he had, for the average cat, led quite an exciting existence. He'd been lugged around the streets of Manhattan in a pocket. He'd taken cab rides and boat rides and train rides. He'd explored the beaches of Fire Island, the snowy peaks of Vermont, and the antique stores of Bucks County, Pennsylvania (a trip that was relatively uneventful, except for the fact that I bought a beautiful eighteenth-century maple cradle that became Norton's favorite and nearly unbearably cute place in which to nap). He'd also become a regular at my office—spending the day with me on the average of once a week—and as soon as that was established as normal behavior, he began coming to company sales conferences. As a corporate guest, he'd been to Phoenix, Arizona; Laguna Beach, California; Bermuda; and various places in Florida. Basically, if the trip was no more than an hour or two on the plane, he came with me no matter how long or short my stay was going to be, even if it was an overnight trip. If it was a cross-country expedition or something else that could turn out to be grueling for him (e.g., more than five hours without a litter box), then I wouldn't take Norton unless I was going to be away for at least five or six days.

One of my fantasies in my pre-Norton days was to have a dog that I could one day take to France. The French love animals; they treat them a lot better than they treat tourists. Even the fanciest restaurants allow dogs to come and make themselves at home during mealtime. It is not uncommon to see tuxedoed gentlemen and fur-clad society ladies dining in Jamin or Rovuchon or L'Ambroisie with their poodles or their dachshunds lounging under the table. Several years ago, a French publisher put out a restaurant guide rating every restaurant in Paris by how they treated dogs: what kind of scraps they gave them, whether they were allowed in leashless or not, how friendly the waiters were when petting was called for.

It had never actually occurred to me to take Norton overseas. I'm not sure why there was this mental lapse. Perhaps it was simply that in the first few years I had him, I wasn't making a lot of European trips.

That all certainly changed in a hurry.

The change came when I got a phone call from Roman Polanski.

"Peter," he said in his distinctive accent, which combines a bit of Polish rebel, French intellectual, English dandy,

American rogue, and Jewish uncle, "have you ever seen Paris at Christmastime?"

Roman and I first worked together in 1982, on his autobiography, *Roman by Polanski.* We'd worked extremely well together and, for some unknown reason, immediately became fast friends. I know he's been surrounded by controversy for most of his life, but to tell you the truth, I've never seen a particularly controversial side to him. We thought alike on a lot of issues, shared the same sense of curiosity combined with approximately the same amount of cynicism. From a friend's point of view, he happens to be an extraordinarily generous guy—there's nothing he won't do for you if he likes you—and he has a great sense of humor. He tells wonderful stories and likes nothing better than to sit around La Coupole, sipping champagne, slurping raw oysters, and swapping good jokes.

I have met a lot of very, very smart people, but Polanski is probably the only genius I know. He speaks something like twelve languages, has one of the most interesting interpretive minds I've ever encountered, has made some of the finest, most original films of modern times, and, to top it all off, knows somewhere in the vicinity of a million long-legged models named Suzette. All of this is to say he doesn't ask questions like "Have you ever seen Paris at Christmastime?" without having something in mind.

"Uh . . . no," I said, cleverly. "I don't think I have."

"It's very beautiful. Very beautiful. The snow comes down, the lights go up. Ohhh, the lights in Paris, mmmmm, magnificent. It makes you cry. And the women . . . there is a tremendous influx of attractive women at Christmas, Peter."

"Can I ask you one question, Roman?" I asked from my New York City apartment.

"Anything. Anything."

"Why are you telling me all this?"

"How would you like to come to Paris for Christmas and help me write my new movie for Harrison Ford?"

The man has style, *non?*

Of course, I played hard to get. No pushover am I. I told him that it would take me at least four or five seconds to pack and catch a plane out of New York. It actually took me a little longer than that—but not much. Within a week, Norton and I were on our way to Europe.

Many people think that taking an animal overseas is some kind of major deal. A lot of them think there's a quarantine (only in England) or that the travel arrangements are extraordinarily complicated or that hotel accommodations are impossible for pets. The truth is nothing could be easier than lugging one's cat to foreign shores—if you do it right. Naturally, the first time I took Norton I did it all wrong.

Polanski was going to be in Amsterdam to promote his newest film. As I was making my—excuse me, *our*—arrangements, he said, "Peter, why don't you fly to Amsterdam? We'll have a great dinner, do our best to get in some trouble, and then go to work the next day in Paris. Amsterdam is the perfect place to recuperate from jet lag."

Makes sense, doesn't it? It certainly did to me. So as a result, Norton's first European stop—after a one-hour layover at Charles de Gaulle Airport—was Amsterdam.

Before we left, I had to take my pal to the vet so he could

get his cat passport. This procedure was quite simple: the vet gave Norton a shot, swabbed his ears out with a Q-tip, looked down his throat, then filled out a small green card saying that Norton Gethers, an eight-pound Scottish Fold, born in Los Angeles but living in New York, was healthy and able to change continents at his owner's discretion.

The flight was a breeze—with one tiny exception. Norton had been on a number of flights on various American airlines. As a result of their rigidity, I was a strict rule follower. I usually put Norton in his box, kept him under the seat for the whole flight, and only dared to bring him up and out onto my lap if a—okay, I can say it now—flight attendant asked to see him, which didn't happen all that often. But on Air France, Norton was greeted as warmly as if he'd paid full fare. The attendants *loved* having a pet on board and immediately told me to take him out of the confining box and make him comfortable. We were flying first class, thanks to Warner Brothers, and we were both treated in a first-class manner all the way down the line. When I was served champagne and caviar, Norton got a little dish of smoked salmon with a cup of milk. At dessert time, I mentioned that Norton had a weakness for chocolate, and *voilà,* his own personal *mousse au chocolat* arrived *tout de suite.* They were so incredibly nice to my traveling companion that I relaxed. I relaxed so much that about two hours over the Atlantic, with Norton resting contentedly on my lap, I fell sound asleep. I would have slept all the way to Paris except for the fact that, at some point, one of the male attendants gently poked me in the shoulder, waking me up. When I rubbed my eyes and oriented myself, I realized that there was no cat on my lap. When I looked up,

I saw that that was because the attendant was holding him by the scruff of his little gray neck. Horrified, I grabbed Norton, put him back on my knee, and began apologizing to the steward. I was so intimidated by the strictness of American stewardesses, I apologized profusely for a good five minutes before I realized the kindly French steward was saying to me, "Eet's all right. We don't mind. 'E was 'aving a goot walk." Eventually I came to understand that the steward really *didn't* mind. So I got up the nerve to ask the one question I really wanted an answer to: "Where did he go?"

At that, the steward crinkled up his nose disapprovingly. Clearly Norton had done something that this man found repugnant. In fact, by French standards, my cat had committed the ultimate sin.

" 'E was back in toureest," the steward told me with disdain, "talking to a *dog.*"

I stayed awake the rest of the trip. Norton spent most of his free time staring out the window, down at the Atlantic. He seemed to find it just as fascinating as the Fire Island bay.

When we landed in Amsterdam, we took a cab to what turned out to be a wonderful hotel, the Amstel. I was all prepared to either hide Norton or lie my head off, claiming that he wasn't actually spending the night there; I was merely dropping him off to some Dutch friend. But there was no need for the cloak-and-dagger routine. The woman who checked us in gave the cat a warm smile, told me to take him out of his bag, and then watched with an amused look as Norton plopped himself down on the counter and made himself at home. The manager of the hotel came over

immediately to get in a few friendly pats on Norton's head; so did a couple of bellboys. The check-in woman asked if Norton was indeed staying there for the night, and when I nodded hesitantly, she immediately asked if he would like a small plate of fish. I sensed that Norton's ears, what there were of them, pricked up a bit at the word "fish," so I told her that would be very nice.

Up in the room, I set up Norton's first international cat litter box, waited for his fish to arrive, then called Roman. After a quick nap, I was ready to go.

Norton was content to spend his first night in Europe sleeping on our down bed while I was wined and dined at a spectacular Indonesian restaurant by a few Dutch journalists. (Okay, Roman was the one being wined and dined— but they let me come along, didn't they? That counts!) The next day was a little more eventful, at least for my gray companion.

I didn't really know what our Amsterdam plans were before I arrived. But I soon found out. We were to check out of our hotel at noon, go to a screening of Roman's latest movie for all the top Dutch distributors, go to a taping of some Dutch quiz show that Roman had agreed to appear on to promote the movie, have dinner with the TV people and some of the distributors, and then catch a late plane to Paris.

It all sounded great except for one thing. What in the world was I going to do with Norton from noon till ten o'clock at night?

Since I didn't really have a choice, I simply took him with me.

The first highlight of the day was our introduction to the distributors. We were at a large screening room and were

seated at a podium toward the front of the room. The studio publicity person assigned to Roman gave a little speech, telling everyone how excited they all should be to be distributing another Polanski film. He went through the litany of Roman's successes in Holland—from his *Knife in the Water* days through *Chinatown* and *Tess*. "And now," he said to the crowd, "I would like to introduce some very special guests. To my right is a man who needs no introduction. One of the great directors of our time, Roman Polanski."

There was a great burst of applause.

"To Mr. Polanski's right is the writer of Mr. Polanski's new film, which they are going to Paris to begin work on—Peter Gethers."

I got some polite applause, considering no one had ever heard of me and probably would never hear of me again. And then came the best announcement, as the publicity person realized there was one other introduction he had to make.

"And to Mr. Gethers's right is . . . his *cat???*"

Rarely have I heard anyone sound as confused. And rarely have I been as proud of my cat. Norton didn't exactly take a bow at the mention of his name, but he did sit up as straight as he possibly could when he heard the very puzzled-sounding applause.

We spent the rest of the day at the taping of the quiz show.

The name of the show translated into "Wanna Bet?" It was the most popular TV program in Holland (also in Germany and Belgium). The only way I can possibly describe it is as a cross between "Truth or Consequences," "Laugh-In," and the ever-popular Vegas review, *Nudes on Ice.*

"Wanna Bet" is ninety minutes long and takes about three hours to shoot. Of those three hours, Norton spent two-and-a-half sitting next to me in the audience—the producers were nice enough to give him his own seat—mostly staring at the flashing sign, which, I assume, said "Applause" in Dutch.

The other half hour he spent in the dressing room— where I was not allowed—being petted by the thirty gorgeous and statuesque topless dancers who participate in the show's sketches.

Norton doesn't usually allow strangers to pick him up and carry him off, but when one of the nearly naked women rushed over to him during a break and asked permission to bring him backstage, he didn't even wait for my okay. He hopped onto the ground and followed her, without so much as a backward glance at his envious dad. When he was returned to me at the end of the show—by three of the dancers, none of whom could bear to part with him—it was yet another time in our relationship when I was very sorry Norton didn't speak English. From the look on his face, however, even if he did, I wasn't ever going to get the details of this particular adventure.

When the show was over, we went to dinner with the heads of the TV studio and several of the distributors who'd earlier been introduced to Norton.

We were taken to one of the city's top restaurants. Norton came along as if he were accustomed to dining out every evening. He hadn't been near his litter box in hours and

hours *and* he'd never been out to eat in public, so I was a tad nervous. However, my boy came through with flying colors. He was the hit of the evening.

The first thing that happened was that our waitress practically fainted when she saw how cute Norton was. When she saw how calmly he sat on my lap, she insisted on bringing him his own chair, which she slipped in next to mine. Next, she brought him his own dinner—a nice little plate of herring and potatoes, which Norton gobbled down appreciatively. He was having such a good time that I was almost insulted when she didn't offer him a glass of wine—although he did seem a lot happier with his dish of milk.

This was supposed to be a business dinner, with Roman talking up his movie, but very little business was discussed. Most of the conversation centered around the newest—and smallest—guest of honor. Every few minutes, someone would insist on switching seats with me or Roman, who was on the other side of Norton, so he or she could be near the cat. By the end of the evening, I was on the complete other end of the table, and Norton was in between the head of the Dutch film distribution industry and the woman producer of "Wanna Bet," doing his best Cary Grant impersonation—politely chewing on his herring, sipping his milk, sitting up in his chair, and basically appreciating the restaurant and the attention.

When it was time to leave, several people offered to let Norton stay in their homes if I ever came through the city again, and several asked if they could visit him on their next trip to New York. By the time we boarded the plane for Paris, he was one exhausted cat. In fact, I had to wake him

up as we circled over the city, holding him up to the window so he could get his first glimpse of the brightly lit Eiffel Tower.

～～

Norton took to Paris like, well, like a *canard à l'eau.*

We stayed at one of my very favorite hotels in the world, the Tremoille, which is on the corner of Rue de la Tremoille and Rue du Boccador in the eighth arrondissement. It is gorgeous, it is small, it is elegant, friendly, it is *very* Parisian, *and* they *love* my cat.

Last year, when I was writing another movie with Polanski, my agent, Esther—she of Norton's encounter with the stewardess from hell—popped into Paris for a couple of evenings of fun and good food. I was there for three months and, to my regret, wasn't staying at the Tremoille—the studio had decided it was too expensive for such a long stay, so I got an apartment—but I insisted that *she* stay there. After dinner, I walked her back to the hotel and talked about how nice they always were to Norton. As I was elaborating, she stopped me on the street and said, "I don't believe you. You are definitely making this up." Indignant, I insisted I was absolutely telling the 100 percent truth. She refused to accept this. So when we reached the lobby, I went up to the front desk, smirked confidently at Esther, and said to the concierge, "Good evening. Do you remember me?"

"Of course," he responded. "And 'ow is your leetle cat? Is 'e well?"

"Very well," I told him.

"Please send him my best," the man said, to Esther's total

astonishment. "Tell 'im to come visit anytime 'e weeshes."

Esther now believes everything I tell her.

Over the years, Norton has stayed at the Tremoille six or seven times, usually when I'm working with Roman. Our writing routine is as follows: start around ten-thirty or eleven in the morning, break for lunch at one o'clock or so, a nice leisurely lunch, then work from three until seven or eight. After an hour- or two-hour break to relax, to have a glass of icy Polish vodka, or just to get away from each other, we usually have dinner. I'd always go back to the hotel to check on and play with Norton, either during our lunch break or our pre-dinner break. After a while, I realized that playtime was unnecessary. Norton didn't need any more playing with. Almost every time I returned to the room, there was at least one maid, usually two, petting him, scratching him, playing with some new toy they'd just bought for him. Once he became an accepted member of the hotel family, they let him hang out in the lobby during the day (one of the people on the desk or one of the maids would bring him back to the room if they felt things were too hectic) and let me bring him down to the formal dining room for dinner.

One day there was a near catastrophe. I came back at seven P.M. for my daily check-in, strolled jauntily into the hotel, and asked for my room key. One of the managers looked at me very gravely and said, "Oh, Monsieur Gethers, your leetle cat, he is very seek."

Without another word, I grabbed the key and raced up the two flights of stairs to my room. When I ran inside, a maid was sitting on the bed, soothingly petting Norton and cooing at him. He was snuggled up on my pillow, curled into a

ball. All in all, he looked pathetic—and was clearly sick.

The maid didn't speak any English, so I didn't catch all of what she said. Basically, I picked up on the fact that she'd come into my room early that morning to clean, began her usual play routine with Norton, only he didn't respond. He wouldn't leave the bed, he wouldn't pick his head up, he wouldn't move at all. She tried to give him some Pounce— I'd brought over a lifetime supply and had shown all the maids where I kept it—and he wouldn't even touch that. This was serious.

Norton had never, ever been sick before. I didn't know what to do. Roman was surprisingly understanding when I told him I was going to skip our usual dinner and carousing because of a sick cat. He was pretty attached to Norton by this time, too.

Norton didn't eat that night. Nor did he move from my pillow (I slept on his side of the bed all night). I did my best to reassure him that everything was going to be all right, but he was not a happy kitten. If you ever hear anyone say that cats don't think or feel, all you have to do is tell them to spend the night in bed with a sick one. If you looked up the word "mournful" in the dictionary, you would have seen a picture of Norton that night. I decided to give him twenty-four hours before calling a French vet.

He seemed to be feeling better the next morning. (I, on the other hand, wasn't doing too well since I'd tossed and turned with worry all night.) He wasn't particularly ac- tive—he wouldn't get out of bed to eat his breakfast—but he did munch on a couple of Pounce when I brought them to him, and he did lick my hand appreciatively afterward. When I left to go to work, Norton roused himself slightly,

standing up for a moment on the bed. I came back, told him he'd be fine, and then watched him settle back onto my pillow.

At lunchtime, I came back to see how Norton was feeling. The manager gave me the thumbs-up sign when I picked up my key. Sure enough, in the room were two maids, hovering over Norton, who was now resting playfully on his back, enjoying their gentle scratching and friendly babbling. They had bought him a present—a little catnip tree, which they'd placed on the end table by the bed. They told me that he wasn't quite ready for it, but they thought it would be a good incentive for him to get well.

I went back to work knowing my pal was in good hands. At that night's dinner break, he was back to normal. Not only did he gulp down his dinner and leap at the Pounce when I held it out to him, he munched a few leaves off his new catnip tree. When it was time for bed, he was well enough to sleep on his own pillow. I had no idea what had brought on his one-day illness—perhaps it was all that rich French cat food—but with a sigh of relief, I told him I was glad he was feeling better and kissed him on the top of his head. He gave me a quick lick with his sandpaper tongue and made me feel as if, at the very least, I'd been an understanding and supportive nurse.

We fell into a fun Parisian routine, Norton and I. Since I didn't have to be at work until at least ten-thirty, I got into the habit of going to one particular café, across the Seine from the Eiffel Tower, for my morning café au lait. After a few mornings of this, I didn't see any reason not to take

Norton. So every day he'd hop into his shoulder bag, we'd leisurely stroll the few blocks to my regular haunt, and I'd sit in my straw café chair, sipping coffee and reading the *Herald Tribune* while he sat in his chair, sphinxlike, watching the passersby and, once the waiters got used to his presence, lapping at a small bowl of water or milk.

After breakfast, I'd usually take him back to the hotel. Sometimes I'd take him over to Roman's apartment. That first trip, when I was rewriting the script for what became the film *Frantic,* Harrison Ford came over to spend a couple of weeks working with us. He was the star of the film and, as such, quite properly wanted to have input into character motivation, action, and thought. He and Roman were friends but had never worked together. I'd never met Harrison before. So the first few days were spent feeling each other out, seeing how we'd all get along, all of us trying to be firm with our convictions for the movie yet flexible and sensitive to the other two's egos and desires. Harrison has a reputation—which my experience certainly bears out—for being a remarkably intelligent actor. It's remarkable because actors, in general, are not considered much higher on the intelligence scale than your basic, everyday dining room table. They are also known for screwing up scripts in order to make their characters look better. Not only is Harrison smart, he's more concerned with the *movie* than whether or not his character is braver, brighter, and cleverer than all the other characters. I liked him and respected him a lot right from the beginning. However, my guess is that Harrison wasn't overly impressed with me the first day he showed up. We shook hands, started discussing the

first draft of the script, which was written by Roman with his longtime collaborator, Gerard Brach—what was wrong with it and what was right with it—and then, just as we were really getting into it, just as some passion was coming out in the conversation, Roman started sniffing the air.

"What smells so terrible?" he asked.

"Wait. Hold it," Harrison said, getting excited. "I think I'm on to something here. I think this guy, this doctor, has to really love his wife, has to be *incredibly* jealous of her—"

"Whoooo, what could smell so bad?" Roman was clearly distracted. His face was scrunched up as if breathing were a painful matter.

"Roman, Roman, listen to me! I think we need a scene between me and my wife, something tender, right at the beginning . . . Jesus, what *is* that smell?"

Eventually, all discussion of the script stopped. The entire apartment was starting to smell as if someone had died— about three weeks ago. Both heads turned to me when I muttered quietly under my breath, "Uh . . . I think I know what it is."

I marched them into Roman's bathroom. There in the tub sat my cat. There next to him sat a very large pile of . . . well . . . what can only be described as cat shit.

"I forgot to bring his litter box today," I explained meekly. "He usually goes in the tub when there's no litter box."

"That's pretty smart," Roman noted.

"This is *your* cat?" Harrison asked.

I nodded.

"You brought him from New York??"

I nodded again.

"I'm working with a writer who brings his cat to Paris so he can shit in the bathtub?"

"I know it looks bad," I said, "but give him a second chance."

"It's not *him* I'm worried about," Harrison said to me.

This was my introduction to a lifetime's fantasy—writing a movie in Paris with a brilliant director and a superstar actor: the brilliant director and the superstar actor on their knees in the bathroom trying to scrub away the smell of cat shit while I held the cat, trying to assure him that he hadn't done anything wrong.

Over the years, I believe Norton has come to prefer Paris to New York, much like his dad. He likes his morning alfresco breakfasts; he enjoys his occasional restaurant dinners. (By coincidence, Norton and I were in Paris when I signed the contract to do this book. He *definitely* enjoyed the celebratory dinner I took him to that night. We went to my very favorite joint, L'Ami Louis, where Norton received his own giant plate of Louis's specialty, the best foie gras one could ever hope to eat.) This cat has even been to a nightclub or two. I will go out on a limb and say, absolutely, that he is the only cat ever to have danced the night away at Bains Douches, one of Paris's very coolest clubs. A lot of people get turned away by the doorman at Bains Douches—but Norton has guaranteed entry when he shows up.

One of my little cat's favorite pastimes was exploring the famous rooftops of Paris. He had access from our room at the Tremoille. The hotel has those old-fashioned, very heavy windows that swing open. (Wait a second—perhaps, at last, I understand why they're called *French* windows!) Norton used to sit with his nose pressed up against the bedroom window, just waiting for me to get the hint that he was desperate to go outside. At first I was hesitant, but once again logic lost out to a cat's desire and the window was thrown open. I held Norton in my arms for a few moments, explaining to him that he was in a strange city and that he shouldn't go too far away—then up over the balcony he went, scrambling out onto the red tile rooftops of the city.

I don't know how far he actually traveled. I once saw him three peaks away—perhaps half a block. He always came back when called, so he couldn't have been out of hearing distance. Eventually, I relaxed with his outdoor prowling, and as soon as I could get the maids to understand that if he wasn't in the room, they shouldn't ever shut the windows, I even began leaving them open during the day so he could strut his stuff when I wasn't there.

The other thing Norton enjoyed for a while was our unusual Paris–New York commute. Although it's usually a safe rule of thumb for a writer to assume that everything he does is either going to fail or never come to fruition, there was a stretch of about a month where everything I was working on happened at the same time—the Polanski movie, a novel I'd written, a TV pilot—and Norton and I

spent this particular February practically living on the Concorde. Once a week I'd go to Paris for a few days to work on the screenplay. Then I'd hop back on the speedy plane, zip back to New York, do whatever I was doing there—I could barely tell one activity from the other by this point—and then head to the airport and jump back on the Concorde. I would spend the quick flight either reading, writing, or rewriting. Norton would spend the few hours wandering around the small cabin, making friends with the attendants and fellow passengers.

This was definitely the height of luxury for a cat and the highlight of his European travels. The Concorde attendants got to know him so well they didn't even make me bring his box. After a while, all I needed was his cloth shoulder bag. He was so much at home on the plane that I half expected, on one of the flights, to hear the following message over the loudspeaker: "Ladeez and gentlemen, we have ze guest pilot for zis flight today. Monsieur, please say hello to ze passengers." Then the pilot would come on the loudspeaker and I'd hear: "Meow."

Things never went that far, of course, but it wasn't for lack of trying on Norton's part.

In fact, if you're thinking of flying to Paris anytime in the near future, I wouldn't rule out the possibility. If you want to make sure your plane lands on time, I suggest you bring a good supply of Pounce.

The cat who fell in love

My cat was getting older, and with age was coming a certain complacency, a slightly existential, lackadaisical attitude. Plus, he was starting to get fat.

So I did what any normal person would do for his cat. I bought a house.

During the summers at Fire Island, Norton would run everywhere, all the time, having a ball, and every season he would lose a pound between Memorial Day and Labor Day. By the time the leaves started to change colors, that Scottish Fold was one lean, mean fighting machine. Over the autumn and winter, however, he never left the confines of my apartment (except for the occasional cross-country ski trip), which meant he did a lot of sitting, sleeping, and begging for Pounce. I knew that wasn't good for him. Since I tended to do the same thing—the lazing around part, not the begging—I suspected it probably wasn't good for me either. So I decided to go house hunting.

Well, I didn't actually house *hunt*. As usual, I house *stumbled.*

Nancy and Ziggy had a place in Sag Harbor, and I went out to visit them one weekend. Norton was supposed to be left at home because Zig is highly allergic to cats. At the last second, however, my trusty cat-sitter wimped out. (I haven't really discussed what happens when my traveling cat occasionally has to be left behind. Luckily, a friend named Lynn Waggoner has decided that sitting for Norton is comparable to chauffeuring Tom Cruise around the city. Well, perhaps I'm exaggerating, but Lynn takes awfully good care of Norton—buying him toys, taking him for walks, all those good things he's come to enjoy and expect. Once, when Lynn was unavailable, my assistant took him for a weekend. She brought him to her in-laws' house in Montauk. Norton had been in the house for all of two minutes when someone left the front door open—and Norton took off. Laura, the by-now terrified assistant, and her husband spent the night in the woods searching high and low for him. They gave up somewhere around two A.M. and came home—to find Norton waiting patiently by the front door. Laura later told me the story—*much* later—and also revealed her strategy on how to break it to me that she'd lost my cat. It was going to be in the form of a suicide note.) Anyway . . . since no cat-sitter was available, I surprised my weekend hosts and brought Norton after all.

My surprise was greeted with all the enthusiasm of an earthquake. He'd be no problem, I assured them. He'd stay outside the whole day. He'd come in only at bedtime, and

then he'd sleep with me. I wouldn't let him out of my bed. Zig would never know there was a cat in the house.

That was true. He didn't know there was a cat in the house—until the middle of the night, when Norton, slipping away while I was asleep, went upstairs and decided he'd sleep on Ziggy's head.

That night at the Aldermans was not dissimilar from what I imagine Krakatoa must have been like. At three A.M. I went upstairs, grabbed Norton off the sputtering master of the house, and took him back into my bed. At three-thirty A.M. he was back on Ziggy's head. We repeated the procedure. At four A.M. Norton had returned to his new favorite spot, covering most of Zig's face with his entire body. At four-thirty A.M. Zig gave up. At five A.M. he realized he wasn't sneezing anymore. By morning, he'd decided Norton was the first cat he'd ever met that he wasn't allergic to. Fury and despair turned to delight and triumph. I was not a favorite house guest (in fact, I won the poll for Most Annoying Weekender)—but somehow Norton had wormed his way into their hearts.

The next day, we went to check out the real estate. My search was only a halfhearted one. I can't say I *really* wanted a house. For one thing, I'm not the handiest guy in the world. I still wake up screaming in the middle of the night at the thought of my high school wood shop. The idea of using a drill or repairing some electrical wiring can quickly bring on my best Curly Howard impersonation, with all the face smacking, high-pitched blubbering, and floor whirling trimmings. For another, I loathed the idea of any kind of commute, even if it was just on weekends. I had no desire ever to do any gardening or to rake up leaves or to shovel

snow off the driveway. In fact, I didn't even want a driveway, since I didn't own a car.

But Norton needed a year-round playpen, so . . .

The first four houses we looked at were all nice, all spacious, and all wrong. They didn't have any personality or
charm. The realtor, a woman named Peggy Meves, to
whom I am forever indebted, asked me to describe my ideal
house—my *affordable* ideal house. I did so: at least a hundred years old, in such good shape it needed no work,
original wood floors and beams, a fireplace or two, eccentric rooms, two stories, an office that was so nice I'd *want*
to go sit at the typewriter, a manageable size—perhaps two
or three bedrooms but not cramped and not so spacious that
I couldn't take care of it. In other words, something that was
so perfect I'd never find it.

When I finished my description, Peggy said, "You know,
I think you should take a look at this one place. But the
people have received an offer on it. I think they've accepted, so I don't think you can have it—but it sounds like
what you're looking for. At least it'll give me an idea of
what your taste is like."

I agreed to go look at the house, knowing that I couldn't
buy it. That was all right with me. Again, I didn't really
want to buy anything. I mostly just liked looking at nice
houses.

I didn't even make it upstairs. One look at the living
room—with its original 120-year-old wood floors, its antique potbellied stove, its *personality*—and I heard myself
saying, "I'll take it."

Peggy, being that rarest of breeds, a completely honest
person, tried to tell me again that I couldn't have this house.

She was just showing it to me for taste purposes.

"This is my dream house," I said. "I think I *have* to have it."

"At least look upstairs before you decide it's your dream house," she advised.

Upstairs made it even worse. There was a tiny, heartbreakingly charming guest bedroom, a large master bedroom (the bathroom had an old claw tub in it!), and to round out my fantasy, there was a small office that hung over the driveway, with French windows that looked out onto the beautifully landscaped garden. I haven't even mentioned the outside of this place, which looked as if Hänsel and Gretel could have comfortably settled in and been right at home.

I ran down the steps, outside to my rented car, and opened the door. Norton came bounding onto the front lawn. He stepped cautiously inside the house, looked around the living room, then plopped himself down in the middle of the floor, directly catching a ray of sunlight streaming in through the window. He looked up at me and meowed happily.

The next day, I bought the house.

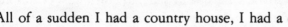

All of a sudden I had a country house, I had a cat, I had good friends for neighbors. I was just missing one little thing.

Despite a rather flip exterior (hiding, many people would say, an amazingly shallow interior), I was becoming a bit concerned that Cindy's parting words—"you don't know what love is"—had more than just the hollow ring of truth

to them. I was beginning to think that too many years of going for the gag, hanging out with Danish models, and working round the clock had possibly limited my capacity for "something more." Of course, every time I began to think this, I tried to imagine what could be "something more" than laughs, Danish models, and satisfying work. I have quite an active imagination, but in this area, my imagination had run totally dry.

And yet . . .

There was Janis.

This was an unusual affair because Janis was not at all my type. Physically she was quite lovely but not the kind of looks I usually go for. She was short and slightly round rather than long and lean. She was extremely classy looking, elegant, and sophisticated, where my taste usually ran to the slightly trashy. She was Deborah Kerr in *An Affair to Remember* as compared to my usual leaning—the soap-covered girl who washed the car in front of the prisoners in *Cool Hand Luke.* Even her personality was off-kilter alongside any past infatuations. I wasn't wild about confrontations. To say Janis was combative would be like saying Lawrence Taylor has an aggressive streak. She had the independence and confidence of British royalty and was as stubborn and opinionated as anyone this side of Saddam Hussein. Yet, despite all our differences—or perhaps because of them—she was the most intelligent, most stimulating, least boring person I'd met in a long, long time.

There was a slight hitch, however, to my having a long-lasting, perfect, satisfying relationship with Janis. She didn't *want* a long-lasting, perfect, satisfying relationship. At least, she didn't want one with me.

The closer we became, the more she'd pull back. Eventually, she pulled back so far I needed a telescope to find her. Which was a good sign the romance was over.

The relationship didn't end, however. What happened was that Janis and I became best friends. Without the threat of a romance, we became as close as two people could be. We even wound up working together. We saw each other during the day, we had dinner several times a week, we even went away on weekends together a few times—strictly platonically. She saw me through a couple of tough romances, through several professional crises. I did the same for her. Despite the Sarahs and the Karyns and the sportswriters and the Dickensian editors, it was Janis who always seemed to be there, whether the "there" was for fun, for support, or for anything that struck either one of us as interesting. We became so inseparable that most people thought we were still a couple. But she didn't want that. She didn't want a relationship because, in her experience, relationships only pointed toward the *end* of relationships. With ending came pain (and the better the relationship, the more painful the ending). With pain came bitterness. With bitterness came sorrow. You can take it from there.

Over time, I accepted that there was never going to be any kind of real relationship with this woman. It took some doing—a lot of teeth gnashing, a good bit of stomach hurting, and way too much head banging—but I did eventually accept it.

Only one person didn't accept it.

And I suppose I have to use the word "person" loosely.

Norton liked Janis.

It was particularly noticeable because she didn't much

care for him. Animals were something else she didn't want to get attached to. She didn't see the pleasure in such an attachment. She didn't see the point. But Norton didn't let up. Usually, when someone ignored him, my cat was happy to be ignored. Janis was the only person other than my father that I ever saw him pursue. When she came over, she wouldn't pet him—but within moments he'd be by her side, rubbing his body up against her leg or trying to burrow his face into the palm of her hand. Rarely did she so much as respond—but over the course of several years Norton never gave up. Whenever he saw her, he rolled over on his back in his best impersonation of the world's cutest cat. If she refused to look at him, he'd move to her, rubbing, cuddling, purring. Janis was tough—she knew the dangers of getting involved. But Norton was tough, too—he knew the *pleasures* of getting involved.

For a lot of this period—Norton vs. Janis—I was content to remain neutral. Then came Sag Harbor.

When I bought the house out there on Long Island, I had already rented a house on Fire Island with Norm for the summer. The thought of one last season avoiding the six-ishes appealed to me (especially since I'd already paid for it), so I came up with the perfect solution. I arranged for Janis to live in my new house for the summer, rent-free, on the condition that she fix it up—furnish the kitchen with utensils, buy and put up drapes, start to get the garden in shape. All the things that I would never have either the time, taste, or inclination to do. It was a fair deal and she accepted happily. At the end of the summer, Norm and I drove out to Sag Harbor to check up on the house and to

have dinner with Janis. She insisted on cooking; dinner was served amidst delicate candlelight on the front porch. When I stepped inside—this was my first time there since I'd signed the papers three months earlier—I was amazed. The place was no longer just charming—it was beautiful. It no longer just had its own personality—it had Janis's. It was clear to me that she loved the house as much as I did. It was clear to anyone who bothered to look inside and see what she'd done with it.

That night we had a wonderful time. The food was delicious, we drank a lot of wine, everyone laughed until we were too tired to laugh anymore, and—for the first time in several years—it didn't feel right leaving Janis. It felt as if there was unfinished business.

Driving back to the city with Norm, we discussed it. He noticed that Janis had seemed softer than usual, that her guard was down, or at least lowered (she usually had barbed wire and German shepherds surrounding and protecting her vulnerability). We discussed the question of the homing instinct—was it actually enough to push two people into a relationship?

Norm thought that it was—if the two people were finally ready for a relationship. He also thought it was interesting that Janis had gone out of her way to do one thing she'd never done before. Right before we got in the car to head back to New York, she'd bent over the couch and petted Norton. Stroked him once, gently.

It had started to rain during our drive, and I remember looking at Norton through the rearview mirror. He was sitting comfortably in the backseat, relaxed, dozing. I won-

dered if I could really use a cat as a gauge for a relationship.

Norton didn't open his eyes to peer back. He wasn't going to make it easy for me.

Janis's birthday comes in the middle of September. It was on her birthday that we decided to bring our relationship to a new level. Or just bring it back to what it had once been. Or bring it back but make it different. As you may gather, we weren't exactly sure *what* we were doing.

What I *am* sure of is that whatever we were doing or becoming, we wouldn't have done it or become it without Norton.

My house became *our* house—mine, Janis's, and Norton's. Norton was fun to be with on the weekends in Sag Harbor, and he made us both laugh. Janis couldn't get over the fact that he'd walk with me to Sean's Murray Hill Market, three blocks away from the house. Unlike Fire Island, Sag Harbor had traffic, so it was difficult to get him to take mid-afternoon strolls. But early in the morning, before cars started clogging up the streets, Norton would leisurely walk along behind us, meowing forcefully as usual. He'd wait patiently outside the market while we shopped, then hike back with us. Initially, Janis would get impatient if Norton decided to duck into the bushes for a two-minute (or ten-minute, depending on his mood) time-out from the walk. She'd try to convince me to leave him behind when it was time to buy groceries. Soon, however, she was coaxing him into taking the walk with us. And once he was along for the journey, if I started walking too fast for the cat, she'd urge me to slow down. "Don't be so impatient," she'd lecture me.

She stopped complaining when he got sidetracked and welcomed him back happily when he rejoined us.

She also liked to watch Norton prowl the garden. There were no bluejays to torment him in Sag Harbor, but there was a mockingbird, and he quickly became my kitten's new nemesis. Once the mockingbird had sized up the situation—the macho-level of the gray, furry animal in the backyard—he started zooming out of his tree, landing on the ground a few feet from Norton, and then would stand there screaming at the poor cat. Norton was totally intimidated. Janis would urge him on, try to get him to beat up on the puny bird, of course to no avail. She began to take it as a personal insult, and I would often find her explaining to Norton—as I had years before on Fire Island—about the law of the jungle and the concept of the food chain.

She grew catnip in the garden for him. It never got high enough for us to cut it and let it dry. As soon as she'd plant it, Norton would make a beeline for the spot, dig up the ground around it, and spend a happy few hours rolling around in the dirt while Janis would mock-scold him.

It was fun to watch a relationship develop between the two of them, both so independent. I'd gotten used to Norton's near-magical powers over the years, so it was rejuvenating to see his effect on her and to watch her witness his effect on others.

Janis was with us one day as we were driving along the L.I.E. out to Sag Harbor. I was driving, Janis was passengering, and Norton was in his usual position, lying down in the back, staring out the rear windshield. (When just the two of us drive, Norton will sit on the front seat, but Janis doesn't like him up there. For one thing, she thinks it's

dangerous. For another—the real reason—Norton's claws will occasionally come out, to help him balance himself if the car lurches, and he will ruin her stockings or rip a small hole in her blouse. So Norton will lie patiently in the back, content to watch the countryside zip by, until Janis falls asleep. Then he'll sneak up cautiously to the front and make himself comfortable.) It was a beautiful day; I was lost in thought and, apparently, also speeding like a lunatic. When the motorcycle cop pulled us over, he already had his ticket pad in hand as he broke it to me that I'd been going seventy-five miles an hour. Before he could write up the ticket, though, he glanced at the backseat.

"Is that a Scottish Fold?" he asked.

I nodded. I'm much better nodding than I am talking to policemen.

"He's beautiful," this leather-jacketed cop said. "I have a Fold, too."

I won't bore you with the sappy details. Suffice it to say that Norton let himself be held and petted by the arresting officer—and the arrest was never made. My record remained unblemished and the ticket was torn up.

Janis was around for another car confrontation with Norton, this one without quite the happy ending of the earlier one.

I had driven to the office that day and had decided to take the cat. He was a perfect corporate companion, spending the whole day either lying on my desk or resting on the couch in the corner. Periodically, he'd wander out of my office and stroll along the hallways, stopping to visit the people he liked. It was no longer a surprise to anyone at the publishing company—even the Chairman

of the Board—when a cat would wander in to say hello.

It was a brutally hot summer day, and naturally enough, the air conditioner in my car was broken. Driving home—Janis in front, Norton in the back hoping she'd doze off—all the windows were wide open. Downtown, in the Village, on the way to the garage, we stopped at a red light. On the street corner was a bag lady, filthy, kind of crazy seeming, clearly homeless. It had been a hard day at work, it was too hot, whatever the reason, but when the woman came up to our car and asked for money, both Janis and I looked right through her. It was as if she weren't a real person, as if she didn't exist. Perhaps we'd been in New York too long, where homelessness is a way of life, something too easy to inure yourself against.

As the car idled, the woman asked me a question.

"Is that a special breed of cat?" she said, pointing to Norton, who was looking out at her, his paws up on the back door, his head sticking through the open window.

Without really thinking about it—except snobbily to decide I didn't want to explain Norton's pedigree to a homeless woman—I simply said, "No. He's a regular cat."

"Oh," she said. "He looks like a Scottish Fold."

The light turned green. Before I could drive on, she added with a wistful sigh, "I used to have seven Siamese."

She stuck her hand through the window, gave Norton a pat on the head, and with astonishing dignity, walked on.

Much to Norton's delight, Janis allowed him onto the front seat for the few-block drive to our garage. She even hugged him. I'm sure also to his delight, neither one of us has ever looked at a homeless person in quite the same way. It was a good cure for our haughty superiority.

Janis was also present for Norton's one and only cat fight, a sorry affair by any standards.

I had long suspected that Norton was no Rocky Marciano. In the garden, he liked to hunker down and stalk the occasional and ever-dangerous butterfly, but that was the extent of his aggressive tendencies. Unfortunately, when one rears an outdoor cat, one must face up to the fact that other outdoor cats will come a-calling.

We had noticed a large orange, furry guy who seemed to enjoy strolling around our backyard in Sag Harbor in the late afternoons. If Norton was outside for these appearances, he would either meow immediately to be let in or he'd quickly disappear around the front of the house to one of his secret hiding spots. If this bully was visiting while Norton was safely inside the house, Norton would bravely stand at the back door, protected by a screen, and hiss loudly. He'd arch his back and release his claws, then he'd look over to us for approval. Either Janis or I would tell him what a tough guy he was and how proud we were of him. Perhaps that's what made Norton cocky.

One afternoon, while sitting upstairs in my office working away, I heard the most god-awful noise. It was a wail of pain and fear, and it seemed to stretch on forever. That was followed by Janis's scream. She screamed my name and then yelled for me to come downstairs.

I made it as quickly as I could, but in the few seconds it took me, I heard violent hisses and howls, high-pitched growls and what sounded like two sumo wrestlers thudding into each other. By the time I got outside, the orange monster was walking triumphantly across the lawn. I

screamed at him and waved my arms. That didn't seem to scare him—he gave me a look that made it clear he felt he could take me, too—but he did get the message that he wasn't welcome. Once he had hurdled the fence and landed in my neighbor's yard, I went looking for Norton.

Now, my cat *always* comes when I call him. *Always.* But not this time. Janis and I spent twenty minutes searching for him high and low. No Norton. I really began to be afraid when I finally heard a very soft and rather pathetic meow. I stopped and listened, heard it again. So did Janis. It seemed to be coming from under my car, which was parked in the driveway.

I got down on my hands and knees to look, and sure enough, Norton was cowering there. It took several more minutes of coaxing, but I finally got him to come out. When he slunk out between the rear tires, Janis gasped. Norton was bleeding above the nose and on his right shoulder. His fur was matted and sticky, and he was so frightened, he seemed to have curled up to half his normal size, which wasn't very big to begin with. When I picked him up in my arms, I realized he had been so terrified, he had also defecated, somehow all over himself.

I calmed him down as best I could, then carried him upstairs to the bathroom. Putting him down in the bathtub, I turned on the water, just a gentle stream from the tap, and did my best to clean him up. He made no effort to resist. Once he was clean, I could see that his scratches and scrapes were minor. The physical wounds were surface, but the emotional scars seemed to run deep. After I dried him off, talking to him and cooing at him the whole time, he timidly went into my bedroom, hopped onto the bed, and crawled

under the covers. He burrowed his way to the foot of the bed and stayed there for the rest of the afternoon. Every so often, I'd try to get him to come out, but, ashamed, he wouldn't even look at me. By dinnertime, he still hadn't poked his head out from under the quilt.

At that point, Janis decided the situation called for a woman's touch. I watched as she sat on the bed and gently pulled the covers back. Norton curled up into a ball, his face hidden. But where he had refused to look at me when I'd tried to cheer him up, he slowly began to uncurl as Janis stroked him and whispered to him. Within a few minutes, his little tongue was out, licking her fingers. When she told him it was now time to come downstairs and eat dinner, he rose, jumped off the bed, and followed her down the steps.

It took Norton a couple of days before he was up to snuff. He didn't look me in the eye for quite a while. It was more humiliating for him to face his dad than his new mom after his run-in with the orange Chuck Norris. I did notice a new bond between Norton and Janis after that. Somehow, he trusted her more than he had before. And somehow, she knew it and responded in kind.

Because Janis was so resistant to a relationship, it was easy to chart her ups and downs by her responses to the cat. When she would be overcome by fear or the claustrophobia of a relationship, she would push Norton away. When she was feeling affectionate toward me, it was easier to show it to the cat. It was safer.

Our biggest arguments at the beginning were over Norton's sleeping arrangements. She *hated* that he slept with us. I had reached the point where I couldn't sleep well if he wasn't in the bed with me. She felt smothered by him—

especially because he insisted on sleeping directly to her left, by her head. Since I was directly to her right, she was caught smack dab in the middle of us—for eight hours a night.

Norton would get in bed before either of us, usually settling down on Janis's pillow (he still slept like a person—head on the pillow, body under the covers). She'd crawl into bed before I would, pick Norton up, and unceremoniously toss him onto the floor. I'd finally come in, ready for lights-out, call for my pal, and he'd come running. He'd start out sleeping by my side, but as soon as it was feasible—which meant as soon as Janis was asleep and couldn't protest—he'd move to her side. She'd start out distant and comfortable, only to wake up in the middle of the night surrounded again.

The First Stage of softening came when she stopped dumping Norton off the bed. She started moving him over to my pillow instead. Then she'd go crazy watching me try to get into bed without disturbing him.

"He's just a cat!" Janis would say. "Throw him off!"

"No, he's too comfortable," I'd say while I was trying to squeeze my tired body into two feet of available space.

"Get rid of him!" she'd say scornfully—but we were both aware that *she* hadn't gotten rid of him.

This stage lasted a long time. Over a year. It was the period in the relationship when neither person knows whether what they have together is permanent, but each is starting to think it *might* be, if such a thing as permanency is humanly possible. She wasn't throwing anything away—not me or my cat—but she wasn't exactly embracing anything either.

During this period, our relationship grew and strengthened—we both relaxed; we both stopped trying so hard and just accepted what was—and so did Janis's relationship with Norton.

Stage Two arrived when I came upstairs one night to find Janis asleep and Norton curled up against her—on *her* side of the bed. He was taking up half her pillow. She hadn't moved to accommodate him, but she hadn't moved him away from her. It was about that time that she first told me she loved me.

Stage Three came months after that, soon after the infamous cat fight. Exhausted, I had fallen asleep early, long before Janis was ready for bed. Norton, overjoyed that he had me all to himself, plopped himself down directly in the middle of her pillow and got into our old sleeping position, me with half the bed, him with half the bed.

I didn't really fall into a deep sleep, so I was half awake when Janis finally crawled under the covers. I was conscious enough to watch her carefully climb over the sleeping Norton—*very* carefully, so as not to disturb him. Exactly as I had done so many times over the years, she scrunched herself into two feet of sleeping space, wedging herself between me and the cat. I fell asleep soon after I felt her gently kiss my forehead—and saw her put her ear against Norton to listen to his purring, then softly kiss him good night.

It was around this time that we began to realize we might be spending a good chunk of our lives together.

Stage Four came about in a complicated and roundabout way. One thing I can say about it is that it was certainly a good test of the relationship. It all happened because I agreed to take my cat *back* to Paris.

It started with another phone call from Roman Polanski, who called to say he thought we should write something

together. Not a rewrite—this time he wanted to do it from scratch.

We decided we would adapt a book. Neither one of us was brimming over with wonderful, original story lines, and we thought an adaptation would be fun, easy, and, from a technical standpoint, interesting. Within moments of this decision, I thought of a book I wanted to adapt. It was brilliant, it was dramatic, it was wonderfully funny and tragically sad. I pulled it down from my bookshelf, stared at it for several seconds, and then stuck it right back where it came from. Too weird, I decided. They'll think I'm crazy. The book was *The Master and Margarita* by Mikhail Bulgakov. I never mentioned it to anyone. Not to Roman, not to the studio.

I didn't find another book. Neither did Polanski. The studio kept sending us thrillers. The director kept rejecting them. Then, a full year after we'd decided to work together, Roman called me. "I know what I want to do," he said. "Have you ever heard of a book called *The Master and Margarita?*"

I thought it had to be a joke. He assured me it wasn't. My heart soared, and two weeks later Norton and I were in Paris adapting one of the greatest literary works of the twentieth century. I do not know if our screenplay will ever get made. Probably not is my guess. Too expensive and too weird. No chance for a sequel. Those are the vagaries and frustrations of working in the movie biz. But I do know one thing about that job:

It was not easy.

The work was torturous. (Or at least as torturous as writing can be. I don't ever like to confuse writing clever dia-

logue with fighting oil fires or harvesting the rice paddies.)
Roman is obsessive about research and meticulously faithful
to whatever material he's working from. He read the novel
in English. Then he read it in American (they are two
different translations). Then in Polish, French, and finally
Russian. Every time he read a different version, it would
spark a different idea or direction. With every new idea,
there was a new night I spent working—and working alone;
nighttime for Roman was definitely not for working—until
two or three A.M.

Thank god for Norton. Never had I appreciated having
him around quite so much. Most evenings, I'd come back
from a day at Polanski's spent and exhausted, intellectually
and emotionally drained. I'd collapse on the bed for an hour
or two, Norton cuddled up against my side; then I'd order
room service or take Norton out to a café for a quick
bite—then back to the apartment for several hours huddled
over the typewriter, trying to make sense of the day's notes
and decisions. Norton would sit on the desk, directly to my
left, watching me struggle trying to whip this book into
shape. By ten in the morning I was supposed to have new
scenes, new ideas, new dialogue for Roman to see.

As I worked, trying to make sense of this twisting, turning novel, as I talked it over with Roman—and over and
over—something started to click. The morass of political
and intellectual theories that abound in the book started to
come into a very definite focus. As we wrote and discussed
and argued and yelled and struggled, this great and dense
fantasy of a novel began to make sense to me in a way it
never had before. Oddly enough—*very* oddly, since my life
could not be farther from the lives depicted in the book—

the sense of the book and the meaning of the screenplay came from the relationship that had developed with Janis. And, yes, with Norton.

The Master and Margarita was written during the 1930s, finished in 1939, and it was considered finished only because the author died, blind and destitute, a victim of Stalin's repression. It is easy to tell what happens in this novel. It is not easy to tell what it's about. The main characters are the Devil, a suicidal writer, a bad poet, a six-foot cat in a top hat and waistcoat, Jesus Christ, Pontius Pilate, and the most beautiful woman in the world. There are brutal murders, public humiliations, crucifixions, and a confrontation with the ultimate evil. There is also sharp satire, laugh-out-loud slapstick, political parody, religious revisionism, and devastating philosophical insight. There are ghosts and people flying through the air and magical transformations. Oh—it also happens to be one of the greatest love stories ever written. All in all, I suppose it's understandable that so far it's been difficult to get a Hollywood studio to give this movie a financial green light: we're not exactly talking sequel to *Home Alone.*

Anyway, after much sifting, sorting, researching, cutting, and stalling, I ultimately made a decision about what *The Master and Margarita* is all about. It all came back to Cindy and her parting words of years before.

You don't know what love is.

Thanks to that trip to Paris, thanks to Janis and our developing relationship, mostly thanks to a little gray cat with a round head and folded ears, I *do* know what love is. I not only know what it is, I've found it. I've seen it work and seen what it can do.

Days before I wrote the ending to the script, I got a call from Janis. She was out in Sag Harbor. It was early in the morning her time, early afternoon for me.

"What are you doing up so early?" I asked.

"I couldn't sleep," she told me. "I haven't been sleeping well lately."

"Why not?" I wanted to know.

"I miss you," she said.

As perhaps you've noticed, I'm a sucker for this kind of stuff. "Awww," I said. "That's so nice."

"But it's not *just* that," she added.

"What else?"

"I don't sleep well anymore unless Norton sleeps by my side."

So it was Janis reaching Stage Four that gave me the nerve to decide that our screenplay for *The Master and Margarita* should be, above all, about love. Love in its most real sense. Love between two people. Two real people. Love surviving politics and oppression and art and history and cruelty and even death. The script for the movie ends the way Bulgakov ends his book. The Master and Margarita ascend, not to heaven but to a world of two, where they can escape the often vicious and always absurd world into which we are born.

My interpretation of this great novel was that the most important thing any of us can do is to live in a world where love is a greater priority than pain. Only in my case, as now in Janis's, it is not just a world of two. As I am reminded by Norton, who this very moment sits on my desk, six inches to my left, watching me write these words, it is very definitely a world of three.

9 The cat who went to Los Angeles

All of our lives, those of us who live in Western civilization, are not really so very different. We all suffer the same constraints—of time, of strength, of laws, of expectations. Within each life there are purely individual peaks and valleys, wild swings of ecstasy and despair, great triumphs, noble failures, yet, taken as a whole, there is a definite commonality of experience. The thrills we experience, which we feel no one can ever appreciate the same way, are thrills experienced by everyone—love, sex, success. The sadness that envelops us, in such a life-changing way that we are sure we are unique in the power of our feeling, envelops us all—illness, separation, poverty, death. There are two ways to go after experiencing one of these highs or lows—one can either withdraw into isolation, or one can accept the commonality and use it as a way of learning more about ourselves and others.

Last year I experienced my first of these sadnesses. Last year my father died.

My mother called, a few days before Thanksgiving. His lung cancer, which had once spread to the hip but had been dormant for several years, had returned and had spread even further. It had recently crushed his hip like an eggshell and was now riddling his back. My father had returned to the hospital, the pain was unbearable, and the feeling was he didn't have long to live.

Norton and I were on a plane the next day. The stewardesses, perhaps sensing my sadness, never said anything when I let the cat out of his box and onto my lap. He spent the whole flight sitting there, letting me pet him, occasionally licking my fingers with his rough little tongue.

I remembered when my dad had had his first operation. He'd had a lung removed. We were all terrified of what would happen, and Norton and I had flown out then, too. When my dad got out of the hospital, he was in tremendous pain. Every breath was agony, and the only way he could get comfortable was to sit back in a giant, ugly, cushiony Barcalounger that my mother bought just for this purpose. He would sit back, practicing breathing with one lung, trying to cope with the agony of broken ribs (that's how the surgeons get to the lung, through the ribs). What I remember most was how afraid my father was. Afraid of death, sure, but even more afraid of the pain.

The Barcalounger was set up in my parents' bedroom, at the foot of their bed. My dad would lie there for most of

the day, watching television, the pain spoiling the concentration required even to read.

He'd been set up in the chair like this for two, maybe three days, spending most of those days just being afraid. I was in my room, maybe forty feet away, when I heard my dad call my name. It wasn't a friendly call, or even a weak one, at least not as weak as he'd been sounding. It was a fearful call and I came running.

When I got to his room, I saw what my father was afraid of. Norton was crouched below his chair, ready to leap, eyeing the blanket on my father's lap. It looked like an inviting spot to sit and be petted—especially since these two had long ago befriended each other. But my father's face was not a friendly one. He was afraid that Norton would jump on him, would jostle him, would possibly even land right on the long, jagged scar, and hurt him even more. My father was too afraid even to move.

I didn't get to Norton in time to stop him. When I came into the room, he somehow took my presence as further encouragement. And so he jumped.

I distinctly recall feeling frozen in time, as if everything were moving in slow motion. The cat was floating through the air, aimed at my father's chest. My father was staring aghast, perhaps as afraid as he'd ever been in his whole life.

Of course it was over in a split second. Norton landed on the cushioned arm of the chair, not even touching my father. My dad sagged back, exhausted from the effort of being so afraid, and Norton, ever so gently, as if he weighed not a pound, settled onto my father's lap and began to lick his hand. My dad, trembling, used his other

hand to pet my cat. The blood came back into his face and finally he looked at me. He smiled—not much of a smile but a smile—and nodded weakly.

I came back an hour later to check up on him. My father was asleep now, his head back in the chair, his body relaxed. His hand was still resting on Norton's body, and Norton was still curled up on the blanket in his lap. My dad woke up when I came into the room, and he smiled again. This time a real smile. Somehow he didn't look as afraid. I think he felt a little foolish that he'd been so terrified of Norton. At the same time I think he was relieved. The possibility of pain had been very real, yet the pain hadn't materialized. I actually think that moment was the first time my father thought he might get better, the first time he realized he wasn't going to die.

Three years later, as I saw him in the hospital room, he *was* going to die and this time he knew it.

My brother, Eric, and my mother had been under an incredible strain, living with this pressure day to day, so I was, by reason of being the newest and freshest face on the scene, elected designated strong person. The decisions weren't pleasant ones—levels of medication, when to stop the therapy, when to stop fighting and give in to the inevitable. Within a few days there weren't many more decisions to make, however. There was very little to be done. My father was in and out of lucidity, usually out. In a ghoulish way, we actually got some laughs out of the situation—final proof that I was right and Sarah was wrong: there don't seem to be any inappropriate times to find humor.

At one point, my dad, totally under the influence of pain-killing drugs, mostly morphine, was convinced Pete

Maravich was playing basketball in the hall. (My dad had never met Pete Maravich to any of our knowledge; however, as Eric pointed out, since Maravich had died several months before this, it probably wasn't a good omen.) In one coherent moment, my dad was confused by the hallucinations he'd been seeing on the wall—confused because they'd suddenly disappeared. "But they were so beautiful," he said.

"At last," I told him, "you can understand why Eric and I took all those drugs back in the sixties and seventies."

"So *this* is why," he said. And then he said, "Now what I don't understand is why you *stopped.*"

My dad did not want to die in the hospital. So when we knew there was nothing else the doctors could do, we brought him home.

A round-the-clock nurse had set up a hospital bed in his bedroom, and that's where he settled. The bed was near his old Barcalounger. For the several days he stayed alive at home, Norton never left that Barcalounger. He stayed there all day; he slept there at night, keeping my dad company.

One night I wanted him in my bed. It was late, maybe two A.M., and I wanted the company. I slipped into my dad's room. He was asleep—rather, by this time he'd slipped into a semi-coma—and the nurse was reading. Norton sat in the chair, awake, staring at my father as if waiting for word that he was allowed to jump onto his bed and comfort him. The word didn't come, at least not while I stood watching. I didn't bring Norton back into my room. I left him there in the chair and went back to sleep on my own. Just in case the word did come, I figured he might as well be prepared.

The next day my father died. It was in the late afternoon. I wasn't there. I'd gone out shopping for groceries. Somehow, pulling into the driveway, I knew. When I stopped the car, my brother and my mother came out of the house. They were crying. I'd missed it by just a few minutes. Eric had been by his side. One minute he was breathing deeply, asleep, the next minute the breaths stopped. That's all there was to it.

I'd said my good-byes a couple of days before. My dad had been slipping in and out of consciousness. When conscious, sometimes he would call for one of us, or all of us. Sometimes when the nurse told us he was awake, we'd just come in, never knowing if it was our last opportunity to speak or listen.

At some point, the nurse told me that he was awake and I should say whatever it was I wanted to say to him. She said I might not have another chance. So she left the room, and I stood next to my dying father, holding his cold, clammy hand. I knew he knew who I was. He couldn't talk by this point, but he was shaking his head, rolling his eyes as if to say, "What a bitch, huh?"

I didn't have anything to say to him. We'd been very close when he was alive—I mean *really* alive, not barely alive—and I'd said a lot to him when it meant something. I didn't have to tell him I loved him. He knew that. I didn't have to tell him I'd miss him. He knew that too. Anything I could say to him now would somehow seem fake or overly dramatic or ultimately meaningless. So I didn't say anything. I just held his hand and waited until he fell back asleep. My dad was never one to tolerate the bullshit. I think he preferred the silence.

That afternoon, Janis had arrived from New York. My dad had been crazy about her and vice versa. They had a great relationship, a lot of banter back and forth. He gave her a very hard time and she returned it with gusto. He appreciated anyone who could give him a hard time.

When she came up the stairs, the whole family was sitting around my dad's bed. He'd been unconscious, but when she walked in he seemed to stir. He was always a bit of a ladies' man.

"Dad," I said, "it's Janis. Janis came here to see you."

He lifted his head, saw us all, then saw her. She smiled at him. He looked back at my mother, at my brother, at me—and rolled his eyes. A big, exaggerated roll, done for Janis's benefit. The roll said, "Jesus—as if things weren't bad enough, *now* look who shows up!"

We all got hysterical; even my dad did his best to laugh. Then he fell back asleep and never woke up.

There's something comforting in the fact that his last act in life was to make people laugh. He kept his sense of humor right up to the end, and it made everything a lot easier on all of us.

We didn't have a standard funeral. We had a party instead. That's the way he would have wanted it—my dad loved parties. He loved being a host.

My dad was in a wine group, and the members of the group brought exquisite wine to toast him. We had one of the best restaurants in L.A. cater the event. Three of Dad's closest friends gave speeches, talking about him. Their talks were wonderfully funny. I would say that, through the tears, there were as many laughs at the funeral as at any party my dad had ever thrown.

That night, after everyone was gone, after Janis was asleep, I went into my bathroom, the bathroom I'd had as a little kid, and I broke down and cried. I cried for perhaps fifteen minutes, real wracking sobs. I cried until I was exhausted, until I not only didn't have any tears in me, I didn't have any emotions left at all.

When I was done, I looked up to find Norton staring at me. He'd pushed the bathroom door open with his nose and had come in to seek me out.

I picked him up, kissed him on top of the head, and held him while I sat in the bathroom, staring out the window at our backyard. Norton didn't meow; he didn't even lick me. He just let me hold him as long as I wanted. I appreciated the silence, too. I wasn't in the mood for bullshit either.

I don't know how long I was in there. I do know it was almost light when I got back into bed.

I lay down, my head on the pillow, closed my eyes, and went to sleep. Norton put his head on my pillow and snuggled in against my chest.

When I woke up, it was a new day. Many things had changed, but not Norton. He was still asleep, still by my side, still content to let me hold him.

Afterword

Sometimes I worry that perhaps it's just me, *that perhaps I make up all this stuff about Norton being so great, being so special. But every so often I'm reminded that that's not the case.*

Not long ago, my friends Nancy and Ziggy had a baby, a truly marvelous little boy named Charlie Elroy Alderman. (Yes, if any of you are wondering, it is indeed Elroy as in "The Jetsons.")

Soon after Charlie was born, Nancy walked him down, in his stroller, from their house in Sag Harbor to mine. It was a Sunday morning and it was early. Ziggy was still asleep and so was Janis. This was Charlie's first trip down the block to visit his neighbors.

Nancy wheeled him up to the back door, picked him out of the buggy, and carried him inside.

Norton, who'd been napping on a kitchen chair, raised his head to check out the newcomer in his life. Nancy took her tiny little baby and held him down toward Norton.

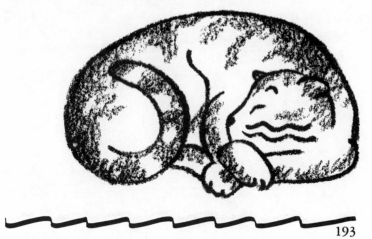

"Look, Norton," she said. *"This is a baby."*

Norton looked up at Charlie, took him in, and sort of nodded as if assimilating the information.

There was a very long pause, and then I heard Nancy gulp.

"You've finally done it," she said to me.

"What?" I wanted to know.

"Most mothers would have said, 'Look, Charlie, this is a cat.'"

I started to laugh.

"Not with Norton," I said.

Nancy started to laugh, too.

"No, not with Norton," she agreed.

A CAT ABROAD

To Danie, Anne, Sylvie, Jean-Guy, Anette, Philippe, Elisabeth, Gwen, Ailie, Jenny, Jim, Maureen, Margit, Georges, Mike, and Deborah, who welcomed us, taught us, fed us, and became friends forever.

contents

Acknowledgments   ix

Foreword   1

PART ONE: A CAT AT HOME

1. A Cat at the Super Bowl   9

2. A Cat Lost   25

3. A Cat on Tour   45

PART TWO: A CAT ABROAD

4. A Cat in France   79

5. A Cat in Provence   103

6. A Cat on the Riviera   147

7. A Cat in Spain   177

8. A Cat in Italy   189

9. A Cat in Sicily (and Other Places)   201

10. A Cat in Goult   217

PART THREE: A CAT RETURNS

11. A Cat in New York   225

Afterword   241

acknowledgments

Leona Nevler and Betty Prashker believed, encouraged, and fixed.

Esther Newberg did her usual tooth-and-nail job and continues to be the perfect agent.

Janis seems not to care (well, sort of), no matter how grumpy I get or how many weekends I work.

And I especially want to thank Norton for letting me share the chair at my desk with him. For the next book, I hope I get a full half, but I won't count on it.

foreword

Recently, I was in Paris with my rather astonishing and extremely handsome Scottish Fold cat, Norton. We were having dinner with Danielle, an old friend of mine who lives in the 17th arrondissement, and her daughter, Priscilla. I met Priscilla when she was four years old and the only English sentence she knew was, "I like ze Beeg Mac 'amburgair." By the night of our dinner, Priscilla was no longer four. She was twenty-three, spoke fluent English, and wanted to take us to a restaurant where her boyfriend worked. Which means I'm getting longer in the tooth (not to mention thicker around the middle).

I say "we" and "us," by the way, because no one was all that excited just to see *me.* Norton was the star attraction. Danielle had made it quite clear that they would certainly be happy if I came along, but they were *really* interested in my little gray pal as their primary dinner companion. Danielle even let me know that the owner of the restaurant,

1

when told about Norton and his adventures traveling the globe, had insisted that *le chat* come to dinner as her very special guest.

When we arrived at the restaurant, Bistro d'Albert, a charming and perfect place that could exist only in France, Norton was greeted the way I imagine Ike was when he arrived at the Champs-Elysées immediately following D-Day. He was given, as he always is, his own chair, which he settled into quite comfortably. The owner, a typical somewhere-over-forty-year-old blond Frenchwoman for whom you'd happily give up the rest of your life if she'd only so much as smile at you, smiled up a storm. But not at me. Oh, no. At my innocent-looking furry friend, who, just to annoy me, I'm sure, purred like a motorboat, rolled over on his back, and practically begged the owner and all of her gorgeous waitresses to come over and scratch his stomach, which, of course, they did. Meanwhile, I was doing my best to order a *kir,* but I couldn't get anyone to even look at me.

Eventually, the waitresses returned to their regular duties, went about their work, and dinner settled into a normal routine. The three humans had a delicious bottle of red wine with their kidneys—the specialty of the house—and the cat worked away on some broiled chicken and a small bowl of milk.

One of the most satisfying things about being in Europe is that animals are treated with enormous respect. You can go into the very best, most expensive restaurants in Paris and it is almost guaranteed that someone will have brought his or her dog along for the meal. No one bats an eye, no one thinks it odd. The general feeling is that a dog has as much right to eat at Robuchon as any human. This night,

at Bistro d'Albert, *five* people brought their dogs along.
Which meant that at some point—I think it was during the
cheese course—Norton looked up from his *lait froid* to find
five curious canines of varying sizes and temperaments sitting in a circle around his chair. One of them growled.
Another worked up his courage, stuck his nose right in
Norton's face, and took a particularly antagonistic sniff. The
dogs seemed to be of the opinion that Parisian restaurants
were *their* domain and that cats should stay where they
belonged—curled up by the fireplace in a turn-of-the-
century apartment or prowling around a garden searching
for tasty mice. Certainly they did *not* belong in places where
they could actually compete for affection, much less the
boeuf bourguignon. For just a moment, the room froze. I
didn't know if French people had ever heard of the Gun-
fight at the O.K. Corral—but I had a feeling they were
about to. Except that Norton, in the peacekeeping role of
Wyatt Earp, simply looked determinedly at his ring of potential tormentors, stared each of them, one by one, straight
in the eye, then calmly went back to eating his chicken and
sipping his milk. When one dog barked, demanding a little
more attention, Norton finished chewing his last piece of
chicken, then glanced at the barker with pity, as if to say,
"Please. This is France. You're embarrassing me. Haven't
you read your Sartre?"

That was the end of the confrontation. Deflated, the dogs
went back to their respective masters and sat under their
own tables, hoping to receive a morsel of food now that
their bluff had been called.

The rest of the dinner went fairly smoothly until it came
time for dessert. Danielle, Priscilla, and I ordered our
mousse and our pastries, and when we were served, the chef

emerged from the kitchen with a big bowl of ice cream. Priscilla had mentioned to him that Norton was an ice cream fiend.

"Zees is for ze incredible cat," he told me. "I made *chocolat*—his favoreet."

Now, Norton likes his chocolate ice cream, no question about it. But he's also quite particular. He loves Ben & Jerry's. Häagen-Dazs gets an A-plus. He will eat frozen yogurt and ice milk but only in an emergency. If offered some chocolate *non*-fat frozen yogurt, he will turn his back disgustedly after one lick, making you feel as if you'd just offered a Sabrettes chili dog to the Queen of England.

The chef dug a spoon into his ice cream and held it up toward Norton. The cat eagerly took a lick, hesitated, gave some thought to what he'd just eaten—and disdainfully turned his back on the chef. I immediately had visions of the chef pulling out a glove, slapping me, and challenging me to a duel—and I was not so far off.

"It's not posseeble," he told me, totally bewildered. "Our ice cream is superb!"

"I'm sure it is," I agreed. "He's probably just full."

"But Priscilla told me he *loves* ze ice cream."

"Why don't you try giving him another taste," I suggested, although I knew my cat well enough to know this would be a useless gesture. By this time, the owner had come to the table to see what the problem was. When I explained, I could see the existential pain in her eyes.

"We have never 'ad a complaint in all our years," she told me. "Zis is outrageous."

"Give him another taste," a waitress urged.

So the chef held out a second spoonful of the stuff. Norton licked cautiously, looked at the brown lump, and, if cats can shake their heads—and I am one hundred percent certain that mine can—he shook his head. *No way,* is basically what he was saying.

Thus ended the meal. The chef stalked back into the kitchen, offended and insulted. The owner made it chillingly clear that the cat was not nearly as special as she had been led to believe. And I was fairly certain that the next time the Larousse French/English Dictionary put in the phrase "ugly American," my photo would be next to the definition.

I gathered Norton in my arms, tried to figure out how I could explain to a cat about the concepts of tact and eating to be polite, gave up, and stuck him back in his cloth shoulder bag, his favorite mode of transportation.

As we were going out the door, one of the waitresses pulled me aside.

"Your leetle cat," she said. " 'E was right."

I looked at her curiously and she explained.

"Ze chef, he made a batch of ice cream and eet was not good," she went on. "He thought he could put one over on ze cat and get rid of it." She put her hand on the top of Norton's head and scratched him, something that ranks in his top three activities. "Zat is a very impressive cat," she said. "And his taste is *soo-pairb.*"

"I never doubted it," I told her and looked at my "leetle cat," just a bit awed. He looked back at me, dubious. "Honest," I said to him, and held my hand over my heart. "I never doubted you for a minute."

PART ONE

a cat at home

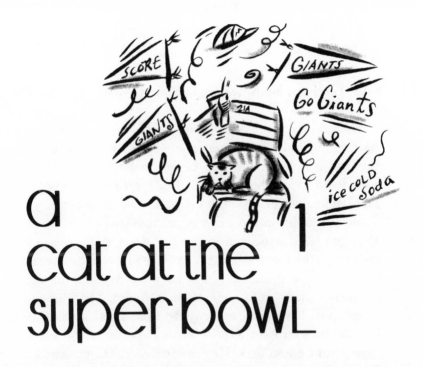

a cat at the super bowl

It's been said—by Edmund Wilson among other scholars—that the only great subject for American writers is the rise of America in the first half of the twentieth century.

That may be true, though I would argue that there needs to be a slight revision to such a narrow way of thinking. Without going off the deep end, let's just say: A very *good* subject for American writers is the rise of the American cat in the second half of the twentieth century. Especially if the cat happens to be a brilliant, handsome, good-hearted Scottish Fold with a round head and flat, folded ears who looks more like an owl than a cat and who has traveled all over the world, having more adventures in his travels than Gulliver.

Of course, I may be a little biased here, especially since this book is a sequel to one called *The Cat Who Went to Paris,* which was all about the aforementioned cat with folded ears and his owner, who happens to have reasonably straight ears.

The cat who did indeed go to Paris is my very own cat Norton. He's also been everywhere else in France you can think of, as well as to Holland, Germany, Italy, Switzerland, and Spain. He's been to baseball's spring training in Florida, to a writers' conference in San Diego, to meetings at movie studios in L.A., and gone cross-country skiing in Vermont. As I explained in the first book, Norton takes walks with me *sans* leash and I can leave him outside almost anyplace, in any situation, and he waits patiently in the designated spot until I come to reclaim him. Those designated spots have been everywhere from hotel lobbies to friends' backyards to airport waiting rooms to the great expanse of Central Park. He has flown on the Concorde. In Europe he goes out to restaurants with me and sits in his own chair, where he behaves like someone who has just graduated from a Swiss finishing school. He is, common to the breed, extraordinarily sweet. He is also, not common to any animal I've ever met before, shockingly smart. I really do take him everywhere I go, have ludicrously long conversations with him, and I like him so much I willingly admit it borders on the demented. Very little is done in my life unless Norton approves of the doing.

Since the publication of *The Cat Who Went to Paris,* I've discovered that, as I venture out into the world, I have begun to fade more and more into the background while Norton has slowly poked his way into the limelight. This is fine with me except it means that too often I find myself being compared, one on one, to something—excuse me: some*one*—I used to foolishly regard as my pet.

Believe me, it is not always a comforting exercise to compare cats to people, particularly if the one doing the comparing happens to be a flawed human rather than a member of the near-flawless feline race. For instance: People lie. In fact, people lie all the time. Cats do not *ever* lie. People happily kill other people in the name of everything from a god to a country to an overly developed sense of annoyance when someone cuts across two lanes on a freeway without signaling. Cats will, on occasion, kill other cats but, for the most part, they are content to puff up their fur, yowl like banshees, and rip the occasional ear off—and all this is usually done for the sake of food or protecting their own territory (which may not be condonable, but it is at least rational). People are often cruel and cause great emotional damage to others, sometimes deliberately, sometimes in blissful ignorance. The worst thing a cat will do, when it comes to inflicting emotional pain, is to make it clear he wants to be left alone. This causes nothing more than a sense of relief in other well-adjusted cats and a sense of rejection in not-so-well-adjusted, much more neurotic humans. People tend to lower their standards (and almost anything else that can be lowered) if they have the opportunity to win approval from a friend, spouse, boss, or even nodding acquaintance. Cats, on the other hand, are relatively indifferent to such emotional stroking. As a result, their decisions—on matters of personal attachments, lavishing affection, and certainly on such questions as whether or not to get off the comfortable couch to join, if they'll excuse the expression, the rat race—automatically fall on a substantially higher moral and ethical plane. All in all, it is not particularly difficult to make the case that cats are, in almost any and all ways, superior creatures to the supposedly dominant Homo sapiens.

That is why, when it came to making the single most important decision of my life—which I did last year—it is not so surprising that that decision revolved around the actions of my moral, ethical, truth-telling, affection-lavishing, semi-couch-potatoish best friend.

To begin to explain, we need to take a look at one area where people seem to hold their own, or at least can compete on the same field, with cats: courage.

Norton, not unlike most humans I have encountered, is an interesting combination of brave adventurer and wimpy coward. Plop my cat in a strange garden, yard, or even forest and he will immediately roar into action, fearlessly climbing trees, playfully slithering under bushes, joyously romping and running wherever his little gray legs will carry him. Put him down in a strange house or hotel room, and he will explore any and all nooks and crannies, generally making himself quite at home without any thought of potential danger—i.e., irate cleaning women, dizzying heights, or wobbly furniture that might not take kindly to an extra nine pounds of fur bouncing around on top of it. He is not afraid of Parisian rooftops or dark and mysterious ruins or airplanes or boats or even most dogs.

However. Two years ago, I replaced the pillows on my bed with nice, soft, down-filled ones. The night they arrived, Norton jumped up on the bed, ready for sleep, got set to nestle into his usual spot by my head, placed one tentative paw on the new pillow, and, to put it graciously, was off the bed so fast, running away from the terrifying pillow at such breakneck speed, that he made Lou Costello in *Abbott and Costello Meet Frankenstein*—and I'm talking the scene with the revolving bookshelves—look like Schwarzenegger in *T2*. It took him six months before he'd so much as *touch* a down pillow again! (Don't worry. For those of you who are already doubting my devotion, yes, I did put the old pillows back on the bed. I kept both sets handy at all times and arranged them so I could sleep on the new ones and Norton could sleep on the old ones.)

Janis—of whom much was spoken in the first book and of whom much more will be spoken in this sequel—and I recently bought a new couch for our Sag Harbor house. Only after the old couch was carried out and far removed from sight would Norton so much as step one gray and black ringed foot into the den. He had an absolute horror of that couch. He was too afraid even to *scratch* it. For those of you who are already wondering to what lengths I'll go to keep my cat happy, no, I *didn't* buy a new couch because Norton hated the old one. We got a new one because the old one was ugly, falling apart, and extremely uncomfortable. The fact that I let my cat live with something he didn't like is, however, totally out of character. In retrospect, I'm already feeling guilty and I just hope he settles in happily on the armrest of the new sofa or I'm sure I'll be furniture shopping before very long.

Janis also just bought a new blanket for our bed. A plain, simple, ordinary, purple, inanimate, wool blanket. There is nothing remotely threatening about this blanket—except to a particular Scottish Fold. To Norton, this blanket has much the same personality as Freddy Krueger in *Nightmare on Elm Street*. The first time Janis picked him up, put him on the bed, and, thus, on the dreaded blanket, Norton did a near-perfect Greg Louganis back flip onto the floor—I gave him a 9.7—and disappeared from sight for the rest of the day.

In addition to the odd piece of furniture and accompanying accoutrements, my dear cat also is terrified of bicycles, jackhammers, and birds. The first two I can sympathize with. Bicycles are ridden by careless humans and are more than capable of squashing a feline flat as a stepped-on morsel of Pounce, Norton's personal favorite between-meal snack.

And jackhammers are loud, earth-moving things and *should* be terrifying to anyone with any sense who's not named Rocco or Deke. The last one on the list, however, is a constant source of humiliation to all who know and love cat and cat owner.

This past autumn, while my round-headed pal and I were spending time in the south of France, I decided to show off *l'intelligence incroyable de mon chat.* We were going out to dinner with a friend and our car was parked several streets away from the house. I decided I'd bring Norton along to dinner—and I also decided I'd let him walk to the car with us. Our friend was a little dubious, especially because the town we were in was a French medieval mountain specialty with winding narrow streets and animals roaming freely wherever they chose to roam. But Norton came through with flying colors: striding boldly out the door, disdainfully ignoring all the dogs and cats frolicking around him, as well as all the kids kicking a soccer ball to and fro and all the adults briskly strolling around with their baguettes tucked under their arms. He followed at an acceptable pace along the cobblestones—until we came to a house, a mere ten feet away from our car, that had a bird cage hanging outside the window. Inside the cage were three tiny yellow birds, whistling and singing away. Norton, having braved all the tough obstacles in town, got within a foot of the cage, heard the birds merrily chirping, turned on his heels, and made a beeline for home, in the process breaking A. J. Foyt's land-speed record by a comfortable margin. I found him huddled pathetically by our doorway, trying his best to make himself invisible.

"They were *birds*," I told him, shaking my head. "*Tiny* birds. *Really* tiny birds. In a *cage*. In a *locked* cage," I added, hoping to shame him.

It's very hard to argue with a cat, however, particularly a nervous cat, and clearly this cat had no intention of getting close to those tiny, caged birds again if he could help it. Which he could. So I picked him up and carried him all the way back to the car. When we passed those tiny little birds, Norton buried his head under my arm, doing his very best ostrich impersonation. Once we reached the safety of our red Citroën, he settled happily onto the backseat, and then, oblivious to the scorn with which he was greeted from his dinner companions, thoroughly enjoyed the rest of his evening on the town. There were no birds in the restaurant to disturb his meal.

While *les oiseaux* seem to be somewhat of an Achilles heel, Norton has a very wide macho streak as far as mice are concerned. This predatory instinct came as something of a shock to me when it finally surfaced. Norton and I had spent many years together without his ever exhibiting one iota of lionlike interest in chasing after big game. Then, one night, while I still had a summer house in the town of Fair Harbor, on Fire Island, the hunter was unleashed.

I was bacheloring it up this particular Saturday night with my friend Norm, the head writer of "Sesame Street" and, as chronicled in *The Cat Who Went to Paris*, legendary lady-killer of the Fair Harbor "sixishes." With us was my cousin Jon, an actor visiting from L.A. The three of us—the *four* of us, counting you-know-who—were having dinner, male-bonding, and basically having a terrific time, all the while wondering how soon we could ditch the other guys and go out and try to find a woman. As we were talking, I noticed that Jon had a big smile on his face and that he was focused on something a few feet from the dinner table.

"What are you looking at?" I wanted to know.

"Nothing," he said. "I'm just enjoying watching Norton play with his mouse toy."

I nodded, smiling at the thought and listening to Norton thrash around on the floor. And then the smile faded. Norm and I looked at each other, confused, and we both said, at the exact same time: "Norton doesn't *have* a mouse toy."

The ensuing action really should have been captured as an Impressionist painting with the title "Three Jews in the Country" because you haven't seen three fairly creaky guys move so quickly in your entire life. Jon, I believe, was standing on his chair. I'm pretty sure that I was all the way up on the table, saying something constructive like "Oh my god, I'm going to be sick!" Norm was the only one with the presence of mind to move for the broom. Using the straw end, he managed to maneuver the thrashing mouse away from Norton, who was playfully batting it around as if the room were one large knock-hockey board game. Clearly my cat did not realize that the small gray thing moving at the speed of light was a disgusting rodent to be feared and avoided at all costs. He didn't even think it was something to kill and eat for dessert. No, judging from this first close encounter of the mouse kind, Norton thought the squeaking, long-tailed prey was something to have fun with, not all that different from a catnip-stuffed beanbag.

Unfortunately for my dignity and sense of self-respect, at some point I had to climb down off the table and hold the door open while Norm swatted the mouse outside, *way* too close to my bare feet, which I pointed out to him later.

Once the creature was out of the house, we settled down and sanity reigned again. We all applauded Norton for his ability to spontaneously tap into his savage jungle instincts, and we all decided that perhaps city life was better for us humans than this dangerous living close to the ocean. More than anything, the three of us were happy we'd all struck out that weekend so that no one of the opposite sex had seen our rather tragic failure when confronted face to face with the wilds of nature. (In later retellings, the mouse became more of a rat—sometimes something closer to a small alligator—and I was the one with the broom, but I'm afraid Norm might read this, so I'd better stick to the sad truth.)

That was only the beginning, however, for Norton, so to speak, had tasted blood.

Fire Island was behind us, the charming country house in Sag Harbor was now before us, and I no longer had to worry about being humiliated in front of strange women because Janis was now a major part of the equation. I could simply worry about being humiliated in front of my very own girlfriend.

Not long after buying our house, I padded downstairs on a perfect autumn morn, went to the market to buy the papers, made a steaming pot of coffee, carried a mug of java into the safe, warm confines of the den, glanced down at the floor . . . and found a half-eaten, dead-as-a-doorknob mouse waiting for me in the middle of the room.

My very own cat had done this. The cat whom I often (probably too often) kissed right smack dab on the lips. The cat who was quite probably the sweetest, gentlest animal in existence. My genius, world-traveling cat had bitten a mouse right in half and left him as a little present for his dad.

I have to admit that, once I got over my immediate sense of revulsion, my chest puffed out a bit with pride. Okay, so birds were scary—but no three-inch-long cheese eater could push *my* cat around.

The only problem left to solve was how to actually dis-

pose of the body. Norton, by this time, was hovering outside the den, waiting for praise for his newfound role as
protector of the household. I indulged him in this, picking
him up and petting him profusely, marveling at his courage and physical prowess. Unfortunately, Janis was also
hovering around, demanding that I get rid of the corpse
immediately.

You may have picked up on the fact that I'm a tad squeamish when it comes to things like dead mice (for the record,
also when it comes to live snakes and any bugs larger than
a quarter). But, since my cat had moved up to a new level
of macho-hood, I was determined to do the same. And
despite what Janis would tell you now if you could talk to
her directly, I did a very solid and impressive job of mouse
removal. It just took me a while, that's all. Like about two
hours, because every time I worked up the nerve to try to
scoop the repulsive little pile onto the dustpan, I'd get dizzy
and go into the kitchen (where Janis, I might add, was safely
sequestered!) and take half an hour to get myself back
together.

After that first kill, however, the routine got a little easier
for all of us. I don't want anyone to get the impression that
our house is a mini-version of *Willard* and that thousands
of mice roam around freely, rearranging the furniture and
making crank phone calls in the middle of the night, but
once or twice a year we do have a little critter who decides
to explore under the sink or behind the refrigerator. And
once or twice a year, Norton goes into action. For a cat
whose favorite hobby, as he gets a little older, is to sit
absolutely motionless for as long as possible, it is a wonder
to behold when Norton's mouse antenna goes up. He will
sit, poised to strike, staring at a crack under the fridge, as
lithe and graceful as any tai chi master. Suddenly, an object

will dart out, so fast it's almost impossible to see, except Norton will not only see him, he'll dart even faster. And before you know it, a victorious Norton will be parading into the living room with a conquered mouse firmly clenched between his teeth. One small step for felinehood, one giant step for a mouse-free home.

I can deal with this sort of disruption much better now. Practice does indeed make perfect. No longer do I freeze at the thought of placing another body into the mouse morgue. No longer does some late, lamented Mickey Doe have to sit in the middle of the floor for hours while I stop my stomach from doing flip-flops. Nope. Now I've got things under control. Either I call my friend David Meves, who lives a couple of blocks away and, as near as I can tell, has no fear of man *or* mouse, or I have David's wife, Peggy, do it.

But I don't discuss Norton's heroics just to show off the fact that, when push comes to shove, my little cat can hold his own in time of macho crisis. I don't want him to turn into a feline Mike Tyson or Stormin' Norman Schwarzkopf. I bring it up because Norton's sense of adventure and general fearlessness had a somewhat larger effect on me and my life than simply getting me to toss out my mousetraps. Last year, I was faced with the major, life-changing decision I hinted about earlier and, as with all life-changing decisions I'd made over the past eight years, Norton was a crucial and essential part of the process.

This particular process began when I was invited to go to the Super Bowl.

I'm your basic sports fanatic, although much less so as I've gotten older, as athletes have gotten greedier, and team owners have gotten stupider. I've been to World Series games and NBA All-Star games and French Open tennis matches, but I'd never been to a Super Bowl, much less a Super Bowl in which my beloved Giants were playing. The thought of seeing L.T. leaping tall AFCers in a single bound was too good an opportunity to pass up, especially since the people who'd done the inviting were the NFL, which meant seeing him leap from fifty-yard-line seats.

Even Janis, who would normally prefer something pleasant and relaxing—like walking across hot coals or discussing the right-to-life issue with Rush Limbaugh—to attending a sports event, decided she couldn't pass up a Super Bowl. So we made our arrangements. A flight into Tampa. A room at the Dolphin Hotel in Orlando. Dinner with a honcho from NFL Properties. A cat who was a big Giants fan.

Norton had, by this time in his life, traveled extensively all over Europe and America. But even for him, Super Bowl weekend was something extraordinary.

First of all, the Dolphin Hotel is part of Disney World. As we were checking in, we were greeted by a bevy of very friendly six-foot-high, three-fingered mice dancing and prancing around the lobby, waving at anyone who'd look at them. For a human being, this is a rather disorienting sight; I can't *imagine* what could have been running through the brain of a reasonably sophisticated Scottish Fold. The prospect of biting one of these suckers in half and leaving him in the den for Dad to clean up must have been incredibly intimidating. Luckily, as I signed us into our room, Norton restrained himself admirably and settled for sticking his head out of his shoulder bag and swiveling his neck in every which direction, awestruck as he peered around the lobby.

When we went out for a stroll to take in the sights—

neither Janis nor Norton had ever been to Orlando before—the atmosphere was no less circuslike. Not only did my cat get a look at thousands of people from all over the country, drinking up a storm and determined to have as wild a weekend as possible, he saw screaming vendors hawking T-shirts and team sweat suits, screaming kids dragging their screaming parents across the street to Disney World, and screaming NFL marketing men trying to stop everybody else from screaming so they could scream louder about their thrice-too-expensive wares. In addition to the giant mice, Norton also got a very good gander at Goofy and Donald, up close and personal, as well as all the real-life (and sculptures of) fish, which were everywhere you looked in the hotel (the designers obviously felt a compunction to create an artistic theme worthy of the hotel's name).

After two days of hectic touristing and socializing, Norton, Janis, and I had a quiet few moments in our room before we were to join all the screaming people on the bus that was to take us to the game.

"Are you glad you came?" I asked Janis, figuring that with only the upcoming game left on our weekend agenda, it would all be downhill from here.

"Sort of," she grudgingly said. "Although I still say it was Goofy who pinched me at that party last night."

"How about you?" I said to my cat. In response, Norton sprawled out on the bed and turned over on his back, his subtle way of telling me he was both tired and wanted his belly scratched.

"What must it be like for him?" I asked Janis. "Giant mice. Lunatic football fans. Kids with buffaloes painted on their chests. For us this is just a weird and fun weekend. For Norton, this must be like going to *Mars.*"

As we talked, I started to obsess more and more about the level of high adventure Norton had reached that weekend. Sure, he'd enjoyed the café life in Paris, liked sunning himself on Florida beaches, even got used to cross-country skiing in Vermont. But this weekend, this was something he'd never come close to seeing or doing before.

"For *real,*" I said, half to Janis, half to myself. "I'm kind of jealous. *Nothing* we do could possibly be as strange and exciting and out of the ordinary as what this cat's doing."

Janis knows enough not to encourage me when I start trying to delve into the mind of my cat (or my own mind, for that matter). So she kept quiet and let me go on.

"It's depressing, is what it is," I began to rant. "We're people, he's a cat! We can't let him lead a better life than we're leading!"

"He leads a better life than anyone else in the whole *world* is leading," Janis pointed out.

"That's beside the point," I came back with. "He deserves it. And I'm not talking about Norton in particular. I'm talking philosophically."

Resigned now, Janis sighed and asked me what I was really getting at.

"Norton's life is exciting. He hunts. He prowls. He goes to Mars. Our life is dull. We go to work, we watch TV. We're stuck in a routine. I want my life to be as adventurous as my cat's!"

"Okay," Janis said, doing her best to humor me. "What exactly do you want to do about it?"

To her credit, when I told her, she didn't gasp, shriek, or faint. What she did was ask me if I was serious, and when I said I was, she said, "Okay."

I decided I wanted us to do something as adventurous as Norton coming to the Mars Super Bowl. So we did.

Which is how I came to quit my very good job, leave my very nice apartment, pack up my entire very nice life, and, with my very understanding girlfriend and my role model of a cat, move to the south of France.

a cat lost

It was not as easy as all that, of course. There were minor odds and ends and major life changes to take care of before the three of us could charge ahead to new glory in the old world.

The first thing we had to consider were our jobs. Janis, who had worked since she was fourteen years old and was something of a workaholic (and a very successful workaholic), arranged for a year's sabbatical from her job in publishing. With that load off her shoulders, she began worrying about a new load: What the hell would she actually *do* for a whole year?

I, as usual, was worried about having *too* much to do. I took care of part of that by resigning as publisher of the company I ran. The chairman of the board I resigned to was quite understanding.

"I no longer get to do what I like," I told him. "All I

do now is talk to lawyers and try to solve other people's problems."

"How do you think *I* feel?" was his response.

I saw his point but I held fast, and he proved he was a good chairman by solving my problem and giving me the perfect job, letting me throw off all the bad parts of what I was doing—the bureaucratic tanglings and business hassles—and go back to what I liked to do, which was working with authors and trying to be creative. And, once he got over the shock, he even agreed to let me do it from France.

The next thing to do was break it to my California agent that my TV and movie career—such as it was—was going to be put on hold for a year. He took the news surprisingly well, which made me think that my TV and movie career probably was *already* on hold. This did not particularly sadden me.

One of the reasons I was able to pack it all in for a while was that my partner, David Handler, and I had been hired to write and produce a TV series that year. It had started out with great promise: a decent premise for the show, a pleasant enough staff of writers, and a terrific cast, TV stars who were actually good actors. The first day the writing staff got together, David and I had visions of a Cosby-like syndication check one day making its way into our dwindling bank accounts.

As is usually the case when one gets one's hopes up in show business, it was not to be.

One of the most amazing things about the television business is the way people delude themselves (which is probably why those delusionless creatures, cats, have never made their mark in TV). People who create shows like "My Mother the Car" and "Pink Lady and Jeff" can't live with

themselves if they actually face up to what they're promul-
gating on society, so they convince themselves that they're
really doing Neil Simon. People who do the *good* stuff on
TV—shows like "Cheers" and "Taxi" and "Hill Street
Blues"—start to think they're Arthur Miller. There's a famous story about a well-known TV producer who had just
produced one of the great disasters of a particular season.
Not only was the show ridiculed for its shockingly low
quality, it was canceled after one episode (which is the only
thing people in TV are *really* sensitive to being ridiculed
about). After the cancellation notice came, the producer
started ranting and raving to his partner. "The problem
was, we were ahead of our time," he insisted. "The show
was too good! The American public wasn't ready for it!"
His partner let him carry on for as long as he could stand
it, then finally interrupted with these immortal words of a
rare television realist: "You know, you're right," he said.
"We *were* ahead of our time. The American public just
wasn't ready for total shit."

Needless to say, the partnership broke up.

Unfortunately for us, however, we had one of those I'm-
a-Genius mentalities running the show David and I had
signed on for. He opened one of our first story conferences
by telling us he thought that a good sitcom script was as
good as the best poetry. Great. He didn't just think he was
Neil Simon or Arthur Miller. We had a producer/director
who thought he was W. B. Yeats. Maybe we could do a
show called "I Love Leda and the Swan" or a "Gilligan's
Island Sails to Byzantium" reunion special.

We knew we were in trouble when, during the course of
writing the first thirteen episodes and shaping the show,
people all around us started to get fired. The co-executive
producer was the first to go. Then a couple of writers fell

by the wayside (including one who, after we'd had a discussion about a zany episode that would center around a botched surprise party, said, "This show has the potential to be so Chekhovian"). New writers were hired and then they, too, were fired (one was hired to be a consultant, came in for one meeting, argued with the boss, and was immediately fired. Actually, not so immediately that he wasn't given a large check to keep him happy. This made the other writers, who were working hard but weren't getting large checks, somewhat cranky). Then, as if things weren't bad enough, we got a close-up gander at the female star, who was, according to the premise of the show, supposed to be gorgeous, sexy, and irresistible. Unfortunately, the only person she could have possibly been irresistible to would have been Dumbo because our star had gained a good thirty pounds since her glory days.

Things went downhill from there. But we knew we were in *serious* trouble after we saw what happened to our first script. David and I tend to take the realistic approach. We were aware we weren't on the Preston Sturges level with our contributions to the show, but we were confident that our forty-four-page work was extremely funny. And while it may not have been Yeats (or even Ogden Nash), it was, we knew, coherent. However, when we were given a cassette to watch after the filming and editing, we were a tad surprised to find that not only were all our jokes cut out, the show made no sense. None. I'm talking total gibberish. Our nemesis had managed to rewrite it and then cut it so any stranger watching it would have absolutely no idea what it was about. Plus, what was supposed to be a lighthearted contemporary comedy now had all the wit and style of one of Eva Braun's home movies. To top it all off, *our* names were plastered all over the credits.

Here's how bad it was: Norton, who liked hanging around the set, had, midway through our viewing of the show's first act, gone and hid in the office's heating duct. He decided that crawling around in old, rusty pipes was a lot more fun than watching his dad's career die a slow and painful death.

As soon as the tape finished rolling, the door to our office was thrown open and it was the producer/director, the man responsible for this entire nightmare.

"I think it's the most brilliant thing I've ever done," he announced.

We said nothing.

"I think it may be the greatest show in the history of television," he now proclaimed. I'm not kidding. He really said that.

We still said nothing. If ever the phrase "Silence is golden" had meaning, this was the time, but we knew that at some point we'd have to work up our courage and speak. The psycho in our office decided there was no time like the present.

"Didn't *you* think it was *great?*" he demanded.

"Well," we both hemmed and hawed, "we thought it was very good. But we think there might be room for improvement. Maybe we can give you a few notes."

"I don't *take* notes on something that's *perfect!*" he told us. He didn't actually say the words "you barbarian ignoramuses" out loud, but his tone made it quite clear that the phrase should have been tacked on to the end of his sentence. Then he slammed the door on his way out, leaving us to realize that we were working for a lunatic and we could forget about making enough money from this series to buy a small, private island in the Caribbean.

David and I lasted for three more painful months before

our greed finally gave way to our self-respect and we quit. The only satisfying thing was that the show folded immediately after we did.

I had learned a couple of valuable lessons, though, which I promise never to forget. One is that I will never again work with people who don't believe that something they do can ever be improved upon in some way, shape, or form. That attitude is the antithesis of all creativity. The second thing I learned is that I will never again doubt my cat's taste. The next time he walks out of a show, so do I.

Free at last, I was in relatively good shape for a change of life. Janis was all set, too. Only Norton now had to be dealt with.

Two things were stopping us from leaving immediately. The first was probably the worst and scariest day of my life: the day Norton ran away and got lost in New York City.

The trauma started simply enough. Janis and I made plans to take a short trip—a trip *without* Norton. This is not something I'm usually wont to do, but my back was to the wall. Janis comes from the South, her family's still down there, she still has enough Southern lilt in her voice to sound as if she could have Stanley Kowalski as a brother-in-law, and, to top it all off, her father had a big birthday coming up—so she decided that we had to venture south of New Jersey for a week before we blew off the United States for good. We decided to fly to Memphis, then spend a week driving further down, through Mississippi to New Orleans. This was not a trip Norton could make. He could happily live with the several hours we'd spend every day in the car; I knew he wouldn't mind moving to a new hotel every night; and I was fairly sure he'd like to discover real Southern barbecue. But it simply wasn't practical. When traveling in Europe, he was used to being greeted with open arms by both restaurants and hotels. On the road in America, however, he couldn't eat out with us and we couldn't be sure that any of the hotels we'd find would take him. I had a crucial decision to make. On the one hand I could leave Norton for seven days with his usual cat-sitter, Lynn Waggoner, his favorite nonimmediate family member in the world. On the other hand, I could try being in the car with Janis on a rainy night in the backwoods of Mississippi trying to explain to her that the hotel we'd been lucky enough to find wouldn't let us in because they didn't take cats. I decided I'd rather face Norton's disappointment than Janis's wrath.

Naturally, I made the wrong choice.

We did nothing different to prepare for this excursion, so don't ask me how my cat could possibly know that he wasn't coming along on the trip—but he definitely, unequivocally, one hundred percent, absolutely knew. A couple of days before we were to leave, I noticed that he seemed to be sulking. Whenever I say things like, "I think Norton's upset because he's not coming on our trip" to Janis, she tries to get me to see a good psychiatrist, so I usually keep such thoughts to myself. This time was no different—I kept quiet. But he was definitely out of sorts.

Janis was going to Memphis on a Friday. That was also my final day in the office, the day of the big farewell party, so I was going to stick around and meet up with her on Saturday. I was also having dinner that night with one of the Random House bigwigs, the nephew of the company's owner. All in all, it seemed worth sticking around for.

We—Janis, Norton, and I—spent Thursday night at Janis's apartment. I woke up bright and early Friday morn, fed Norton his breakfast, then went in to take a shower. When I came out, I got dressed, kissed my still-sleeping girlfriend on the top of the head, and went to gather up my cat to take him to the office. When the company told me they were going to throw me a farewell party, they made it fairly clear that they wanted the chance to say farewell to Norton as well.

I called him, waiting for him to come as usual, but there was no response. I waited patiently—still nothing. I began poking around in some of his usual resting places—but no Scottish Fold anywhere. I then spent twenty minutes looking through Janis's apartment and could find no trace of Norton. Annoyed—what a time for him to decide to act like a regular cat—I went in, woke Janis up, and told her I was going to leave Norton behind.

"He's hiding," I said. "I'm sure he'll come out as soon as I leave. Have a good flight and I'll just come back and pick him up after work. See you tomorrow."

And off I went.

At noon Janis called my office.

"I'm leaving for the airport," she told me. "Norton still hasn't come out. I don't know if he's still in the apartment."

"Of *course* he's still in the apartment," I told her, a little annoyed. "Where could he have gone?"

"I don't know," she admitted. "I can't figure out any way he could have gotten out, but I really looked for him. And I don't think he's here."

"He's just being a cat," I said confidently. "Cats hide all the time. We're just not used to *Norton* doing it. He'll be waiting for me when I come to get him."

She acknowledged that I knew my cat better than she did and went off to Memphis. I stuck around, ate some cake and drank some wine at the farewell party, then around four in the afternoon I went back to Janis's to pick up what I was sure would be a repentant Norton.

When I walked in the front door I called his name. Silence. I tried again, gently cooing for him. Zilch. For the first time since cat and I had joined our lives together, I got a nervous flutter in my stomach.

I began to *really* search the apartment.

I looked in the closets. I took things out of the closets. I stood on chairs and peered into corners of the highest bookshelves. I crawled under beds. Gently calling Norton's name every few seconds.

No cat.

Now, I am a reasonably mature person. I have had my share of traumatic experiences and emergencies and have handled them all with, I like to think, a certain amount of grace and strength. I'm not prone to overreaction, panic, or hysteria. But, at the moment I decided that my nine-pound, extremely trusting, wonderfully sweet, and extremely protected cat was outside, loose on the mean streets of New York City, I overreacted, panicked, and became completely hysterical. To make matters worse, the weather immediately turned hurricanelike: Gusts of wind, explosions of thunder, flashes of lightning, and sheets of rain took over the city. As I pictured little Norton outside in all that, I lost whatever inner fortitude I'd ever pretended to have and simply began blubbering pathetically.

The first thing I did was call my friends Kathleen and Dominick. Kathleen is one of my very closest pals and would do anything for me. Dominick speaks with a British accent, so I knew he wouldn't go emotional on me and would keep his head. Through pathetic gasps and strangled sobs, I managed to spell out the problem. Half an hour later, they were down at Janis's apartment, helping me rip the place apart.

"Norton is *definitely* here," Dominick said. "There is no question about it."

His confidence buoyed my spirits a little, but the buoy sank fairly quickly as we kept searching the place to no avail.

We moved couches. We took every single item out of Janis's closets. We lifted radiator covers and floorboards, shifted large, unbelievably heavy kitchen appliances, and called Norton's name as calmly as we could—but there was no sign of him whatsoever. That was when I spied the open window.

You must understand something: We kept the windows closed, except for a crack, whenever Norton was staying in that apartment. But as my eyes were scanning every inch of the place, desperate for any sign of feline life, I spotted a living room window that was open at most three inches—and open from the top, perhaps twelve feet off the ground. It would have been a herculean feat, involving a jump to a chair, another jump to the top of a bookshelf, then an incredibly difficult leap up to and through a three-inch-wide crack—but I was convinced that it was through that crack Norton had disappeared. No matter that the trip down would have been even more difficult—either a tough jump up to the roof and then on to who knows where or a very difficult shinny down the front of the building to the street. I was positive I'd discovered the escape route. So we went in search of the escapee.

We immediately began a tour of the Soho neighborhood, in weather that now seemed to be a full-fledged tornado.

The three of us went to every store within two blocks of the apartment and asked if they'd seen a small, gray, wet cat with folded ears. No one had seen anything except three drenched, crazy-looking people in search of a lost feline.

We then scoured every nook and cranny and back alley-way within the same two-block range, screaming out Norton's name whenever we saw a potential hiding place for a wayward cat. But no wayward cat appeared (and the only positive that came out of this exercise is that I learned Linda Winer's Cat Law #3. Linda Winer is a columnist for *Newsday* and friend of mine who, at various points in her life, has owned several dozen cats, including one named Ishkabibble. Linda's Cat Law #3 is a simple one, written in stone after Ishkabibble disappeared one day and Linda had to search high and low for him all over her neighborhood: Never Name Your Cat Something You Are Ashamed to Yell Out Loud at the Top of Your Lungs).

We split up at this point, having failed to find Norton close to home. Dominick and Kathleen broadened our horizon, moving several blocks farther away, still checking for any buildings and alleys that might look inviting, warm, and dry to a frightened cat. My assignment was to get Janis's landlady to take me into their backyard. They had a decent-sized garden and patio, with a garage/workshop. It was reasonably familiar territory, I realized. Norton might have fled there figuring I'd be able to find him eventually. I was just hoping-beyond-hope that he'd figured right.

Janis's landlady wasn't home yet, but the landlady's mother, who also lives in the building, was. She was kind enough to use her key to let me back. Unfortunately, she also decided to accompany me.

She's a terrific woman, Mrs. Flaymen, but she's also eighty years old and has a slight hearing problem—as in, she can't hear anything anyone says. It's difficult to stress exactly how upset I was; just accept the fact that I was bordering on irrational behavior. So I was not at my best for the conversation that transpired in the pouring rain, in the nooks and crannies of Mrs. Flaymen's backyard.

"Ohhhh, the poor cat," she began.

I didn't want to hear about the poor cat. I wanted to hear

that he was dry and safe. So I acknowledged her despair only with a grim nod.

"How old is he?" she wanted to know.

"Eight years old," I told her.

"Four weeks old!" she screeched. "Oh my God!"

"Eight *years,* " I said again. "He's *eight!"*

"How could you let a four-week-old kitten outside?! And in weather like this!"

Normally, I would find this kind of inane miscommunication fairly funny. Perhaps even hilarious. However, in the midst of my desperate search, I had, possibly for the first time in my life, completely lost my sense of humor. So I did my best to ignore her and started looking through the garden.

"What's his name?" she asked me as I prowled.

"Norton," I muttered.

"Morris?!" she said.

"Norton!" I told her. *"Not Morris! Norton!"*

"Morris!" she began to call. "Come here, Morris!"

"Norton," I growled. "His name's Norton!"

"Morris!" she kept shouting. And then she started muttering about how stupid I was to let a one-week-old kitten outside in a hurricane.

"His name's not Morris!" I finally screamed. "His name's Norton! And he's not one week old! He's not even four weeks old! He's eight!"

"One week, four weeks, eight weeks," she said. "What's the difference?"

"Eight *years!"* I yelled as loud as I could yell. "Eight years!!!!"

"I don't think it makes a difference," she said with a shrug. "I'm sure he's dead."

I'll skip the rest of the conversation, as well as any detailed description of the veins bulging in my neck, and just say that my scrupulous search of the back of the apartment house was as fruitful as the searching I'd done up till then. There was nary a sign of my beloved cat.

I met Kathleen and Dominick back at the apartment at the appointed time. They were as wet as I was and had also had the same rotten luck. I called the number where Janis was staying in Memphis and left the following message on her friend's phone machine, in a monotone that could, putting the most positive possible spin on it, only be described as zombielike: "Hi. It's me. Still no sign. He's gone. I don't know what to do. I'm not coming tomorrow. I have to wait here until he shows up." I don't think I was even able to say good-bye. I just choked my message off in mid-sob and hung up. That was the fourth or fifth such message I'd left for her.

By this time, the entire block was involved in the search. Janis's landlady, Sylvia, had come home, heard the frantic activity, and learned what had happened. She started calling all her neighbors and pretty soon everybody was calling everybody else, seeing if anyone had seen a lost cat with strange ears. One kindly person called Janis's apartment and told me that she had definitely seen Norton. But, as I probed a bit, it turned out that she'd spotted a stray cat in her yard the day before. Sorrowfully, I explained that Norton had only gotten out that very morning, and that it was some other miserable person who'd be searching for yesterday's stray.

It was now seven-thirty at night, so in addition to the storm, it was getting quite dark. It was also time for my dinner with Mr. Random House. There was nothing I could do for Norton—not at this point—so I did my best to look presentable and went off to the restaurant. I decided I'd

return to Janis's after dinner and spend the whole rest of the
night waiting and/or searching.

The dinner was a disaster from start to finish. I'd be asked
a question along the lines of, "Well, what kind of direction
do you foresee for the company over the next few years?"
and I'd come back with a morose reply along the lines of,
"Huh?" Then I'd stare vacantly at the wall for five minutes,
the silence being broken only by my long and loud sighs.
We made it through the salad and main course and on to
the dessert in a leisurely twenty minutes or so. I had no
appetite and my total depression put an obvious pall on the
executive's appetite. I think it also put the same pall on his
opinion of me, but what could I do? As far as I was concerned, life as I knew it was over.

As we were waiting for the check to arrive, the waitress
came over to our table and said to me, "Excuse me, but are
you Mr. Gethers?" When I told her I was, she let me know
that there was a phone call for me.

The call was from Janis and it was the most wonderful call
I'd ever received in my life.

"You're not going to believe it," she began, "but go to
my apartment immediately. Norton's waiting for you in the
living room."

I let out a very loud yelp, tried to calm myself down since
I was in public, then said the hell with it and let out another
yelp, louder than the first. I pleaded with Janis to tell me
how this miracle had occurred.

"I told you you're not going to believe it," she said, and
then proceeded to relate the entire story: After landing at
the airport and going straight out to dinner, she'd finally
gotten to her friends' house in Memphis, where she found
my many suicidal-sounding phone-machine messages wait-

ing for her. Not knowing what else to do, she called her
landlady and asked her to send her husband up onto the
roof in one last desperate attempt to find the cat. According
to the landlady, her husband's not unwarranted response
was, "What are you, out of your mind?!" and her response
to that was a slow, quiet, and obviously quite effective:
"Get . . . out . . . on . . . the . . . fucking . . . roof. *Now.*"

She then went up the two flights to Janis's apartment,
figuring that if Norton was indeed up on the roof, he would
be so petrified and hard to handle that her husband would
need someone to hand him to, through the window. She
turned the key to the front door, stepped inside . . . and
sitting in the foyer, curled up in a calm, peaceful, untrauma-
tized, toasty-warm ball, was none other than Norton the cat.

Stunned, she ran to the phone and called Janis in Memphis, who immediately called me at the restaurant. I hung
up the restaurant phone, told my confused dinner partner—
who'd clearly crossed my name off his list marked "People
with a Future to Whom I Might Pay Lots of Money Some-
day"—that life was good again, then I raced back to Janis's
in a cab, taking the three flights up to the apartment two
stairs at a time. By the time I got there, Sylvia had put
Norton in one of the apartment's two bedrooms, closing
the door behind him so he couldn't possibly get out and
hide again. When I inched the door open—still not believing the little guy was really there—I found Norton sound
asleep on the bed in his usual position: head on the pillow,
body tucked under the blanket. When I stepped inside, he
opened one eye and began purring.

I gently walked over, picked him up, and began a rather
lengthy petting, scratching, cooing, and kissing process.
When both of us had had enough of that, I called Janis.

"He's actually here," I told her. For the first time in fourteen hours, my voice didn't have that despairing rasp to it.

"And he'd *never* been outside?" she asked, incredulous.

"Nope. He's as dry and happy as could be."

"Then where was he?" she wanted to know—the first of several million times we asked ourselves that question.

We never found out where he was. We did eventually figure out that this day-long hide-and-seek experience was Norton's little way of letting us know he didn't like being left behind for a week while his parents went off on a fun vacation (and, believe me, now Janis accepts it as gospel when I tell her that Norton's looking a little subdued—she instantly goes through her apartment, closing the door to every room). But, more immediately, as we spoke on the phone, as I did everything but collapse in relief and exhaustion, Janis got angry. In her own way, she'd been as unnerved by the experience as I'd been, and she had the same feeling, I imagine, one has when a child falls off a high swing yet doesn't hurt himself. At first you're so relieved he's okay, you'll do anything to make him happy. Then, when the scare's over, you want to kill him for putting himself—and you—through the trauma.

"Don't let him get away with this," Janis told me. "I don't think you should feed him tonight."

"You're right," I agreed, nodding vigorously. "I definitely won't feed him."

"And don't pet him and kiss him and tell him that everything's okay," she ordered.

"Absolutely not," I said. "I'd never do that. I'll be strict and firm."

"Yeah," she said dubiously.

"Yeah!" I said strictly and firmly, if a bit guiltily.

"I'll see you tomorrow," she said, unconvinced. "And I'm glad your stupid cat's okay."

"Thank you. I'll tell him."

"And don't feed him. I *mean* it. It's for his own good."

"As of now," I insisted, "he's on bread and water. Think of me as George Kennedy in *Lonely Are the Brave*."

When I start making movie references that she doesn't get, Janis usually figures it's time to hang up. I knew, at that very moment, before the phone even clicked down into the cradle in Memphis, she was turning to her friends and telling them there was no way I wasn't going to cave in. I could tell she thought I'd be feeding and petting my cat within seconds. But I was determined to toe the line. Tough love was my new motto for the evening.

Unfortunately for my new motto, it's almost impossible to resist a meowing Scottish Fold. Especially one of his special "I'm hungry" meows.

"No dinner for you," I told him as definitively as I was able. "*You* are being punished. And that is *all* there is to it." I figured he might be intimidated by my refusal to use contractions, but no such luck.

He meowed again. I thought of the anxiety and horror he'd put me through all day long. I remembered how I'd felt trying to imagine him wandering the streets of New York City, wet, lonely, frightened. I remembered my vision of seeing Norton's picture on the side of a milk carton, with the phrase "Have you seen this cat?" All of seven seconds had passed since I'd gotten off the phone with Janis.

"Well, maybe just a snack," I allowed, and instantly opened up a can of his favorite food, scooped it into his bowl, and set it down in front of him. Grateful, Norton munched until satisfied. Then he came over and tried to get back on my good side, once and for all. The first thing he did was look me straight in the eye and start purring.

"No way," I announced. "I was given explicit instructions not to be nice to you. I can't let you starve to death, but I don't have to be friendly."

He jumped up onto the bed, looking shaken and, if truth be told, extremely pathetic. This may have been the first experience of rejection in his life. I reached out and stroked his head in a moment of forgetfulness. Norton immediately took the reassuring gesture as a sign of capitulation and he went in for the kill, rubbing his nose firmly up against my cheek, something I'm usually a sucker for. But not this time.

"Uh-uh," I told him, drawing back. "I am *not* weakening."

He now began rubbing himself against my leg.

"It's for your own good," I tried to explain. It had sounded so convincing when Janis said it.

The purring grew louder, the look in his eye more tender. My resolve, I do have to admit, was weakening rather quickly. After several minutes, when he turned over on his back and wiggled his paws around in the air, my resolve was about as firm as my backbone—which was clearly the consistency of mush.

"All right," I sighed. "C'mere."

That was it. I was a goner. Discipline was thrown out the window and I was on all fours, petting and scratching and telling him that everything was fine, I really didn't mind that he'd put me through the worst day of my life, just as long as he was okay.

This went on for quite a long time—until he was sure I'd forgiven him completely and until I was sure he understood that this hiding business was not something to be repeated in the future.

Peace made at long last, I went into the kitchen and poured myself a well-deserved beer. Then I came back to my cat and spoke two more sentences.

"Don't tell Janis," was the first thing I instructed. After all, there was no real need for her to know the extent of my wimpiness. Luckily, from the look in Norton's eye, I knew my secret soft side was safe with him. I took another long swig of beer. "And where *were* you?" was the second thing I said, very quietly.

But this time Norton only turned his head to avoid my stare. After a few moments, he glanced back at me, quietly closed his eyes, and went straight to sleep.

There are certain secrets a cat just won't share, I suppose, not even with his best friend.

3

a cat on tour

We made the decision to rent a house in Provence.

There was no particular reason for this, although we did have a certain guiding logic. We wanted to be in the country, not in a city. We didn't want to go *too* exotic since I needed to be somewhere I could get a fax machine repaired at the drop of a hat. Janis wanted warm, or reasonably warm. We wanted good food and we wanted someplace beautiful. This narrowed it down to approximately half the globe, then we got serious and started picking, choosing, and eliminating.

First we ruled out any countries with whom we didn't share an alphabet. Then we crossed off anyplace that might be under attack from Scud missiles. Next we eliminated any country that ate cats. Pretty soon, and without too much difficulty, we boiled things down to Italy and France. We winnowed out a few regions in both of those countries— Sicily was a possibility but I decided I wasn't in the mood to get blown to smithereens in my car; Burgundy was a very real consideration until Janis got it in her head that the weather was exactly like England and thus she'd be cold and damp all the time. Picture the creature in the Schwarzenegger film *Predator* and you've pretty much got Janis's personality if she was cold and damp all the time. Soon we were down to Tuscany and Provence. We compared wines and cheeses, we looked at the dollar against the lira and the franc, we did everything you were supposed to do, and then we made our decision based on one key factor: We didn't speak a word of Italian and we did speak a tiny bit of French. So we settled on Provence.

A couple of years before, while I was working with Roman Polanski on a screenplay, Norton and I'd lived in Paris for three months. Almost every night, Roman and I would go out to dinner, usually with friends of his. Roman had friends who were Italian, Polish, French, Russian, you name it. So during our meals, someone would say something in French, someone would answer in Polish, someone would then respond to that in Italian or Danish or Upper Slobovian. Every fifteen minutes or so, Roman would interrupt protectively and say, "Come on, fellows, speak English for Peter" (translation: "Come on, you guys, we've got a cretinous American here, so say something he can understand"). Rarely had I felt so inept, so when I returned to New York I was determined to learn at least one other language.

I'd had two years of high-school French, but that was so long ago I could really only remember the bare essentials. I could conjugate the verbs *aller, avoir,* and *être;* I could ask for the location of the nearest apothecary; and if someone served me the proper vegetable, I could show my appreciation by saying, *"Bravo! Des asperges!"* Braced by such a substantial background, I began taking French lessons from a rather eccentric woman who lived on the Upper East Side and who had, in a one-room apartment, six birds (including a blind pigeon she'd found in the park), one dog, three cats, and several mice (I *think* the mice were pets, though I wouldn't swear to it). She also liked to keep the room temperature somewhere near a hundred and forty degrees at all times. But I slogged through my lessons and, when the time came to *choisir un pays* (don't applaud, really), I thought my French might come in handy.

Once we'd settled on Provence, the next step was finding a house. This was something I had absolutely no concept of how to do, but I made a decent stab at it. I called the French embassy. They sent me to a French realtor with an American outlet. They in turn sent me to some company that mailed me a videotape showing all sorts of *châteaux* for sale for a mere three million dollars. I even called a realtor in France who told me that what I was looking for didn't exist and that I should stop bothering her.

Eventually, we found a house through friends of friends of friends. It sounds farfetched, but that is the absolute best way to find something. Just start telling everybody you know that you want to rent a place in the south of France. Someone is bound to say, "Oh, Fred did that two years ago. Got a great farmhouse in the country—and boy, was it cheap." It may not be in Provence—but, hey, the Dordogne ain't Pittsburgh—and the odds are that Fred's farmhouse has tripled in price since then, but it's also probable that Fred learned about other places while over there or knows somebody who knows somebody who knows somebody else who has a house for rent.

When word got out that we were looking to shove off, I got a call from a writer friend of mine. His wife was friendly with someone who lived in Paris who had a *deux-ième maison* in Provence that they sometimes rented. I called the people in Paris, who told me that they were no longer renting their place out. But—and this is key; this is why it pays to talk to anyone, anytime—they loved where they lived and were very happy to find someone who also wanted to live there. So, trying to see if they could help me in some way, they asked me what I was looking for. I told them: I wanted a three- or four-bedroom house in the Lub-éron. I wanted old, I wanted charming, and I wanted a garden. I also wanted something that was in a small village rather than in the middle of the countryside (Janis didn't want to feel too isolated). And we wanted something that had a few conveniences—a dishwasher and a washer-dryer would be nice—but that wasn't so modernized and Ameri-canized that we'd feel we were renting a condo in Atlantic City. In other words, I wanted perfect. And not incredibly expensive.

Much to my surprise, they didn't tell me to rent myself a nice little room in an insane asylum, they told me they thought they could help. They had a friend who had exactly what we were looking for. They'd mention our search to her—and if she was interested, she'd get back to me.

The next day, I received an eight-page fax from a woman named Elisabeth, who turned out to not only have the perfect house but who was a classy, honorable, and gener-ally wonderful person. Her fax described the house in great detail—it was three hundred years old, stone, four bed-rooms plus an office, and it had a football-field-sized garden. It also had a dishwasher, a washer-dryer, and a BMW which we were welcome to use. She was French, her husband had been American (he'd died a couple of years earlier), so the house was half-French (the charming part) and half-American (the convenience part). Ooh-la-la! She stressed that it was very countrified, although very comfortably outfitted. "Don't expect a pancake flipper," she warned. "It's still France." Which was okay with me. I wanted a crepe pan, not a damn pancake flipper.

So we were all set. I had an office, Janis had a garden, Norton had three centuries' worth of mice to chase after. There was only one thing still left to do.

Unfortunately, to write about what it was I had to do, I have to break a solemn vow I took with someone very near and dear to me.

Years ago, I made a pact with my writing partner, David, who has as much integrity and taste as it's possible to have considering what we do to make a living. The promise we made to each other was that we would never—artistically speaking—eat our own entrails.

This is not nearly as repugnant as it sounds. Honest. It simply means that when we were younger we decided that if we ever became successful writers we wouldn't join the Philip Roth School of Writing About How Successful We Are. Uppermost in things to avoid: writing about how hard it is to be a writer; writing about how no one ever appreciates how hard it is to be a writer; writing about other writers or editors and critics, because they're all incredibly boring; writing about how all those boring writers, editors, and critics don't like you either; and absolutely first on the list, never, ever, *ever* write about your own publicity tour. It's unseemly, it's uninteresting, and it's just plain obnoxious (as in, "Oh, yeah, sure you've got it rough over in Bosnia, but you should have been in *my* shoes when this little short guy with a bad rug got my *name* wrong on 'Good Morning, Schenectady.' Now, *that* was a nightmare!").

Anyway, Dave, I'm not really writing about *my* publicity

tour. I was all set to go over to the three-hundred-year-old house in France and keep my last few shreds of artistic dignity. I swear. Nobody wanted to talk to or see *me*, anyway. But before I could hop on a plane and hightail it out of here, I had my last little detail to take care of. It turned out that a lot of people wanted to meet my cat.

The tour officially began in Los Angeles but, in the publishing equivalent of spring training, we got a practice appearance in, on a show on a small cable station in Connecticut. Everyone thought this was a good idea since no one really knew how the cat would behave in front of the cameras and, probably more pressing, everyone wanted to see if I'd turn into the Chef of the Future once the little red light went on.

Basically, it went well. Norton was, of course, his usual perfect self. We arrived early, as instructed, and were led to the greenroom, which, in case you're interested, was brown. (Later, in several weeks of touring, I was in many, many greenrooms. Not *one* of them was ever green. I'm thinking of calling "Sixty Minutes" to see what they can do with this.) I paced the room for half an hour, looking in the mirror constantly, running my hand through my hair, straightening my tie, doing everything but going "mi mi mi" and gargling. Norton was already acting as if he'd been on as many talk shows as Teri Garr. He sat on the couch, let a few stagehands come over and pet him, and was even nice to the guest who was to follow me, a woman who'd written a book about the proper way to pack a suitcase. Ah yes, there's nothing like doing publicity to make one feel like an important cultural influence.

Once we went on the air, the host and hostess of the show couldn't get over the way Norton just sat on my lap for the whole interview. He even would sit up and look straight into the camera, thus making sure all thirty-five people watching the show would stop listening to me and pay sole attention to how cute he was. (I think he did this whenever he sensed I was going on too long and was becoming boring.)

For my part, I was fine, except that, being as vain as possible, I'd worn a dark blue suit and blue shirt, figuring that would be my best look for my TV debut. It was, I suppose, at least at the beginning. But as the show went on, Norton began doing what all cats do, especially when they're under hot lights—he began to shed. And he began to shed all over my dark blue suit. By the end of the interview, I had so much gray fur on me that I looked like nothing so much as a large, talking prehistoric bird.

But we'd not only survived the first test, it was clear that Norton was such stuff as stars were made of.

As I said, this was an early interview, a trial run. The book was still a few weeks away from being published. So all we had to do now was wait for the book to exist and then, having passed our test, wait to throw ourselves on the mercy of America.

For a writer as well as a cat, waiting is the hardest part. But, from a literary point of view, the end of the wait is usually worth it.

There is something very special about seeing one's book for the first time as a finished product. No matter the quality—whether you're Daniel Defoe or Danielle Steele—writing a book is damned difficult. Everyone *thinks* he or she can write, but it's fairly daunting to take a look at a blank page and then decide that you have the audacity to fill not only it up but many more like it. So when you finally have finished the first draft, then the second, then the third;

when you've corrected the copy-edited manuscript, then the galleys, then the bound galleys; when you finally get to hold the finished, published product in your very own hands—several hundred pages long, a real jacket, flap copy that hypes till even *your* face turns red, something solid and permanent—it provides a moment pure and satisfying. Bad reviews haven't come in yet, nor have the agent's calls telling you that three days after the pub date the book's already on the remainder tables. All that exists is this physical *thing* that somehow is a mental extension of yourself.

That lasts for all of a minute or two. Then, of course, reality comes a knockin'.

The Cat Who Went to Paris gave me a particularly satisfying couple of minutes because it was so personal and because it had extraordinarily handsome photos of my beloved companion all over the front and back jacket. The day before Norton and I were to leave on our publicity tour was the first time I saw it in a bookstore, B. Dalton's on Eighth Street down in the Village, where Norton and I were making our first public bookstore appearance that evening. I was supposed to sign books and be witty. Norton was supposed to look cute and let people admire him. I can't tell you how often, as the tour progressed, I wanted to switch roles, but everyone from the publicist to the editor to my very own girlfriend told me I'd be making a *big* mistake.

Several hours before the signing, I took Norton and we snuck into the store, incognito. (It wasn't very difficult. No one recognized me since no one had ever heard of me. And Norton's very good—when he wants to be—at slipping down into his shoulder bag and becoming almost invisible. It's why I've always thought he'd make a superb private eye.) As I casually checked the store out, trying not to look too much like an annoying author checking out the store,

I was surprised to see that the book was very well displayed—there was even a giant poster of Norton in the window. Ecstatic, I bought a copy for good luck—figuring it was probably the first hardcover sale in New York— rearranged the remaining books on the shelf so they lay face out (yes, we really do that; any writer who denies it is lying through his teeth. I didn't want the copy I bought to also be the *last* hardcover sale in New York), then practically danced back out to the street. Outside, I showed the book jacket to Norton, who seemed singularly unimpressed, perhaps wondering why I got my name on the front of the jacket but he didn't.

Later that night, we went back to the same store, boldly striding in this time, Norton fearlessly taking in the sights, both of us hoping the clerk wouldn't recognize me as the nervous, sweaty guy who'd earlier bought a copy of his own book. There were perhaps fifty people at this first signing and three speakers. The first speaker was a woman who'd written one of the all-time great cat books, *The Natural Cat.* The second speaker was a man who'd put together a superb cat encyclopedia called *The Cornell Book of Cats.* (His only flaw was that he spent *way* too much time lecturing about the tragedy of cat prostate problems. It was all I could do to keep myself—and Norton!—from passing out during that particular section of his speech. At one point, I'm afraid I did have to cover my ears and quietly hum all the words to "A Hundred Bottles of Beer on the Wall," but I'm sure no one noticed.) When it was my turn, I talked about how I came to write the book (an editor thought it was a good idea to have a book about a *bon vivant* who traveled around the world with his cat; I was so thrilled that somebody thought I was a *bon vivant,* I immediately agreed to do it), and then told several of the most amusing and amazing

Norton stories in it. Nothing was as amusing or amazing, however, as my cat's behavior during the speeches. When the first two speakers were on, Norton lounged politely, barely paying attention. When I stood up to begin, my little gray partner sat straight up on top of his table, staring right at me in rapt attention, occasionally glancing out at the audience as if to encourage them to laugh. The only problem came at the end of my talk when the cat fans in the store decided to applaud. At the first sound of enthusiastic clapping, Norton spun around so his back was to the crowd and he snuggled down out of view inside his bag. I immediately figured he didn't like my speech and was trying to discourage the positive reaction. It took me a little while to realize that, while he was otherwise totally unintimidated, the loud applause frightened him. For the rest of our tour, I would always begin my talk—even on a TV show if there was a live audience—by explaining that I had the greatest, most courageous cat in the world but that applause scared him, so could they please refrain from clapping when we were done, even on the slim chance that they felt like doing so. That made Norton much happier all along the way. And, of course, made me a bit neurotic. There's nothing like giving what you think is a slam-dunk winner of a talk, then walking off the stage to total silence. But, you know me—anything for El Foldo.

After the seminar/signing at B. Dalton, Norton and I headed back to my apartment. Still basking in the glow of our literary triumph and certain we had a big hit on our hands, I went to my phone machine to check my messages before I began packing for our next day's journey. I had only one message; it was from a middle-aged-sounding man and here it is in its extremely polite entirety:

Uh, hello, uh, I'm looking for Peter Gethers, if this is the same Peter Gethers who wrote a book called The Cat Who Went to Paris. *I'm calling all the way from California and I bought this book for fifteen dollars. I'd just like to say that my wife and I both read it and we'd like our money back. This is the worst piece of shit we've ever read. I mean it. What garbage. Total, absolute shit. You should be ashamed. Thank you.*

In a mild state of shock, my first reaction was to wonder which one—the man or his wife—had read it first. And whoever did, did they then turn to their partner and say, "Honey, I just read the biggest piece of shit I've ever read. You've *got* to read it, too"? And then, did the other person read it, curled up in front of a fire, turn to the first reader and say, "Sugar pie, you're sure right with this one. Hooo-eeee, this stinks to high heaven! Let's call the author long distance and tell him"?

Once I decided this probably wasn't a healthy road to pursue, I called my partner, David, to play him the message. He didn't seem too surprised. Not because he agreed with their assessment but because he's written several mystery novels, one of which won an Edgar Award, and thus he's come across his fair share of wackos. (It's a publishing rule of thumb: Science fiction fans are absolutely the weirdest. No question. Many of them think they're from another planet—and, in fact, a good many of them probably are. If you ever want to convince yourself that the nihilists are right and that life has no meaning, go to a science fiction convention. After the sci-fiers, though, come the mystery fanatics. They all dress in black and have memorized every-thing Arthur Conan Doyle ever wrote. They also meet at conventions two or three times a year, where they attend panel discussions on things like "What's the Best Murder Weapon?" and "Who's Zanier: Cornell Woolrich or James Cair?") David topped my anti-groupie without hesitation. He told me about one particular fan of his who called him on a regular basis, usually early in the morning before he had the wits about him to screen his calls. David described the fan as sounding a little bit too much like Hal the computer in *2001*.

"Daaave," the guy would say. "I just read your first novel again. Sixth time. And I'm gonna read it *again. Tomorrow.*" Then he'd usually say something like, "I'm in Chicago today, Dave"—a mere thousand miles from David's house. "How about I drive up and we meet for lunch?"

I felt a lot better after talking to David—demanding fifteen dollars back seemed a lot saner than a twenty-two-hour drive for lunch—and started packing for the tour. I knew enough to pack mostly gray clothes, thanks to my Connecticut experience. I also had the presence of mind to give Norton many extra Pounce that night and to pet him for a particularly long time before working up the nerve to ask him, "Do you have any idea what we're really in for?"

I don't know if he did or not, but he was certainly a good sport about it, and purred contentedly on my pillow until I fell asleep.

~~~

The first stop was Los Angeles and the Four Seasons Hotel, home to several impressive Nortonian moments in times past.

The Four Seasons is where I always stay in L.A. It's convenient, classy, and perfect for conducting business. The staff is also extraordinarily nice to Norton. In fact, every Four

Seasons is particularly gracious toward pets. In the Boston
Four Seasons, they even have a pet room-service menu. I
know this because when we stayed there, I was happy to
find a large bowl filled with nuts when I walked into the
room. Only I soon realized they weren't nuts but dog biscuits—and fairly tasty dog biscuits, I might add. Under the
bowl was a small, printed sheet which was titled "Doggie
Delights." The rest of the menu read as follows:

BARK, BARK!

(Main Courses)

#1   Ruff, Ruff, rrr . . .
(Quickly Broiled Beef Filet with natural broth $6.00)

#2   Aowh, Aohw, Aohwooooooo!
(Boneless "Safe to Eat" Lamb Chops $7.00)

#3   Woof! Woof! Grrr!
(Roasted Chicken Breast with natural gravy $5.50)

BARK!!!

(Side dishes)

#1   Awwrr, Yip, Yip!
(Brown Rice $1.75)

#2   Grrrrrr . . .
(White Rice $1.75)

ARP! ARP!

(Assorted Ice Creams $2.00)

Needless to say, I called down to check this out. At first I
thought it was a joke, but when the room-service person

indignantly assured me it wasn't, I wanted to know why the menu was geared only for canine guests. The voice at the other end of the phone hemmed and hawed over that one but finally said he was sure that cats would also find the food quite delicious; the hotel was happy to admit that dogs were not the only four-legged connoisseurs.

It turned out the room-service maven was correct. Twenty minutes after I hung up, a waiter arrived. On the cart he wheeled in was an array of fine china. And on the china was a delicious—judging from Norton's considered reaction—chicken breast.

But even with the usual fine Four Seasons treatment, I still wasn't prepared for the greeting we got upon our arrival in L.A.

First of all, as the cab from the airport dropped me off in front of the hotel, I heard two men in black suits say, in muffled tones, "He's here." Surprised, I put the cat in his shoulder bag and we headed into the lobby. As we stepped inside, two more men in black suits said, "He's here. Get ready."

I knew Norton was popular, I thought to myself, but I felt a surprise party was just a tad excessive.

The entire lobby seemed abuzz as we walked toward the desk. There was a flurry of activity, people rushed toward me—reporters, hotel staff, more guys in black suits. I smiled broadly and Norton stuck his head out of the bag, craning his neck in his best E.T. impersonation—who are we to reject V.I.P. treatment?—and then we watched as everyone rushed toward us . . . and right past us. As even more guys in black suits stampeded by, saying things under their breath like, "Moving toward the elevator. Cover the doors," Norton and I casually glanced behind us—where the President of the United States was standing. Yup. George Bush was there for some kind of money-raising, glad-handing function. I suppose, if I'd really thought it through, I would have realized that Norton didn't need *all* of those Secret Service guys. Nonetheless, I confess to being just a tad disappointed.

Not for long, however.

With Bush out of the way, I found that cat and I were the only guests remaining in the lobby. So when I heard a woman's voice say, "Wait a second, I think he's here," I again turned behind me to see which top-notch celebrity had breezed in. Mel Gibson? Liz Taylor? The cast from "Beverly Hills 90210"? I was determined not to be sucker-punched again.

So I was even more confused when I realized there was nobody behind us, not even Herve Villachaize. Norton and I were *it* as far as lobby loiterers.

Another woman, this time from behind the check-in desk, said, quite clearly, "It *is* him. He's here!"

This led to a couple of exclamatory bursts from other women, all exceedingly attractive—one at the cashier's desk, one from behind the concierge's counter—along the lines of, "We've been waiting for you! We're *so* glad you're here!"

I decided that this was definitely more like it. Until, naturally, I was forced to accept the fact that once again I was not their obscure object of desire. The real target was not nearly so obscure.

"*Norton,*" the woman at the front desk cooed with her arms held out in welcome, "we are *so* glad to see you!"

Now, I've stayed at the Four Seasons ten or fifteen times. When I'm there by myself, they're certainly friendly—but no one ever holds her arms out to me and scratches me under the chin while shrieking how cute I look. Norton had stayed there four or five times—and no one had really even done that to *him* before. At least, not quite in this fashion. Because that night, as we checked in, just about every person who worked on the ground floor came out to fuss over their smallest, grayest guest. It turned out that the publicist for the book had sent a few copies over to the hotel several days before. They'd been passed around and read and Norton was now clearly on the Four Seasons' "A" list of desirable celebrities.

"We've upgraded you to a Four Seasons suite," the desk clerk said, smiling at the cat.

"We think you'll like it," another said, petting him.

"And we've got a few surprises for you up there," another one told him, scratching his stomach (by this time, he was lying on his back on top of the check-in counter; I was a little startled at how easily he'd succumbed to life in the L.A. fast lane).

I was starting to wonder if they were going to take Norton's credit card, since it was pretty obvious I was an afterthought, but no such luck. For that part they deigned to talk to me.

When we were finally shown to our room, we had indeed been upgraded to a suite. Norton also had a litter box already set up in the bathroom. On the floor by the TV were two elegant dishes, one for water—with a bottle of Evian next to it!—and one to fill with the cans of food that were stacked on top of the end table. And on the desk in the living room was a gift-wrapped box with a note taped to it.

Flattered and pleased, I tore open the package—only to find that it was a can of shrimp-flavored Pounce. Deflated—I don't know what I'd expected; I think I had my heart set on a lovely crystal goblet—I also opened the note, which was from the manager of the hotel. It read (handwritten):

> *Dear Norton,*
> *Welcome back to the Four Seasons! My cats, Nicholas and Alexandra, would love to meet you someday . . . you sound like a really neat guy.*
> *Enjoy your stay.*
>
> > *Kathleen Horrigan*
> > *Hotel Manager*

I prowled around the room (both rooms!), hoping that perhaps Kathy Horrigan had also left a small basket of fruit lying around for me, but not a chance. It was clear from the very beginning that Norton was the star of this little sojourn. And from his contented meowing—over by his bottle of Evian water—I could tell he was not unhappy about it.

~~~

The highlight of our travels around the country came at the very beginning of the trip in L.A. when the publisher threw a party to celebrate publication of the book. It wasn't just a regular humdrum party with potato chips and clam dip. For Norton, they threw a bash at Spago, the most famous restaurant in the country, run by Wolfgang Puck, arguably the most celebrated chef in the world.

Not that I'm jaded or anything, but I'd been to Spago plenty of times. In fact, my mother works with Wolf (she helped him write his last cookbook) and she's part of the unofficial Spago family.

Norton had never dined there, however. In fact, no cat

had ever dined at Spago before—until Norton broke the barrier that night. Broke it in style, I might add.

They closed the restaurant for a few hours for our private party. The guest of honor—a hint: not me—was given his own table, upon which he sat in a princelike fashion and let all the guests come over and pay homage. Wolf, whose renowned specialties are pizzas covered with such delicacies as smoked salmon, wild mushrooms, or caviar, made Norton a pizza covered with Norton's favorite delicacy—Pounce. The pastry chef, an amazing woman named Mary (who, in honor of an annual trip I make to Las Vegas with a bunch of friends, once made a cake in the shape of Sammy Davis, Jr.), baked small cakes and cookies with cat paws and cat whiskers all over them. I was congratulated once or twice by the fifty or so guests, but mostly they fussed over Norton. Many of them had never been out in public with him and they couldn't believe how human he acted (they thought that was a compliment; we know better). During the several hours we were there, Norton perched himself on his table/throne, ate when he felt like it, drank a little milk when he was in the mood, allowed journalists to take his picture, let children talk to him as if he were a grown-up (and I mean a grown-up person, not a grown-up cat), and permitted all his admirers to pet him, stroke him, and compliment him. He even let the manager of the restaurant repeatedly refer to him as "Norman" without swatting at his ankle.

The highlight of the evening, however, was Wolf's wife, Barbara Lazaroff, the designer of and guiding force behind Spago and all of Wolf's other restaurants. Barbara, who's extremely attractive and even more flamboyant, strode into the party wearing a cat outfit. We're talking cat slippers—

with whiskers and everything—cat pants, a cat sweater, and a cat hat. Norton, for one brief, shining moment, thought he'd met the ultimate member of the opposite sex, but eventually, to his disappointment, I'm sure, he realized that Barbara was just another admiring, if stunning, human.

After the Spago party, the rest of our tour was fairly typical—considering that one of the authors on tour was a four-legged feline. Following L.A., for the hardcover and the paperback versions of the first book about our adventures together, Norton and I went to San Diego, San Francisco, Portland, Seattle, Miami, Dayton, Rochester, Detroit, Dallas, and Philadelphia. (After the West Coast tour, I told the publisher that a city a day was just too tough on my little pal. He was an extraordinary trouper and shockingly well behaved—just ask any of the couple of thousand people who came by to meet him—but, still, I felt it wasn't fair to cart him around all day, then put him on an airplane. So, for the other cities, we were put on what I heard referred to as the "old author's tour." That meant we got an extra day or two in each city to ease the travel burden. Me, Norton, and James Michener.)

The routine was pretty much the same in each city. An escort would pick us up at the airport. I carried the portable litter boxes—I had about twenty of them in my suitcase when I started, just in case—but each escort was instructed to show up with a bag of cat litter in tow. As soon as I picked up my bags and got into the car, out would come a collapsible litter box, then I'd rip open a new sack of litter, and the whole thing would go on the floor behind the passenger seat. Then we'd get taken to our hotel. As soon as we were checked into the room, it was time for another fold-up box and more litter. This way, not only was Norton assured of never having to go too long *sans toilette,* I was assured that none of the escorts would sue me for ruining the upholstery in their Buicks.

In each new hotel room, Norton would stake out his territory. He'd prowl around, sniffing along each of the four walls. If there was a desk or chest of drawers, he'd hop up on that and check out the comfort level. If there were thick curtains, he'd disappear behind them, checking, I imagine, for scratching texture as well as hideability level (thick curtains are very nice to hide in when a noisy room-service cart careens into the room).

I had many, many cans of Norton's favorite foods and a reasonable supply of Pounce. (Although once the book came out and people read that Pounce was his favorite treat, a can of the stuff became the gift offering of choice at all autographings. On the paperback tour, Norton received, in two weeks, sixty-four cans of Pounce.) Norton's food and water were usually set down in the bathroom. I don't actually know how a cat can tell which room is a bathroom, but I do know that if he was hungry and I hadn't set down any food yet, he'd go right into the correct room and start meowing his starving head off.

San Diego was Norton's first official TV show after the Connecticut dry run. We went on "Inside San Diego," which proved once and for all that Norton had the potential to be another Lassie if he so chose.

For the entire interview he sat on my lap, not thrilled with the lights and the background noise but certainly not uncomfortable or nervous. Subdued and alert would be my description. The hostess of the show—a cat lover—couldn't get over how adorable and intelligent he seemed throughout our chat. But even she wasn't prepared for Norton's finale. As the show was ending, the director decided to put the camera on Norton as the final credits rolled. They wanted to use Camera 3 (it was a three-camera show, as are most TV interview shows) instead of Camera 1, which was the one focused on Norton during the rest of the program. Just as the countdown began to signal that the credit roll was about to start and that we'd be back on the air, the director's voice boomed from above, over the microphone linking him from the control booth to the set: "Do you think you could try to get the cat to face Camera Three?" Without missing a beat—and with no prodding or prompting from me—the newest TV heartthrob sat up on my lap, turned a hundred and eighty degrees, and made sure he was directly facing Camera 3. Just a split second before the countdown ended and the sound and cameras went on, the director summed up what he saw quite magnificently, also over the mike. "Holy shit," he said. "That cat's a fucking genius."

As we did more TV and radio, Norton became even more at ease in front of the cameras and the mikes. On various radio shows, I'd try to be my usual witty self, while Norton would sit next to me, probably wondering why he was there, since no one could see him and no one was asking him to talk. The deejay would usually exclaim, several times for his listening audience, "I know you can't see this cat, ladies and gentlemen, but he really is unbelievable!"

In San Diego, we did Michael Reagan's radio show. Much to my surprise, he turned out to be Ronald Reagan's son. I wasn't looking forward to the interview, since Reagan ranked up with Iago and Roy Cohn in my top five list of villains, but the son wound up being perfectly pleasant and funny. He also turned out to be highly allergic to cats.

The entire week before we arrived to do the show, he'd been going on the air talking about how he was dreading meeting this genius cat. He was afraid he'd be sneezing during the entire interview. Naturally, as in all cases, Norton managed to accomplish the unexpected. Not only was Reagan *not* allergic, he wound up petting him and declaring over the air that he was now going to get a Scottish Fold.

We went back to L.A. to do a Book and Author Luncheon. What happens at these lunches is that a group of book lovers, usually women, decide it would be fun and interesting to bring in two or three authors to lecture and discuss their latest works over a lunch of overcooked vegetables and undercooked chicken. I was chosen for this particular lunch and thus was up on the podium, speaking to a lot of fur-clad women, along with a woman who wrote about the emotional problems children were having in high school, a man who had an easy, step-by-step formula for everyone to reach inner satisfaction, and a woman who wrote best-selling true-crime books and lectured about the mind of the psychopathic killer. It didn't really matter what I said to this group because Norton decided to steal the show. I stood up in my nice new suit (the gray one, where all the cat hairs weren't nearly so visible), glasses perched, looking as professorial as I can, and began to talk. In the meantime, Norton decided to plop himself down right next to the podium, looking for all the world as if not only did he belong up there as one of the speakers, but as if he were, in fact, my translator. The whole time I spoke, he kept glancing back and forth between me and the audience, as if to say, "Come on, folks, he's really trying hard." Whatever I was doing, it worked. In order of popularity, I think I came in a solid third. The psychopathic killer came in second, and Norton, of course, finished first.

Seattle, Portland (it was Norton's first trip to the Pacific Northwest), and San Francisco all went as smoothly as possible. Outside of San Francisco, in Larkspur, we made an appearance at a wonderful bookstore called A Clean Well-Lighted Place for Books. The evening was sponsored by the local SPCA. I spoke, Norton sat by my side, translating as usual, and several cats found new homes. So the entire evening was a terrific success. (Not to pat myself on the back, but I do find it admirable that throughout this entire book as well as the first one, never once have I succumbed to the temptation to say things like "a purrfect success." I just wanted to point that out to anyone who felt that, in general, cat books are too cute to bear. Although I don't have any compunction about relating stories of *other* people who show overly cute tendencies in front of Norton. Once, when we were in Philadelphia, I ordered up my dinner from room service after another grueling day of being witty and charming for TV, radio, and print. When the woman from room service brought me my dinner, she couldn't help but notice Norton and give him a few friendly strokes. She left, then fifteen minutes later reappeared. This time with a bowl of cat treats and a small catnip ball. These gifts arrived with a note. The envelope was addressed to "Kitty Cat Gethers" and the note read, "Hope your stay with us is pu-u-urfect!" It was signed: "The cat lovers in Room Service." You didn't *really* think I could write an entire book like this without having one of those "pu-u-urfect" anecdotes, did you? Grow up!)

In Seattle, I did have the stupidest experience of the entire tour. What people have to understand is that while writers are thrilled to have the opportunity to promote their books, since that's the only way they can possibly hope to collect any royalties, it really ain't a lot of fun. The reason it's not is because most of the talk-show hosts and interviewers who you're talking to haven't read the book and have no idea what you're doing there with them in the first place. At one newspaper interview in San Francisco, I went into the reporter's office, sat down, and after he introduced himself, I told him who I was, then pointed to the sack on my shoulder and said, "And this is Norton." His eyes widened and he said, "You brought your *cat* to the interview????" Slightly taken aback, I shrugged and said, "Well, yeah. He goes everywhere I go." "He *does????*" the guy responded. "That's unbelievable." About this time, I began to suspect that the reporter hadn't actually read the book, so I said, "Well, see, the book's called *The Cat Who Went to Paris* because I travel all over the world with the cat." "And he's actually been to Paris?" the guy now asked. "Uh-huh," I cleverly responded. "That's where we got the title from." "Wow," the guy said, stunned at this heavy new info. "This is unbelievable. Well . . . what do you want to talk about?"

Some of them are bad but not quite as bad as that. One otherwise well-done newspaper story that came out in Boston repeatedly referred to me as *Sam* Gethers (I'd spent two hours with the reporter, but I guess I didn't really make a big impression). I did one radio interview outside of Detroit and moments before it was was supposed to begin, the hostess of the show rushed in, introduced herself, and said, "We only have a minute. What's the title of the book, what's your name, what's the book about, and what the hell are we going to talk about?!" Refusing to panic, I calmly gave her the title, my name, the subject of the book, and fed her several reasonable questions to ask. We were then given the signal that we were on the air and she began the interview by announcing to all those listening, "I have here today an author, Peter Gethers, who wrote a book called *The Cat Who Went to Paris.* Now, I have to be totally up front about this: I hate cats and I hate cat books."

One good thing about that opening: The interview had nowhere to go but up.

Throughout the entire tour, Norton behaved impeccably. Rarely did he stumble and start to act like a . . . well . . . like a cat. I think he was fairly exhausted by the end, as was his dad, but generally he got to eat a lot, sleep a lot, and have tons of people tell him he was the greatest thing that ever walked the earth. So, while I was glad to get him back home, where he could curl up in his favorite and familiar spots, I think he had a fine time overall on the road.

In San Francisco, I realized he'd just about had it, though, when, one day at a radio interview, he decided to hide.

When I was being interviewed, he'd usually sit right by my side, but this afternoon he was restless. The interviewer, a woman named Ginnie Waters, who hosted a show on KKSF Radio called "Something Different," loved cats and encouraged Norton to stroll around the little broadcast booth as much as he wanted. Since he'd been absolutely purrfect . . . uh, perfect (sorry) . . . for the entire tour, and this was the very last stop for a while, I relaxed and didn't bother to keep my eye on him. The interview took half an hour, went quite well, and when it was over, I called for Norton to come and hop into his shoulder bag. Only there was no Norton. I knew I was in trouble because he'd been a little cranky all day. I should have seen it coming—he'd had a tough trip and was just plain tuckered out—but his timing was not great. For one thing, we had a plane to catch. For another, I'd just spent half an hour telling a good chunk of San Francisco about what an extraordinary cat he was and now I had to spend another half an hour crawling around on my stomach, peering under desks, climbing up on shelves, and searching through strange electronic equipment, while a bemused member of the media watched me try to find my cat. Finally, I heard a meow—he'd decided to let me know he was okay—but there was still no cat in the booth. He meowed again—and kept meowing for another fifteen minutes—but I absolutely could not find him. It wasn't until one of the engineers came in and suggested I look inside one of the speakers that the hiding place was discovered. How he managed to get in there, none of us could figure out. But, cat extraordinaire that he was, he'd managed to slip into the one place in a ten-by-ten room where he couldn't possibly be spotted. He didn't resist when I picked him up, and I sure didn't scold him. He wasn't angry; he wasn't even really hiding. He was just letting me know, in his own inimitable way, that he'd had enough. And I sure couldn't blame him.

But none of this holds a candle to the moment in Seattle. It came at exactly 6:05 A.M. Now, I'm not really the greatest morning person. I can survive it, but I'd gotten into Seattle about 10 P.M. the night before and, between one thing and another, hadn't gotten to sleep until well after midnight. So I wasn't thrilled about getting up at five, slurping down a cup of coffee, and then waiting for the radio station to call me in my room for their morning phoner. Reliable author that I am, however, I did it with as big a grin on my mug as I could muster. And, sure enough, just as I was stifling a major yawn, the phone rang and it was the drive-time radio show. They told me to hold on a couple of minutes while they did the traffic report and then they'd get back to me. So I yawned and held on and eventually heard a typical frenzied deejay's voice saying, "And in just a moment, we'll be talking to Peter Gethers, author of *The*

Cat Who Went to Paris, and his amazing cat, Norton. Hello, Peter . . . are you there?" I told him I was here—and he then asked, in his best slick radio cadence, "Tell me, Peter, what does Norton think of relationships in the nineties?"

I should say right now that I'm usually a fairly glib person. It takes a lot for me to be stumped. Maybe it was the fact that it was the middle of the night, as far as I was concerned. Maybe it was that we'd been touring for too many days in a row. But all I could think of to say was a not-very-glib, *"What?"* And when he repeated the question, I came back with, "Uh . . . well . . . he approves of them."

"Thank you very much," I heard. "That was Peter Gethers, author of *The Cat Who Went to Paris,* and his amazing cat, Norton, on relationships in the nineties." And then he hung up.

I decided I had nobody to blame but myself, wondered how Tolstoy would have responded if he'd been out promoting *Anna Karenina*—"Tell me, Leo, what does Count Vronsky think about relationships in the 1800s?"—then got dressed, kissed the cat, and went on to our next interview.

~~~

The best part of being on tour was going to bookstores. Not only was it exciting to see truly great stores—and once again be reminded why I do what I do to earn my keep—it was extraordinarily fun to see how people reacted to Norton.

One woman at the Boston University bookstore showed up at a signing with photos of her family—which consisted of *six* Scottish Folds.

Two women who came to meet Norton at the Village

Green in Rochester were Scottish Fold breeders who appeared with their impressive brochures filled with cute photos of Fold kittens. These two charming women, Barbara Meyers and Grace Sutton, are responsible for the fact that Esther, my agent and lifelong die-hard resister of cats, finally gave in and now has a folded-eared pal of her own named Tate.

When I would sign books, people lined up for books while I sat behind a table and Norton sat on the table. Someone would hand me a book, ask me to sign it (scarily enough, often to someone named Fluffy, Spitball, Pooh, or Peanut Butter), and while I was doing so, he or she would pet Norton, coo over him, and, as often as not, hand him a can of Pounce as a present (one woman tentatively presented me with some M&Ms because she felt guilty that I wasn't getting enough attention; other than that, I was strictly in the background).

If someone had never heard of the book but just happened to be wandering by, they'd usually give me a perfunctory glance, spot Norton doing his shtick, widen their eyes, then sidle over to me to ask a few questions. The questions would usually range from "Is he a trained cat?" (Answer: No) to "Why does he look so funny?" (Answer: It's the breed) to "He's so calm. Did you drug him?" (Answer: No!) to "Did you clip his ears?" (Answer: NO!!!!).

At Gene's Books in King of Prussia, Pa., they had a photo contest. People brought in a picture of their own cute feline and I was supposed to pick winners in the following categories: Fattest Cat, Most Amazing Cat, and Cutest Cat. This was not unlike being put in the delicate situation of having to choose which person's baby is better looking. I did my best, being careful not to always choose photos of Folds, since I didn't want to appear to be too biased. Overall, the winners were gracious and the losers didn't either hit me or tear up my book, so I suppose it could be considered a successful contest.

At Liberties Books and Fine Music in Boca Raton, Florida, people were encouraged to bring their own cats to meet Norton. One guy brought a large St. Bernard dog, for some strange reason, and one couple brought a large black cat who was the calmest cat I've ever seen. Norton, when he's in public, is not particularly nervous or hyper, but he does stay extremely alert. If I lecture for more than half an hour, he may doze off, or may turn over on his back, purr, and demand to be scratched, but usually he sits calmly, checking out the situation, making sure that there aren't going to be any unpleasant surprises. But this black cat didn't care about surprises or anything else that I could see. He simply sat in the audience and was about as tense as a bowl of jello. One of his owners brought the cat over to meet me—and the cat was hanging upside down from the guy's hands like a side of beef in a meat locker. I couldn't tell if Norton was a little jealous or if he was merely scornful of the black cat's eagerness to please. I like to think it was the latter, as I presume he's above any feeling of petty jealousy, but he was definitely standoffish toward this feline competitor.

At Books & Co. in Dayton, Ohio (the country's second largest independent bookstore and a book lover's fantasy), I was the second speaker of the evening. The only problem with that was, while the first speaker was going on—her book and talk were both quite charming, all about various American family traditions—Norton and I stood off to the side, preparing for our own little seminar. So while this other poor author was speaking, people started spotting the cat and coming over to pet him and say hello. Pretty soon, there were fifty people surrounding Norton, praising him to the skies, while three people were left sitting in front of the family traditions woman. I got the distinct impression, when we were both dropped off at our hotel later that night, that her family's newest tradition was going to be hating authors who write books about their cats.

In Dallas, not only did Norton finally get his first taste of real barbecue, he was now so relaxed about appearing on television that he actually fell asleep on a local talk show. The setup was vaguely "Tonight Show"-ish—the host sat in a chair while the guests lined up along a couch. Norton and I were the only guests. He sat closest to the interviewer and I sat next to him. The woman who was the star of the show was a fanatical cat lover and I think she was never really sure to whom she should address her questions, me or Norton. Every so often, I could see a look of surprise on her face after she'd ask something and I was the one who responded. The whole time I was talking, I was rubbing Norton, until somewhere in the middle of the interview, the host said, "Well, I can see the problem with Norton is that he's just too tense under the scrutiny of public life." I looked down and, sure enough, the Perry Como of the feline world had his head tucked into his body, all curled up in a ball, and he was sound asleep, purring away. By the time we got to Taylor's Bookstore the next day, I could tell that Norton was beginning to take seriously to the celebrity life. As the hundred or so people lined up to meet him, I had the distinct impression that he was disappointed there were no cameras around to record his every movement (which, I must admit, weren't many; mostly he would stick his head up to be scratched or stick his head down to be hand-fed a couple of treats. He's kind of a minimalist when it comes to actual public activity).

When the tour for the hardcover book was over, I believe that Norton felt much as I did. There was a sense of relief—it was nice to be home rather than in a new hotel room every day, and it was even nicer to be alone, without having to constantly be performing, something neither writers nor cats take to naturally or are great at. At the same time, there was a little bit of a letdown. For a short burst of time, we were center stage. Don't panic, neither one of us ever fully turned into Sally Field at the Academy Awards, but I do think there was a slight addiction to the public acclaim. Cats and writers are both loners for the most part and there was something gratifying, however uncomfortable it sometimes felt, about people personally acknowledging that we had given their lives some pleasure.

I believe, after the tour ended, that Norton had a slightly different relationship with the human race. Prior to this experience, I was basically the one who'd provided him with the most protracted and strongest feelings of affection and love. Several girlfriends over the years adored him and let him know it, and he'd met all of my friends, who fussed over him more than enough to keep him happy. In our various travels, he'd also encountered plenty of strangers who certainly pumped up his ego. But on this trip it was the first time he was able to sense that *many* people, *thousands* of people, wanted to love him. If not him specifically, then something—or someone—very much like him.

It was an interesting switch. Cats often affect people in strange and mysterious ways and, for the most part, change our lives for the better. It's what they do. It's one of the things that makes them cats. But this was a rare occasion when people were able to substantially change a cat.

Since Norton can't really talk—even though I'm able to interpret many of his meows, it's fairly difficult to have a philosophical conversation with him—I can't be absolutely certain that this change was as strong as I suspect. But I can turn the tables on my cat and observe him, sit back and watch him in action, and I *am* certain, from my observations after the tour, that he was different after coming in contact with so many people who so clearly adored him, and who just as clearly yearned for him to adore them.

He certainly didn't turn into a lap dog. God forbid. Nor did he lose any of his independence or his individualistic spirit. But I noticed that when a stranger came in the room and reached out a hand, Norton's neck would move just an inch in the proper direction, an admission, however grudgingly, that love was not a one-way street.

For a cat, that ain't bad.

And for a cat, an author, and an author's girlfriend, it also meant it was time to put our past lives behind us and head off across the Atlantic.

PART TWO

a cat abroad

4
a
cat
in france

Then there was the bad weather.

Just kidding—that's the opening line to *A Moveable Feast*. I always like to see who's on their toes.

Unlike Papa, as I call him, when we arrived in Paris the autumn weather was absolutely spectacular. Getting there was not quite as pleasant, however.

One of the drawbacks of giving up the life of semi-high-powered publishing executive was that I also gave up the semi-high salary that went along with that life. Saving money just happens not to be my strong point (I'm much, much better at spending it), so, trying to show me that a careful, considered, budget-conscious life could also be fun and rewarding, Janis convinced me to get tickets using our American Advantage Miles. In other words, we could fly to France for free.

I don't know how many of you have ever tried to actually order whatever Advantage Miles are due you. But let me

assure you, if you don't have a Ph.D in Reading Instructions, give it up. Don't bother. As a publisher, I had to wade
my way through many a complicated contract. I know all
about options and step deals and various parties of the first
part and even something about a few parties of the second
part, but trying to order Advantage Miles was something
substantially beyond my intellectual capabilities. I couldn't
figure out how many miles it took to get an international
flight. Then I couldn't figure out how many more it took to•
get a seat in business class. Then, to make matters worse,
I absolutely couldn't figure out what dates were restricted
or what dates were okay to fly. The nearest I could come
was that, with the mileage I'd accumulated, I could either
fly nonstop to Asia or I could get an upgrade on a flight to
Seattle, but I couldn't fly anywhere else unless I wanted to
go after two A.M. on the eighteenth day of every other
month. After several hours of trying to make sense of the
back of my Advantage Miles statement, and finally realizing
that whatever I did was going to be one hundred percent
incorrect, I called American Airlines and threw myself on
the mercy of whoever answered the phone. I promised
them that I was a reasonably intelligent person who normally could function in the real world, and then I confessed
that trying to figure out their simple system for free flights
was the equivalent, for me, of those spatial-relations tests
they used to give in junior high school. Sometimes I still
wake up screaming as I remember sitting at my desk, looking at a drawing of two gears, and staring at the caption
which read: *If the gear on the right spins counterclockwise and
strikes the gear on the left, which way will the gear on the left turn?*
Not since those mind-numbing sessions—where I would
spend the entire hour twisting myself into a pretzel trying
desperately to figure out the proper movement, then trying

even more desperately to even figure out what a gear *was,* after which my friendly counselor suggested that I try to stay away from all activity that ever involved any form of mechanical skill or abstraction—had I felt the way I felt reading those Advantage Mile forms.

My only consolation was that the woman at the airline was very understanding, leading me to believe that at least some other customers had run into the same roadblock I had. Not many, but some.

We finally figured out what I needed to know and our tickets were ordered. But after this was all done, Janis asked if I'd made a reservation for Norton. I hadn't yet—that had to be done separately; I was afraid of overloading my sympathetic airline friend—but I assured her it would be no problem.

As usual, I was completely wrong. It was a huge problem. American Airlines no longer allowed pets to fly in the cabin on international flights.

This was absurd, and I said as much to whoever I talked to at the American reservation desk. That may be, she said, but it was also company policy. So I asked to speak to the manager. He was quite nice and friendly, but he also told me it was company policy. But, I argued, I fly American everywhere in the States just because they let me take my cat in the cabin with me. Yes, he assured me, that was correct. But not for international flights. When I asked why that was, he told me it was the law.

Granted, I'm not a lawyer, but I seriously doubted there was a law on the books that forbade cats to fly with their owners from New York to Paris. I was also fairly sure it was nowhere to be found in the Constitution of the United States. And while I knew that such a right wouldn't be covered in the Bill of Rights (I can see it now—Thomas

Jefferson stroking his chin, deep in thought . . . "Hmmm. Let's see . . . let's give everyone the right to freedom of speech . . . the right to privacy . . . I know! And the right to bear cats on airplanes!"), I had a distinct feeling that this guy from American was not telling me the truth. So I did what any normal, cat-loving person would do. I called the president.

Give me a break—not the President of the United States. I'm not a total lunatic. But I did call the prez of American Airlines. I explained to him that I had just written a best-selling book about traveling around the world with my cat, that I was going to be writing another, and that, for some weird reason, his airline, which was always so nice to my little furry friend, would not allow him to fly with me to Charles de Gaulle Airport. I'm a little ashamed to mention it, but sometimes this mention of the book works when all else fails. Once, when Norton and I went down for our annual spring training trip to Florida, the Rotisserie Baseball guys who organized the trip decided to change from our usual hotel. No more Belleview Biltmore, where they loved the cat—despite the time he fell fifteen feet through the dining-room awning and almost gave two seventy-five-year-old women heart attacks when he landed on their table. We were now staying at a large, pink monstrosity called the Don Cesar. Because Norton had been going on this baseball trip for so many years, it never occurred to me to make a reservation for him, which turned out to be unfortunate because the Don Cesar didn't take cats. I won't give all the gory details, but there was no chance of getting into another hotel within a hundred miles, so I wound up sneaking Norton into my room. The next morning, the manager of the hotel accosted me, drawing himself up to his full height of five feet six inches, and telling me that he heard I had a cat in my room. I stared him straight in the eye—I had to stoop a bit—and, looking as indignant as possible, lied my head off. Later that morning, when I returned to my room after breakfast, who was there but the manager, snooping around. Not only did he find the litter box, the cat food, and the bowl of water, he found the cat. I tried being outraged that he'd broken into my room, but it's hard to sustain outrage when you're caught in a total lie. So I did the next best thing: I offered to bribe him. When that didn't work, I became desperate and told him that I had a book coming out in several months, that the book was expected to be a best-seller, and that if he didn't let my cat stay there, I'd make sure I wrote terrible things about him and the hotel in the book. Even Norton was embarrassed by this feeble attempt to keep him sheltered, but much to our shock, it worked. The manager suddenly looked at Norton, smiled somewhat sycophantically (a trait I personally like in hotel personnel), and said that Norton certainly looked like an extraordinary cat and he didn't see what harm a feline could do for just a few days. Now I know how it feels to abuse the power of the media. It feels just *great!*

However, such a ploy didn't work with American Airlines. The president (to be honest, he was sort of vague about his title; he never actually *told* me he was the president even though that's who I asked to be connected to. My own opinion is that he was a fake president, someone they use when dealing with crackpots on the telephone) told me that the several people I'd already talked to were absolutely correct. It was against company policy to fly a cat in the cabin internationally. "Why is that?" I asked as politely as possible. "I think it's against the law," he told me.

At this point, I had visions of a major Supreme Court case. *Norton* v. *the United States of America.* It had a nice ring to it. I was already beginning to fantasize about Clarence Thomas catching Norton alone in a hallway and making a pass, but, as always, Janis pulled in the reigns on my sanity and convinced me that it would be a lot easier to simply get a ticket on another airline.

So on the day of our departure, Janis flew for free on American Airlines. Norton and I flew—not even remotely for free—on Air France. I was not unhappy paying for the flight, since there was no way Norton was ever flying in the baggage compartment. And for some reason—and this will definitely be brought up when I appear before the Supreme Court—it is not illegal for Air France to fly their cats in comfort and plush surroundings up with their two-legged customers, only for American-based airlines.

Norton and I had a delightful flight. I'd found a brand-new traveling kennel for him. Instead of those hard, heavy cases that fit under the seat but force him to assume a pancakelike position for much of his air time, I'd discovered these wonderful shoulder bags made out of a very tough cloth and which are airline approved. There's mesh in the back, so Norton can look out, and it unzips, so he can even stick his head out, which is his favorite way to travel. For takeoffs and landings, the thing zips up and fits under the seat, but it's extremely comfortable and makes Norton's trips a lot more luxurious.

Of course, on Air France, they are incredibly nice to a certain Scottish Fold, and this trip was no exception. The business-class cabin was nearly empty, so Norton got his own seat, as well as his own meal of smoked salmon and baked *lotte*. All in all, he was quite a hit on the flight. A very attractive and very French woman sat next to me, curled up in a little ball under a blanket. When she saw Norton up on my lap, she squealed and said, "Oh, ees he an American

Curl? I joost saw one of zose." I did my best to explain the concept of Scottish Fold—which, in French, translates vaguely into *Écosse Plier*—but I don't think it really came across. Norton's personality did come across to the two stewardesses, who spent an inordinate amount of time making sure that he was comfortable and well-fed. As we taxied into Charles de Gaulle, one of the attendants made the following announcement over the loudspeaker: "Please remember to take all packages weeth you. Except for ze passengaire in fourteen A. Eef he would like to leave his leetle cat, Norton, we would be very glad to take care of heem. Sank yoo."

Janis and I decided, due to several factors—the number of suitcases we had (whenever we moved, I felt exactly like the elder Charles Foster Kane: baggage stretched out for miles before us); our impatience to get started with our new lives in the house we'd rented down in Provence; the fact that Paris costs several million dollars per minute—not to dawdle in the city for too long. We were headed to the countryside, so to the countryside we decided to head.

We stayed at a friend's apartment for the night, determined to get an early start in the morning. Once we were over our jet lag and had our espresso and croissant the next morning, the first thing that had to be done was to pick up the car we'd rented. One nice thing about moving abroad for a year is you learn all about these strange businesses and services that, ordinarily, you'd never discover. One such business was something called Europe by Car. Instead of renting a European Ford from Avis at a cost of thousands of francs a week, Europe by Car leases Citroëns and Peugeots for up to six months at a time at a very reasonable rate.

We'd ordered a brand-new, shiny red Citroën for ourselves, and all I had to do was go pick it up.

Easier said than done in Paris.

Janis stayed at the apartment; Norton and I headed for some strange part of south Paris that we'd never been to before. I don't think too many other people had been there, either. And those who were wandering the streets all looked like they were trying to collect the reward for killing Salman Rushdie. I did manage to find the garage eventually, and once that was done also managed to polish off all the paperwork and other rigamarole one has to do. Then I was pointed toward another room, followed instructions, and went to get my car.

A very Parisian auto mechanic—overalls, a beret, a thick black mustache; he looked like he'd fix your transmission with a loaf of bread rather than a wrench—insisted on showing me all the fine points of my new vehicle before letting me drive off. I tried to tell him that I had a hard time understanding car talk in English, let alone French, but he paid me no mind. I vaguely followed his explanations of the clutch and the trunk and the hand break, and Norton seemed satisfied with the seating room in the back, which of course was of primary importance, but my interest really perked up when he pointed to some little lever to the right of the driver's seat.

"Ne touchez pas, monsieur," he told me. *"Ne touchez jamais."*

"Why shouldn't I ever touch it?" I asked back.

He gave me one of those French looks. The look that says, "Why do Americans insist on asking questions when all that is called for is simple truth?" And he wagged his finger at me, looked down at the lever, and repeated his words of warning. *"Ne touchez pas,"* he said and shook his head solemnly.

"But what does it do?" I asked.

He looked at me incredulously. *"C'est très important,"* he whispered. The whispering meant it was even more important than I'd already suspected. *"Ne . . . touchez . . . pas."* There was a good ten-second pause before he added the word I knew was coming. *"Jamais."*

I decided to give it one more shot.

"I promise I won't touch it," I said. "I swear. But just give me a hint. What does it do?"

My French mechanic zipped up the front of his overalls, wiped his hands on his pant leg, and walked over to me. He put his hands on my shoulder and stared me straight in the eye.

"Monsieur," he said, in a tone worthy of a head of state announcing the commencement of war. "I would like to say just one thing to you."

"I think I know what it is," I told him.

He spun around, took two steps toward the exit, then spun back around to me. He held out his arm, extended a finger of his hand, and pointed toward the lever in the car.

"Ne touchez pas," he ordered.

"Jamais?" I asked.

Pleased—but still grave and unsmiling—he nodded. *"Jamais,"* he agreed, and left for lunch.

I never did *touche* that lever. I also never found out what the hell it was for. All I know is, for the rest of the year, I lived in mortal fear that a stranger would get behind the wheel of that red Citroën, spot an interesting lever to his right, and either some poor passenger would be catapulted through the roof or some city in China would actually be wiped off the face of the earth.

Of much more immediate concern, however, was getting back to Janis and the apartment where we'd left her.

Aside from my lack of mechanical ability, I have possibly the world's worst sense of direction. I can get lost in New York City—where the streets are arranged numerically!— so driving in Paris turned out to be somewhat of an adventure. All streets in Paris are one way, usually going exactly the opposite direction from the one I wanted to go, and very few streets go for more than a block or two without turning into another name. Which makes it very difficult to get around if you don't know where you're going. It's hard enough driving and simultaneously reading a map, but it's especially hard in Paris, where every two seconds someone either's honking at you or screaming at you or trying to get you to buy some pastry.

I did learn one very important lesson, however: Cats may be wonderful at many, many things, but reading maps is not one of them.

It took me two and a half hours to make the twenty-minute drive to the apartment. But once there, we were all packed and, once Janis was placated, we were also ready to move out.

And so, only a few hours behind schedule, we began our drive down south.

～～

Norton had never been through the Loire Valley—the Valley of Kings—and for that matter neither had Janis, so we decided to spend a few days meandering through that region's *châteaux* and drinking its superb wine.

Once we finally figured out how to get out of Paris (I don't think I can stand to recount how many times I actually had to drive around the roundabout at the Arc de Triomphe; let's just say it was not a pretty sight), we decided to drive the ninety kilometers to the town of Chartres and begin there.

Perhaps you have picked up on the fact that I am not, in any way, shape, or form, a religious man. I relate to my own culture as I relate to most every other culture—through its food and its women. Thus, except when I once dated a dental hygienist named Rachel, a satisfying Sunday brunch of lox and bagels is about as close as I get to any sort of mystical experience involving my own heritage. Other religions and religious rites leave me cold, too. I'm not much of a believer in spectacle (I can pass just as easily on the Rose Bowl Parade as on midnight mass at St. Patrick's). Neither fear nor guilt work well for me as motivating forces, and I've never thought much of dressing up in long, flowing robes, heavy crowns, and millions of dollars' worth of jewelry except to think that the Pope and Allan Carr would probably have a lot to talk about. I don't believe in heaven or hell (unless you count Anaheim) and I don't think praying for one's soul does any good other than to absolve one from an awful lot of responsibility. I sort of understand the fatalism of various Eastern religions, but I can't say I see much sense in climbing incredibly steep mountains just to find inner peace. I can do that watching Dwight Gooden throw a perfect Lord Charles. As far as walking over hot coals and doing the thing where you sleep on a bed of sharp nails, ix-nay on that. Redemption in the form of pain *really* doesn't cut it with me. All in all, I can't say I believe in god. If, in fact, I ever find out that he does indeed exist, I think I'll stay away from him, because if he's responsible for half the things he gets credit for, he's got to be one mean son of a bitch.

To walk into the cathedral at Chartres, however, makes one understand religion and everything that created it. It's not as if I feel that god was behind this remarkable structure, but it's impossible not to feel the power that *was* behind it—that power being the *belief* in god.

There has been a church at the site of the current cathedral since the fourth century, though the cathedral that stands now wasn't built until 1194. Well, at least it was begun in 1194, and was finished, remarkably, in only thirty years. I am not a student of architecture and this book is not meant to be used as a travel guide, but to stand before the church's facades, the flying buttresses, the *Clocher Neuf,* the overwhelmingly beautiful thirteenth-century stained glass and the fourteenth-century stone choir screen is really to stand before the beauty and power of history. It is as overwhelming a visual experience as I can imagine.

Norton seemed quite floored as well. The three of us toured the inside of the cathedral—Norton on my shoulder, as usual—then sat in a pew to rest and try to absorb what we were looking at. Usually, in such situations, Norton will either be oblivious to his surroundings—i.e., sleeping the sleep of all cats—or he'll be looking every which way, trying to see everything that can be seen, as well as keeping an eye out for any potential dog alerts. At Chartres, however, Norton sat on the pew, head up, and very slowly swiveled his neck, looking first at the huge organ, then studying the pulpit, then taking in the sculptures and paintings and thousands of candles. At one point, a representative of the church ambled over to us and started to say something—I'm fairly sure what he was trying to articulate was that cats weren't allowed in places of worship—but then he saw Norton respectfully eyeing the carved wooden archway to our right, so he ambled back from whence he came. It looked to me as if he realized the cat was appreciating what he was seeing just as much as any other tourist, and he decided the no-cat rule probably wasn't apt in this instance. If only he'd worked for American Airlines instead of god, my life—and probably the lives of countless others—would have been a lot easier.

Going from the splendor of the cathedral to the backseat of the red Citroën, Norton was clearly psyched for his first car trip through the French countryside.

Our next stop was the splendid town of Amboise. Amboise is known for several things: It's where Leonardo da Vinci was buried in 1519; it's where the Mona Lisa was first brought to France; it's where Charles VIII died after hitting his head on a very low doorway. (I'm not making that up! And that would definitely rank near the bottom of ways I personally want to leave this earth.) It's also where Norton jumped out of his shoulder bag and ran away for the only time in his life.

Amboise is down by the river and its amazing *château* is terraced high above it. Before touring the castle, we decided to explore the town, since my favorite thing in France is simply to walk around, watch the people, and stop into as many *pâtisseries* as possible. Janis likes to see how many museums and ruins she can visit in one day; my idea of being a tourist is to find an atmospheric café and spend the day sipping espresso and pretending to be French. For this, our first day in the Loire, we decided to compromise. We'd take the *château* tour, but first I got to walk, drink, eat, and pretend. Norton, of course, accompanied us everywhere. Strolling, sightseeing, caféing. He was right at home.

At one point, we decided to stop at the post office to send back a few postcards. The Amboise *bureau de poste* was in the busiest part of town. After we'd bought our stamps and done our mailings, we headed back to the old town, but before we got there, a large truck decided to barrel past us, its horn blaring, at the exact same time that a bicycle decided to nearly sideswipe me and knock me into the bushes. I was a little unnerved—mostly by the jarring honk from the truck, which wasn't all that close, just loud—but nothing seemed out of place until I heard Janis scream. I turned back to see what she was screaming at, reached into the shoulder bag to make sure Norton was okay, and then realized why she was shrieking—because Norton had jumped out of the bag and was streaking off down the street. He was already a good twenty feet away from us and running as fast as he could. Before Janis could even get out the words "Go get him!" Norton had rounded a corner and disappeared into the heart of a medieval hill town.

I will say one thing for my relationship with my cat—at no time have I ever condescended to him. I refuse to believe he would ever do anything completely untoward. I don't mean something annoying like hiding for the day, I mean something permanently improper—like running away.

Janis, on the other hand, panicked. She kept yelling for me to chase after him, even after I pointed out that even in my best years, I could not run fast enough to catch a cat who didn't want to be caught. Instead, I took a deep breath and told Janis that he would be waiting calmly for me to come get him around the next corner.

Still calm, I led her to the street down which Norton had disappeared. Together we walked—not ran but walked, albeit with a fairly quick stride—the two hundred feet or so to the next corner . . . and there, sitting in the middle of the street, waiting for us, was Norton. He had quietly planted himself in front of a dry cleaner's and had an expression on his face that, without a doubt, was meant to convey, "So where were you? I've been waiting."

He sat there until I went right over to him, picked him up, and set him back in his bag.

Janis merely scowled and shook her head.

"He won't run away," I told her.

"Yeah, well *I* might," she said.

I stroked my cat, gave him a quick look, which I'm sure he knew meant I'd been a lot more worried than I'd let on, and then we went up to see the Amboise *château*.

It was spectacular. Even Norton thought so (although every time he shifted in his bag to get a better look at his surroundings, Janis practically jumped out of her skin). We saw Leonardo's tomb and the plans and models of his early inventions (how is it that someone was able to sketch plans for an airplane and automobile in the early 1500s and I can't touch my fax machine without getting a paper cut that slices my finger practically to the bone? It doesn't seem fair). We also got our first inkling of how far we had to go with our grasp of the French language.

We'd decided to take a tour of the place, led by a woman who explained—in French—what we were seeing. She was obviously well schooled when it came to tourists because, realizing that very few of us were linguists, she spoke ve . . ee . . rr . . yy . . . sllooowwwllyy. I thought I was doing rather well, following almost everything, until afterward I asked Janis what in the world the guide was talking about when she told us the story about the shoemakers.

"*What* shoemakers?!" Janis demanded.

"You know," I said. "The shoemakers in the forest who

ran around and—here's where I'm a little fuzzy—found shoes and brought them back for the king?"

I'll actually never forget the expression on my darling's face (or, as they say in France, on the face of my *petit chou-chou*—my little brussels sprout) when she realized to what I was referring. It was a look that combined astonishment, awe, and not a little bit of terror.

The guide had told this long, I thought convoluted story, about the *chasseurs* going out to do their thing for King François Premier (or, François the First to you). I couldn't begin to fathom why *chasseurs*—which I thought were shoemakers—would go searching for pumps and loafers in the woods. It turns out that cha*u*sseurs are shoemakers. And they weren't foraging for leather goods in the king's backyard. Ch*a*sseurs are *hunters*. And they weren't bringing back boots for Frankie either, they were bringing him wild game that they'd shot. To say I missed the point would be a slight understatement, especially since my slant on the entire rest of the guide's story revolved around this whole shoe issue. I was particularly bewildered about the annual "Feast of the Open-Toed Sandals."

Oh, well. So I wasn't ready to resume my dinners with Polanski et al. and seize control of the conversation. Soon, I assured my two traveling companions. But neither Janis nor Norton looked convinced.

I *was* ready—and so was at least one of them—to drink some wine. So we began the *dégustation* part of our Loire trip.

The first place we stopped was Azay-le-Rideau, which in addition to delicious white wine, had a world-class castle. We hit a few *caves,* sampled the local *vin,* then took Norton to see his second *château.* I remembered going to Azay-le-Rideau nearly twenty years before, and I was positive that the word then was that this was the place where the Sleeping Beauty legend grew up.

"Just think," I kept saying to Janis, "this is where Sleeping Beauty was supposed to have slept."

"Prove it," Janis kept saying back to me, because, sure enough, nowhere—in any guide book or anywhere at the castle—was this rather wonderful fact mentioned.

"That's the problem with the modern world," I muttered, when I realized it was my word against Michelin's. "No romance."

"Maybe some shoemakers used to come here," Janis told me, but I made sure she knew that that tack was not going to make me feel any better.

We wound up spending three more days touring *châteaux* and beautiful Loire towns. We never planned ahead, just took our chances on finding a hotel. Twice we went for local dives, which were just fine; once we stayed in a converted castle. Norton liked that room best of all, because it had a beautiful large red satin chair that he used to much the same effect as a throne.

The first couple of hotels we stayed in, I followed the same routine. I'd pull up in front, have Janis wait in the car with you-know-who, then I'd timidly ask the desk clerk or innkeeper if they would let a cat spend the night. Each time, I got exactly the same response.

"Why not?" was the standard reply. "We'd let *you* stay here. Why wouldn't we let a cat stay here?"

I must say, I thought this attitude remarkably healthy, and so, obviously, did Norton. Not only did he make himself comfortable in each room we spent the night, he came down to dinner with us also, and generally had the run of each establishment.

We took Norton to some of the most beautiful places in

France over these few days. We went to the *château* in Blois. (Two interesting facts about Blois: The first is that the name of the town is Celtic and it means "wolf"—and, by the way, so does almost everything else in French; anywhere we'd go for dinner, we'd ask what the name of the restaurant meant and at least fifty percent of the time it was some ancient language for "wolf." The second is that the entire town smells like chocolate. Don't ask me why. I will just assume there's either a large chocolate factory nearby or a really, really fat person with no willpower lives there.)

Norton toured the *château* in Chambord, which looks English to me, perhaps because it was a famous hunting lodge in the 1500s, as well as Cheverny, which still has much of its original furnishings, and he was definitely the first cat since the time of Henry II to tour the two most amazing *châteaux* in the Loire, Chinon and Chenonceau.

Chinon, for those of you who know their history from movies rather than reality, is where Peter O'Toole imprisoned Katharine Hepburn in *The Lion in Winter.* It is mostly in ruins but, perhaps more than any other structure in all of France, strikes me absolutely dumb. It sends shivers up and down my spine. Part of it, I'm sure, is my overactive imagination. Nonetheless, the ruins and history of Chinon inspire dreams and fantasies unlike anyplace I've ever seen.

Chinon is where Joan of Arc stopped to meet the Dauphin—and miraculously recognized the heir to the throne, even though he was dressed a lot like Red Skelton in the guise of Freddie the Freeloader. When Janis, Norton, and I stood above the Chinon moat, having seen Joan's bedroom, and the prison that held Eleanor of Aquitaine, it was a wintry, blustery day. There were few tourists around, fewer cars, and it was remarkably easy to imagine life five hundred years ago. It was not hard to picture oneself in armor, another Richard the Lion-Heart, fighting against Moslem infidels (something I've always wanted to do) and for the survival of civilization. Except in my case, of course, it would be Pete the Cat-Heart.

I let Norton out of his sack for a while and, after he sniffed through the ruins to his satisfaction, the three of us sat in the mostly crumbled courtyard, shivering slightly while we all pictured the past.

The present wasn't too terrible, either. We had a wonderful dinner that night at the Château de Marcay, near Chinon. The hotel is actually a fifteenth-century fortress, surrounded by its own vineyards, with forty rooms which are filled with antiques as well as whirlpools. There, they looked askance when I asked for a bowl of water for Norton—and insisted on bringing him milk instead—and looked absolutely horrified when I ordered the wine I wanted. The *sommelier*, a woman, which is rare over there, quietly and tactfully shook her head and offered to suggest something we might prefer. Although neither Janis nor I are ignoramuses about wine, we put ourselves in her superior hands and we were not disappointed. She brought us perhaps the most delicious white wine I've ever sipped, an Anjou, a Château d'Epire, produced by a M. et Mme. Bizard. I've never seen it before or since, but the taste will stay with me for the rest of my life. Of course, it didn't hurt that we were sipping it on giant oak chairs in front of a roaring, twenty-foot-wide hearth. My guess is that the atmosphere will help Norton remember the taste of that milk, too, a Château Borden, produced by Mme. Elsie.

The local Chinon wine was quite delectable as well, as we discovered the next day (and, if you go there, try the red, which is rarely imported to America—it's superb). We also discovered that small towns in America are not the only places that tend to be rather . . . uh . . . shall we say, rinky-dink.

Picture going to San Antonio to see the Alamo. As soon as you get within thirty miles, you start seeing The Alamo Motel, The Alamo Diner, The Alamo Bar & Grill, and The Alamo Fertilizer & Seed Shop. Everywhere you look, you see nothing but people using the name Alamo to promote something that has about as much to do with Davy Crockett and Jim Bowie as it does with life on Neptune. It's the same thing in the Loire Valley, although most of the touristy come-ons are somewhat more attractive than anything found in San Antonio. When you spend the night in the lovely villages of Loches or Ambois or Blois, every sign in town says something along the lines of CAFÉ LOUIS XIV or BOULANGERIE HENRI VIII or BLANCHERIE HENRI II (Henry the Second's Cleaners—it doesn't have quite the same ring in English, does it?).

One thing in the Loire that absolutely cannot be ruined by commercial greed is the wondrous *château* at Chenonceaux, built on top of a five-arched bridge over the river Cher.

I was first at Chenonceau (And so you don't think I'm a careless speller, please note that the French, typically, spell the town Chenonceaux, but the actual *château* is spelled Chenonceau. What can I say? That's why they're French.) in the summer of 1976, when I was young and hippieish. The place was crawling with tourists and it was brutally hot, but it was so wonderful it didn't matter. I was with David, my partner (yes, we go back that far together, although we didn't know what we were doing back then when it came to writing scripts), and our respective girlfriends (we didn't know what we were doing with them, either, but they're long gone from our lives), and we took rowboats on the river, rowing right under the castle as the sun was setting, then we sat in the middle of the Chenonceau grounds, amidst the alley of plane trees, drank wine and watched the incredible *son et lumière* show explaining the history of the castle.

Years later, when Janis, Norton, and I made our pilgrimage, there were no rowboats and no sound and light show and practically no tourists. It was cold and windy and, if possible, even more perfect than that summer day of long ago. As we toured the castle, nearly by ourselves, all the fireplaces had crackling fires in them. Looking through the windows, it was as if we were looking back into a glorious yet sobering past. We could palpably feel the plagues, the beheadings, the treachery, the splendor, the royalty that had all passed through the stone walls. None of the guards questioned that we were bringing a cat to study the Flemish tapestries, the four-poster beds, the Renaissance furniture, and the mind-boggling underground kitchen. I suppose with all that treachery and all those plagues, a Scottish Fold was no big deal.

Our last stop in the Loire—we were now getting eager to reach Provence—was in the lovely wine village of Sancerre.

This town has always had a fascination for me. When I was twenty-five, I had a novel published, called *The Dandy,* in which the lead character moves to France and chooses the town of Sancerre as his home because it produces his favorite white wine. Years later, the town—and the wine—didn't let me down. We wandered through the old part of the city, parts of which go back to the eleventh century, then we went a tastin'.

Sancerre happens to be Janis's favorite white wine, too, so we didn't hesitate to do as much sampling as we possibly

could. And in this town, it's possible to do a *lot* of sampling.
There must be over a hundred vineyards in a two- or three-
mile area, each producing a wine more delicious than the
last one. My favorite, and Janis's, was a small local *cave* right
in town run by a father-and-son team. They were shut tight
the day we were there, but a sign was posted saying that
anyone who really wanted some wine should go three
blocks further, make a right, then knock loudly at the door
of the second house on the left. We followed the directions—a miracle in itself, nearly on a par with Jeanne d'Arc
and the Dauphin—and found ourselves in someone's
kitchen. The mother of the whole family, a rather chubby
lady in her seventies, was making a huge vat of soup. We
talked about their various wines while she stirred; then we
sipped some different vintages while she stirred. We kept
talking and sipping, she kept stirring, and finally we bought
several cases to stick in the trunk of our car. I don't think
she ever let go of her spoon the entire time.

Norton's favorite vineyard, however, was called the Cave
Fouassier, right outside of town on the Route de Bourges.
Norton didn't actually taste the wine, but he was very impressed with the vintner's dog, who, when he wanted to go
out, would stand up on his two hind legs, put his two front
paws on the doorknob, turn the knob, open the door, and
scamper outside. It took us so long to taste and decide what
to buy that by the time we were ready to leave, the dog
wanted to come back in. So he went back on his hind legs,
grabbed the doorknob with his front paws, and in he came.

It takes a lot to make Norton feel insecure. But I could
tell from his expression that he was a bit awed by this feat.

"Hey," I told him, "practice makes perfect. It'll give you
something to work on while we're here."

"You're talking to your cat again," Janis told me.

Norton didn't tell either one of us anything. He just stuck his head down inside his shoulder bag and thought about what he'd seen and what he was going to do about it.

We loaded our wine into the back of the car—there was now barely room to even put gas in—found the big high-way, the *péage,* on our map, and, satiated with history, beauty, spirits, and genius dogs, sped on down to our new home.

5
a cat in provence

The house was perfect. And so was our new hometown.

The photographs we'd seen, convincing as they'd been, hadn't done either of them justice. The house was indeed three hundred years old. It was tucked away in a tiny side street (since the whole town was basically one street long, it wasn't difficult for the side streets to be tiny), the facade for the front was a pinkish, rough stucco, and the back was all the original stone. Downstairs was a small living room (very comfortably furnished), an eat-in kitchen with a fireplace (and no pancake flipper), a small *toilette,* and a separate bathroom with a tub and shower. On the second floor (which, mysteriously, the French call the first floor) were three bedrooms—one quite large, two smaller ones which formed a kind of mini-suite—another *toilette,* and another bathroom with tub. On the third floor (which the French call the second floor—if you think *you're* confused, try having a conversation with a French person about finding

something on one of these floors!) was a large, sprawling
office, sparsely furnished with a few chairs and a long, glass
desk, and then another bedroom, large with its own sink
tucked off to the side. There were also closets and cupboards everywhere you looked, all of which were filled with
Provençalian napkins and tablecloths and linens and towels,
as well as china and such essentials as an iron, a vacuum
cleaner, and lightbulbs. The furniture was old and comfortable and inviting; the kitchen was splendidly equipped. Best
of all, for my taste, was the sprawling *cave* underneath the
house. Using an old turnkey to open the thick wooden door
from the street, you then stepped into a stone dungeon. In
addition to such modern essentials as a washer/dryer and
a boiler, the *cave* was the place to stack the winter's supply
of wood and preserved jellies and jams. It also had a wine
cellar, protected by an iron gate, which needed another old
turnkey in order to pass through. Every time I went into the
wine cellar, I was positive some forty-pound guy with long
white hair was going to spring out at me and beg me to put
in a kind word with the captain of the king's guard.

All in all, this house was made for me.

More important, Norton took to it immediately.

Before we did anything else, I showed him the plump
couch and two easy chairs in the living room, explaining to
him that this was not our furniture and that he was not
allowed to scratch it. Ever. Janis, as usual, thought that I'd
lost my mind and that these complicated instructions probably would not penetrate the mind of a cat, but I do have to
say—and feel free to call our landlady anytime to verify
this—at the end of our year there, not a chair or a couch in
that house had so much as one scratch on it.

As soon as the rules were laid down, Norton went exploring. He sniffed around the living room and immediately

discovered his favorite exit from the house. The old-fashioned windows that swung open, looked over the backyard—and the entire Lubéron valley as well. A roof extended from right below the window, which functioned as an overhang for a patio. Norton immediately hopped up onto the window ledge, looked plaintively back in my direction until I figured out how to swing the window open (something I learned to do smoothly just about the time our year was up), then he hopped out onto the roof, stretched leisurely, lay down directly in the middle of a ray of sun, and began his life as a Provençal cat. All he needed was a beret and a baguette and I guarantee people would have come up to him and started to ask him what life was like in the *résistance.*

Another window swung open over the kitchen table, and Norton liked hopping out that one, too. He was also happy with the placement of his litter box, on the stone floor right by the back door. It became fairly standard procedure, during our time there, for Norton to pay a visit to his litter box, then immediately stand by the back door, waiting to be let out. Once out, he'd jump up onto the stone wall that ran up alongside the back steps to the house, assume a sphinxlike position, and spend as much time there as direct sunlight allowed.

The garden was a cat's delight (as well as Janis's greatest pleasure, since there is nothing that gives her as much pure joy as sticking her hands in dirt and either planting a beloved perennial or ripping out some dreaded weed). Our Provençal garden was roughly the size of a football field, divided up into four distinct square levels and sections, each square separated by an ancient stone wall. Directly out the back door, the first square had an enormous spruce tree in the middle of it, and next to that, a small fig tree. Around the perimiters were roses, pansies, tulips, wisteria, and lots and lots of herbs—including huge hedges of rosemary. Up against the house, an extension, really, of this part of the garden, was a stone patio, set up with several chairs and a small dining table. The weather was so beautiful that we ate outside almost every day until mid-December.

If you made a right turn out the back door, took ten paces, and then went down a couple of stone steps, you'd reach the second square of the garden. This one was dominated by a large lavender garden; the well-defined rectangle of lavender was probably twelve feet wide and fifteen feet long. Past the lavender, and running along the boundary of the property, was another patio, also set up with a small table and chairs. Built into the wall there was a stone barbecue, complete with grill.

Facing straight ahead, still standing on the right side of the yard, you could go down a couple of stone steps to the third quarter of the garden. This one was dominated by a luscious cherry tree and a round stone table, the perfect place to sit and sip a late-afternoon *kir*.

To the left, and down six or seven more steps, was the last part of the garden, this one fairly sparse. An olive tree sat toward the right of the space, as did a bay laurel tree, and the left boundary was lined with raspberry bushes (we were eating ripe, delicious raspberries for breakfast until the first week in December).

Norton spent hours and hours exploring every nook and cranny of this garden. He loved it out there. For one thing, there were no mean mockingbirds to torment him, as there were in Sag Harbor, only a bunch of fairly pleasant black and white magpies. Plus, I'm sure the mice were particularly delicious, since they had been fattened up on camembert and roquefort since birth.

As much as we adored the house—and we gradually added our personal touches to it: the occasional quilt here, a piece of rough hewn pottery there—the town in which we now resided was even more special.

Goult truly is a village touched by magic. It is as lovely as any of the small towns in the entire region yet has escaped any trappings of tourism, managing to remain completely unspoiled. It's small, approximately eleven hundred people, has a thousand-year-old castle, and is nicknamed "Le Village Caché" ("the hidden village") according to local legend because it's tucked away on top of a hill and seems to disappear, à la Brigadoon, when one is trying to spot it from the road down below. Up until the spring of '92, there was only one restaurant in town; now there are two. Up until that same time, there was one *épicerie* in town; now there are two. There have always been two butchers, though I can't fathom how a town of a eleven hundred people supports two butchers, especially since—and this could only be in France—they are right next door to each other, keep the exact same hours, and are closed the exact same day of the week.

We—the three of us, with Norton lagging behind and periodically disappearing into strange alleys and *caves,* including someone's garage, which turned out to have once been the town's ancient olive oil mill—toured the town and oriented ourselves, once we explored the various rooms and gardens of the house. Satisfied that we'd done well— having no idea yet quite *how* well we'd done—we returned to the house to begin the process of making it our home. The first step was to unpack the various boxes we'd sent on ahead (yes, yes, we had even *more* stuff than the millions of pounds we lugged in our suitcases). There was only one problem: There *were* no boxes.

This brings us to an important rule of thumb that one must understand before ever moving to France: When it comes to anything involving rules, regulations, and laws, absolutely nothing in the country makes any sense whatsoever.

A case in point:

Since I was neither retired nor wealthy, and since my cat was expecting to be kept in the style to which he'd become accustomed, I had to do some work while we were in France. As this is the twentieth century, I needed a computer, a fax machine, and a telephone answering machine to do that work. And thus the nightmare began.

My first mistake was shipping those key items over instead of packing them away and carrying them (this was important because in all the trips we made in and out of the Marseille airport, we never even *saw* a customs official, much less one who would rummage through a suitcase). My second mistake was being honest. On the UPS form, right below the line where they promise you'll receive your goods in two days, is a blank space where you're supposed to list exactly what it is you're shipping. On my form, kook that I was, I put exactly that: a fax machine, a laptop computer, a telephone answering machine, three electrical transformers (which weigh twenty pounds apiece, cost eighty dollars apiece, and are an absolute necessity for any American spending time in France), and some sweaters (which, along with bubble wrap, were used to cushion all the machinery so they wouldn't be smashed into little bits). UPS couldn't have been nicer or more efficient and they weren't even that expensive. All my stuff even arrived in Paris exactly on time. And when it arrived, I got a call from someone named Monsieur Kebé at French Customs. We had a very pleasant chat—although Monsieur Kebé spoke no English and, at this point, my French sounded a lot like Inspector Clouseau; I was basically speaking English with a French accent and hoping that would pass—until I was told that it was impossible to allow my cartons into the country. It seems that the French phone company, which is government-owned, has a monopoly on phone machines *(répondeurs)* and fax machines. So no such machines are allowed to be brought in. Ever. Never.

I was told that no amount of money, no amount of pleading, no amount of *anything* would ever convince them to let me bring these machines into France. It was impossible. Out of the question. End of story. *Tout est dit!*

I did some checking. There really did seem to be a law against bringing in phone machines. The government made everyone buy only French phone equipment. As near as I could tell, however, there were no exact laws against bringing in computers—they're not owned by the phone company, thank god!—but it seems the French just don't really *like* it when one is brought in. They prefer you buy one of their own *ordinateurs.* As far as the sweaters were concerned, they were a little concerned that I'd be opening a sweater store, which would be illegal for an American, so they thought they'd keep those, too.

I'll skip most of the unpleasantries. Like anything else in France, what was needed most here was neither money to bribe nor logic to convince. What was needed was patience. And a French friend named Nicholas who lived in Paris and went to see Monsieur Kebé in person. After three days of conversation, Nicholas called me to say that he explained to Monsieur Kebé that I was a writer and a publisher and that these machines were not to be sold in France but were the tools of my trade. Ah! Although it was still out of the question—absolutely and finally—Monsieur K wanted me to fax him my passport, a letter from my French publisher, and a copy of the jacket of my latest book. I was happy to do that, I explained—except that Monsieur Kebé had my fax machine. That was why we were having this conversation in the first place!

They acknowledged a certain logic on my part, but nonetheless they wanted what they wanted. I found a public fax in the nearby town of Murs and was able to send them what they'd asked for. It only took me six hours, which means I could have taken the TGV up to Paris, dropped the material off, and trained it on back home in the same amount of time it took me to fax something. The reason it took so much time was also fairly typical Provence (and fairly typical me). Janis decided to stay home to begin work in the garden. So Norton and I got in our car and went exploring. First we went to the town of Apt, the largest nearby town. After asking in the bookstore, a café, and a pottery store, I found out that there was no public fax in Apt. The nearest one was in Murs, a town of perhaps seven hundred people. No problem. We headed off to Murs and got to the *mairie,* the town hall, just a few minutes after noon. Which was a few minutes too late because the *mairie* was closed until three. No problem. I was in France; I could adapt to a different speed and lifestyle. I'd simply go to a café in Murs, have a little wine, read a little bit, pet my cat, and wait for three o'clock to arrive. Except that Murs didn't *have* a café. It was too small. So Norton and I drove back to Apt, where we found a café and a carafe of chilled rosé wine. Two hours later, it was back to Murs. But there was some sort of emergency and the *mairie* still wasn't open. (Later, I think I pieced together the emergency: The woman who worked at the *mairie* had a daughter who'd had a fight with her husband. I couldn't understand what they fought over, though I think it had something to do with a beef stew the daughter either had or hadn't made for that night's dinner.) At 3:45 the woman arrived and, apologetically, opened up the town hall. She reminded me of Jo Van Fleet in *Cool Hand Luke,* wheezing and creaking and coughing while she talked. We climbed the two flights of stairs together, then, exhausted, she had to rest for a few minutes before we could get on to business. I showed her my passport and the other things I'd brought and asked her if I could use the town's fax machine. *Of course,* she told me. *Absolutely no problem. Fine,* I told her. *Well, maybe there's* one *little problem,* she said. Then she told me she didn't know how to work the fax machine. No one had ever asked to use it before. So we had to wait for her coworker, a man of sixty years or so, to come huffing and puffing up the stairs, too, to try to send the material. He was the French William Demarest, grumpy, mumbling constantly, very concerned about everything, and extremely tan and leathery.

An hour later, we'd all basically figured the sucker out. Sure enough, when I tried faxing everything through, it worked. (Although when the first sheet of paper passed through, both William Demarest and Jo Van Fleet did double takes. "What eez zat noise?" she asked. "I think it's the fax being transmitted," I told her. She looked at him for confirmation and he just shrugged; now that it was working, he'd washed his hands of the whole matter.)

I then asked how much I owed—and this was a major stumper. She had no idea, so she paced for a while, pursed her lips in that French way, shook her head, and muttered to herself. She tried asking Bill Demarest, but he could only make puffing noises with his mouth and slowly shake his head back and forth. I just let them talk and pace and puff, and at some point they settled on twenty francs, about four dollars.

On Day 5 of the Fax/Computer Hostage Situation, customs told me I should forget about what they'd said earlier: I could have all my things after all—for a mere fifteen hundred dollars in import tax. Outraged, I told them to ship it all back to America. I'd rather buy new equipment, I said. (A mistake: A French phone machine, even a crummy one, costs four hundred dollars. A fax machine goes for about fifteen hundred. Don't even *think* about buying a computer there. Anything electric costs two to three times as much as it costs in the USA.) Luckily, however, they paid no attention to me. French people hardly ever pay attention to anything stupid we foreigners say.

Day 10: They asked me to send them a copy of *The Cat Who Went to Paris.*

Day 14: Monsieur Kebé liked the book. I decided he's more suited to be a literary critic for *The New York Times* than a French Customs official. He also says I can have my equipment for a mere thousand dollars. I get angry but, keeping his superb literary taste in mind, I don't go berserk.

Day 17: My friend Nicholas calls me to say I'm getting everything—for free. No problem whatsoever; it'll all arrive within two days. He said the final conversation in the customs room between Monsieur Kebé and his superior went as follows:

"Hmmm, he really seems to be a writer."

"What should we do?"

"Hmmmm. More wine?"

"Thank you. Do you think he's importing these things to sell them here?"

"No, do you?"

"I don't know. I don't think he could get very much for those sweaters."

"Oh, let's send the stuff to him. It takes up a lot of room here."

"It certainly does. Okay, let's send it. Could I have a drop more of the white?"

〰

Once my home office was set up, I could relax, rather than spend most of the day pacing around the town of Goult muttering about the end of my career. This final settling in also meant that our family of three could develop a routine. (Although here are two hints to help you relax a bit more if you're American and you ever set up a home office in France. Hint #1: Bring a spare phone machine because you will definitely blow up the first one trying to figure out how to hook it up to the transformer without blowing it up on the different current. Hint #2: After you finish ripping your hair out of your head because you can't figure out how to plug an American phone into a French phone jack, go to a French hardware or electrical appliance store. They have special plugs that fit American phones—even though they're not supposed to, because, as we all remember, it's illegal to have an American phone. Don't ask questions, just get one.)

Our routine was a fairly relaxed one, since the purpose of this whole trip was to exchange our insanely hectic New York lifestyle for one that made some philosophical, psychological, and emotional sense (and, since we were in France, we figured we also had to eat and drink as much as we possibly could). I would get up, have my early-morning two-mile run through the vast expanse of vineyards, then, huffing and puffing on my way back up the hill to Goult, I'd stop off at the patisserie in Lumiere, the town closest to us, for a baguette or a couple of croissants. By the time I'd get to the house, Janis would have made coffee. We'd have our breakfast—bread, honey, jam, and coffee—together, on Elisabeth's china and in her giant, soup-sized bowls; sometimes Norton would join us, sometimes he'd already be perched on the roof or the wall outside. Then I'd go upstairs to work for the morning while Janis would garden or go off to a museum or just study her French. Come lunchtime, we'd rendezvous, deciding, depending on our mood, whether to have a luxurious and extravagant lunch, or a quick peasant lunch at a *routier* (truckstop) followed by a two- or three-hour session exploring the region. If I didn't have to work in the afternoon (I was busy working for Random House as well as writing a screenplay and a book; I know that doesn't sound like much of a vacation, but believe me, after running a company and producing a TV series and writing a book all at the same time, working two jobs on my own time was the equivalent of lying on the beach in the Caribbean), we could explore further. For dinner, we'd either hit a local restaurant or expand our culinary abilities (not to brag, but we both became fairly proficient in the kitchen while we were there) or, as our circle of friends expanded, hope that one of our new pals would invite us over for an *aïoli* or a *maigret de canard.*

Norton's routine became fairly standardized also, once we worked out his sleeping arrangements. For the first couple of weeks we were there, we had a tiny bed and he was too outraged at the lack of space to sleep with us. There was barely room for the two humans to get through the night without tumbling onto the floor, though of course this didn't stop me from trying to squeeze Norton in. But he would have none of it. Needless to say, this didn't sit well with me; I do not sleep well unless my cat is within hugging distance at almost all times. So I was delighted when our landlady agreed to buy the house a new and much larger bed, although, like everything else, having a bed delivered in France is not like having a bed delivered anywhere else. More than anything in the world, French people love to talk. It doesn't matter if the tone is argumentative, questioning, sympathetic, informational, or philosophical, as long as talk is involved. So the first thing was that the guys from the furniture store came over to take a look at the house—and talk about it. They examined the front door to make sure the bed would fit. That was good for a five-minute chat. Then they examined the hallway. That seemed worth talking about for ten minutes or so. They examined the curved stone stairway that led up to our bedroom. That was a particularly interesting topic of conversation. How old was the stairway? Was it original? How many steps were there? How steep was it? Did I ever slip and fall down it in the middle of the night?

They managed to examine the bedroom—as well as the three other bedrooms in the house, just in case the bed wouldn't fit in the room for which it was intended. Then they discussed the door and the hallway and the various bedrooms some more. After forty-five minutes of this, I suggested that perhaps it might work best if they actually measured the doorways and the width of the stairs. Yes, they agreed. That was a very good idea. Did I happen to have a tape measure? I did happen to have one, and after another forty-five minutes during which we discussed the furniture in the house, the weather, the advantages and disadvantages of Goult, a date on which they could deliver the bed, and, finally, drank a couple of cups of coffee, they left. A week later, when the bed came, the problem with

Norton was solved. He had enough room to be comfortable and went right back to his usual spot of sleeping near
my neck and chest.

The first night of the new bed, we went to the local
restaurant in Goult, Le Tunneau, owned by a charming guy
and good chef, Patrick, to celebrate. It was Norton's first
time at Le Tunneau and he was served a little duck by way
of introduction. He was accepted as just another customer.
There was no fuss whatsoever, even from the dog dining
there that night. During the course of the meal, Norton
wandered a little bit (the restaurant is a converted *cave,* so
there were plenty of interesting sniffing and scratching
places). Every so often, he would hop back up on his seat
and help himself to a taste of my rabbit or Janis's chicken.
After dinner, stuffed and quite content, the three of us
headed home and went to sleep. Janis woke up in the middle of the night to the following picture: I was sound asleep
on the left side of the bed; she was lying on the right side.
Stretched out exactly in the middle, head on both of our
pillows, body under the blanket, was our Scottish Fold,
sound asleep yet purring so loudly he'd woken her up.

Once the sleep routine was settled, Norton's day was not
so different from our own. After a fine French breakfast
(canned rabbit was the clear winner as far as he was concerned), he would sun himself outside in one of his three
or four favorite spots. He would, as often as not, come out
to lunch with us and explore whenever it was appropriate.
Depending on how hard we'd judged his day, he'd either
dine out with us or stay home like a normal cat, content to
eat more canned rabbit and then fall asleep.

Norton had never been a particularly social animal, not
when it came to other four-legged creatures. He was not
around a lot of cats in New York (he'd been in one fight—

recounted in extraordinary dramatic detail in the *very* un-
derrated yet moving and puckish *The Cat Who Went to
Paris*—which did not end happily or with much of Norton's
dignity remaining) and his exposure to dogs, while harm-
less and uneventful, had also been infrequent. That all
changed in Provence.

At my last count, there were forty-two million cats in
Goult, give or take a million. They were all over the place,
everywhere and anywhere you turned. None of them, it
seemed, had a home, although every person in town knew
every one of the cats, usually by name. Our landlady, Elisabeth, was a longtime cat lover and, even though she didn't
have any of her own, she used to leave food out for *tous les
chats Goultois.* Which meant that we usually had several cats
strolling the property in search of nourishment.

I don't know whether it was the fact that Norton felt, as
an expatriot cat, that he was intruding on the Goult cats'
turf, but he was far friendlier and more relaxed around
these fellows than he ever was with the felines in Sag Harbor or Fire Island. There was the occasional hiss and unmistakable cat-fight screech, and every so often he'd try to act
like a tough guy (usually when he was safely inside and
knew all doors and windows to the garden were closed),
but on the whole, Norton seemed to accept the French *que
será, será* way of life and actually made a few pals.

One of his closer friends was a solid black cat, whose
name we learned was Othello. We never learned who
Othello's owner was, but Othello's demeanor was befitting
of his regal name; he used to preen all around the town,
though his special spot was a bench that was placed in a
small grass triangle—a *very* tiny public park—from which he
liked to survey the townspeople's comings and goings.

I don't think Norton and Othello used to go to soccer

matches together or exchange Christmas presents, but there was a certain amount of male bonding that went on. I do know that one day, as I was strolling to one of the village butchers, I did see Norton and Othello together sitting outside the café. Don't worry: They weren't being served. At least, not when I passed by.

Probably the funniest animal in town was a bulldog named Archie (pronounced Ar-*shee*). Archie was as solid as bulldogs usually are and he was a dead ringer for the older J. Edgar Hoover, except I never saw Archie wearing a dress. Archie's owner was a young woman who would often walk him through town on a leash, but just as often, we'd find Archie hanging out around our front door, leashless and ownerless. Everyone in town knew Archie (I think he must have, at one point or another, drooled several kilos of saliva on every person in Goult), but he handled his celebrity status quite well. He was always friendly, to humans and to Scottish Fold cats. After several weeks of eyeing each other warily, Norton and Archie achieved a certain comfort level. When in each other's presence, Archie would do his best not to snort and breathe so heavily that he scared Norton, and Norton eventually got to the point where he would stroll within inches of the bulldog without having to sprint, hiss, or make all his fur stand up on end.

I know everyone likes a happy ending, but I'm sorry to say that Norton never did come to grips with those little, friendly birds who were in the outdoor cage a couple of blocks from our house. After his wimpy run-in with them, which I mentioned earlier, he stayed as far away from that part of town as he possibly could.

Norton got to be pals—or at least nodding acquaintances—with several animals outside of Goult, too.

One of our favorite restaurants, a breathtakingly charming place up in the mountains, the Auberge de la Loube, in the town of Buoux, was wonderful not only because of the owners/chefs but because of the cats and dogs who populated the place.

The restaurant is a four-hundred-year-old stone farmhouse, quite small, maybe twelve tables, dominated by an enormous fireplace and decorated with all sorts of horse accoutrements—everything from photos to bridles to reins to saddles. The owner, Maurice, is a terrific guy, quite friendly and elegant, a little bemused at how successful his country inn has become since Peter Mayle rhapsodized about him in *A Year in Provence.* (The reason there's so much horse memorabilia around is that Maurice restores antique carriages—as in horse and carriages. Some of them are nineteenth-century American carriages, most are French, all are exquisite. When the weather's nice, it's possible to arrange for a carriage ride in the mountains and a picnic lunch or dinner. One other thing about the Auberge de la Loube: For months, we assumed "Loube" was some variation on the Lubéron valley and mountain range, of which Buoux is a part. However, we asked Maurice one night and he explained to us that—and remember, I warned you about this earlier—*loube* is, in fact, Provençal for "wolf.") His wife, whom we knew only as Madame Maurice, is equally terrific, and she took particular pleasure in Norton's visits to the Auberge.

Maurice and his wife have three dogs, a gorgeous Irish setter, a black lab, and some kind of very friendly mutt, as well as a big, fat, easygoing orange cat. The dogs roam the two rooms of the restaurant, camping under the table of whoever looks most likely to drop food on the floor, either unintentionally or out of pity for the tortured, starving look the dogs can assume at a moment's notice. All three of the canines also spend a lot of time burrowed in the two hollows that are dug into the stone underneath the huge hearth. The cat, naturally, is much more dignified. He strolls around the restaurant, quite haughtily, until he finds a willing sucker, then he jumps up into his or her lap and settles in for the night (or until Madame Maurice spots him and swats him away, yelling at him to leave the customers alone). The dogs and cat get along famously, and they all switch back and forth effortlessly from being outdoor to indoor animals. There is a famous local story about the Irish setter, who tends to roam more than the others. He was spotted one day in the town of Apt, which is a good seven or eight miles away from the Auberge. When he was recognized, as he was walking confidently through the town, some concerned friend convinced him to hop into his truck and brought him back to the Auberge, where they suspect he makes such lengthy sojourns on a regular basis.

The first time we brought Norton up to meet the gang at the Auberge, he was greeted warmly by all concerned and fit in as if he'd been born to the French mountain life. He had quite a few dinners up there, and humans, dogs, and cat were always glad to see him. When the restaurant wasn't crowded, he'd be allowed his own chair. When it was crowded—which was more often than not—he'd either sit on my lap or find a nice spot on the table in which to settle in. If we got a window seat, he was also more than happy to dine in comfort on the stone window ledge.

The food at Auberge de la Loube is a cat's delight, as well as the delight of any sane person, because it's delicious and completely satisfying. They also do something that's common in France, which is take the pressure off the diner as far as having to choose is concerned; basically, they order for you. When you sit down at Auberge de la Loube, an enormous tray of Provençal appetizers is placed before you. On the tray are small dishes, filled with local delicacies. A typical sampling will include onion marmalade, tiny quail's eggs, the best *tapenade* ever made, candied carrots, rabbit pâté, a very garlicy yogurt, *anchois* and pickled cucumbers. All to be eaten with a basketful of French bread, which is sliced before your eyes with an antique bread cutter which resembles nothing so much as the guillotine that sliced off the head of Marie Antoinette and probably a whole bunch of other cake-eaters.

Once sated, you're left only with having to make choices from the good, inexpensive, and mostly local wine list and four or five options for a main course. In the fall and winter, the possibilities range from *sanglier,* which is wild boar (often served in a stew, with a thick, very dark sauce, called a *civet*), rabbit (sometimes served in the same kind of stew, sometimes served roasted), stuffed or roast veal, and occasionally a fish, usually salmon or *lotte.* In the spring and summer, the choices are usually the same base foods, although prepared in a somewhat lighter fashion. Oddly enough, restaurants in Provence rarely serve chicken, as that's perceived, historically, as poor people's food.

Perhaps it has occurred to you already, but when one lives in the south of France, one becomes totally obsessed with food. We would get calls from friends back in America wondering whether we'd lost our minds because they'd just received a three-page letter from one of us which was about nothing but one luscious and delicious tomato we'd bought at the market. It reached the point where people were expecting daily faxes from us to find out what we'd eaten for dinner the night before.

It didn't take long for each of us—me, Janis, and Norton—to grab hold of this obsession and refuse to let go.

After we'd been there several months, we had the ultimate compliment paid to us by an elderly French woman, who prepared us dinner one night. As we were eating her succulent lamb, we were discussing other great meals we'd had since we'd been in Europe. We're munching on her roast potatoes talking about a pasta dish we'd eaten in Tuscany; we're scarfing down her white beans in *vinaigre* while extolling the virtues of a bouillabaise we'd had in Marseille; we're moaning over her *tarte aux pommes* but manage to get in a few highly charged words about a raspberry beignet we'd stumbled upon at an open-air market. Finally she says, in a throaty voice with just a touch of a French accent, "Congratulations. You are now truly French. To eat a fine meal and do nothing but talk about other foods means you're now one of us."

Hey, when in Rome (or Provence), you know what I mean?

Our days began to revolve around food.

One of the great thrills of living there is to shop at the open-air markets, which move from town to town, depending on the day of the week. When we finally figured out the schedule, we began to move along with them. Tuesday was a small market in the village of Gordes. Saturday was Apt. Both towns were convenient to Goult, so we became Tuesday and Saturday regulars. The biggest and most spectacular market was on Sunday, in the town of L'isle-sur-la-Sorgue. There the appeal was not just food but miles of stalls filled with splendid antiques. Going to market on Sunday became, to me, the equivalent of a five-year-old kid going to Disneyland.

L'isle-sur-la-Sorgue is not a large town—perhaps three thousand people—but on Sunday mornings it quadruples in size. The village itself is quite beautiful. It's flat, unlike most of the towns around it, which are perched on hilltops, and has winding cobblestone streets lurching in every direction. It's also built on a series of canals, which surround the town and, thanks to the clear, rushing water and the waterwheels and the wooden bridges, give it much of its atmosphere. During the week (except Thursday, when there's a mini-version of the big market), the place is subdued, quiet, and charming. But on Sundays, from seven in the morning until one o'clock in the afternoon, it's a madhouse. Every inch of the cobblestone streets is packed with vendors and shoppers. The vendors have staked out their particular territories over a period of years (in some cases, I'm fairly sure that certain families have been selling their wine or their potatoes in the same spot for about three *hundred* years or so); the shoppers mill aimlessly until they see what they want or, especially as the seasons get warmer and more tourists show up, shove their way through the crowds to try to get the best of everything. It's so European it can make you cry with pleasure, especially when the local organ grinder, who happens to look like a young Maurice Chevalier, strolls through the crowded market in feathered cap and glowing cape belting out his romantic ballads.

Norton quite liked being lugged through the L'isle market in his shoulder bag. If he played his cards right, which he usually did, he could come away with little bits of everything from homemade sausage to strong, smelly goat cheese to chocolate tarts. Janis and I also usually played our cards right. It didn't take us long to find our favorite vendors and become regular buyers (many of the same vendors also went to the Gordes and the Apt markets, so we'd see them two or three times a week). One of our favorites was a small, wonderfully nice and cheery man who made mouthwatering tarts and sold them from his truck, with the aid of

his eight-year-old daughter. He baked in the town of Ve-
nasque, about forty-five minutes away, via a curving, mountain road, and then carried his scrumptious works of art to
the marketplaces. His artichoke tart was like nectar of the
gods, as was his *poireaux* (leeks) creation, but his shallot tart
was his masterpiece, as delicious as anything I've ever tasted
that wasn't covered with chocolate. And while we're on the
subject, he happened to make a chocolate and caramel tart
that, in my humble opinion, belongs in the Louvre. Luckily
for everyone's cholesterol count, we figured there couldn't
possibly be more than seven or eight pounds of butter in it.

   In addition to our tart guy (that's the way we started
thinking of him: Our Tart Guy), there was a Cambodian
man who made the most delicious *poulet rôti* that was ever
*rôti*ed. He was a lawyer in Cambodia but wasn't allowed to
take the French bar (or whatever the equivalent of the bar
is in France) and so made perfect roast chickens instead.
There was a young Algerian who aggressively sold vats of
incredible *tapenade* and *anchois* (crushed olive paste and
crushed anchovies). There was also an old, cronelike
woman who was missing at least two-thirds of her teeth and
who sold goat cheese so strong you could barely stand up
after a small taste. She sold them in little heart-shaped
cheeses, each one flavored with rosemary or garlic or shal-
lots or—and this one I'm guessing on but I think I'm
close—really old socks. We bought cheese from her every
week and her products became a benchmark for any and all
of our visitors. It was simple: Someone would arrive from
New York, exhausted from the long flight and drive from
Marseille. We'd sit him, her, or them down, set up a glass
of wine from a nearby *cave,* and place a plate of the crone's
goat cheese before them. If they tasted it, and then hungrily
dug in for more, appreciating the earthiness and power, we

knew we were in for a good visit. If, on the other hand, the guest or guests got a slice of the garlic cheese halfway down their throat, then started gasping and calling either for water or a gun with which to shoot themselves, we knew that we'd have trouble sharing our Provençal tastes and pleasures.

Norton, in the meantime, was developing his own very particular tastes and pleasures when it came to French food.

With all our travels, prior to and including this year abroad, Norton seemed to prefer French cat food to any other. His favorites were Whiskas, Gourmet, and the French Friskies. Gourmet was the cheaper brand, more of a peasant cat food, but at times clearly satisfying to the cat palate. The nice thing about Gourmet was that they sold it in a handy three-pack *(le menu 3 étoiles; 3 boîtes de 195 grams)*. They had many different flavors, most of which pleased my cat. In the category of *Les Pavés Mignons,* they had your basic *Délice de Viandes,* your fresh *Au Saumon,* and the ever-popular *Au Foie et Volaille.* In the category of Best Supporting *Terrine,* they had an overload of delicacies: *Au Lapin et Foie* (definitely in Norton's top three); *L'Agneau et Volaille* (yummmmm), *Au Foie et Veau, Délice de Colin, Aux Trois Volailles, Au Foie et Volaille* (a certain pattern does seem to be emerging, though I'm not sure if Norton ever noticed that there were the same basic ingredients, cleverly mixed together in as many different combinations as those Gourmet folks could think up), *Au Boeuf et Rognons* (also quite a favorite), *Panache de Poissons* (not a chance; Norton never succumbed to this one), *Au Gibier* (Norton was quite fond of this can; Janis would leave the room as soon as it was opened—a *boîte* filled with all sort of giblets is not her idea of culinary heaven), *Au Poulet et Rognons* (boring but a solid choice), *Au Lapin et Foie* (now you're talking!), and just before we left, Gourmet introduced the *nouveau* flavor of the year, *Au Rognons et Volaille* (bravo!). As if this weren't enough, they also had a category called *La Mousse*, which only had one flavor, but was nothing to sneer at, *Au Rognons et Volaille.*

Although Gourmet was not, in fact, the crème de la crème of French cat foods, I had a soft spot for them because of the Club Gourmet one could join. On specially marked cans of their food was an announcement: *Vous qui êtes passionnés de chats, rejoignez vite le CLUB GOURMET, un club spécialement crée pour vous: vous bénéficierez des privilèges d'un club prestigieux et des conseils châteaux de CATY.* Translated as best as I can manage, this means: You who are passionate about cats, quickly sign up for the Gourmet Club, a special club created for you: you benefit from the privileges of a prestigious club and the counsel of the cat castle.

Friskies wasn't bad, if you go by Norton's appetite, and they had the advantage of being slightly healthier. Well, okay, I wouldn't call it health food, but at least with their *Au Foie et Volaille,* they added *petits légumes.* After Norton munched on these, I didn't feel so bad about giving him a lick of my dessert.

Whoever was the creative force in the Whiskas kitchen was a fine *chef de cuisine,* also. Norton's favorite *boîte* on their list was the clever combo of *Au Lapin et à la Dinde* (rabbit and turkey; you've got to admit it sounds good). Whiskas also was thoughtful enough to tell you a little bit about their food on the back of each box top:

● *WHISKAS a préparé pour votre chat les "Petits Régals":*
● *des recettes richement elaborées avec de delicieux petits morceaux et une odeur appétissante*

- *une présentation soignée, en portion repas, facile à utiliser, avec un couvercle refermable*
- *Pour varier les plaisirs de votre chat, les "Petits Régals" vous proposent trois variétés raffinées: Au Bouef et aux Rognons, A la Volaille et au Foie, Au Lapin et à la Dinde.*

Words to bring comfort to any cat and cat owner:

- *WHISKAS has prepared for your cat the Little Meals:*
- *recipes richly elaborated with delicious little morsels and an appetizing odor*
- *a careful presentation, in meal-sized portions, easy to use with a recloseable top*
- *To vary the pleasures of your cat, the "Petits Régals" proposes to you three refined varieties: Beef and Kidney, Fowl and Liver, Rabbit and Turkey.*

Bon appétit.

~~~

At the beginning, it all seemed exotic and quaint and a little eccentric. The more time we spent there, however, the saner life in Provence became. What was happening, without our realizing it, was that we were becoming part of the community.

Though we'd only been gone a few months, America was receding into the distance. We didn't have a television in Goult—a deliberate choice, mostly Janis's I have to say, but a very wise one—which cut us off from a lot of our own culture. Our French, at this stage, was barely serviceable, but almost no one we were spending time with spoke any English, so we quickly got out of the habit of speaking the only language we could communicate with.

That left us in a strange though not unpleasant kind of limbo.

There were all sorts of things we had not anticipated before we moved from one country to another. Or if we had anticipated them, they didn't turn out quite the way we'd expected.

We knew we'd have to do something about money, which meant we'd have to figure out what to do about using a French bank. Cleverly (I thought), before we left New York, I'd spoken to someone at Crédit Lyonnais, the second largest bank in France. The person in their New York office told me that they did indeed have a branch fairly near Goult, in the town of Cavaillon.

Perfect.

After our arrival and two or three days of doing nothing but soaking in atmosphere, appreciating the local beauty, and screaming at the customs officials, we decided we had to do something practical, so we drove into Cavaillon and found Crédit Lyonnais.

It was easy. The very first street we turned down, once we hit town, had a bank on it with a big LYONNAISE sign. We parked in front of the bank and went inside. (Which was not very easy; the French have a strange system where you have to punch a buzzer to get in one door, then you're trapped in a tiny room before you can open the other door. The problem is in trying to open the second door, which can't be done until the first door is completely shut. Janis, Norton, and I spent a good ten minutes trapped in between doors, until some kindly soul in the bank finally started waving his hands and pointing and shouting and showed us how to get through.) Once inside, we were golden. The bank was very small, almost sleepy compared to most banks. In very simple French, I asked if anyone spoke English.

They told me that the manager, Monsieur Gilbert Rebattu, spoke a little English, and moments later we were ushered into Monsieur Rebattu's office.

When they say "a little English" in Provence, they mean a *little* English. Monsieur Rebattu, a slight man with a dark mustache and a somewhat nervous but absolutely charming manner, knew how to say "hello" and "good-bye" and practically nothing else in between. He was, however, extraordinarily nice and helpful, and spent almost an hour with us, helping us fill out the forms. (Normally, this would have been a five-minute meeting. But between my French and Monsieur Rebattu's English, we needed the hour.) He told us what type of banking would be best for us, he explained how we should write checks, he even explained the French banking system, which makes a lot more sense than the American system. In France, no one asks for I.D. when you write out a check. You don't have to show a driver's license or a credit card; it's exactly the same as handing over cash. Monsieur Rebattu explained that that was because people in France don't bounce checks. There is no system of credit there (one of the reasons that the country's not in debt for hundreds of billions of dollars, unlike other countries we might name). When a French person pays with a Visa card, that money is taken right out of his or her bank account. If a French person ever bounces a check, he loses all banking privileges for a year—which basically means he can't live. I think Monsieur Rebattu also said something about never again being able to drink wine or watch Jerry Lewis movies or eat *tarte tatin,* too, but, again, my French was still pretty rusty.

Once this was all explained to us, we put in enough money to ensure we'd never lose our banking privileges. We received our temporary checks right away—Monsieur

Rebattu had the good sense to ask if Norton would require his own checkbook; the answer was a definite no—and then we were all set. But as we thanked our new bank manager and stood up to leave, Monsieur Rebattu put his hand on my arm and said, in a very soft voice, "Excuse me, *monsieur*. But what is it that made you choose our bank?"

I explained that it was quite simple. We'd been told that Crédit Lyonnais was the most convenient place to bank because there were branches all over the country. We'd also been told that the Crédit Lyonnais in Cavaillon was the closest to our town. There was nothing more to it: the biggest, the best, the closest. *Voilà.*

Monsieur Rebattu nodded unhappily. The smile that had been on his face disappeared. He was not a physically imposing man to begin with and he seemed to shrink before our very eyes.

"Yes, I thought it was something like that," he sighed.

"Is there a problem?" I wanted to know. I didn't really want to know, but I sensed it was a question that had to be asked. I was right.

"This is *not* Crédit Lyonnais, *monsieur.*"

"It's not? But the sign out front . . ."

"This is Lyonnaise de Banque."

I looked at Janis. She looked at me. Norton refused to look at either one of us. "That's not the same thing?" I asked, trying my best not to look as miserable as I felt.

Monsieur Rebattu nodded knowingly and wistfully, then, looking much unhappier than I could possibly be, he shrugged and gently said, "It's not too late to change. I will understand."

By this time, Janis was practically in tears and half in love with Monsieur Rebattu for being so kind and thoughtful, so we both shook our heads—after a moment's hesitation—and boldly declared, "Absolutely not. Lyonnaise de Banque is the bank for us!"

They didn't bring out a band or have a parade but it was close. I don't know when they last had a new customer, but clearly this was an event of the first order for the gang at Lyonnaise de Banque. Monsieur Rebattu shook our hands (and petted Norton) and thanked us profusely. Then he proudly took us through the rest of the bank, which took all of fourteen seconds, introducing us to all the other employees, who looked at us as if they couldn't comprehend that we were actually putting money in their, shall we say, "modest" place of business.

It turned out to be a great move. (Except for the time our friend Norm came over from New York and wanted to change American dollars into francs. That really threw the entire bank for a loop. They didn't know the rate of exchange—I swear! I asked three times to make sure I could believe my ears—so they had to look it up in the paper. Then Norm watched in astonishment as they scurried around trying to find five hundred dollars. They looked in drawers, in cabinets, under stacks of paperwork. Finally, they scraped up enough francs and proudly turned them over.) For the entire time we were in France, whenever we went into our bank, Monsieur Rebattu would stride out of his office, smile broadly, pump our hands, ask about our health, and usually give us a calendar or a pen (if anyone needs six or seven Lyonnaise de Banque wall calendars, just give a holler). We got a lot of funny looks when we told people where we were banking, but other than that we never had a problem. In fact, I've never had better banking or more personalized service anywhere, proving Red Auerbach or Leo Durocher or Vince Lombardi or someone like that to be a genius when he said, "I'd rather be lucky than good."

One of our next points of business was to become fairly familiar with the local wine growers. After a few weeks, we stumbled into a vineyard, only fifteen minutes or so from our house, that sold a local Côte Ventoux. Monsieur Bonnelly et Fils. Monsieur Bonnelly was a man of eighty years or so. As we were tasting his delicious '86 red wine, we struck up a conversation.

"What do you do?" he wanted to know as he was petting Norton. When I told him I was a writer and had, in fact, written about the very cat he was stroking, he asked if I'd ever heard of a Monsieur Beckay. I shook my head and his eyes widened in shock. "Beckay?!" he bellowed. "You've never heard of Samuel Beckay?!!" I finally realized we were having a pronunciation problem. Samuel Beckett is who he was talking about, and when he calmed down I told him yes, indeed, I'd heard of Monsieur Beckett.

"He used to buy his wine here," Bonnelly told me. "Before the war. While he was working on *Waiting for Godot*. He lived in Roussillon and used to come in every Wednesday. He'd buy three bottles of red and flirt with my wife. She was much better looking back then."

Monsieur Bonnelly pulled out a tattered copy of *Attendent Godot*. Not only did Beckett buy his wine there, he wrote about it. In the middle of the French edition of the play, one of the tramps actually says, "Let's go to Bonnelly's for some wine."

Since Beckett is a god to me, in my opinion the greatest writer of the century and the author of the great English novel (a trilogy of novels, actually: *Malloy, Malone Dies,* and *The Unnameable*), this was fairly impressive. Not to mention inspiring. Sparked by the ghost of Godot, we bought several more bottles of wine from Monsieur Bonnelly than we'd originally intended. And as we were leaving, Monsieur Bonnelly called after us. "Perhaps in twenty years, I'll tell people that Monsieur Norton also bought wine from me."

Which is how this book almost came to be called *Meowing for Godot.*

Two of the more interesting local characters whom Norton won over were Gianni Ladu and his wife, Chantal, Sardinian goatherders who ran a rustic *auberge* up in the mountains above Sivergues. Gianni was very much a Sarde, which meant he always had a three-day growth of beard and liked doing nothing so much as slicing open and skinning a goat right in front of you. That could be a little intimidating while trying to have a conversation, I have to admit, but Norton seemed to soften Gianni up a bit. He liked to roam about Gianni's property—not exactly mingling with the goats, but not really avoiding them either. Norton seemed fascinated by those animals' bleats and bla-aaa-aaas, and I got the distinct feeling he wouldn't have minded taking a day-long trek in the mountains with them. Gianni had seen many things in his day, but he'd never seen a cat in his restaurant, especially one who'd hang out with his herd. The restaurant was usually fully booked—they served their meals to a select few at long tables in an ancient room of stone and wood beams—but when I'd call to say we wanted to reserve a table, he'd say, "Is the cat coming?" If I said no, it was fifty-fifty at best that we'd get in. If I agreed to bring Norton, Gianni would usually say something along the lines of, "Okay. We're full—but for you and the cat we have room." We'd then get to sit up in the mountains and eat a whole roasted goat (Norton, for some reason, didn't mind that one of his pals was being consumed right before his very eyes), some of Chantal's homemade lasagna and their fresh goat cheese, and drink way too much of Gianni's homemade *eau de vie.* After a lot of goat and liquor, Gianni's thirteen-year-old son, David, would usually serenade the diners with some ear-splitting Hendrix on his electric guitar, which was a little unnerving for Norton. Other than that, it was a perfect place for a cat to feel as if he were very much the rustic, French mountain *chat.*

The only unpleasant thing that had to be dealt with quickly after we arrived in Provence was that Janis didn't know how to drive a stick shift. Before coming over, I'd assured her that it was no big deal and that I could teach her easily. She was a good driver, I was a good teacher, what could be easier? It turned out that climbing Mount Everest naked while surrounded by a swarm of killer bees would have been easier. A *lot* easier. There were a few elements of the equation that I hadn't counted on. First of all, it's never a good idea to teach one's mate how to drive. That's a lesson I should have known just from watching sitcoms all my life, but I chose to ignore it. The second warning sign I ignored was that I'm not the most patient person in the world. If I tell someone what to do, I expect them to do it perfectly. I'm aware that that's an unreasonable expectation, but that doesn't stop me from expecting it. The third thing that made our driving lesson difficult was that I'd never quite realized before that Janis was a total nut.

Norton and I took her out in our leased Citroën. Norton hopped into his usual spot, perched on the shelf of the rear windshield. He stretched out, expecting to whizz along to another great lunch spot. Instead, he got taken down to the soccer field below town, the only level place within thirty miles that wasn't a highway.

It had been a long time since I'd tried to teach someone how to shift and use a clutch, but I explained it plainly, simply, and calmly. After the explanation, Janis, who tends to be slightly negative in her approach to life, looked at me and said, "I will *never* be able to do this."

I took these words as a challenge and told her that within fifteen minutes she'd be speeding along the highway, confident as could be.

Two hours later, after lurching around the soccer field, nearly getting squashed by a truck at an intersection, and almost driving off a cliff, I would have told Janis that she was right, she'd never be able to drive a stick, except I couldn't tell her because we weren't speaking to each other.

Norton was not taking sides. Once, when she was trying to pull onto the highway and it looked as if there was a fifty-fifty chance we were going to die, Norton meowed a fairly firm meow. Janis turned and glowered at him, and he quickly decided that meowing was not the way to go. But by the third time I'd made her cry and said something along the lines of, "Even Norton would have learned to get up this hill by now!" Norton would have none of me either. Either I'd offended him by saying *even* he would have figured it out or else he was just fed up with all the lurching about and wanted to go someplace where there was peace and quiet.

The thing was, Janis *had* to learn how to drive. I couldn't be her chauffeur for the year and, despite my assertion, Norton was way too short to reach the car's pedals.

She came through, of course, with flying colors. Once we started speaking to each other again, I reassured her that no one could actually learn all this in fifteen minutes. It would take a few days, perhaps a week, but she would definitely learn. Janis is the type who doesn't like to learn: She likes to be perfect. Since learning, or at least the *process* of learning, is antithetical to short-term perfection, she tended to get rather cranky when doing things like stalling in the middle of a big intersection or coming to a stop at the top of the hill and then rolling half a mile backward before being able to get the car moving forward again. She had the same problem learning French. She didn't want to speak the language until she actually *knew* the language. This was not a very practical approach, not if she ever wanted to go anywhere or do anything. So she gritted her teeth and, not exactly happy but not completely miserable, learned how to drive a stick shift and how to speak French.

Another thing we never anticipated was the French mail system.

It can take two weeks for a letter or package to make its way from America to a small town in the south of France. One of the reasons, we eventually discovered, is because somewhere there is someone who has something to do with French mail delivery who is always on strike. After we'd been there a few weeks, we stopped getting mail. For three or four days straight we'd check the box at the back of the garden and *rien.* Zippo. Not even the *Herald Tribune.* We finally worked up the nerve to ask at the post office and they told us that the Avignon mailmen were on strike. Since Avignon was fifty kilometers away, you might ask yourself what that had to do with us. Well . . . we never quite got a satisfactory answer to that question. The nearest we could tell was (1) most mail had to go through the large Avignon post office before it was sent on to Goult's little, tiny post office and (2) because Avignon was more important than

Goult or any of its surrounding towns, the local Lubéron mailmen were being enlisted to deliver the Avignon mail.

That strike lasted two weeks. When it was over, we got our mail for three days in a row, then it stopped again. On the second day (of the second round) of no more mail, we went back to the post office to see what the story was. The story was that the Avignon mailmen had ended their strike in victory; they'd gotten raises and better benefits. Now the local Lubéron mailmen were striking because they were making less than the Avignon mailmen.

If the mailmen weren't striking, the truckers were striking, which meant no packages could be delivered. If the truckers weren't striking, the railroads were striking, which somehow still meant that no packages could be delivered. If the railroads weren't striking, then the farmers were protesting the horror that's known as EuroDisney and were blocking all the roads and railroads, so no packages could be delivered.

One day, after we'd been in Goult for several months, we noticed once again that the mail had stopped arriving. We trekked back to the post office (all of a two-block trek) to find out who was on strike. No strike, we were told. But our mailman had had an accident. He'd fallen off his scooter—a tiny motorbike, at least a foot too short for his long legs, with the world's loudest engine—and broken his collarbone.

"Oh, that's terrible," I sympathized. "Please send him my best. But what does that have to do with why we're not getting any mail?"

Which is when I realized that there was only one mailman for Goult. If he wasn't able to deliver mail, no one was. He was the only one who knew how to sort the letters, he was the only one who knew where everyone lived, and my guess is he was the only one available for the job who had a motor scooter.

It was two weeks before we got our mail again. And the mailman, a gangly, unhappy-looking man, looked even more solemn than usual as he chugged around town on his motorbike, his arm in an uncomfortable-looking sling.

Norton was, for a while, our only touch with regularity. He was awake and waiting by his food dish at the same time every morning, curled up in the same two or three spots every day, meowing hungrily for dinner at the same time every evening. Everything else in France seemed to us to operate on a whim.

One morning we woke up to find that someone had dumped approximately a ton of rocks in our backyard. This seemed quite mysterious to us, since we were positive we hadn't ordered a ton of rocks. We called our landlady, Elisabeth, in Paris, who was equally mystified. She said she'd get back to us. A week later, the mystery was solved. Several months before, she'd spoken to a *maçon* about rebuilding the stone wall at the back of her garden. She'd asked him to get back to her with a price. He never did. But he did wake up one day, remember that she'd wanted her wall fixed, so he thought he'd just get started. His start was to dump all the stones needed for the job in the yard and leave them there.

After Elisabeth figured out that he must be the culprit, she called him to say that we didn't appreciate the gesture. The next day, he came and gathered them all back up, I assume to dump in somebody else's yard.

Dumping clearly was a major activity in our new neighborhood (or *voisinage,* as I was now learning to call it).

As winter started to settle in, we realized we'd better

store up on our wood for the fireplace. We'd heard all sorts of horror stories of the Provençal wind and cold. When the *mistral* came whistling through the trees, word was that it gave new meaning to the words "when hell freezes over."

We followed a series of crude hand-made signs—WOOD FOR SALE: simple, straightforward, and effective advertising—that led us perhaps a mile away from Goult, to a small farmhouse. The owner shuffled out, smoking a cigarette, beret tipped at the jauntiest of angles over his head, and I couldn't help but notice a disturbing pattern: All small-town French men over the age of sixty-five reminded me of William Demarest.

It's worth bringing up here that there's such a thing as a Provençal accent. It is, in fact, so thick as to render normal French completely incomprehensible, until you get used to its twangs and blangs and various nasal inflections. A Provençal accent puts a "g" at the end of just about everything. The French word for tomorrow is *demain*. With a Provençal accent, it's *demaing*. The word for hand is *main*. With the southern accent, it becomes *maing*. By way of example, take a sentence in English: "When did the man ban guns, John?" An easy sentence, right? Well, pretend you're hearing it for the first time, and with the Provençal accent added to it. It becomes: "Wheng did the mang bang gungs, Jong?" It sounds more like Chinese than English. That's about what Provençalian sounded like to us when we first arrived: some strange tongue spoken only in places where you have to ask directions of Sherpas.

The man selling the wood had the thickest, most impenetrable accent I'd ever encountered. The only thing I was able to clearly understand was when he looked at Norton, who was busy poking around the man's garden, and said, *"Votre chat. Il est très sage."* Several French people made this comment about Norton when we were on our travels. Most Americans, when they meet the little guy, say, "Oh, he's so cute" or "Oh, he's so calm." I much prefer the French way and I think it's indicative of their true respect for cats as well as life: "Oh, he's so wise." *Il est très sage* indeed.

Aside from the flattery about Norton's sagaciousness, after half an hour of conversation this is what I'd learned about the winter wood situation: We either could or couldn't buy it from him. Either his son or his daughter would come visit us or we had to go visit them, although they seemed to live in Spain. If we could get wood at all, it would either come that night, the next week, or never. And it would either cost a million dollars or would be free. When we finally left, my head was spinning, but I was fairly sure I'd ordered a small amount of wood that would be reasonably inexpensive.

I was right about the inexpensive part; I was wrong about the small amount. Three days after our conversation, a dump truck backed up in front of our house, which was no mean feat in itself because the truck fit on our narrow street with perhaps half an inch to spare on each side. When it arrived, the son of the man I'd talked to pulled the lever inside the truck, the back began to rise, and in moments, enough wood to rebuild the Brazilian rain forests came tumbling out onto the street. It took perhaps three minutes for all the wood to empty out of the truck. It then took another two minutes for the truck to make its way back to the end of our street and hightail it out of there. And then it took six hours for me and Janis to carry it, stack it anywhere there was a spare inch—in the three outbuildings in the backyard, in the *cave,* in the kitchen, in the stone hallway by Norton's litter box—and then collapse in an exhausted heap on the floor.

In some odd way, we felt comfortable being in the midst

of such eccentricity. It made us feel a part of the town. And this feeling was magnified because we were accepted by the local Goultoise with surprising ease. We made friends with a French neighbor, who also became our French teacher. She in turn introduced us to another friend, who became our Goult version of Millie in "The Dick Van Dyke Show"—she would pop in at any hour of the day or night; we were free to do the same. She also spent a couple of hours a week teaching us French; we spent the same amount of time teaching her English. And from there, our circle of friends expanded until, by the time we left, we numbered as lifelong friends four French women, one Swedish woman, and two French guys (one of whom became my sports buddy; since I couldn't get my much needed football, basketball, or baseball fix, Norton and I would go to his house to watch the soccer matches. Olympic Marseille became, to me, nearly what the '86 Mets had once been).

We also fell into the extraordinarily interesting expatriate community that populated the Lubéron. Most were Brits, a few were American. Expatriates are usually running away from something. Some from work. Some from politics. Some from relationships. Almost all, in one way or another, are running away from themselves and feel that a new life in a new place, particularly a place like Provence, will help them re-create themselves. Sometimes they like to start from scratch, sometimes just partial replacements are needed.

Almost every expatriate we met had some sort of secret. There were messy divorces in their pasts. Some had left husbands for younger men. Some had left *wives* for younger men. There were vaguely sinister stories: violent ends to affairs; suicide attempts; the mysterious loss of millions of dollars. Everyone we became friends with had a vague shadow hanging over them—and that made them all the more interesting. It made them appealing. Couple that with the fact that they'd all made the same choice we'd made—to leave one life behind and resettle in a French paradise—and it created an instant bond, one not felt to this extent, from my end, since I'd been given a certain six-week-old Scottish Fold kitten.

We went with these people to the opera house in Avignon to see Mozart concerts and we practiced our French reading from the *Provençal,* the local newspaper equivalent of the *National Enquirer* (their favorite thing to write about is how many people were killed and injured on the highway during the week: 4 MORTS ET 7 BLESSÉS! is a typical headline of the *Provençal*). We went to harpsichord concerts in local churches and trudged to Avignon to see English-language movies. We hiked for miles with them, exploring the wonders of the mountains, and went on treasure hunts and once, on a magical New Year's Day picnic, even danced around in a circle, holding hands, singing the words to "Sur le Pont d'Avignon" (although if you tell that to any of my close, personal friends, I'll deny it). We stayed up late nursing them through broken hearts, we lived through their affairs with married men, we ate in their homes and cooked for them. We told jokes—in various languages—and made one another laugh. And we slowly learned a lot about a group of people—English, American, French, Swedish, you name it—with whom, ostensibly, we had nothing in common, yet grew to treasure.

Not all of our treasured memories, however, revolve around people. Or even cats, for that matter. Every so often there were other—if you'll excuse the expression—catalysts working their magic.

By far the strangest and, in some ways, the most delightful experience we had the entire time we were in Goult was when Janis came running into the house late one afternoon. Excited, she told me to hurry up, get Norton, and jump in the car. She wouldn't tell me what was going on, she just insisted I follow instructions.

She drove—she was becoming quite proficient with the Citroën and by this time could almost get up a steep hill without my head banging against the windshield thirty or forty times—until we came to the town of Menerbes, another perfect Lubéron mountain village, ten minutes away from Goult.

Just outside the town, Janis stopped the car to let an animal cross the street in front of us. It was a goat. I was about to say, "What's a goat doing in Menerbes?" when I looked to the right of the car and saw two lions lounging by the side of the road. Next to them was a friendly but quite large elephant. Before I could get too disoriented, Janis drove a little further and we came to a small tent that had been set up. In front of the tent was a man in a clown outfit and five or six small children running around in front of him, giggling and yelling with pleasure.

"We're going to a circus?" I asked Janis in disbelief.

"We're going to a circus," she answered.

I would love to report that this charming country circus was an artistic triumph, everything that the overdone and overhyped Ringling Bros. type of show is not. Unfortunately, if I did report such a thing, I'd be lying through my teeth. This little circus that Janis brought me and Norton to was the cheesiest, most pathetic, most hilarious thing I'd ever seen in my entire life:

The human troupe consisted of a ringmaster, two clowns, and a woman acrobat who, every time she so much as did a simple somersault, looked as if it was going to be her last act of life. She tripped and fell down *twice* while walking across the arena to encourage us to applaud the ringmaster. The clowns also were not of the highest possible caliber. One clown's wig kept falling off, and you could tell he wasn't happy about dressing up in the stupid-looking costume anyway. The other clown's sole job was keeping the bouncy music going, but the tape machine was on the old side, so the music wasn't all that bouncy because it was played somewhere around two speeds too slow. When it came time to bring the speakers inside—they'd been outside to help broadcast the exciting news that the circus was in town—the whole troupe chipped in. It was a struggle for all of them to lift the things—enough of a struggle that they almost knocked the entire tent over in the process.

Once the show started, things managed to get lots worse. The opening act was Minou the Dog Genius. Minou's trainer (the ringmaster) strode out into the middle of the ring, announced that we were about to see the smartest dog in the world, then, with a deep bow and a majestic wave of an arm, called for Minou to come running. No such luck. Minou was either asleep or hadn't been paid in a week, because there was nothing they could do to get that dog into the ring. The ringmaster kept calling him, but Minou never showed up. Finally, one of the clowns had to carry the pup into the tent and plop him down in the center. The ringmaster then told the genius dog to leap up onto a stool—and he announced to the audience that we were going to see the most amazing mental feat ever performed by a member of the canine race. It really wasn't as amazing as all that—because all Minou did was turn around and run out of the tent again.

The ringmaster began to realize that Minou was off his

performance that night, so he called for JoJo the Brilliant Horse. Norton enjoyed JoJo tremendously, especially when JoJo refused to do anything except trot around the ring. "Up, JoJo!" the ringmaster would thunder, and JoJo would trot some more. "JoJo! How much is two plus two?" the ringmaster asked. Unless I lost count and JoJo trotted around the entire ring four times, I don't think he had any idea how much two plus two were. That didn't stop the ringmaster from thanking everyone for watching JoJo the Brilliant Horse (*"Mes amis, messieurs, mesdames, les enfants, JoJo le cheval génie!"*), and then introducing The World's Most Intelligent Monkeys. Their entire act was to eat their dinner as fast and as messily as they could in front of the rapt crowd.

By the time of the monkey act, Norton was getting a little bored. I'm sure it was beginning to occur to him that if these animals were making a decent living, he could become a millionaire without too much trouble if he ran away to join a French circus.

That was when he got his moment in the sun.

There were not a lot of people in the audience. I'd say perhaps twenty small children, two or three mothers, and us. But when I heard the ringmaster say, into the mike, *"Monsieur! Monsieur, s'il vous plaît,"* I really didn't think anything of it. Not, that is, until Janis pointed out that he was talking to *me,* since I was the only adult *monsieur* in the joint.

"Monsieur," he repeated, when he finally caught my eye. "Come here," he said. *"Venez."*

If I knew what I was in for, I don't think I would have brought Norton into the ring, but I truly wasn't expecting anything other than semi-funny banter. Even if I did have to participate in something physical, I figured I could just eat some food quickly or jog around the ring twice when they asked me how much one plus one was. Even when they brought the camel center stage, I still didn't understand what I was supposed to do. Only when the camel knelt down and one of the clowns led me over to it, did I realize I was supposed to get up on the thing and ride it around the tent.

Norton was a real trouper, I'll say that for him. He let me hold him as the clown boosted us up onto the camel's back. I held on to the cat with one hand and on to the camel's hump with the other. As the *dromadaire* sped faster and faster around the ring, and Norton got more and more relaxed, the children in the audience went wilder and wilder. Out of the corner of my eye, I'm pretty sure I saw Janis laughing uncontrollably, though she swore to me later she was impressed with how well I'd maintained my dignity.

The main thing I remember is the ringmaster, who realized that with all his trained elephants and monkeys and horses and dogs, a nonprofessional cat was stealing his show. To his credit, he went with it. Standing off to the side, he began bellowing into his microphone as we rode past and the cheers grew louder and louder and Norton sat up straighter and straighter on the back of the camel. "Ladies and gentlemen, boys and girls," he was saying. *"Messieurs et mesdames, les enfants, mes amis! Je vous present le monsieur et son chat extraordinaire!"*

a cat on the riviera

6

One of the strangest things about living abroad is being away from home for holidays.

I'm fairly big on tradition. Every Christmas Eve I go to my friends Glen and Sharon's apartment for dinner. Every December, on the first weekend of the month, I throw a waffle and champagne party and make everyone I know watch *It's a Wonderful Life.* Thanksgiving is my favorite holiday of all and for ten years I've been going to other friends, Kathleen and Dominick (of the traumatic Search for Norton Day), to eat a major feast, drink many bottles of delicious port, and play a killer game of charades. In general, I'd have to say that Thanksgiving is my very favorite day of the year.

In France, Thanksgiving doesn't exist. I experienced this once before, when I went to college at the University of London. I gathered a few American students over at my flat, along with some newly acquired British friends. It turned out that none of us Americans had a very firm grasp on exactly what Thanksgiving was. We knew it had something to do with the Three P's: Pilgrims, Plymouth Rock, and Pocahontas. And we were pretty sure we were supposed to be giving thanks for religious and political freedom and for the fact that only in America could there be an official holiday that enabled some creative entrepreneur to actually make millions of dollars off those little orange and black candy corns. Other than that, all we knew was we were supposed to eat a lot of turkey and pumpkin pie. (Although pumpkin pie is not a well-known treat in England and, being college kids, we didn't really know how to make one—so we tried doing it with a real pumpkin rather than canned pumpkin. It's difficult to describe the actual taste of our dessert that night. The closest I could come, I think, would be to say it had the delicate texture of a terry-cloth robe and the subtle taste of a whole lot of unsweetened chocolate.) To this day, I think there are several English people walking around London who think that every final Thursday in November, Americans celebrate a bizarre Pilgrim-Indian sex rite by eating terrible food.

We did slightly better in France, though not at first.

Two weeks before the big day, we went to one of the two butchers in Goult—we'd settled on one we preferred, though for no logical reason—and told him we'd like to order a turkey *(un dinde)* for the end of November.

"You mean the end of December," he said.

"No," I said. "I mean the end of November."

"That's impossible," he told us.

"And why is that?" we wanted to know.

"Because the turkeys are not fat yet," he said.

It turns out that no one in the south of France ever eats turkey except for Christmas. So, especially in such rural areas as the Lubéron, November and December are months spent feeding the birds and getting them plump enough for *le diner de Noël.*

"But it's a very important American holiday," I explained to Monsieur Isnard, our butcher of choice. "What if we order a pathetic thin turkey?"

Non.

We debated having a Thanksgiving feast of chicken and shallot tart, but we were spared such an agonizing break from tradition when our friends Nicholas and Linda called and told us to come up to Paris to have Thanksgiving with them.

Nicholas is French and Linda is American and they've been living in Paris for five years now. They also have twin five-year-old daughters, Naomi and Gala, possibly the most gorgeous, sweetest children who ever lived. At the time, they were refusing to speak so much as one word of English, even though Mom was American and they absolutely could understand anything spoken in English that they wanted to understand. Instead, they would look adorable and speak perfect French, saying such cute little *enfant-*like things as, when riding in the car on a cold winter day, *"Oh, maman, j'adore la musique et la chauffage!"* which means, "Oh, Mom, I adore music and the heating system." I know it doesn't sound nearly as good in English, but nothing does, and when they'd spew out these accented epigrams, my heart would melt so quickly it was pathetic. So we were in the mood to see Linda, Nicholas, and the kids anyway, and our choice was made easier yet when we took into consideration that Linda was a cook of the first degree. So it was on to Paris for Thanksgiving.

The TGV—*train de grande vitesse* ("train of great speed," or "big, really, really fast train," as I like to call it)—has changed everyone's life down in Provence. In the old days, it was a seven- or eight-hour train ride from Paris to Avignon. By the time you got to the train station, waited for the train, stopped a hundred times along the way, and got to your final destination, it was an all-day trip. Now, with the fast train, it takes three hours to get from Provence to Paris, and you get there in extremely luxurious fashion. The drawback is that wealthier and more annoying Parisians are now able to consider Provence something of a weekend retreat. On the other hand, it makes it awfully nice to live down there, knowing how simple and hassle-free it is to get up to the greatest city in the world.

Norton was a big TGV fan. Human seats need to be reserved but pet seats don't. And because the train is built for comfort as well as speed, there are thick, plush armrests which, when pushed down, make the perfect seating arrangement for Scottish Folds. Norton could stretch out on the armrests and do his favorite thing in the whole world: stare out the window at the countryside as the train sped along at a hundred miles an hour. Since it was only a three-hour trip, he didn't even need a litter box.

This was our first weekend in the big city since we'd moved down to Goult, and we decided to live it up. We stayed in L'Hôtel, a very beautiful hotel on the left bank on the rue des Beaux-Arts, celebrated because it's the house where Oscar Wilde died. It's even possible to stay in the very room—and bed—Oscar Wilde died in, although why anyone would want to do that I'm not exactly sure. The rooms are tiny (unless you take the suite on the top floor, which is huge and looks like a very classy nineteenth-century whorehouse; unfortunately, the cost is more like a twenty-first-century whorehouse) but are filled with antiques and decorated in lots of bright red and green velvet.

The colors somehow work, though they tend to be just a tad overpowering. In fact, as the bellman was opening the door to our room, he said softly, *"J'espère que vous aimez la couleur rouge"*—"I hope you like the color red." It was a fair question because *everything* in our small room was bright, shocking red. The wallpaper, the bedspread, the chairs, the towels. We got used to it in a few moments, but I must admit that for several days after we left, everything we saw looked rather drab and bland.

As usual, the hotel was totally taken with the cat. Within minutes of checking in, the concierge sent up a bowl of milk for Norton's cocktail hour. Just to be on the safe side, I checked to see whether Janis or I had gotten any fruit or chocolates, but as usual it was only *le chat* who received any complimentary calories.

The first day we were there, we did a lot of Christmas shopping at the antique stores along the nearby rue Jacob and, farther away, rue St. Paul in the Marais. One St. Paul store particularly impressed me. They remembered me from previous shopping sprees—usually to bring something back to Janis when I felt particularly guilty about being there without her—and even remembered most of the things I'd bought there over the years, which I have to admit made me feel about as sophisticated as I can feel. They clearly had no idea what my name was but they did remember my shopping companion. When I strolled in with a cloth bag on my shoulder and a gray cat poking his head out of the bag, they greeted us with the warm words, *"Bonjour, monsieur! Et bonjour, Monsieur Norton! Ça va?"* It never fails.

The night before Thanksgiving, Norton met his French *attaché de presse. The Cat Who Went to Paris* was being published in France before too long and the editor, an American woman named Nina Salter who was an editor at the Parisian publishing company Albin Michel, decided it would be wise if Norton met the woman who'd be doing the publicity for the book.

Janis, Norton, and I went to a restaurant called Le Square Trousseau, a smoky bistro populated with a lot of publishing and show-biz types, near to the Bastille. Nina and Kathy, the publicist, were regulars but the place was jam-packed, so even at nine-thirty at night we had to have a drink at the bar before being seated. No problem for Norton. He took a stool at the end of the bar, his little head popping up over the brass railing. Kathy sat next to him, petted him, and clearly fell in love. What's not to love, I guess. Norton's a great date.

Dinner went smoothly as the relationship between Norton and his publicist proved to be the real thing. Norton sat in his own chair, and nothing going on around him disturbed him—not the noisy crowd, not the giant St. Bernard who camped under his chair almost the entire evening, not the patrons of the restaurant who, periodically, would come over and ask me if that was a real cat.

Kathy made his life a lot easier—and mine a lot harder—by giving Norton the full star treatment. She hand-fed him some of her foie gras, then some of her chicken. For dessert, she ordered him a plate of chocolate ice cream (it was far superior to that of Bistro d'Albert). As an after-dinner drink, she ordered him some milk and, since he is the world's sloppiest milk slurper, Kathy even wiped his mouth with her napkin after each session with the milk bowl. That was the final straw as far as Janis was concerned. For months afterward, she complained vociferously that no one ever wiped her mouth after she ate. I tried pointing out that perhaps someone would if she would agree to bend down and eat out of a bowl, but she never took my advice to heart, which was probably all for the best.

The next day, we were all slightly hung over. Janis and I from too much wine and *eau de vie,* Norton from too much spoon-fed foie gras. We were content to linger in our red velvet room for most of the morning. I was especially content because there was a TV in the room and I'd been having sports withdrawal down in Goult. Much to Janis's horror, I watched a Pistons-Pacers basketball game on an English cable station, then, much more to her horror, proved how desperate I really was by watching almost all of a Hulk Hogan versus The Undertaker wrestling match. Our only interruption came when two of the hotel maids knocked at the door. Janis told them we'd be out of the room in another hour or so, but they weren't there to clean—they were there to introduce themselves to Norton and play with him. We told them we'd leave him in the room for the afternoon so they could pet him to their heart's content.

That night was Thanksgiving dinner over at Linda and Nicholas's apartment. I believe this was Norton's first official Thanksgiving (he's never gone to Kathleen and Dominick's because they have two cats, Lulu and Zonker, who don't cotton to any feline competition in the annual charades game). He was made to feel welcome by the twins, Naomi and Gala, who crayoned little place settings for everyone. They drew a picture of me and set it in front of my plate on the table. They did the same for Janis and for their mom and dad. For Norton, they drew a lovely picture of him, complete with flattened ears, and put it on the floor, right next to my chair, along with a bowl which happened to be perfect for holding bite-sized morsels of turkey scraps.

The dinner was a grand success. In Paris it was not only

possible to get fattened turkeys at the end of November, it was possible to get everything needed for stuffing and sweet potatoes and mashed potatoes and all other Thanksgiving delicacies.

By the end of the weekend, we felt we'd had a touch of home, which we'd needed. Norton felt as if he'd had a *new* home since, when we checked out of L'Hôtel, I believe that every single employee came to say good-bye to him and wish him *bon chance.*

Norton, Janis, and I had the next several weeks to ourselves, during which we continued our Provençal explorations and our Provençal ritual of stuffing our faces at every possible moment. And then, right at Christmastime, a new ritual began: Company started arriving.

Our first guests were—and don't start any gossip, this was strictly a platonic arrangement—my friend Norm Stiles, the "Sesame Street" maven, and my friend and book agent, Esther Newberg, the well-known cranky person. Neither Esther nor Norm had ever been to Provence before and we were determined to show them how perfect life could be.

It wasn't as difficult as we thought.

It turns out it's not hard to convince people that life is perfect—not when they're in Goult for Christmas.

The lights in town are, of course, tasteful and elegant. Strings of colored lights ring the tower of the church in the lower part of the town; a strand of white lights sits over the thousand-year-old vaulted arch that leads to the town *château.* Along the main street, artfully decorated lights run, every ten yards or so, across the width of the street, from one building to another.

In our cozy house, we got two Christmas trees—a large

one for the living room and a small one for my third-floor (or second-floor, if you're French) office. Both trees were decorated Provençal-style: with various fruits (tiny tangerines, which are called *clementines,* small apples, and pears) and strands of nuts.

On Christmas Day, Janis, Norton, and I strode around Goult, enjoying the simple fact that we were there and nowhere else. Norton started out in his shoulder bag but before long hopped out and walked with us. The town was fairly empty—even the tiny caged birds were inside—so we had a relaxed cat on our hands, one who was ready to stroll anywhere.

We passed one house we'd admired since the day we'd arrived. It was off a small grassy triangle at the top of the main street, before one reached the castle. From the outside, Janis had picked this as her favorite place in town—it was quite old and at one time had been the Goult post office, but had obviously long ago been converted to a spectacular home. They'd been doing some work on the house, fixing up the courtyard, and I'd peeked my head through from time to time, admiring and envious. On Christmas Day, as we passed by, a grungy-looking workman in overalls was busy poking and scratching at the stone outside the house. The doorway leading to the courtyard was open, so I pulled Janis in to show her the work that had been done. The workman looked at us but didn't say anything, but after it was clear that we were so admiring of the place, he asked us if we wanted to see the rest of the house. Since looking in other people's houses is our favorite thing in the world, we immediately said yes. The workman started leading us through the entire home, which was much larger than it looked from the outside and even more spectacular. It was restored magnificently and furnished to the period, the late 1500s. After twenty minutes or so, we arrived at the kitchen. Sitting around the kitchen table were two women—clearly a mother and daughter—and two young children. The younger of the grown women looked at us—two strangers, a workman, and a cat—and asked the workman what he thought he was doing. The workman replied that we—the strangers and the cat—had admired the house and he thought we might like to see it. She sighed, they discussed the situation, and pretty soon Janis and I realized that the workman wasn't a workman—he was the owner of the house. We'd just managed to worm our way into his family's Christmas celebration.

We immediately apologized and tried to leave, but now the family would have none of it. They insisted we see the rest of the house, which got better and better with each room we toured, then they made us stay for a drink (okay, okay, they didn't *make* us, but it would have seemed inhospitable just to tour and run). The man who'd been showing us his place turned out to be a Belgian architect who lived, most of the time, in Algiers. This magnificent home was his weekend retreat, which he used only three or four weekends a year, plus Christmas week.

After our drink, we realized Norton had wandered off to examine the house on his own. I'm sorry to report that I panicked briefly; in that house he could have hid for days at a time and I had a sudden vision of not only ruining these people's Christmas but their New Year's as well. Luckily, he came the moment I called him, hopped into his shoulder bag, and Janis and I took him back to our house on rue St. Frusquin.

It was still relatively early, and we decided now it was time to open Christmas presents. Janis and I exchanged first. I got an ancient hanging oil lamp (I have a fetish for old lighting fixtures) as well as something I'd been looking to get for myself for over five years: a beautiful bowl and matching pitcher to go in a wooden dry sink I'd bought long ago. I'd never been able to find one I liked, but Janis had spotted this at the weekly antique mart in L'Isle-sur-la-Sorgue and hidden it away some weeks before. She received, in turn, an eighteenth-century iron (she has the same fetish for old irons that I have for lamps) and two nineteenth-century casserole dishes in the shape of hearts. Aaaaahhhhhhhh.

Norton did all right, too. He received several cans of Pounce (which I'd had someone send to me from New York; good cat treats are the one thing France seems to lack) and two fine catnip toys, one in the shape of a mouse, one in the shape of French bread.

For dinner that night, we did it up. We invited several Goultois to join us and devoured our very own fat turkey, chestnut stuffing, *patate douce avec cognac* (sweet potatoes drowned in brandy, to you), and some of the old toothless crone's killer goat cheese.

All in all, it was a perfect French Christmas and we were now ready to face Americans.

The next morning, we drove down to the Marseille airport, an hour away, to pick up Esther and Norm. They are both very dear friends and we were thrilled that they were our first guests, but, to be fair, I've got to paint a realistic picture. Neither of them had ever been in the European countryside before. This was Norm's very first trip to France. Within moments, he was so overjoyed at being there, he was speaking "like zees: I luf ze French. Zay are ze best. Oui!" and thinking that he was already able to communicate with the French on their own level. Esther, on the other hand, is not a person who's very comfortable when she's away from her office (picture a small, tightly wound Ethel Merman and you'll have the picture—I won't have an agent, but you'll have the picture). By the time we got back to Goult, she had three faxes waiting and two urgent calls to return. So while we showed them their rooms and helped them get settled, Esther spent an hour on the phone negotiating various deals and Norm walked all over the garden, speaking to the trees and stray cats in some language he was convinced was French. "Allo, leetle tree, 'ow aire yew? Et bonjour, Monsieur Bird. Eet ees very nice tew see yew. *Oui?*"

Our rule of thumb with jet-lagged arrivals was that they had to stay up until ten P.M. That way they'd be exhausted, would sleep through the night, and would wake up refreshed and back on a regular schedule at nine or ten the next morning.

That afternoon we took them to a cocktail party at our neighbor's (she was English; it was a Boxing Day party). Then we took them up into the mountains to Auberge de la Loube. We were the only people in the restaurant that night, so they moved a big table right in front of the fireplace. Norm toasted everybody and everything, while Esther dozed off in her chair (in addition to jet lag, she was also carsick from going up the winding road to the restaurant). Norton was now on such friendly terms with the three dogs that he hopped into their hiding place under the hearth with them for much of dinner.

We had a few days to be tourists with our guests and we enjoyed every moment of it. The next day, we began running them around to all our favorite places. We made them climb to the top of Oppede-le-vieux, a medieval village dominated by wonderful ruins at its peak. There is a straight drop from the cliff when you get to the top of the town. I, myself, never ventured too close, but Janis liked to teeter on the edge and drive me crazy. Once, while she was doing that, a private airplane flew by *below* her. The passengers waved while I held on to a tree, getting dizzy just thinking about it.

After Oppede, we had lunch at an amazing *routier* called Bistrot du Paradou in the very small town of Paradou. The restaurant is a four- or five-hundred-year-old stone house divided into two dining rooms. The front room has an enormous bar, usually surrounded by local truck drivers swigging wine and *pastis* and telling stories. The back room is perhaps twenty tables along with a fireplace, which usually has a *rôti* going, with lamb or chicken or rabbit on it. In wintertime, the Bistrot is only open for lunch, and only during the week, and each day they serve only one thing. You call up and ask what their menu is that day and they'll tell you they're having a *pot-au-feu* or an *aïoli* (which they have every Friday) or a *coq au vin* and then you decide if that's what you feel like eating that day. They also serve a delicious salad and as much red wine as you wish to drink (the bottle's waiting for you on your table when you sit down; it's produced directly for the restaurant and is *biologique*—organic—which means there are no sulfites or other nasty chemicals). The owner was a successful advertising executive who decided one day he'd had enough of selling Perrier or whatever it was he was selling, so he opened up the perfect fantasy of a French restaurant.

The Bistrot du Paradou is one of Norton's top three Provençal restaurants as well as ours. I think this is due to a combination of the fact that one particular waitress there likes him very much and is always telling him how much smarter he is than her dog, and the fact that the hearth is so large, Norton can sit almost anywhere in the whole restaurant and be warmed by the blazing fire.

After lunch, we went several miles down the road to the best olive oil mill in all of France, the cooperative mill in the town of Maussane. Maussane happens to be Janis's favorite town in the south of France, with the possible exception of St. Remy. It's built right onto the road, is small and charming yet extremely sophisticated, and looks exactly like the kind of place where Sergeant Saunders always used to get wounded in the show "Combat." More to the point, their olive oil is so delicious that we have personally risked lengthy prison terms smuggling many liters of the stuff back to New York.

After watching them crush olives, then buying enough oil to pan-fry half of Western Europe, we drove back to Goult. That afternoon, we had a party of our own, a cocktail party from five until whenever, so all our new friends could meet our two old friends. We had about thirty people in all, some Brits, one expatriate American, a couple of Swedes, and mostly French. We served leftover turkey and a giant ham and lots and lots of delicious cold *champagnoise* from the *cave* in Coustellet, but the biggest hit was the bagels and cream cheese that Norm and Esther brought from New York. The French people thought this was the most delicious thing since the invention of the croissant and gobbled down the onion bagels like there was no tomorrow.

The biggest surprise of the party was not that all our friends got along so well. It was that Norton, for the very first time in his life, not only spent most of the evening attending a party, he let all the children there come up and pet him.

I have not discussed the dark side of Norton's personality, mostly because there really isn't one. If he has a flaw at all, it's that he doesn't much like children. Small children, to be exact. I suppose it's understandable. Children are very volatile and loud and move in sudden herky-jerky motions. As a grown-up, I find them scary enough, so I really can see why Norton has always shied away from them. If we're in public, which we often are, Norton doesn't hiss or scratch them or anything like that. He simply gets very passive and withdraws into a shell, or else, if he's able, he'll make sure to just stay out of their way. At our first major Goult cocktail party, however, we had many children underfoot. They ranged from five years old to twelve, and somewhere around eight at night, I saw Norton calmly sprawled on the living-room floor, letting one of the five-year-olds try to crayon the top of his head.

France was clearly having its effect on the star of my family. And I must say I approved.

The next couple of days went by in a blur of tourism.

We all went to Arles and tried to find some semblance of Van Gogh but, except for the ultramodern Van Gogh Café and a Van Gogh gas station, hardly a trace remains. It is a beautiful town, however, and Norton was fascinated by the bullfighting school that practices in the town's Roman coliseum. We also went to Avignon, a truly great city. I don't know if Norton was able to appreciate the Palais du Papes or the spectacular wall that rings the town or even the Utopia, the only English-language movie theater south of Paris. I do know he definitely appreciated the *manège,* the merry-go-round, that sits in front of the opera house, gloriously lit, and spins around all night. Norton would have been happy to sit there with it, watching it go until dawn.

We took our visitors to the market at L'Isle-sur-la-Sorgue, of course, where we bumped into every single person we knew in Provence. By the end of the shopping trip, I'm sure Esther and Norm thought we'd bribed total strangers to pretend that they knew us and fake our guests into thinking we were popular. After buying our weekly supplies, we then took a wine tasting trip to Châteauneuf-du-Pape, which was only forty minutes from Goult. (In case no one seems to be making the connection between all these places with the word *pape* in them, here's a very brief and probably inaccurate history lesson: When the French government was trying to, more or less, take over the Vatican, they wound up installing their own Pope and luring the Catholic Church headquarters over to France. When you tour Avignon and Châteauneuf, it's not really hard to see why they came running. The palaces are awe-inspiring and the wine is, arguably, the best in the world. When the corrupt French Pope finally died, he was replaced by a corrupt Italian Pope who went back to Italy, but the palaces and the wines remain, with Avignon as their approximate center. End of lesson.) Janis and I had made several trips out Châteauneuf way and even knew some of the owners of the smaller vineyards (we're easy to remember: There aren't many American couples who come wine-tasting with a Scottish Fold). Typical of the Provençal French—of their class, their warmth, and their style—one of the *cave* owners we'd previously spent time talking to about wine gave a half bottle of his newest vintage to Esther and one to Norm as presents. He also offered one to Norton, but I decided my cat had already picked up enough bad habits and, since Norton was technically a minor, I declined for him.

By the time Monday rolled around, Esther and Norm

were fairly convinced that we were living in paradise. And then we decided to *really* go wild.

One of the best things about Goult was its location. Not only was it in the heart of the magnificent Lubéron, it was a two-and-a-half-hour drive from skiing in the Alps, it was two and a half hours down to Barcelona, it was two hours from Nice and Cannes, and it was two and a half hours to Italy. So we decided to have an adventure and go visiting foreign lands.

Norton had already spent lots of time in Italy and down on the Riviera. Nice (which is pronounced Neese; trust me: This will come into play later) was one of his favorite towns in France. He liked the accommodations, the food, and found the Niçoise particularly friendly. We'd been down there often, partly for business, mostly because we had friends living there.

An old friend of mine was Joel Douglas (Kirk's son, Michael's brother, a successful film producer in his own right). I'd known Joel and Michael when we were youths and had kept in touch over the years. Michael, of course, went on to become a zillionaire movie star and Oscar winner and even see Sharon Stone naked (for which I would happily give up the zillions and the Oscar). Joel wound up living the perfect life, moving to Monaco, marrying a ter- rifically nice woman from Nice (or neese woman from Nice; uh-oh, don't get me started), and was running the oldest working film studio in Europe, which he and Michael were in the process of buying. (Just to clarify: They were buying the studio, not Europe, although I have a feeling Michael could afford to actually buy the Continent if he so desired.) I was talking to them about doing some work out of the studio, so after we'd been in Goult a few weeks, we went down to talk some new business as well as catch up on old times.

Norton, Janis, and I met Joel and his wife, Paddy, at the commissary at the old Victorine Studios. After a very tasty lunch and even tastier conversation—we hadn't seen each other for years and had a lot to catch up on: brothers, parents, work, ex-girlfriends or ex-wives as the case may have been—Joel took the three of us on a tour of the studio. I was in heaven, because Victorine is like an old Hollywood studio from the twenties and thirties. It's got all the atmosphere and magic and romance that studios used to have (they still have them in L.A. to a certain extent, but it's all tempered by the fact that Sam Goldwyn and Harry Cohn have been replaced by either agents, morons, or corporate Japanese people). On the lot we saw the places where they filmed Truffaut's *Day for Night* and Hitchcock's *To Catch a Thief,* and the greatest French movie of them all, *Children of Paradise.* Joel also showed us a rough cut of a promotional film they were putting together about the history of the studio. It was put together by the studio projectionist (whose father was the studio projectionist, as was his grandfather. This guy *lives* for the studio). Unfortunately, despite the best of intentions, it was a *very* rough cut—dominated by a lot of unknown actors in period wigs—but the screening room was very luxurious. After half an hour or so of the film, Norton stretched out on the chair next to mine and took a little cat nap.

That night, we had dinner at a fish restaurant with Joel and Paddy and their small, very friendly if somewhat overactive dog. Norton and the hyper pup got along quite well, though Norton spent a little more time on my lap than he usually does.

The next day, we strolled around Old Nice, where I

could happily live. The new part of Nice couldn't be uglier (actually, that's not true, it could be Cannes, which is perhaps the ugliest beach city in the world), but Vieux Nice is full of cobblestone streets and ancient churches and wonderful little shops and restaurants. Since it's so close to the border, only fifteen or twenty minutes away, Nice is as much an Italian city as it is a French one, and the combination definitely works.

Norton made several trips to Nice while we were in France and, while that may be his city of choice on the Riviera, I think he found St.-Jean-Cap-Ferrat a close second.

The day we went to Cap-Ferrat—or as I like to think of it, "The Village That Only Donald Trump Can Afford to Live In"—we were visiting Nina Salter, the editor of the French edition of *The Cat Who Went to Paris* (the translated title: *Le Chat Qui Dinait Chez Maxim's*). It's not that French publishers pay their editors so much more money than American publishers do, it's that Nina was visiting a childhood friend of hers, whose parents had a nice little mansion in Cap-Ferrat, right on the sea.

Norton took to it immediately, ignoring the scrumptious repast that was set before us when we arrived, preferring to stroll the grounds and sniff out the new surroundings. After lunch, he came for a walk with us, along the boardwalk and up into the rocky crags of the shoreline. Norton was not as foolhardy as Nina, who dove into the sea and took a lengthy swim (this was in early March, when the temperature was all of forty degrees). My little cat much preferred the dry rocks and, while various swimmers trembled and turned blue, Norton found the only ray of sun to luxuriate in.

It really *is* hard to argue when someone says that cats are a lot smarter than people.

Norton also spent some time in the ultra-chic town of Ramatuelle, just outside of St. Tropez. An author and friend of mine, Edward Behr, was based in Paris but had bought a house in Ramatuelle in 1966, for something like forty dollars. It was a modest little joint: a one-time hotel with six or seven bedrooms, a professional kitchen (including walk-in freezer), an uncountable number of dens and offices, a balcony overlooking St. Tropez and the Mediterranean, and, surrounding the swimming pool, sloping gardens that rivaled those at Versailles. That's all.

Norton, jet-setter that he is, liked Ramatuelle fine, but he really took to St. Tropez, where he got to sit on the bay and sip—or, more accurately, slurp—a *café liegois,* a fancy name for a cross between an iced coffee and a coffee sundae, the first nonchocolate concoction I've ever seen my cat flip over.

All of this is by way of pointing out that Norton was a far more experienced traveler in the south of France than either of our Christmas Week human guests.

The first thing we decided to do with Esther and Norm was to stop off in Nice to walk them through the old town. This we did, and all went smoothly, except for the moment when Norm, forgetting once again that he couldn't speak French, got into a conversation with a shopkeeper. He was buying a few presents for people back home, and the woman at the store asked him a question in her native tongue. Norm, still refusing to acknowledge that he didn't understand the language, nodded and responded, *"Oui. Un peu."* (Yes. A little.) This confused the woman no end, since the question she'd asked was, "Would you like this gift-wrapped?"

You try gift-wrapping something just "a little."

Being the ultrasophisticates that we were, we decided to

venture into Italy for lunch. We also decided that spontaneity was the way to go for this brief two-day trip—we would just do whatever the hell we felt like for thirty-six hours. Naturally, the first thing we felt like doing was eating. So we drove half an hour to the town of Ventimiglia, the Italian/French equivalent of Tijuana.

Janis, Norton, and I had done this trip several times. Nothing made us appreciate our year more than saying, spur of the moment, "Let's drive to Italy for lunch." And Ventimiglia happens to be a perfectly nice town. It's not Rome or Verona or Venice, but it *is* Italy, so what could be bad?

We had a delicious lunch right on the sea. Norton got his own plate of scampi and the restaurant made him feel so at home, he did a little wandering, checking out a few of the other diners, moseying into the kitchen to see what else he could dig up in the way of antipasto. After lunch, we did what people seem to do in Italy: We spent two hours waiting in line at a bank trying to change our francs into lira, and then we went to an open-air market to buy yet more food. The only hitch in this part of the operation was that Norton single-handedly almost started World War III.

As we walked into the market, the little guy was in his usual position, sitting up with his head swiveling out of his shoulder bag. The Italians feel just as warmly toward cats and dogs as the French do—they see nothing even remotely strange about a cat visiting a restaurant or a market—so as soon as we stepped inside, one of the vendors sprang into action and offered Norton a fresh sardine. Norton looked at him as if he was insane, sniffed at the fish rather rudely, and turned his attention elsewhere—mostly toward the *gelato* stand.

"What's the matter with him?" he asked me. "He's too good for my fish?"

"No, no, no," I hurriedly assured him. "He just doesn't *like* fish."

"He's a cat, isn't he?" the fish vendor wanted to know.

"Sure, he's a cat," I agreed.

"Then he should eat fish."

"I know he should"—and here I shrugged very philosophically; that usually worked with French people—"but he seems to be more of a meat eater."

I should point out here that what I was speaking was NormLanguage. I don't speak a word of Italian, so I was mixing in a little French with a little English, and a lot of a Vito Scotti–like Italian accent.

"This is a *fish* market," the guy now pointed out to me. By this time, several other vendors had gathered around to see what the commotion was. No one was happy to see it was a cat who didn't eat fish.

"Yeah," another one grumbled. "Why bring a cat who hates fish into a fish market?"

Smiling at all of them, I mumbled to my cat under my breath, "Norton, sweet little cat, *please* eat the sardine."

No chance. My sweet little cat simply doesn't eat fish. But the vendor held it out in front of him again and Norton practically gagged. Before there was a full-scale riot, Janis wandered over, took me and Norton by the arm (and paw), and led us back out into sunlight and safety.

"*What* was that all about?" she demanded.

"He's got fussy eating habits," I said, pointing to our gray companion. "It's not his fault."

"No, it's not *his* fault," she said and rolled her eyes, leaving no doubt whose fault she thought it was.

Full and now feisty—and still living on spontaneity—we

all piled back in the car and decided to keep forging further into Italy.

"What about the French Riviera?" Esther wanted to know.

"Italy's great," I told her. "It'll be fun. We'll just drive until we get to someplace nice and then we'll find a hotel."

"What about a reservation?" she asked, and we all explained to her, once again, this whole concept of spontaneity. Reluctantly, Esther agreed to go along with the crowd.

And the crowd proceeded to drive into five hours of hell.

We checked a map and decided we'd go on to San Remo, a supposedly nice resort town, supposedly only another hour or so further into Italy. Note the key repetition of the word *supposedly*.

The first part of the drive went smoothly. Then, as we approached San Remo, we noticed that traffic was slowing down. The last mile or so into town took a little longer to travel than it should have—by about an hour. The next thing we knew, we were on the outskirts of San Remo stuck in the worst traffic jam in history. The first half hour, we were all calm. The second half hour, Janis went to sleep. We had now progressed about a hundred feet into town. The third half hour, Esther started to whine. The fourth half hour, Janis woke up again and she joined in the whining. We were now all of a hundred and ten feet into town. Somewhere in there, Norm snapped. He began talking in a thick Italian accent, pretending he was a native of San Remo. "Excusa me," he said, tapping on the window as if he were outside the car. "I'ma liva here an' Ia been inna my car fora fourteen years. The radio no work—hassa anything happened?" I started giggling, which was a bad sign, and only egged him on. The Italian accent continued. "Excusa me. I justa bringa my new son homa from the hospital. It taka me eighteen years and now I have to finda the college." By the time Norm was through with his riff, we learned that no one in the town of San Remo had ever been out of their cars, no one in town knew how to walk, and that forty-two percent of the town's population had the first name of Fiat. This went on for nearly an hour (or another hundred and fifty feet). Janis and Esther were in a total panic by this point. They not only hated being in traffic, they hated me and Norm, who were laughing so hard as to be near some strange form of mental illness. Norton was the only one keeping his head, but I maintain it's because he was in the backseat with Esther and Janis and simply didn't want to face their wrath if he started laughing along with us.

In addition to his take on San Remo, Norman also explained a word game he'd invented several years before when the Ayatollah Khomeini was first popping up in the news. Norm was obsessed with the whole Ayatollah/Salman Rushdie business ever since he found out that Salman Rushdie had gotten engaged. Norm figured that he, Norm, went out almost every night in search of the perfect woman—or even a date who'd see him a second time—and had never been able to find her. Now, here was a guy who was in hiding, under the threat of death, and he was getting married! My pal Norm didn't think this was fair or just. So he created a game about the Ayatollah hoping perhaps an entire religion would put a price on his head and he'd get to meet an attractive woman.

The game he invented was that you had to come up with a new type of Ayatollah, defined by his job or his attitude, but one who rhymed with Khomeini. For instance: The Ayatollah who loves dogs is the Ayatollah Great Daney.

The Ayatollah mystery writer is the Ayatollah Ed McBainy. The weird Ayatollah is the Ayatollah Insaney. Okay, granted that on paper it might not look like much, but after hours of being stuck in the car with crazy Italian drivers honking their horns every fifteen seconds, it was the greatest thing that had happened to me since I was twenty-one years old in St. Tropez and saw a gorgeous blond woman walking along the beach wearing nothing but sunglasses, a thong bikini bottom, and white cowboy boots. For the rest of our trip—which at the time seemed as though it would probably be spent on the not-all-that-attractive road leading to San Remo—I became obsessed with rhyming Ayatollahs. Some of the better ones: The accordion-playing Ayatollah (the Ayatollah Lady of Spainy), the mogul Ayatollah (the Ayatollah Citizen Kaney), and the spitfire-singing Ayatollah (the Ayatollah Abbe Laney). My guess is, if I keep this up much longer, my editor will cut all the rest of them out anyway, so I think I'll stop here with the Ayatollahs.

We did finally get out of San Remo, at which point Esther seized control of the situation. We stopped at a not-fancy-looking hotel, desperate for accommodations. It wasn't seedy but it also wasn't the Ritz. Esther strode in and asked if they knew of a nice hotel anywhere in the vicinity that had a room. They asked if she wanted a room there and she said no: She wanted a *nice* hotel. (Okay: Here's where that whole Nice pronunciation comes in handy. The same way I overdid the Thanksgiving jokes when Janis and I were once in Turkey, I became a little too vigorous about switching the uses of Nice, the city, and nice, the adjective. I can't tell you how many times one of us would say, "That looks like a nice restaurant," and I would respond, "Do you mean a nice restaurant or a Nice restaurant?" I can't really defend myself on this matter, but I found it funny every single time this came up in conversation, until Janis told me that if I said "Nice" for "nice" one more time, she'd kill me.) Anyway, despite Esther's insult in the roadside hotel, she did find out that we were never going to be able to stay anywhere on the coast of Italy that week. It turns out that the whole country has Christmas Week off for vacation and, apparently, everybody *in* the whole country comes down to the coast. What was causing the traffic jam is that there is exactly *one* coast road. That's right. If you want to get anywhere on the Italian (or French, for that matter) Riviera and you don't use the highway, there is one tiny, winding road and that's it.

It didn't take us long to change our plans. We turned around immediately and headed back to Nice (which seemed like it would be nice). There we decided to treat ourselves to a magnificent evening, since our day had been so completely miserable. Instead of staying at the nice (sorry! I can't help myself) but small and moderately priced hotel Janis, Norton, and I usually stayed at, we checked into the Negresco. And we didn't just check into the Negresco—we checked into the most expensive, luxurious, over-the-top two-bedroom suite they had. For you prudes in the reading audience, don't worry; Esther checked into a third room far down the hall. She didn't want to be anywhere near any of us.

We went to a lovely restaurant, Coco Beach, right on the water, and had a perfect fish dinner. The owner—I know you'll think I'm making this up, but he really did remind me of a French William Demarest—prepared a few grilled shrimp for Norton when he got word that the cat wasn't wild about regular fish. The shrimp seemed to do the trick. As a matter of fact, ever since Coco Beach, Norton has been willing to chow down on all shellfish as well as the occasional bite of salmon. Tuna, however, remains out of the question, as do sardines.

After dinner, we went to the Nice casino. (Don't worry: My lips are sealed. I will make no comment on whether the casino was . . . ummm . . . pleasant or not.) Norm was the big winner. Not only did he pocket several hundred dollars, he came up with the world's stupidest Ayatollah (the Ayatollah No Brainy).

The next morning, we drove back to France along the glorious Mediterranean, stopping off in Eze, probably the most touristy village of its type but nonetheless a spectacular medieval town that cannot be missed. We had lunch at the Grill du Château at the very top of the town, where the waiter went crazy over Norton.

"Vôtre chat," he told me. *"Il est superb!"* He was the first cat, the waiter gushed, he'd ever seen behave like a human being.

That night was New Year's Eve and we spent it back in the Lubéron in fine style. We had a few French friends come over for some champagne—no *champagnoise* that night!— then the five of us went to Auberge de la Loube for their special New Year's dinner.

I've already described the delectable appetizers at the Auberge, but on New Year's Eve Maurice puts on a special spread. It starts with a truffle omelet—two or three eggs scrambled with the scrapings of wild, black French truffles, mushrooms so strong and delicious they are considered one of the great delicacies in the world (and priced accordingly, although Maurice doesn't charge for this dish—it's his gift to his regular clients). I don't think Maurice was all that thrilled when I gave Norton a taste, but he softened when he saw how much Norton enjoyed it.

The rest of the dinner was on a par with the *truffes,* then exactly at midnight, Maurice poured champagne for everyone and we all toasted and hugged and meowed appropriately, welcoming in the New Year.

Thursday was Esther's and Norm's last night in Provence, so naturally we had to eat even more food by way of a fond farewell.

I'd lost a bet to Esther before leaving for France—I'd said that Clarence Thomas wouldn't be confirmed; she told me I was a naive ignoramus and, of course, she turned out to be right—so my payment was to take her to Oustau de Baumanière, the legendary restaurant which is the best and most famous in this area of Provence.

Janis and I had been there before. The owner and chef, Jean André Charial, is a friend of Wolfgang Puck's and so I'd heard about this place for years and years. In fact, it's thanks to Baumanière that Janis and I really wound up in Goult. Several years before, we had stayed at the hotel (it's not just a restaurant; it's one of the great hotels in the world, too). As if the feather beds and down comforters aren't enough of an enticement, the town of Les Baux is spectacularly set into white Bauxite mountains. When you first see the town, and the hotel right outside of town, it's as if you're Ronald Colman in *Lost Horizon* and have just found Shangri-la. Over the years, we'd stayed and/or eaten there several times. Since we'd been in Goult, we'd made the forty-five-minute drive a couple of times to worship at the feet of the two-star chef. More important, Baumanière was, no question about it, Norton's favorite restaurant. The staff loved him and usually greeted him with affection and a bit of wonderment. He was automatically given his own chair when we were seated at a table, and often had a special dinner prepared for him.

This night, the restaurant outdid themselves, both for humans and for cat. Esther agreed she'd never eaten a meal like that, even in her dreams. Norm could barely say he'd had a Nice time. Janis, as usual, kept her dignity until the huge cheese cart arrived, then she lost any sense of propriety and basically just kept screaming out, "More! More! More!" to the server. Norton was served a small dish with three separate specialties—duck, scallops, and fish. At Baumanière, even Norton will eat the fish.

The *pièce de résistance,* as usual, was the dessert.

Each of the humans had ordered a specialty of the house—a hot soufflé, covered in *crème fraîche* and the appropriate sauce (if a raspberry soufflé, raspberry sauce; if chocolate soufflé, chocolate sauce; if gingerbread soufflé, their newest and possibly greatest creation, gingerbread sauce). Each of the soufflés is presented on a covered silver dish. The soufflé is brought before the diner, placed on the table, and then with a flamboyant but spritely motion, the cover is whisked away and the customer usually goes something like "Oh my God!" or "Ooooooooohhhhhhhh!" or, if you're our friend Dominick, "Is that all?!"

Four times we witnessed this ritual, first for Janis, then Esther, then Norm, then me. Then we realized there was a fifth silver dish and it was placed directly in front of Norton.

Before I really had time to ponder what they could have possibly made for my cat—a Pounce soufflé??? a Whiskas Chopped Chicken and Cheese soufflé????—the waiter whisked off the silver cover to reveal a small, gray, marzipan mouse, complete with tail, pink eyes, gray whiskers, and black marzipan nose.

The creation drew well-deserved applause—not just

from us, from other appreciative diners as well—and the pastry chef received Norton's permanent and undying gratitude.

Deep down, despite all the proof to the contrary, I know that Esther, my own agent, thinks I make all this stuff up about Norton. This night, I made a special point of watching her as she stared at the cat, who was calmly taking a few licks of his mouse on a silver tray in a two-star French restaurant as if this were something he was used to every night of the week. The look in Esther's eyes at that moment told me it was almost worth having Clarence Thomas on the Supreme Court. Not quite but almost.

The next day, my gourmet cat was most sorry to see Norm and Esther go back to New York. It meant that life, for him, was going to return to normal.

Or as normal as Norton's life ever gets.

a cat in spain

For the month of February, my old pal and writing partner, David, came to pay us a visit. It was not entirely social; we were writing a screenplay together and we decided there was no better place to write together than in my temporary office on the third (or second) floor overlooking the Lubéron valley.

In a sense, history was repeating itself as far as David and I were concerned.

So many years ago it's a little depressing, we went to the south of France together for our first collaboration. He had just graduated from journalism school and was taking a year off to travel in Europe with his girlfriend. I had just finished writing my first novel and was certain it was only a matter of time before I would be rich, famous, and a celebrated literary man about town. I was young and headstrong and thought I could do anything. One of the things I thought I could do was to quit my first real job at a publishing company and my $135 a week salary and go off and spend a year in the south of France. This was a concept carefully planned and maturely thought out in the manner of most of my plans in those years: David and I got extraordinarily drunk and stoned on a train ride from Boston to New York and at some point during the five-hour trip, we decided we'd rendezvous in Europe and write a movie together. This was in 1976.

Several terrific things came out of that train trip. We actually did write a movie together, which was flat-out horrible, but which eventually was sold as a television pilot, helping us to break into that charming business. We're still writing partners, after all these years, which was another nice result of that fifth or sixth Jack Daniel's on wheels. The best thing that happened, of course, was that we wound up rendezvousing just north of the Spanish border halfway in between the towns of Collioure and Port Vendres, which was about as close to heaven as two young, broke, would-be-screenwriters and novelists could possibly come. We had a dirt-cheap apartment and we could actually jump from our balcony into the clear, blue Mediterranean (we never did, but we *could* have, if we were really the Ernest Hemingway clones we thought we were instead of two fairly cautious Jews who didn't want to have to learn the French phrase for "Excuse me, do you have a very large bottle of iodine and several hundred yards of bandages?"). We shopped at the open-air market, which magically appeared in the Port Vendres square every Saturday, and bought fresh fish direct from the fishermen during the week (Port Vendres was still a mainstream fishing village in those days). Wine was twenty-five cents a bottle and we were too young to have ever heard about cholesterol, so we basically spread cheese on anything or anyone we possibly could. Nobody in town spoke a word of English, the temperature seemed to be eighty degrees every single day, and there was one great café in Collioure, an amazing place called the Templiers, which astonishingly had original Picassos on the wall because old Pablo and Braque and Matisse used to trade paintings for food when they were mere pups (or *petits chiens,* if you want to be technical) and lived down there. We went into the Templiers every single day after we were done writing, for a cognac or a *pastis* or just a cold beer, and when the eighty-year-old owner of the Templiers actually deigned to shake our hand one day when we came in—the ultimate sign that we were considered regulars and were now accepted by the town—we knew that, indeed, life was a very, very good thing.

We were young and even though we ran out of money in several months and had to return to New York—my novel had indeed sold to a publisher, but I learned the harsh truth that while an advance paid for a first novel does allow one to actually buy meat once in a while, it doesn't allow one to lead a Scott Fitzgerald–like lifestyle—I was under the impression that this was the way my life would be lived from then on. I did not appreciate that the daily handshakes at the Templiers and the Brigadoon-like fog of perfection surrounding Collioure were not things simply handed over on a regular basis to anyone who thinks he deserves it. It was the zenith, the goal that one strives for throughout one's life. It was, in a sense, a dream, but it was a dream I had actually experienced—and one I would not and could not forget.

Clearly, since I was now, sixteen years later, doing my best to repeat it.

I'd even gotten my old buddy Dave to repeat it with me.
And what better way to do this than by returning to our old
stomping grounds? With Janis and Norton, no less.

～～～

Janis had heard our romantic rhapsodizing and seen several
million photos of Collioure over the years. She also knew
me and David too well, and was aware that as soon as we
were back in the town for a weekend, we'd be laughing our
heads off over things unexplainable and want to see places
that had no interest for anyone who wasn't personally involved in the sightseeing. So she decided that Collioure
could not be our one and only destination. After a brief
discussion, we all agreed to stop off in Collioure Friday
night, spend some time there Saturday, then drive on down
into Spain for the rest of the weekend. We settled on Barcelona as our final destination, as neither Janis, David, nor
Norton had ever been there.

France has changed quite a bit since David and I first
discovered what it was like to live there. French people now
use English words like *parking* (as in "Make ze first right
and zen go to ze parkeeng") and *fax* has actually been given
a gender (it's male, in case you're interested—*le* fax).
Plenty of McDonald's do, indeed, dot the landscape, and
French politicians are now more or less as corrupt as their
American equivalents. (They probably were always corrupt
but it seemed as if the corruption always revolved around
sex and food. Now French corruption has been Washingto-
nized and the scandals have become financial.) Even so, we
were not prepared for our first look at the 1990s version of
Collioure.

It looked a lot like Miami Beach.

When we'd lived there, it had been a sleepy village. It

was a resort town but was not considered chic or hip and was known mostly to French people who lived in the southwest part of the country. We lived in one of the few modern apartment buildings; it was on the southern outskirts of town and was one of perhaps five or six buildings in the complex. Now, as we pulled up in our Citroën, it was almost impossible to see the village, which was completely hidden behind a skyline of giant condominiums. It was a lot like the scene in *It's a Wonderful Life* where Clarence the Angel takes Jimmy Stewart back to Bedford Falls to see what it would have been like if he'd never lived—and sleepy, all-American Bedford Falls has turned into Pottersville, where every other store is a nasty-looking saloon and naked dancing girls are everywhere you turn. Perhaps Collioure wasn't *that* bad, but it *was* a shock to the system. Everything was new and everything was ugly. Janis had that look in her eye, the one that said, *"This* is the place you've been telling me about all this time?!"

I didn't panic, however, and my patience was rewarded once we made it into the old part of town. The French may put up truly ugly new structures, but at least they don't tear down the old beautiful ones in the process. The old village was left untouched and was exactly as David and I remembered it. Once we were safely ensconced within the medieval walls of Collioure, everything was fine.

We had booked rooms at the hotel Templiers. This was not a coincidence—the Templiers was the place with the Picassos and Braques and Matisses, our old watering hole. When we lived in Collioure, we had never been able to afford to eat there, much less stay there, though the old man, Monsieur Pous, had once shown us through the whole building, pointing out some of the famous artists whose paintings also adorned the hotel walls and corridors.

The restaurant was Norton's kind of place. Very casual, very friendly, a little bit of sawdust on the floor. An excellent eatery for a cat to wander through and poke around in.

David and I were thrilled to be eating there. It was as if we'd been in there drinking our *kirs* just the day before. Some of the old-timers sitting playing cards at the back table even looked familiar. Exactly as we remembered, every inch of the walls were covered with paintings and sketches. Some of them were awful, some of them were wonderful. Some were done by absolute nobodies—if *I* gave the owner a drawing or painting, he'd put it up; and, believe me, my artistic ability stops at stick figures—but some were, incredibly, original Picassos. Right in the middle of the room was a large photo of Monsieur Pous, the owner, with his arm around Pablo himself. Framed with the photo was a Picasso line drawing of a reclining nude.

One thing had changed, sadly, in the years since we'd last been there: The old man, Monsieur Pous, had died. But his sons now ran the place, and they obviously had a keen sense of tradition. We were glad we'd had the opportunity to shake Monsieur Pous's hand back when we were young, and we'd seen enough of the way he'd run his place to know he'd approve of the way his family was carrying on.

The meal was exquisite. Norton came back from his tour just in time to share my plate of grilled squid and garlic, and stuck around long enough to have a reasonable amount of my bouillabaise. He didn't taste any of the local wine, which was very dry and very good. (In fact, the wine from Collioure is now the latest "hot" wine in France. It's still fairly inexpensive and really is delicious. It makes me proud to realize that many years ago I used to practically bathe in the stuff.)

The next day, David and I took Janis and Norton on a

nostalgic trip through our past. I sensed that Janis was a little bored but Norton seemed interested. His head was out of the shoulder bag the entire trek. I think he was glad to find that I'd actually lived a life before he'd arrived on the scene.

We took them first around the old village. We went into the *pâtisserie* I used to go into every morning to buy breakfast. Every single day for three months, I'd go in and ask for *"deux pains au chocolat"*—two chocolate croissants. Unfortunately, my *"deux"*—two—sounded like *"du"*—some. So five days a week, four weeks a month, for three full months, I'd ask for *two pains au chocolat*, and each one of those days the woman behind the counter would smile and say, "Very well, monsieur. And how many would you like?" It didn't matter how I pronounced the *"deux,"* it didn't matter that I sometimes repeated it three times, as in, *"Je voudrais deux, deux, deux pains au chocolat"* and hold two fingers up in front of me. Every single time she would ask me how many I wanted and every single time I'd want to kill myself because I couldn't make her understand my French. Years later, a dear friend of ours in Goult, Danie, showed me how to distinctly differ my pronunciation when saying *"du"* and *"deux."* Still psychologically scarred after all that time, I worked up my nerve, went into the Goult *pâtisserie*, and asked for *"deux pains au chocolat."* "Very well, monsieur," the woman behind the Goult counter said. "And how many would you like?" Crushed and humiliated, I went running to Danie for consolation. She told me how to avoid this problem forever after: I should, from here on in, order *trois pains au chocolat!*

We walked out to the old stone lighthouse and in and out of the town's alleyways and cobblestone paths. In these sections, nothing had changed at all and that stability was, to me, remarkably reassuring and exhilarating.

After we got through walking Janis and Norton all over town, we drove out to see our old apartment building. This was the worst change of all. It was no longer one small ugly building surrounded by four or five other small ugly buildings. It had turned into a giant and horrendous apartment complex. There were probably a hundred and fifty hideous condos built at the spot. We still were excited to see it— although Janis couldn't understand why we'd get excited visiting the ugliest place she'd ever seen in France.

By late Saturday morning, we'd gotten the past out of our system and were now ready to head to Spain.

Collioure is only a few miles north of the border. We drove past Port Vendres, which was just as lovely as we remembered, past the towns of Banyul and Corbere, and then we were in Spain. Or nearly in Spain.

Going from France to Italy with a cat is no problem. In fact, the Italian border guards never even look at Norton when we drive there. The same for Switzerland. Luckily, I'd brought Norton's papers along, because it turns out the Spanish are very strict about bringing pets into their country.

"You have a cat," one of the six border guards told me.

"Si," I said. (Spanish is one of the many languages I also don't speak. I tried French and English and even a word or two of Italian, hoping one of those would work. They didn't.)

"He has a cat," the guard now said to another guard. Why they needed six border guards when clearly ours was the only car that had passed through all day was beyond me. But I didn't want to ask. I was already in enough of a jam.

"Si, si," one of the guards now chimed in. *"Uno gato!"*

"Do you have the papers for the cat?" I was now asked.

It turned out I *didn't* have the papers for the cat. I had

papers, but not the right papers. In Spain, you need some special permission from the embassy or some such place. But, happily, the guards didn't really have any idea what the right papers were either.

"He has papers," one of them announced.

"Are they the right papers?" another one asked.

"I don't know. They're in English."

"Ask him if they're the right papers."

"*Señor,*" the first guard now asked me. "Are these the right papers for the cat?"

"Yes," I lied and nodded very convincingly.

The guards relaxed and smiled—all six of them—and waved us through.

Now we were in Spain.

Our first stop was Cadeques, one-time home of Salvador Dali as well as a lovely northern beach town. The drive there was fairly uneventful, except that the road was particularly winding and curving and both Janis and David got kind of woozy. They wound up in the backseat feeling sorry for themselves. Norton sat happily beside me, the perfect passenger.

After lunch in Cadeques, we took the *péage*—the high-speed toll highway—to Barcelona.

Barcelona may be the perfect European city. It's small, stunningly beautiful, very sophisticated. The people are friendly and the food is delicious. And they like cats. As I said: perfect.

Norton toured the city with us from morning till night. He saw the spot from which Columbus set sail for America, he took a walking tour of the Barri Gòtic (the Gothic Quarter), he visited several Gaudi buildings, including the still-being-constructed Sagrada Famillia cathedral, he ate a special Catalanes paella for dinner at the restaurant La Cuineta.

Then, to top it off, he—and we—saw one of the great sights of the western world.

In front of the cathedral, which dominates the square in the center of the majestic Gothic Quarter, we witnessed a hundred Barcelonians dancing the official dance of Barcelona—the almost indescribable "sardana."

Night had just arrived, candles were flickering on the tables in the outdoor cafés, there was mystery and romance in the darkness and shadows. Suddenly ten circles formed, rings of ten people each. Every member of the circle held hands, the hands raised triumphantly above their heads, and all had replaced their regular shoes with white espadrilles. The ritual had begun. They stood like this, motionless, for perhaps thirty seconds, then an orchestra, tucked into a corner of the massive square, began playing lively, sensual, exquisite Spanish music—and then a hundred grown-ups began spinning and dancing and flailing exactly like Jerry Lewis on the bandstand in *You're Never Too Young.* It was the scariest, most inane sight I've *ever* seen. If a hundred people did this in New York, I guarantee they'd be beaten to a pulp and then arrested—and deservedly so. Forget the ritualized beauty and power everyone talks about. Forget all that passionate blood coursing through Spanish veins. I'm telling you, this was worse than the clog dancers on the Labor Day telethon.

That more or less ended Norton's first visit to Spain. I believe a statue was later erected after our weekend trip, commemorating the very spot on the square where an American tourist actually laughed so hard, he almost passed out.

We did stop for lunch on the way back, at a tiny café on the coast. The sun was shining, so we sat outside and drank sangria while Norton ate to his heart's content off an enormous plate of grilled shrimp.

The waiter came by at some point; he stood over our table without saying anything, watching the cat. Finally, he turned to me and said, "Your *gato*. He is Spanish?"

"No," I told him. "American. By way of Scotland."

The waiter stayed by our table for another few minutes, watching Norton munch on the *gambas*. Before he turned to go back to the kitchen, the waiter tapped me on the shoulder, then pointed at Norton.

"He is handsome enough to be Spanish," he announced.

We finished our sangria, gathered the cat up, and headed back for the car and for France.

"You are handsome enough," I said to my little gray pal. "Just don't try puttin' on those espadrilles. Even *I* have my limits."

Forty-five minutes later we were back on French soil, where the border guards didn't ask to see Norton's papers, only welcomed him into the country with a very polite *"Bonjour, Monsieur le chat. Ça va?"*

It felt a lot like coming home.

a cat in Italy

8

At some point, before we settled on Provence, there was a very good chance that Norton was going to have to learn Italian.

I think he would have adjusted with few qualms. For one thing, he's very happy with Italian cat food. He still won't eat Petreet's *Tonno con Riso* (although I definitely would, in a pinch; it looks *good*), but the Gioie di Miao version of *Pranzo Regale con Gamberetti* is, judging from the way Norton attacks it, as good as anything he's had in the finest restaurants. He even enjoys, when the mood strikes, the Italian dry food, the Brekkies *con pollo* and *con manzo*. And Norton usually feels about dry food the way I feel about movies where Barbra Streisand plays the sex object.

Norton's spent a lot of time in Italy over the years, as have Janis and I. Since Goult was so close to the border, and since all three of us had travel in our blood, we spent a lot of time in Pastaland during our year abroad.

Our first foray came only a few weeks after we'd arrived in France. We went down to Nice to visit our friends the Douglases, and the next morning, instead of turning back and heading home, we ventured twenty minutes further away and went to Italy for lunch.

The moment you cross the border, everything changes. The French plant in straight, orderly rows. Their vineyards are organized and perfectly manicured. In Italy, nothing is straight or orderly. Everything looks as if it's been planted by Foster Brooks. Five minutes away from France, the cheese is completely different, the vegetables are different, the whole way of life is as if it's another planet.

This was always difficult to explain to our Goult friends, who usually thought we were nuts when we'd tell them we went to Italy for lunch or drove to Barcelona for the weekend. That's not something they ever would have done. We would explain that in America you can drive for three days straight, and still be in the same country and the same basic culture. If you start in Goult and drive for three days straight, you're in a completely new world.

So we would pop over to the border town Ventimiglia for lunch on occasion, usually to the *ristorantes* La Caravella (on the water) or Cuneo (right in town; very near the market where Norton refused to scarf down a sardine). At Cuneo, the proprietors, Beraudo and Figli, were particularly nice to Norton. By the end of our first visit, it was clear he was free to wander through the restaurant; what was theirs was his. One thing I'll never know is how or why cats pick their favorite spots, but pick them they do, and at Cuneo Norton's favorite spot was underneath a large, elaborately carved wooden hutch. That's where he'd eat and that's where he'd stay until we'd polished off every last drop of our Chianti.

The first time we made this sojourn to Italy, we had a little surprise waiting for us back in Goult.

We left Ventimiglia soon after lunch, at three-thirty or so, and arrived in Goult at six P.M. As we pulled into town, we were a little startled to find somewhere around two hundred and fifty people—approximately a quarter of the town—marching around the streets, up, over, and down, starting and ending at the Salle des Fêtes (literally, the Holiday Room, but what it is is the town meeting place, where they have everything from political rap sessions to the weekly bingo festivities). As if it weren't strange enough to find the whole town on parade, they were being led by twenty guys dressed like Richard Burton at the end of *Beckett*. They had on red and green robes, pointy hats, and were wearing religious-looking insignia and necklaces. As if *that* weren't enough, they would stop walking every ten feet or so and blow into long trumpets, blaring something vaguely heraldic. Every time they stopped and blew, the whole town would cheer wildly.

Needless to say, we parked our car and joined the rally, curious to see what could possibly be going on. I assumed Goult had won the French version of the World Series or else it was Bridget Bardot's birthday, which I'm sure must be a national holiday over there. It turns out I was wrong on both counts. The guys in the red and green robes were The Brotherhood of Wine Growers (those religious necklaces weren't religious or necklaces, it turned out: They were silver wine-tasting cups), and this was the annual march to celebrate the new vintage Côtes du Ventoux wine. They didn't just march, either. They gathered the whole town in the Salle des Fêtes and handed out free glasses of red, rosé, and white to anyone who wanted to taste it. We followed the parade from beginning to end, went into the

Salle des Fêtes, happily drank our glasses of wine, shook hands with the silly-looking guys in the robes (there were also two silly-looking women in robes, to show how far the French have progressed), then we went home, wondering if this is what would happen every time we went off to Italy for a day.

It wasn't. But that didn't stop us from going there. And we did venture further than Ventimiglia on several occasions.

My mother came over from Los Angeles to visit us for a while. We decided, on the semi-spur of the moment, to take a few days off and head toward Tuscany, which, unbelievably to us, was only a five-hour drive away. Going there is like driving from New York to Boston, except when you arrive you don't have to listen to Red Sox fans feel sorry for themselves. Plus the food's a lot better.

Our first stop was the town of Levanto, in the provence of Liguria, and the hotel Stella Maris (Roger's wife—and yes, I did say that at the time, and yes, Janis did swat me on the arm). The hotel is really nothing more than a bed and breakfast, slightly run-down but very cozy, and only a block from the beach, which is nice in season. But what really makes it special is that there are huge and spectacular sixteenth-century frescoes all over the ceilings, and the people who run the hotel make you feel as if you're a member of their family. Norton was the first cat who'd ever stayed there and at first they didn't know what to do for him. They kept knocking on our door and offering food, then milk, then they knocked just to see if he was content and comfortable.

We'd had a bit of trouble finding the Stella Maris the night we pulled into town. After driving aimlessly for a few minutes, we decided to stop at a café and see if we could figure out how to ask directions. The café we stopped at had nothing but Italian men standing around swigging down beer and anisette. Norton and I went in to see what was what. At first, the guys in the café stared at me as if I were from Mars. Not because I had a cat on my shoulder, but because I kept asking for a street called the via Marconi. After a while, one of the grizzled regulars came over to me and said, "Via *Mar*coni?" "Sì, sì," I said. "Via *Mar*coni." They all got a major laugh about the fact that I thought such a street might have been pronounced via Mar*co*ni, and then the real laughs started when they tried to give me directions. At some point, the same grizzler took me by the arm, put his hand on Norton's head, and yanked me out of the bar and into my car. He then shoved Janis over, climbed in, and began barking out orders 'that we interpreted, sometimes correctly, sometimes not, as things like "Go!" and "Right!" and "Left!" After fifteen minutes, he said something we were pretty sure meant "Stop!" and when I did, he hopped out of the car, disappeared around a corner, and we found our car parked right in front of the hotel Stella Maris.

Our second night in Italy, we stayed in the truly extraordinary town of Lucca and in the even more extraordinary hotel (a misnomer; it really is a castle), Villa S. Michele.

Villa S. Michele was originally built in the fourteenth century, added on to in the seventeenth century, and has been magnificently restored by the owner, whose name actually was Giuseppe, an Italian charmer in his late fifties or early sixties.

We spent the day touring Lucca, an old walled city that has to be seen to be believed. After many months in the small and relatively unsophisticated environs of Goult, we were surprised at how sophisticated and stylish the Italian version of the Lubéron really was. The chicest thing one could buy at the L'isle-sur-la-Sorgue market was a fancy apron. In Lucca, built into the ancient stone and rock, were row after row of designer clothing stores. Even Norton seemed to get a little bit of a lift spending the day around so many gorgeous and well-turned-out people.

At lunchtime, at another superb Italian restaurant, Bucadisantantonio, Norton was paid the supreme compliment. The four of us were quietly making oohing and ahh-ing noises over our pastas (or our small ashtray full of diced-up grilled chicken, depending on whom we're talking about), when I noticed a man at a nearby table doing nothing but staring at Norton, who, as usual, was sitting next to me on his own chair, eating and minding his own business. I smiled at the man but he didn't smile back—he just kept staring. Finally, after he and his wife paid their check and stood up to leave, he hesitated, then approached our table. He said something to me in Italian and when I indicated that I didn't understand, he asked whether I spoke French. When I nodded, he said, as solemnly as could be, *"Votre chat, monsieur. Il est très sage."*

Your cat, sir. He is very wise.

Yes, I agreed. I'd been told that before. Very wise. And the man, content to have paid homage, turned and left the restaurant.

We got back to the hotel, exhausted, having covered every inch of Lucca on foot (Norton was sound asleep in his shoulder bag long before we made it back to the hotel). When we arrived, the owner/restorer was behind the desk. He was a friendly sort, so when we asked for our key, he started talking, asking us what we'd done all day, etc., etc. As we were starting to trudge upstairs to our rooms, for some reason he stopped us and said the magical words, "Do you like to eat?"

I don't know what made him ask that. Perhaps it was the strands of pasta that were still dangling from my mouth, several hours after lunch. Perhaps we just had that lean and hungry look (well, hungry look, anyway). Either way, his eyes lit up when I said to him that yes, not only did we like to eat but that my mother was a fairly well-known cook and cookbook writer back in the United States.

Our new best friend got incredibly excited.

"Where are you going for dinner tonight?" he asked, and when I told him, he shook his head and said, "No, no, no." Then he paused and asked, "Do you like truffles?"

We all looked at one another, shrugged, and went, "Sure." (By the way, this conversation was not as easy as it looked—our new pal didn't speak a word of English; we compromised on a fairly rocky bastardization of French.) "I will take care of you," he announced and immediately went to the phone, dialed, waited a few seconds, then spoke rapid Italian for several seconds and hung up. He turned to us proudly and said, "I called the best restaurant in the region, told them a famous chef was coming, and told them to prepare a masterpiece for you!" He then insisted that we come down an hour before dinner, so he could serve us a drink and some cheese.

After a brief nap, we rendezvoused back in the lobby and met our new protector. He took us downstairs to his private bar, in the hotel's *cave,* where he poured an ice-cold local white wine for an aperitif. Just in case we weren't going to eat enough food at the restaurant he was sending us to, he also cut some slabs of fresh Parmesan cheese and homemade sausage (which Norton thought was the single most delicious thing he'd ever eaten).

Our host, Giuseppe, had thinning white-yellow hair, thick black-framed glasses, and wore a black turtleneck. He looked like a worker; his hands were rough and strong when he slapped you on the back (as he was wont to do) or clasped your hands in friendship. He was extremely energetic, full of life and lust (I'm fairly sure I caught him batting his eyes at dear old Mom once or twice). He also loved to talk, and thus told us his entire life story. He spoke French because he'd learned it in school. While studying, his teacher had given him the name of a girl in Paris—a countess. They exchanged letters (supposedly as language practice) and he fell in love, going back and forth between Rome and Paris to see her for eighteen years. (I don't know what happened after the eighteen years. At that point in the story, I started to be able to think of nothing else but how delicious that cheese was and concentrated on eating as much as possible before we had to leave for the restaurant.) He used to run a modern hotel on the island of Elba, then decided to come to Tuscany, where he renovated S. Michele over a period of three and a half years (it had just opened a few months before we'd accidentally stumbled in there).

By the time we'd polished off his bottle of wine—for which he refused to charge us—it was time to leave for our truffle extravaganza. It turned out to be far more than we had bargained for.

The restaurant Solferino, just outside of Lucca, was nothing fancy. Quite the contrary. It was a family-run joint, divided up into seven or eight small rooms. The bar was filled, as so many Italian places are, with locals playing cards and arguing over something or other. But we did happen to have the best dinner I've ever had in my life.

Nobody in the restaurant spoke a word of English. Or French, for that matter. So we were helpless captives. One of the waiters recognized us as the Americans they had been told about, so he ushered us to a table and just started bringing food over. Since our friend at the hotel had told them we liked truffles, it was truffles we were served. The first dish was sliced raw beef topped with thinly sliced truffles and olive oil. Then came a pasta dish—ravioli stuffed with truffles and topped with truffle cream. Then came another pasta dish—gnocchi in red-pepper truffle sauce. Then came *another* pasta—ravioli stuffed with roast pheasant and, you guessed it, truffles.

Before we came into the restaurant, Janis had made a point of saying that she wanted to pay for dinner; she hadn't been allowed to pay for anything on the trip so far. My mother agreed to keep her hands off the check, as did I (Norton's only flaw is that he *never* picks up the check, so we didn't bother to clear it with him). However, at this point in the meal, as we realized there was more food still to come, I pointed out to Janis that, with all the truffles we were getting, this meal was likely to cost several million dollars (or several billion lira, as the case may be). That certainly didn't stop us from eating, however. We were then served a guinea hen roasted with truffles—that was the highlight, for me—and then, believe it or not, we were each served a small beefsteak topped with truffles and grated fresh Parmesan cheese. At this point, I thought there was a fifty-fifty chance I was going to explode.

Even Norton had had enough by this time. Still exhausted from his tour of Lucca, he even decided he'd get off his own chair and snuggle up onto my lap for a while. He figured he deserved a soft lap and some petting while we were waiting for dessert.

All during dinner, there was a man sitting at the table behind us. He had a loud, gravelly voice; he sounded as if Lucca Brazi had, some years earlier, removed his vocal chords with a fork. The entire time we were there, he would point over at Norton, pound the table, laugh incredibly loudly, and scream out to the entire restaurant, *"Il gatto! Incredibile!"* This went on for hours.

The incredible *gatto* was now sound asleep on my lap, but the humans were still going. The waiter brought out some chocolate-covered grapes and three round custard-filled doughy pastries, with miniature American flags stuck into them.

Finally, when we were finished stuffing our faces, the owner of the restaurant made an appearance. He sat down with us and we did our best to converse, although there really was a serious language barrier. We got him to understand that my mother worked with some famous chefs back in Los Angeles, and he got all excited, ran back into another room somewhere, then returned with his scrapbook. As we were flipping through it, admiring his various clippings and credentials, we realized that many of the chefs my mother was friendly with had come to study under or work with this guy. Suddenly she was looking at pictures of her L.A. cooking pals, all with their arms around Mr. Truffle. Needless to say, this lent a whole new air of excitement to our evening. Everyone started talking loudly and waving their hands, even though no one had any idea what anyone else was saying. After we'd gone through all the clippings, he took us on a tour of the kitchen and the rest of the restaurant and then introduced us to his mother—who was eighty-three years old and was still the chef for the restaurant. She'd done all the cooking that night—and did all the cooking six nights a week. We learned that it was her father who'd started the restaurant sixty years earlier.

The check came—and it was embarrassingly low after my snide comment; he hardly charged us for anything, much less for the truffles—and with it came a complimentary bottle of *grappa*. Even for us, that was just too much. We told him we couldn't possibly eat or drink one more thing, so our host and new pal wrapped up the bottle and told us to take it back to France, which of course we did.

As we left, we got hugged and kissed by the old mother, and we were hugging and kissing anyone else who got in our way. Norton had revived himself, so he came in for some heavy petting, too. As we stepped out the door, we were told that we—all four of us—would be welcome back whenever we happened to be in the neighborhood.

a cat in sicily (and other places)

One of the things Janis most wanted to do on her year's sabbatical was travel. Unlike me, who left to my own devices would have been content to plop down in Goult and plop up a year later when it was time to leave, Janis wanted to visit as many places and see as many new things as possible.

Having positions that couldn't be more polar opposites, we compromised. We would travel and visit and see as much as we could until I got too cranky and started complaining. At that point, we'd either return to Goult or find a nice, quiet beach somewhere where the most active moment would be turning over from back to stomach to tan another side of the body.

We wound up moving around quite a bit and, of course, wherever we moved, Norton moved. We and he would have it no other way.

One of my fantasies in life is to, one of these days, spend a month or two being a ski bum. I don't actually ski very often or very well, although I can get down a not-too-difficult slope without killing myself. But I enjoy it and it seems like something worth mastering. The idea of paralleling down a mountain at breakneck speed is extraordinarily appealing to me, although I know if I really went at it, there's a good chance I'd wind up in a Swiss emergency room looking a lot like the Boris Karloff version of *The Mummy.*

Norton had been cross-country skiing in Vermont, where I must confess he spent most of the trek on my shoulder, though he did run around in the bushes, following the trail for part of the time. I decided he'd like to see the Alps, so we drove up into the mountains for a weekend.

Janis's idea of fun, in case you were ever in doubt, does not include skiing. It does not, in fact, include any activity where it's possible to break a bone, scrape skin off the body, or ever possibly see one's own blood. But even she was charmed by Aix-les-Bains, on the French side of the Alps.

She got her hopes up as we pulled into town, when she saw there was no snow on the ground. I pointed out to her, however, that the skiing—and thus the snow—was several miles higher. We would stay in Les Bains for two nights, but most of our activities would take place up by the ski slopes.

At this point in the narrative, I would like to interrupt to give a free lesson to everyone reading this book: Don't, under any circumstances, ever try to teach your spouse to ski. It's much, *much* worse than teaching the proper way to drive a stick shift.

I think it sufficient to say that Janis fell down fourteen times in the first three minutes of our lesson. Most of those were directly in front of the ski shop where we rented our equipment. She never even made it to the beginners' slope. Within seconds of her final tumble, her skis were off and she was sitting in the warm restaurant trying to decide which she hated more, skiing or me.

Even Norton deserted me on this occasion. He just wasn't in the mood to frolic in the snow, so he joined Janis for the cat equivalent of a hot toddy.

By the time I'd gotten in my ski time, both girlfriend and cat were, luckily for me, warm and relaxed. They liked the *raclette* dinner I took them to much more than they liked battling nature.

A *raclette* is a very special Alps experience. *Raclette* is a type of cheese that comes in a large brick. When it's served up in the mountains, it's placed on a special *raclette* oven that gets extremely hot and melts the cheese down layer by layer. As it melts, people at the table reach over and use everything from bread to *vinaigred* onions to *cornichons* to tiny baked potatoes to scoop the now-gooey cheese up and eat it. Add some good beer or a cold bottle of white wine, plus a stunning view of the snow-covered Alps, and you've got a memorable dining experience.

Norton was quite pleased with his first *raclette* experience. He was also pleased with the owner of the restaurant, who kept wagging his finger at Norton and enticing him through the swinging door into the kitchen. Every few minutes, we'd hear a "Psssttt" and turn to see the owner, visible through the small porthole in the kitchen door, motioning for the cat to join him. Norton would hop off his chair, disappear for a few moments, then return happily licking his lips.

~~~

As our year abroad was drawing to a close, *The Cat Who Went to Paris* began to be published in various countries around the world. Several of those countries wanted Norton to come do publicity.

England was the one country Norton couldn't visit, since they still have that horrendous six-month quarantine for all animals. But at least the Brits could understand the language and most of the references made in the book. The Japanese translator had a few problems.

While we were in Goult, she wrote me the following note:

> *Dear Mr. Gethers,*
> *It was my great pleasure to translate your book. I can't believe there is such an amazing cat as Norton. I have been a dog lover and afraid of cats since my childhood, but through the translation of this book, I have changed greatly. Now I can walk up to a cat, say hello, and scratch under his (or her) chin. I am surprised to know how beautiful and elegant the felines are.*
> *While translating Norton's story into Japanese, I came across a lot of phrases and a lot of proper nouns which I couldn't understand. I will be very happy if you kindly answer the following questions.*

She then proceeded to list all the things she couldn't understand. By the time I got to the end of the list, I was not only amazed that she liked it, I was shocked she had any idea at all what I was writing about. Plus, when I saw the particular references she was questioning, I became a little worried about my own sensibility.

Her first question was: "Is Eric your older brother or younger brother? I have to know which, because in Japan we use a different word for each of them." (More than anything, this made me happy I was only learning French, not Japanese.) Her next question was: "Tarte tatin. What is this? How do you pronounce these words?" (This also made me happy I was living in France rather than Japan.) The list went on: "P. 20. Willie Davis, Willie Wilson, Willie Mays. Who are they? Please explain about them." "P. 20: Who is Roger 'the Dodger' Staubach? Is 'the Dodger' his nickname?" "Grand High Exalted Wizard. What is this?" "What is kibble? Cat food?" "Ted Bundy. Please explain." "Who are the Seven Santini Brothers?" "Who is John Gotti? A real man or an imaginary one?" "What are the Rams? And why do they stink? Please explain." "What kind of shop is Victoria's Secret?" "What is the Liberace Museum in Las Vegas?" "I do not understand the phrase 'Jack La Lanne's personal hell.' Who is Jack La Lanne?"

It went on, but you get the idea. More than anything else, I wondered if there was any other book ever published that had references to Willie Mays, Ted Bundy, kibble, Victoria's Secret, and the Seven Santini Brothers. Probably not. And that was probably a good thing.

The Dutch had a few problems, too. They didn't know the reference to The Grand High Exalted Wizard either, which, of course, is from "The Honeymooners," from whence Norton derives his memorable moniker. They also didn't know who Laura Petrie or Oscar the Grouch were. They did know who Willie Mays was, which made me feel somewhat better. I never heard from the Italian, German, or Swedish translators, so I assume those countries all watch old Seven Santini Brothers movies and shop mail order at Victoria's Secret.

The Dutch publisher invited us to come up from Provence for the publication in Holland. In Amsterdam— where, several years before, Norton had taken the town by storm when we went there with Polanski—my cat picked up exactly where he left off.

The afternoon we arrived, the publisher, a delightful woman named Hanca Leppink, who ran the firm of Luitingh Sijthoff (don't worry: I can't come close to pronouncing it either), had a pub party for Norton up in her conference room. The entire staff turned up to shake hands (or paws) with *De kat die naar Parijs gin.* The humans all drank champagne and munched on Dutch hors d'oeuvres while the star of the party, a certain Scottish Fold, sat in the center of the room munching on his own special plate of herring while everyone at the company took turns petting him.

After the party, Hanca and a few other people from the office took Janis, Norton, and me out to dinner. Norton, still a bit full from all that raw herring, barely nibbled at his share of the *rijstaffel,* though he enjoyed the evening immensely.

The next two days in Amsterdam were spent being interviewed and photographed by Dutch and Belgian newspapers and magazines. The interviews proved to be remarkably similar to the American interviews we'd done—with one exception. There was one question that all Americans stayed away from. But every single Dutch journalist made a point of bringing this up: They wanted to know what I would do when Norton died.

I was so startled by the question and the topic that the first time I had to give an answer, I fumbled and stumbled through some complete piece of pap. By the third or fourth time this came up, I was at least composed, though I never was able to come up with anything satisfactory, much less glib. Basically, what I said is exactly what I felt: This was something I would have great difficulty dealing with and I didn't think I had to begin dealing with it yet. There was a good chance Norton would live for another ten years, at least. Who knew what would happen in ten years? Who knew if *I'd* be alive in ten years?

To be honest, Norton's death is something I'm not able to think about. I know it happens to the best of us; I've certainly been through it with humans, with those closest to me, those whom I've loved the most. Yet, somehow, it's different with my cat. Maybe it's because there's no formal language with which to directly communicate caring or sorrow. When a parent is old or dying, it's easy (unless you're British) to say the words "I love you." And once those words are said, it makes everything less difficult, even the pain of a final separation. Perhaps that kind of verbal communication assuages guilt. Perhaps it's merely a soothing way to release emotions. But with an animal, words are meaningless. It's actions that count (which, strangely enough since I'm a writer, I prefer. I don't really trust words. They can be used to manipulate too easily). In a sense, there's no way to finalize and communicate grief to an animal. And somehow that makes grief all the more difficult to comprehend and come to grips with.

There's no real point to this diatribe except to say that, after my morbid grilling by the Dutch, I think I've become even more solicitous of Norton. When it does finally come time to say good-bye to him, I want to be sure he knows how much he's meant to me.

I may not be able to *tell* him I love him, but I sure can *show* him.

~~~

Our brief trip to Amsterdam was notable for a few other memorable moments. I don't know whether I'm responsible for this great cultural leap forward, but I do know that the week Norton and I were there promoting our book, "The Honeymooners" made its first ever appearance on Dutch TV. In the television listings, under the heading for 7 P.M. on the channel Nederland 3, it read: *"Honeymooners. Is een in 1955 opgenomen komische Amerikaanse serie over twee echtparen. De opschepperige bus-chauffeur Ralph Kramden en zign vrouw Alice, en hun buren Ed en Trixie Norton."* I have absolutely no idea what that means, but I desperately hope *opgenomen komische* is the Dutch translation for "Raccoon Lodge."

I'd been to Amsterdam for the first time twenty years before. What I mostly remembered from that trip was that hashish was legal and that, if you took the boat trip up and down the canals, you heard the single most annoying phrase in the world over and over and *over* again. On those trips, the tour guides repeat everything in four languages: English, French, German, and Dutch. So, near the beginning of the tour, when they tell you the history of how Amsterdam got its name, you hear this, in a lilting, lovely accented English: "First the town was built around the Amstel River. And the dams were what made the river function. So you see? Amstel . . . dam . . . Ams*tel*dam . . . *Amster*dam!" Then, once the English version is finished, a couple of minutes later, you hear the guide, blabbing away in German. You don't understand anything you hear until the guide comes to the phrase "Amstel . . . dam . . . Ams*tel*dam . . . *Amster*dam!" A few minutes after that, the French begins and you can maybe pick out one or two phrases, and then comes "Amstel . . . dam . . . Ams*tel*dam . . . *Amster*dam!" And there's still one more to go. There's some guttural Dutch, then some more guttural Dutch, then even more guttural Dutch, then, that's right: "Amstel . . . dam . . . Ams*tel*-

dam . . . *Amster* dam!" Believe me, this is not something you can get out of your mind easily. Twenty years later, if someone orders an Amstel Light, I find myself going, "Amstel . . . light . . . Amstellight . . . Amster Light!"

I'm almost over the fixation now, and I suppose I should get serious psychiatric help, but I did refuse to take another canal tour with Norton and Janis. I didn't want to be repeating that phrase over and over to myself when I'm eighty years old and living in the home for aged cat owners.

One thing I did revisit while in Amsterdam was the Anne Frank house.

Janis and I walked to the famed hiding place with Norton on my shoulder. Two blocks away, Janis suddenly went sprawling in the middle of the street. I helped her up, concerned but certainly not overly concerned, figuring she'd merely tripped. But when she was back on her feet, tears were streaming down her cheeks and she grabbed me, bordering on hysteria. Astonished, I asked her what the hell was going on.

"You don't understand," she sobbed. "I sprain my ankle almost every week! My ankles are so weak I can hardly walk and it hurts so *much!*"

"Don't cry," I tried to soothe. "It's not the worst thing in the world."

That only made her sob harder. "It *is* the worst thing in the world. I can't walk without hurting myself! And I look like an idiot, falling down all the time! *What could be worse!!!*"

"Well," I said slowly, holding her in my arms and thinking about where we were headed, "how about being forced to hide in an attic for three years and then being killed by Nazis?"

That ended the ankle problem and any ensuing complaints. We then walked—slowly—to the museum and, with a subdued cat, saw where the tragic story had all transpired.

Afterward, we walked back to our hotel in silence—it's almost impossible to talk after being enveloped by the sadness of that house. Janis didn't mention her ankle and, for the first time in months, Norton didn't meow repeatedly to let me know it was past his feeding time.

~~~

Our last major trip of the year was to Sicily, a place I'd desperately wanted to visit after sitting through *Godfather I* and *II* forty-seven times each.

We were particularly excited about going. It seemed more exotic than our other travels yet not at all intimidating. It promised to be luxurious yet still mysterious. There was Italian food, but even better than normal because it was *garlicy* Italian food. And we knew Norton would be accepted. He'd seen *The Godfather* at least as many times as I had.

Getting there was your basic nightmare, unfortunately. This is the worst thing about traveling with a cat: If a plane's late, a person can relax in the bar, go to the bathroom, do whatever he wants. But it's extremely difficult for a cat to cope when takeoff is delayed by an hour or two. I do everything possible to keep things under control for Norton. He has access to his litter box until the last possible moment. He's free to roam around at all times except for when airline officials tell me he must be in his traveling kennel. And, of course, Norton is an experienced traveler, so he rarely panics. But it's not fair to keep a cat away from a litter box too long (even Norton has his limits), and though I try to make traveling as comfortable as possible for him, it has to be faced that he must go through some inconveniences if he wants to come along.

The plane leaving for Rome was an hour and a half late. Luckily the plane was fairly empty and, having learned my lesson from a couple of accidents early in our traveling experiences, I brought a portable litter box on board. I didn't fill it up with litter—that would have been a little much—but I did unfold it and put it under the seat in front of me. Every twenty minutes or so, I'd put Norton in the box until he got the urge to use it. Then I was able to get rid of the box in the bathroom—and no one on the plane was ever bothered.

The airline officials in Italy are even more relaxed than in France. For both takeoffs and landings (from Marseille to Rome, then from Rome to Catania in Sicily), the stewards let Norton sit calmly on my lap. I think he reminded them a little bit of Marcello Mastroianni, so they just decided to leave him be.

Supposedly, our hotel was about an hour's drive from the Catania airport. There was one small problem, however: It's not possible to get *out* of Catania. We picked up our rental car (and immediately put a litter box *with* litter on the floor in the back), took a look at our instructions, drove away—and got hopelessly lost. We were told to leave the airport and look for signs that lead to the autostrade, then take that in the direction of the town of Enna. We left the airport—and there were no signs. Not one. Not even a stop sign at the intersection. We took a guess and made a right, heading down a road that looked like something out of *Mad Max*. After fifteen minutes of aimless driving through slums

and totally deserted, burnt-out areas, we stopped and motioned to a pedestrian. "Autostrade?" we said pathetically.
"Enna?"

We got directions promptly (and loudly)—but they were
the wrong directions. After another bewildering fifteen
minutes, we stopped and asked somebody else. This person
shook his head gravely, started doing "tsk tsk" with his
tongue, and told us we were lost. Thanks a lot, pal. He then
gave us long, complicated *new* directions, which also
proved to be completely wrong. Eventually we struck out
on our own again and found the autostrade, although we
never saw a sign that said anything even remotely resem-
bling ENNA. However, we did see something that pointed
us toward Messina, which the map showed was approximately the right direction. The miracle of it all was that we
were told it would take us an hour to get to Taormina,
where we were staying, and when we pulled up to our
hotel, the trip had taken exactly an hour. The moral of that
story is that normal directions in Sicily seem to be, "First
you pull out of the airport. Then you get lost for half an
hour and feel like an idiot . . ."

I don't want to turn this section into a travelogue. Let's
just leave it that Norton did all the usual touring. He went
to the Villa Romana, near the Piazza Armerina, which has
incredible Roman tiles (Janis liked the ones of the birds
with bright plumage; I preferred the bikini-clad women
dancing arm in arm). We went up to Castlemodo, a little
town that overlooks what seems to be the entire world.
Norton got lugged to Siracusa, which once was the center
of the world and, judging from everything I've seen, probably should be again. He went with us to Noto, an eighteenth-century village which is entirely gold-hewed. Even
the white wine has a bronze tint to it. He also went to

Agricento and the extraordinary Valley of the Temples and to the town of Sciacca, a city of thermal baths (I'm sure this doesn't need to be said, but yes, I did drive Janis crazy doing a lot of Sciacca Therapy jokes). We had dinner one night in a total nontouristy town called Forza d'Agro. We ate at a small café as farmers walked by, carrying on their heads baskets of grain and fruit and even chickens, on their way home from the fields. Wild cats kept coming up to our table to beg for food, which I think made Norton feel a little guilty. Also somewhat thankful that he was with us, rather than out on his own.

The only place Norton didn't go with us was to see Mount Etna—while it was exploding. We went at night and it was an awesome sight, beautiful and terrible at the same time. Everywhere we looked there was molten red lava flowing down the mountain toward small besieged villages. I figured Norton was better off in the hotel. I didn't know if he'd be feeling adventurous, but I didn't particularly want to deal with having a Scottish Fold Red Adair on my hands.

Of the places we stayed, Norton much preferred Taormina. We stayed in a fifteenth-century castle that stood on a cliff, looming several hundred feet over the sea. And when I say looming, I mean *looming*. The first thing Norton did when we checked in was to dash out onto our balcony and go racing—much too fast to do my heart much good—across the very narrow ledge, the entire length of the hotel. Practically every minute we were in our room, Norton spent on that ledge, staring out over the water far below. If he wasn't there, he was outside by the pool, which was also located high above the sea. He liked it there, too, mostly because the waitresses would bring him little strips of chicken while he sat on his chaise longue.

The highlight of our Sicilian trip, without question, was

discovering an inn and restaurant in the middle of nowhere (or near the town of Gangivecchia, to be more precise, absolutely smack dab in the middle of the island). The restaurant is called The ex-Convento di Gangivecchia. It's called that, cleverly enough, because it's an ex-convent, dating from the thirteenth century.

It's a giant and magnificent structure, over forty rooms, surrounded by two hundred acres of gardens and farmland—everything served there is grown or slaughtered there, too—and it's run by two women, a mother and daughter, the Baroness Wanda Tornabene and Giovanna Tornabene. We made so many pleasurable groaning noises while we were eating the asparagus fritter, the fresh *tapenade*, the homemade gnocchi in eggplant and tomato sauce, and the homemade cannolis and hot lemon-curd fritters, that the Baroness came over to our table to talk (I think she was just happy to get us to stop eating). She admired Norton right off, which endeared her to us, and told us that the last such distinguished visitor at the ex-Convento was Prince Charles. Personally, I think Norton could have held on to Di if he'd had the chance, so I didn't think much of the comparison, but I thanked her for the compliment anyway.

Despite the fact that the ex-Convento was three hours from anywhere a normal person might be in Sicily, the three of us drove back there four days later—when I told Janis that I might kill someone if I saw another Roman temple. Since it was his second visit, Norton felt right at home and made himself comfortable while he explored various rooms supposedly off-limits to customers. But the Tornabenes didn't mind. In fact, when we left, we discovered there was no check.

They felt honored to be able to treat Signore Norton to a good lunch, they said.

Touched, I told them that Signore Norton was equally honored. I, however, was happy the next day when it was time for the gray Signore to return to France. If he spent much more time in Sicily, I believe his little folded ears might just have been overwhelmed by his ever-larger swelled head.

a cat in goult

On New Year's Day of last year, our French friends gave us a present: They provided us with the most wonderful day I've ever spent. In so many ways it's what our entire year was all about.

Our friends in Goult had a tradition. For ten years, they'd hiked up into the mountains on New Year's Day. The hike was a relatively easy one, beginning just above the town of St. Saturnin d'Apt. Each year, they started at the same spot and hiked about an hour until they reached an old deserted stone village, abandoned over a hundred years ago when the town's water supply ran out. Everyone who hiked had to bring some form of good food or drink; when they arrived at the abandoned village—called Travignon—everyone then ate and drank, napped in the sun, celebrated another year of good living, wished for a new year with more of the same, then hiked back home, happy, tired, a little bit drunk, and more than a little bit filled with good cheer.

A few weeks before Christmas, Janis, Norton, and I were invited on their hike. Touched and honored, we agreed immediately, though we warned them that two other Americans would also be with us—that was the week Norm and Esther came visiting. No problem, we were told. We were official Goultoise now and we could invite whomever we wanted.

The day before New Year's Day was cold and wintry. The day after New Year's Day was even colder and rainy. But our *bons amis* had assured us that the weather for their New Year's hike was always perfect—and when we awoke that day, the sun was shining down and the sky was blue and clear.

I had crudités and wine stuffed into my backpack and a curious cat stuffed into my shoulder bag as we hiked up into the hills. We all bounced along, chattering in bizaare pigeon-English and pseudo-French, everyone being ultrasensitive to everyone else's inability to communicate properly. We took in the glory of the countryside until we reached Travignon, situated at the top of the mountain. It was a kind of hippie camp now. In the structures that still had roofs, there were mattresses, tattered sleeping bags, and crude tables made out of large rocks. There was also a nice tradition: In some of the ruins, there were full bottles of wine, left by the last person to sleep there, waiting to greet the next camper.

The sun was shining and warm (the official weather word on Provence from the locals: a cold climate with a hot sun—and that's the perfect description) and it was now time to eat. Blankets were spread on the ground. Cheese and fruit and bread were spread out; wine was opened. We gathered kindling to build a campfire, on which was cooked delicious homemade sausages.

After lunch, some of the group went off hiking and prowling. Two American pseudo-Goultoise lay down on a large, surprisingly comfortable rock and took naps in the sun. The smallest, grayest, flattest-earred member of the hike did his best to poke through the campfire and eat as many leftover sausage bits as he could find before joining his dad in the midday snooze.

Years of tradition broke on the hike back. We all realized we weren't ready for the day to end, so we went back to one of the hikers' houses to prolong the warmth and good cheer. We ate pasta and sat around until one in the morning listening to our friend Jean-Guy, a musician, play the guitar and sing his own, romantic compositions. Norton was having such a good time, I'm sure that if only Jean-Guy knew any tunes in English, one member of the hike would have happily meowed out the words to "Michael Row the Boat Ashore."

By the time we made it back to our house, the day had become a dreamlike experience. Friendships were cemented, new traditions were established, new levels of communication had been reached. Sometimes when I'm lecturing about the wonders of my cat, I do feel a little guilty and feel as if I should add a P.S., which I will add here, that occasionally people—even relative strangers—can also provide an awful lot of the good things in life.

There is a New Year's superstition in France. It is believed that the first twelve days of the year are crucial to one's happiness. If the first day is a good one, you will have a good month of January. If day two goes well, so will February. If day three is fine, March will be a lucky month, and so on. I don't remember all the details of our first twelve days of last year, but it's certain we were living under a lucky star. Or perhaps it's easier to make your own luck when surrounded by true friends, Monsieur Bonnelly's wine, and a cat who appreciates the splendor and glory of the hot Provençal sun.

~~~

As all good things must, our year abroad did end.

Duty, not to mention the need to make a living, called.

In our last weeks, we went from town to town—from nontouristy Jucas and Murs to the magnificent red cliffs of Roussillon to the chilly ruins of Oppede-le-vieux—soaking it all in, trying to sere into our brains not only the magnificent sights but the European attitude and the feeling of appreciation for life which we hoped to carry back to America. We lunched in the wonderful villages of Manosque, stuffed ourselves with desserts from the *pâtisserie* in Cabrieres, toured the beauteous St.-Rémy and the rest of the region known as Les Alpilles, and often just sat in our house in Goult, sipping a glass of cold rosé wine and marveling at the splendor we could find in our own backyard.

Our last night in Goult, our friend Anne had a small dinner party. Just our close circle of French friends (though one woman, Anette, was Swedish, she was considered honorary French, having lived in Goult for years).

We sat around Anne's dining table—Janis, Norton, myself, our new friends—talking easily and eating well, of course, and, naturally, drinking a lot of good red wine. And during the evening, our sense of sadness lifted. We somehow knew we'd be back. Or these new people in our lives would visit us in New York. Or that, even if we never saw them again, they'd all somehow be with us for the rest of our lives.

At midnight, we knew it was finally time to say good-bye. Everyone kissed and hugged and exchanged small gifts of farewell and of thanks. Then Janis, Norton, and I strolled the two or three streets back to our house. When we rounded the corner across from the restaurant Le Tonneau, walking along the front of Goult's thousand-year-old castle, we found ourselves at the very spot of the dread outdoor bird cage. But the birds were not there; for some reason they'd been taken inside. Norton, not believing his good fortune but wanting to take advantage of it, hesitated, then walked to the front door of the house and sniffed cautiously. Proudly, he turned toward us and took one strutting step forward. At that moment, we heard the loud chirp of a bird from somewhere within the house. A final farewell.

Norton led the way, of course, but Janis and I sprinted after him the best we could, running and laughing—and meowing—all the way back to our three-hundred-year-old home.

And the next morning, we were still laughing—and meowing—as we left Goult and headed back to America.

PART THREE

a cat returns

a cat in new york

11

Janis and I returned home wondering exactly how we were going to resume our previous lives. Our careers were up in the air—her sabbatical was over and she had to find out what, if indeed any, job was waiting for her; I had to decide whether or not to return to corporate life—as were our living arrangements, our relationship, and all sorts of other loose ends.

Norton had none of those questions to resolve. He returned to find himself a changed man (I know that's not exactly right, but it sounds a lot better than "a changed cat"). He returned to find himself a celebrity.

Soon after arriving back in New York, Norton and I were on the road again, traveling to Los Angeles for business and venturing around the country for the paperback publicity tour for *The Cat Who Went to Paris*.

The first indication I had that, in the year we were away, fame had found a certain Scottish Fold, came in Boston.

Norton and I were sitting in the lobby of the Boston Four Seasons, being interviewed by a reporter for a Boston paper. All of a sudden, three women walked by—a fiftyish mother and her two thirtyish daughters—and the mother stopped short, turned, and stared straight at us.

"Oh my god!" she said slowly. "Is that *him?*"

For one brief, shining moment, I, of course, thought she was referring to me. Yeah, *right.*

"Is that *Norton?!*" she squealed and came rushing over to pet him.

When I acknowledged that the creature now on his back and purring loudly was indeed Norton, she called her two daughters over to meet him. It turns out she'd read the book a year earlier and, since she traveled a lot, had kept her eye open for you-know-who whenever she was on the road.

"I *knew* I'd run into him one of these days," she gushed. "Do you think he'd ever want to come up and visit us on the Cape?"

This was by no means his only brush with Fold groupies. When I—excuse me, we—appeared at Books & Company in Dayton, Ohio, one woman came up and shyly told me she'd driven over a hundred miles just to meet Norton. Since she'd come so far, I introduced the two of them and left them alone for several minutes. When their chat was over, the woman didn't seem at all disappointed. In fact, she had a big smile on her face. I have no idea what they discussed and decided I was better off not knowing.

In Detroit he was recognized in the airport. As we were boarding the plane, a woman came over and asked whether that was that strange cat who went to Paris. When I said yes, she asked if she could have his autograph. I tried to explain to her that even though he was a very smart cat, he couldn't actually hold a pen and write. So she wouldn't be too disillusioned, I told her I was sure he could spell his name, but the problem was a lack of opposable thumbs. That seemed to satisfy her.

In Los Angeles, a bellman at the Four Seasons told me a great story. He said he was helping two women up to their rooms and he overheard them talking about a book they'd read about a most amazing cat.

"Ladies," he said to them. "Excuse me for kibitzing your conversation, but are you talking about Norton Gethers?"

Astonished, they said that they were. "But how did you know?" one of them asked him.

"Because he stays here," the bellman told the women. "I know him. This is Norton's hotel of choice."

Norton and I were in L.A. that trip to talk about selling the movie rights to our book. Initially, quite a few producers and directors were interested. There was a lot of talk about Mel Gibson as me (a natural, I figured) and Michelle Pfeiffer as Janis (a natural, she figured). Norton was tough casting—I thought maybe they'd get a dog who was an impressionist—but that wasn't really my problem. We narrowed the list down to five producers, then those five took it to their respective film studios. That's when we ran into a bit of trouble.

The first executive called me from 20th Century-Fox. "I like it," she said. "But I think it's a little soft. Explain to me how you'd turn it into a movie." So I did. I went through Act One, Act Two, and Act Three. I told how I'd develop the characters and I told exactly what role the cat would play. "I still like it," she said when I was finished. "But I still think it's a little soft. Is it possible that we can add some sort of thriller element?"

"Like a Cat-Meets-Clint-Eastwood-kind-of-a-thing?" I said. *"Dirty Norton?"*

"That's interesting," she said. "That's a very interesting way to go."

"Not for me," I told her and hung up.

The next executive I had to go through was at Warner Brothers. She, too, felt it was a little soft for a movie. So I went through the same pitch, told her how it would work, and she said, "I like it. But do you think it would be possible to have the cat talk?"

"You mean like *Look Who's Meowing?*"

"Exactly," she said.

"I'm hanging up now," I said.

The third person worked at the Imagine film studio. We went through the usual exchange—Her: too soft; Me: here's how to do it—and then when I was all finished, we had this memorable exchange:

"I love it," she told me. "I really do." (Important Aside: The phrase "I love it" is totally meaningless. Studio executives want you to like them, so they never tell you face-to-face that they think anything is bad. Afterward, they just refuse to take your phone calls, so you get the hint that they don't want to do your project.) "But," she went on, "you have to help me with one thing."

"Anything," I promised.

"What do I do when my boss comes into my office and says, 'How is this different from *Turner and Hootch?*' "

"You mean the Tom Hanks police thriller about a cop and his dog?" I asked.

"Uh-huh," she said.

"Welllll . . . that's a tough one," I agreed. "How about telling him this *isn't* a police thriller, there's *no* cop and *no* dog?"

"I don't know if that'll do it," she said.

That's when I called my agent and told him I didn't want to have any more conversations about turning the book into a movie. So Norton wouldn't ever get his paw prints in front of Mann's Chinese Theater—we could live with that. At least I could.

This isn't to say that he was ignored by his adoring public. I would guess that, over time, we've received a thousand letters from people who've read *The Cat Who Went to Paris*. Every so often, someone mentions that they liked the book. Mostly, people ask questions about Norton. Or just praise him. Some people send him presents. Norton has received his own Feline Passport (a popular new product, so I'm told), he got a self-published book of poetry that was dedicated to him, and he was sent several inspirational poems, framed quite nicely. One woman sent him a package that included a couple of cans of Pounce, a lovely salt shaker (don't ask me—I just report the facts!), a Christmas tree ornament, and a photo of her car, which she thought he'd be interested in seeing.

Many people send photos of their cats. I'm glad to report they usually preface these with the words "Dear Norton, I know my little [fill in the blank: Daffodil, Sarge, or Ezekial] isn't as handsome as you are but . . ."

Most of the letters are actually wonderful. A lot of people were moved by the story of the death of my father and wanted to let me know that by sharing my grief I'd helped them with theirs. Many letters began with phrases like "Dear Peter and Norton, Excuse the familiarity of the greeting, but I feel like I know you both so well now. You seem like old pals." Many letters, amazingly enough, were simply addressed to Norton, Sag Harbor, New York. Don't ask me how the post office knew to deliver them, but they arrived.

Norton and I got letters from ninety-year-old people letting me know that my book inspired them to get one last cat before they died; women who sent semi-suggestive photos or suggestions along with invitations to visit anytime (my favorite enticement was from one woman who ended her letter with: "I keep a can of Pounce handy at all times. One in the kitchen, one in the bedroom. You're welcome to use either one." I don't know about you, but a can of shrimp Pounce by the bed turns *me* on!); letters from people with AIDS who told me their cats provided them with enormous solace and comfort; and one extraordinarily moving call from a woman who had a retarded daughter and wanted to tell me that the only thing that made her daughter smile was when she looked at the photo of Norton on the cover of our book.

Some people wrote eloquently of being touched by my relationship with Norton and by his unique personality. Others wrote simply to tell me that my feelings about Norton made them realize how much they loved their own cats.

I got several angry letters and calls, too. Several people worried that I placed my cat in too many dangerous situations (which I don't—honest), and one man wrote me an extremely nasty letter, telling me that just because my life was so interesting was no reason to write a book shoving his face in the fact that his life was so boring.

The ASPCA got in touch with me. They were putting out a book of photographs of famous animals. Would Norton agree to be included? It was for a good cause, so I agreed. Then they called back and said that the person in charge of the project had just read my book—and he was shocked to find that I let Norton eat ice cream and jelly doughnuts. He found that so offensive, he wouldn't allow Norton to be associated with his work.

And people wonder why organizations have trouble getting donations.

My two very favorite letters came from young girls (get your mind out of the gutter!).

One was from a thirteen-year-old in Greater Manchester, England. After telling me that *The Cat Who Went to Paris* was her favorite book ever, she added such gems as: "We have a cat named Floyd and he is just like Norton except (1) he has blue eyes, (2) he is not a Scottish Fold and (3) he is not very smart." Other than that, exactly alike. My English fan also told me that she "ranked the book as one of the greatest modern books ever written." Ah, yes. *The Brothers Karamazov, The Great Gatsby,* and *The Cat Who Went to Paris,* not necessarily in that order.

The best of them all, however, came from an eleven-year-old girl in Colorado. Here's how her letter began: "Dear Mr. Gethers, I just want to tell you that your book is one of the *absolute best* books I have *ever* read (and believe me I read almost everything). I'm in love with Norton!" She also had this to say, which I liked quite a lot: "To tell you the truth, when I first got your book (for Christmas) I thought it was going to be another hummdrumm book (like us kids so commonly get). But it definitely wasn't!" What made her letter so memorable, however, was her spelling. Among the misspelled words: seems (seams), believe (belive), commonly (comenly), commonly (comonly), definitely (defenetly), wasn't (wasen't), perfect (perfict), writing (writeing), and please (pelease). At the end, she added these two wonderful addendums: "P.S. I admire your work because I want to be a author also and I hope I can be as good as you. P.P.S. Sorry my spelling isn't grate."

One of the most amazing side effects of writing about my cat is how interested people are in Norton. They've taken to him as if he's a member of their own family. The nice thing is, people seem to appreciate him. They "get" what it is that makes him so special. Another amazing thing to me is how interested people became in *my* life. It's a strange sensation to open yourself up to a hundred thousand people or so, telling very personal stories about everything from idiotically talking aloud to a cat to coping with the death of a parent. But all of a sudden, I find that Norton and I have this kind of odd (sometimes very odd!) extended family all over the country. All over the world, in fact. When we're on the road or via letters or even in the occasional stray phone call, people tend to want answers to the same questions. I think it might not be a bad idea to answer them all here. Not only will this save you the twenty-nine cents for a stamp, it'll keep me from losing my voice on the next tour.

The single most common question—usually asked by women with thirty-year-old unmarried daughters—is: "Are you and Janis married yet?" The answer is no. We lived together for the year we were in France and, except for the several moments per week when we wanted to kill each other (especially when she refuses to put the open milk back in the refrigerator), we did okay. But I don't seem to be the marrying (or even the living together) kind and neither does she. We're also both children of the sixties and we share the same view of marriage: It's only a piece of paper and a relationship doesn't have to be made legal for it to be a good one. To top that all off (since you're so nosy), and I realize this is a character flaw, I figure there is a reasonable chance I'll one day meet either Sarah Jessica Parker, Michelle Pfeiffer, Katie Couric, Uma Thurman, or Sandra Day O'Connor (okay, okay, I don't *really* think she belongs on this list of sexy women, but I don't want people to think I'm shallow) and if I do, I just don't think I could bring myself to say the words "Hi. Meet the wife."

The second most asked question: "How old is Norton?" Here are all of his vital statistics: By the time this book comes out, he will be ten years old. I'm expecting him to be around at least ten more years (and every time I see an item in a newspaper or magazine about a twenty-two-year-old cat, I make sure I read it aloud to him). He weighs nine and a half pounds, is still pretty trim, is in excellent health (he's been sick twice that I can think of, both times with a touch of the flu), and yes, he does like traveling with me. I am starting to think of getting another cat. I think it would be good for him; it would help keep him young. But I'm still too selfish to do so. Traveling with two cats would be too difficult. Perhaps in another few years, when Norton really starts to slow down and traveling becomes less fun for him.

In descending order, these are the other questions I'm usually bombarded with:

3. *Do cats need passports?* No. When traveling internationally, all they need is a health certificate. They need to have their shots within a week of leaving for Europe—and be sure to keep the record because, to return to America, you have to prove that those shots were received within a year of your return. Any vet knows exactly what shots to give and what papers are needed.

4. *How's your mom?* She's great. I just threw her a surprise seventieth birthday party at Spago (Norton didn't go but he

did send a telegram). She's writing two new cookbooks, travels constantly, is so busy it's hard to get her to sit still for more than two minutes, and generally is quite happy.

5. *Will you publish my cat book?* No.

6. *Will you read my cat book?* Not unless I have to.

7. *Do cats get jet lag?* Think about it. Cats sleep *all* the time. They're not awake long enough to get jet lag!

8. *Why won't my cat act like Norton?* I have no idea. Do you talk to him constantly, pet him incessantly, give him whatever he wants whenever he wants it, and pamper him at first-class hotels all around the world? This may have something to do with it.

9. *Is* The Cat Who Went to Paris *ever going to be a movie? And is Norton going to play himself?* Believe it or not, after the nightmare of trying to sell the book when it first came out, it looks like things worked out after all. The book has been bought by Paramount and the screenplay is in the works. Norton is definitely *not* going to play himself. That's where I drew the line and demanded a stunt cat. However, we did have to go to L.A. recently for a movie pow-wow. Norton and I went onto the studio back lot for our meeting. (The best thing about going to the Paramount back lot are the names of the buildings. You can sit around a conference table in the Bob Hope Building or stroll by the Edith Head Wardrobe Building. If you prefer, you can also rendezvous at the Ernst Lubitsch Annex, at the corner of Rudolph Valentino Place, in the Mary Pickford Wing, or my favorite—and this is where I got to have my meeting—in the Jerry Lewis Building.) We met with the studio executive in charge of the project and the producers of the film. When we walked in, I think they were all a little nervous that Norton would turn out to be somewhat of a letdown. But, as usual, he was anything but. He sat on the couch next to

me for the first part of the meeting, then as he got a little bored hearing all the stories about his life repeated for the umpteenth time, he began to explore. First he sized up the producer's gigantic office, sniffing at the various cupboards, shelves, and tables. Then he hopped up onto the desk and snooped around there, probably trying to catch a glimpse of the contract to see if he had script approval. Then, while we story-conferenced the movie, Norton went out into the hallway and introduced himself to the various secretaries and story editors in their nearby offices. By the time he came back, the script was ready to be written and I think the Paramount executive was thinking of starring Norton in a remake of *Gone With the Wind*. The producer also had a vision of screening the movie, if it's actually made, at the White House. I think he figures we can get a good quote from Socks. My hope is merely that Norton is the first cat invited to a state dinner. Or that he receives some kind of official post (even if it's only a Scratching Post).

10. *Will you write another book about Norton?* No. I think this is it. It's time for me to reclaim my own life as a human being able to stand on my own two feet (or nearly) and to let my cat return to his anonymous, if still extraordinary, ways.

The first book I wrote about Norton ended with the death of my father. Luckily for me, this book does not end with anything nearly so dramatic or traumatic. However, that doesn't mean that life has and will continue to sail a smooth course.

The Cat Who Went to Paris ended with everyone living happily ever after. But, of course, nobody *really* lives happily ever after. Things happen.

Things change.

That's what makes life interesting, if not always sane.

But, to steal from a fairly respectable poetic voice, most things change with a whimper rather than a bang.

My father's been dead three and a half years now and the pain has certainly subsided, but it's a very strange thing: His death has left me with a perpetual sadness. There is a great poem by Gerard Manley Hopkins called "Margaret Are You Grieving?" It's ostensibly about the grief one feels for a loved one who dies, but it's *really* about the fact that what we're feeling is grief for *ourselves*. That what we're all crying about is our own mortality. While I can honestly say I miss my dad every single day in all sorts of little ways—I constantly think how he would have loved a particular movie or book, or how I'd like to get his opinion on something, or how happy he'd have been that Clinton won the election—I know that some of that sadness I'm feeling is for myself. I remember how upset I was when my grandfather died. Then, of course, the pain of my father's death is still a wound, perhaps not so raw anymore but certainly still tender. And then I think, Uh-oh—guess who's next in line?

So, happily, there are no recent deaths to deal with these days, but there is still grief nonetheless. I find myself crying at movies I never would have cried at in the past. Every so often, I'll even find myself crying at bad sitcoms that deal with the subject of loss (and believe me, something's a little screwy when you cry at the rerun of "Family Ties" when Alex goes off to college). There's nothing to do about this. It doesn't affect my life. I have as much fun as I've always had. I laugh just as much as always. It's just that, as one gets older, life gets slightly and irreversibly sadder.

Relationships change, too.

I am, of course, still crazy about my mom. She's as cool

as a mother can be. But, though she's coping wonderfully well with widowhood, she's more nervous about things than she used to be. She spent her whole life taking care of my father. Now there's a void: She needs something and someone else to take care of. I find I'm a lot less patient around her, that I get irritated over practically nothing. This has nothing to do with her. She's still great. It has everything to do with my reaction to the fact that she, too, is getting older and isn't—and couldn't be—the same person she was in the past.

I guess I don't like when things change, although I have yet to discover any way to stop them from doing so.

My brother, Eric—the one who's responsible for giving me Norton—and I don't speak anymore. I thought he was screwing up his life and made the mistake of telling him so, in no uncertain terms. He was equally certain I was wrong. Also that it was none of my business, which in retrospect is hard to argue with. So in a particularly painful conversation, he made it clear that, though at one point when we were younger we were very, very friendly, our lives are no longer entwined.

I've come from a family that was extremely close and loving. And we've been close my entire life. That foundation has always been a big part of my identity. But somehow, inexorably it seems, that family and foundation has eroded. The family no longer exists. It's gone, and that is a change most difficult and painful to adjust to.

Friendships, too, alter themselves. It was interesting to see the reactions when Janis and I left for France. Many of my relationships are professional ones. As a publisher, I buy books from agents, I work closely with authors. Once I stepped down as the head of a company, it was extraordinary to see which agents stopped calling because they decided I was no longer useful, and which authors suddenly realized there might be someone who could be a more beneficial dinner companion. Some people, I think, were resentful that I was actually trying to make my life better. Some didn't give it nearly that much thought and simply moved on to someone else who could help them more.

Even more personal friendships went through changes. Some very close friends resented our leaving, didn't understand why we'd want new friendships and new experiences. They felt that our leaving was some form of rejection. So, much to my surprise, certain relationships were altered, some subtly, some not, for reasons that were beyond my control as well as my comprehension.

One big change, of my own doing, is that I have made my escape from corporate life a long-lasting one. Recently, I was offered the chance to get back on the publishing fast track and run a very large company. This would have meant quite a bit of prestige and more money than I'd ever thought I'd make. But after an agonizing week of worrying about my future and dreaming of a large house in Provence that would now be affordable, I turned the job down. I decided to follow my cat on this one and stay as independent as possible. I may regret it—and already have, on occasion—but when I finally rejected the offer, it was as if a five-hundred-pound weight was lifted from my back. This is one instance where change might be for the better.

Janis and I haven't changed very much. We still have our separate apartments and our separate lives, yet we still have our life together. We both seem to like it this way. Is it permanent? Is it unchangeable? I don't have the foggiest. But we've been through too much together and care about each other way too much to even conceive of anything else. I like our chances.

However, as life shows us over and over again, things do change.

Except for one.

I've spent a lot of time thinking about what it is that makes cats and our relationships to cats so special. Yes, they are extraordinary in their wisdom and their independence and their beauty. Yes, they provide comfort and company and, of course, fun. But it's more than that. I think cats provide permanence.

Cats don't change.

Certainly they get older and certainly they die, but while they're here they are what they are and that's *all* that they are.

Yes, Norton has a tiny touch of arthritis now and can't jump quite as nimbly onto the kitchen cabinet as he used to. And yes, occasionally he will not make the jump at all because he doesn't think he'll make it—which pretty near breaks my heart. And I think he sleeps a bit more than usual and he's no longer quite so eager to go on walks with me—he'd rather stay home and conserve his energy.

But he *is* under my cheek every morning when I wake up.

He meows for breakfast every single day the moment I swing out of bed and my feet touch the floor.

When I come home at night, he's waiting by the front door as soon as my key turns the lock.

When I'm home working, I know that all I have to do is turn slightly to my left and he'll be stretched out on the back of the couch, basking in any sun that might be streaming through the living-room window.

There is absolutely nothing I could do—or ever would do—that could stop him from loving me. And vice versa. There is not much else in life you can say that about.

I'm not old and neither is he, but we're getting older. Just recently I turned forty and Norton turned ten. To celebrate, Janis and I went to New Orleans with some of our closest and dearest friends. We ate *beignets* and oyster po' boys and obscene amounts of crayfish and drank a whole bunch of spicy Cajun martinis and celebrated what's been a pretty damn good life, which is going to, I hope, get even better. We stayed at a beautiful small hotel in the French Quarter called The Lamothe House. When I called to make the reservation, I asked the manager, whose name was Brant, if I could bring my cat.

"I'm terribly sorry," he told me, "but we don't allow pets."

"See, it's my birthday," I started to explain. "And Norton, my cat, kind of goes everywhere I go and this is going to be a big celebration and—"

"Your cat's *Norton?*" Brant asked over the phone.

"Yes," I said, a little taken aback.

"Oh, Norton can come," he then told me matter-of-factly. "Norton's different."

So Norton came. He basked in the sun in the hotel's courtyard, got powdered sugar all over himself eating *beignets* at Café du Monde, charmed the hotel maid, and generally had a good time as we both eased into the next stage of our lives.

And while the older I get, it seems the less I know, I *do* know one thing: For the next important day of my life, whatever and wherever it is, Norton will be there also—to celebrate, to participate, to do whatever it is he decides to do. But he'll be there.

That will never change.

afterword

Janis and I learned all sorts of things from our year living in France.

We learned about wine. We learned how to cook and how to speak a different language. We learned how to balance work with life. We learned how to put a lot of different things in perspective.

Norton learned something, too, which we just discovered.

In our house in Sag Harbor, our bedroom door locks in two ways. It's really two doors that close and meet in the middle of the doorway. On one of them there's a small hook, waist-high, that flips over and catches onto the other door, keeping the doors closed but somewhat flimsily. Then, on the bottom of one of the doors is a latch that slips down and fits into a notch in the floor. This secures both doors as well as our privacy.

We don't usually lock or even close the bedroom door

except when we have overnight guests, because our second bedroom is very nearby. I don't mind being behind closed doors and neither does Janis. Norton, however, doesn't care for it one iota.

He must have a touch of claustrophobia. He almost always spends the entire night in bed with us, but I guess he likes it to be his option because as soon as the door is locked, Norton hops out of bed and decides he has to escape the confines of the room. This is one of the few times in his life he doesn't get his way. When the door's locked, it stays locked. His litter box is upstairs, he's got water upstairs—there's no need for him to leave. So he stays, even if it's against his will.

Until recently, that is.

Before we left for France, Norton could not solve the system of the two locks. Soon after we got back, however, he did something that even I found a little scary.

We had guests one night, so the door was locked. Somewhere around two in the morning, I heard a scratching noise. I tried my best to ignore it, but after a minute or two that proved impossible, so I leaned over the bed to see what the hell was going on.

What was going on was that Norton was trying to lift the latch on the floor with his paw. I watched him claw at it once, twice, three times. Around the sixth or seventh time, he caught it and lifted it out of its notch. He then jumped straight up four or five times until he managed to swat at the waist-high hook that held both doors shut and unlatch that, too. With all the hard work done, Norton gently butted his head into one of the doors, swinging it wide open, then stepped nonchalantly out into the hallway and disappeared.

By this time, Janis was also wide awake and staring down at our little cat.

"You don't think . . ." she started to say to me.

"I *do* think," I told her, in a hushed tone.

We didn't have to say more than that. We were both remembering a moment in France. In the town of Sancerre, at a vineyard. It was the moment Norton saw that amazing dog stand on his hind legs, turn the doorknob, and open the door when he wanted to come in and out. That was the one thing in France that had seemed to overwhelm my cat. It was the only time he'd seen an animal do something he himself couldn't do.

"I don't believe it," Janis sputtered. "He couldn't still remember that. And even if he could, he couldn't make the connection . . . I mean, he just couldn't see that dog and . . . *Could he?*"

"Trust me," I said, nodding as her voice trailed off. "I know my cat."

THE CAT WHO'LL
LIVE FOREVER

CONTENTS

Foreword   1

1. A Cat Rethought   5

2. A Cat Revisited   10

3. An American Cat   14

4. A Cat in the Spring   31

5. The Cat Who Went Back to Paris   52

6. A Cat in Retirement   76

7. The Cat Who Turned Middle-Aged   113

8. The Cat Who Stayed Home   149

9. The Cat Who Had a Will to Live   167

10. The Cat Who Went Back on the Road   192

11. The Cat Who'll Live Forever   219

Afterword   245

DEDICATION

There's only one possible choice for this . . .

To the greatest little cat there ever was.
Au revoir, pal o' mine.

ACKNOWLEDGMENTS

've got to thank everyone who helped and loved my amazing Scottish Fold. Particularly Dr. Jonathan Turetsky, Dr. Andrew Pepper, Dr. Dianne DeLorenzo, and Dr. Marty Goldstein. I'd also like to thank all those who greeted him on his travels and took care of him along the way—but to list them all would take pages and pages and would need a better memory than mine.

For this book in particular, I'd like to thank Steve Rubin, the perfect publisher, Lauren Marino, the perfect editor, Esther Newberg, the perfect agent (and the only person who blubbered more than I did during this whole process), and Leona Nevler, because no one would be reading about Norton if it weren't for her.

Thanks, too, to all those who let me write about them, particularly my dear old mom and my dear young girlfriend.

FOREWORD

One of the reasons I moved to where I live now is because it's right near Washington Square Park, in the heart of Greenwich Village, and ever since I came to New York City, this is exactly where I fantasized about living. For human beings, however, wanting to do something and actually doing it are often two very different things. Which leads me to confess that the *real* reason I finally made the move is because my cat wanted to live on Washington Square Park.

Do me a favor and please don't ask how I know that this was his abode of choice. I know many strange things about my cat and I'd rather not discuss them because anyone who's not a cat fanatic will think I'm insane and anyone who is a cat fanatic (or has read about my particular fanaticism) will not even question the above statement. In fact, the only question those readers might ask is, "What took you so long?"

What took me so long was that I never realized that Norton, my exceptional, geniuslike—and did I mention dashingly handsome?—Scottish Fold pal, liked the dog run quite as much as he did.

My ignorance lasted until one day, when we were strolling around the Village on a sunny afternoon. Well, I was strolling; Norton was in his usual position, relaxing, half in, half hanging out of his cloth-and-mesh bag that hung on my shoulder, swivelling his head at everyone and everything around him. At some point we found ourselves in the middle of the park. In addition to the sounds of guitars and bongos (I know it sounds like you've suddenly been plunged into a Dobie Gillis episode, but I swear there really were guitars and bongos), there was also the distinct and incessant sound of dogs barking. We made our way to the south side of the square and, sure enough, there was this caged-in stretch of land—some grass, mostly dirt—in which twenty or thirty dogs of all shapes and sizes were rolling, running, jumping, fetching, yapping, growling, howling and generally acting like happy, idiotic canines. Norton was fascinated by this undignified but free-spirited behavior, so we mosyed up as close as we could to the wire fence that separated the dogs and their owners from non-dog-owning humans. Norton twisted himself further out of his bag, sticking his head—which would easily have fit whole into most of those dogs' mouths—as far across the boundary as he could muster. Several of the dogs raced over and barked hysterically but Norton stayed fairly serene, safe in the knowledge that none of the barkers could quite reach

him and, if they could, all I had to do was take a step backward and he'd be out of harm's way.

I knew he was enjoying all this so I found a nearby
bench, sat, and spent a decent part of the afternoon watching him watch the dogs. (I think I'll skip over the fact of
how much time I've actually spent during my adult years
doing nothing but watch my cat do things that most people would not find all that entertaining. All I'll say, so I keep
some modicum of self-respect, is that I'm a total Knicks fanatic and I tend to live and die with that very aggravating
basketball team. Nonetheless, if forced to choose, I'd have
to say, "Watching Norton do just about anything, one;
watching Latrell Sprewell juke to the basket, two.") A few
days later we went back to the same bench and my little pal
seemed to have just as good a time, so after that we started
going more often. And very soon after that I bought my
new apartment, which I tell people I bought because it's
right on Washington Square Park but which I really bought
because it's only about fifty yards from the dog run. Even
though I don't have a dog.

Once we were so conveniently located, Norton and I
went by there almost daily. We liked to take little strolls together in the afternoon; it got me away from the stress of sitting at my computer for hours on end and it got him away
from the stress of . . . well . . . napping by my computer for
hours on end. After a few weeks, we didn't just sit on the
bench on the outsider side of the fence, we started sitting *inside* the dog run. At first, the regular inhabitants (both human and canine) were not thrilled to see a feline intruder.
They (the canines, not the humans) would come running
up, barking ferociously, and my cat would retreat hastily into

his bag. But gradually, the ferocity stopped and curiosity took over, and then it was even possible to spot a kind of friendly wariness. Norton, throughout this process, usually just nestled calmly on my lap, half in, half out of his bag.

One day, the two of us were sitting in the sun, in the middle of the dog run, and a woman came in and sat down beside us. I was reading, Norton was sitting on my lap, totally out of his bag now, soaking in the rays. The dogs were basically ignoring us, except for one small one, a Scottie, I think, who didn't seem to understand that Norton wasn't a dog, because he couldn't seem to comprehend why Norton had zero interest in running around and playing fetch with him. The woman next to us sat there quite a long time; I was vaguely aware that she kept staring over in my direction. Then, finally, she nudged me. When I looked up, she didn't make a big deal out of it, she just said, "That's Norton, isn't it?" I nodded once, muttered something like, "Yup," then she didn't say anything else for a while. She did start nodding, though, repeatedly, as if finally grasping some long-sought knowledge. Then, her head still bobbing slowly, her voice betraying just the tiniest bit of awe, she said, "So it's true . . ."

I knew immediately what she meant. She had read about Norton. She had heard about him. His travels, his adventures, his remarkable effect on everyone around him. And now she had seen him in the flesh (or the fur, as it were), which is all it ever really took for people to understand how genuinely special he was.

I looked at my little cat and patted him on the head. My hand lay there, taking comfort in the smallness and the familiar fit within my palm.

"Yes," I said, smiling down at my beloved gray pal, "it's definitely true."

CHAPTER 1

A
CAT RETHOUGHT

Ever since I made the decision to write this, the third book about my gray, floppy-eared Scottish Fold pal, Norton, I have been trying to decide exactly how to begin.

That very human, very non-cat-like flaw called over-thinking settled in all too quickly, and, as a result, more and more time passed while I sat, stared into space, and didn't type. This book would, I thought, for many reasons, be somewhat different from the others and there were distinct choices that had to be made. Each choice would clearly alter style, tone and philosophy, if I can be pretentious enough to suggest that the books about my cat actually *have* a philosophy (and, please, don't worry; believe me, I know enough to understand that I'm writing something much closer to *Tuesdays with Norton* than I am to *Meowing and Nothingness*).

My first instinct was to begin like this:

One of the reasons I became a writer is because using words the way I do is as close as I can get to putting some kind of order in this rather crazy world of ours.

I was then going to go on and describe that one of the things in life that drives me most crazy is the way the English language is constantly mangled. As always, this is an area in which we should learn from the feline way of doing things. Cats have a way of speaking that is direct and unmistakably clear. Their words might all be the same but the meanings behind them are just a tad less ambiguous than human-speak. There is no mistaking a meow that means "feed me" for one that means "scratch my stomach." Has anyone who has been owned by a cat for any length of time ever confused an "it's nice sitting by the fire" meow for one that says "let me out" or "sorry, there's no way I'm going to the vet"? The answer's no. Of course, not only is cat body language less inhibited than ours, cats tend to speak in commands, which does make life easier, at least for them. The only question I can come up with that a cat might ask is, "Are you okay?" And, if you're not, the follow-up meow is usually another directive: "Here, shove over so I can snuggle up to you and make you feel better." Cats have definitely gotten the act of communication down to an exact science.

But when humans open their mouths, the screw-ups are endless. The constant misuse of "I" for "me," for example (hint: If you don't wish for me to publicly humiliate you, never say "Just between you and I" or "Come with Freddy and I" in my presence). And the addition of the word "very" when describing something "unique." That's the same as saying "very one-of-a-kind" which is linguistically impossible. Then there's the fact that no one seems to know what the word "irony" means. It does not mean funny or snide or coincidental or satirical or anything along those lines. If you don't believe me, here's the definition straight from the *Random House Dictionary of the English Language*: "The use of words to convey a meaning that is the opposite of its literal meaning." If it's raining outside and you say, "Beautiful day, isn't it," that's irony. And the reason this matters to me is that the title of this book is, to a large extent, meant to be ironic, and it's important to understand that going in. Nothing and no one lives forever. Not plants, not people, and most unfortunate of all, not cats. In some ways, "life" itself is the ultimate ironic word because to live means that, eventually, you'll die. And that realization, that experience and understanding, is partly what this book is about.

But only partly.

I'm mainly trying to convey the feeling and the strength that come from being in contact with a truly amazing life force.

All of which is a long-winded way of explaining why my first choice for an opening didn't make the final cut. That and the fact that irony is not a concept that cats even understand. And although this book is written for humans, since cats can't read (unfortunately for me; if they could there's a reasonable chance I'd be the richest person on earth!), I didn't think it was appropriate to begin with something that went so against their nature.

A second possibility was to go for pure drama. For a long time, this was my intended first sentence:

On the day I moved into my dream apartment, I found out that my cat had cancer.

I'm sure you can see the value of that. I mean, it's definitely a grabber. And, like everything else I've ever written about Norton, it's true. But ultimately, I rejected that, too. Too sad. Too self-pitying. Way too cloyingly sentimental. And definitely *not* what this book is about. Most certainly not what Norton is about. What you're about to read is, I hope, anything but sad. It is not about illness, it is about health. Rather than the trauma of being sick, it is about the satisfaction and the bonds that arise as we age and learn how to care for each other—and learn how to accept that caring from others.

Anyone who has read earlier tales of life with Norton can tell you that I will almost always go for the gag—on paper and in life—and also that I am not a big fan of fake sentiment (several ex-girlfriends would say I'm also not a fan of real sentiment). But I *am* a fan of genuine emotion and, luckily for me, rarely is that exclusive of laughter. So in no way is this book depressing. It is, I hope, hilarious and joyful and as life-affirming as it's possible to be without turning into a Steven Spielberg movie.

In a way, this rambling and overthinking has actually done what my two initial openings couldn't possibly do. I did manage to bring some order, not just to this book but to my thought process. And, probably more important, I realized that, despite what I wrote earlier, the title is not really ironic.

The more I thought about it, the more I understood that in many ways my little gray pal will indeed live forever. And live exactly the way he'd like to: bringing pleasure and, on occasion, even meaning into other people's lives. I guess that's why, when push came to shove, I decided that what this book really is about is quite simple.

It's about my cat, Norton.

Exactly the same as the other two books. And that's why the real opening is as follows:

The wonderful thing about having a relationship with a cat—one of the many wonderful things about having a relationship with a cat—is that you never have a clue where that relationship will lead you . . .

CHAPTER 2

A CAT REVISITED

The wonderful thing about having a relationship with a cat—one of the *many* wonderful things about having a relationship with a cat—is that you never have a clue where that relationship will lead you. It can, and often does, lead toward love. But it can also lead toward frustration. And sometimes heartache. Or comfort. It can lead toward other relationships, feline as well as human. Sometimes it can lead to all of the above—in various combinations and even at the same time.

That relationship can also bring you to something truly extraordinary and life-changing, as has been the case with my extraordinary and life-changing Scottish Fold, Norton.

If you've read the many words I've already written about my amazing pal over the years, you won't need to be convinced of his ability to astound. You have already witnessed how he is—in no small way—responsible for my love life, my house, my travels, my professional success, and whatever emotional maturity I've managed to achieve. If you haven't read my rapturous descriptions, here's a little something to chew on (or scratch on, as the case may be) . . .

The backstory:

When we first met book publisher and writer Peter, he was your basic, insensitive oaf. Also a cat hater.

Enter Norton, age six weeks, a gift from one of Peter's girlfriends, Cindy.

Cindy goes. Norton stays. Peter becomes so attached to his kitten it borders on insanity (but is also totally deserved). Many other girlfriends come. Many other girlfriends go. Norton clearly has to take things into his own paws if he's ever going to have a stable home life.

Peter has to travel for business. So Norton travels with him. This changes in the years to come. *Norton* eventually has to travel for business so Peter travels with *him*. They go to Fire Island (Norton is stunned by how low his owner will sink to get a date for New Year's Eve), California (Norton meets the folks), Vermont (Norton goes cross-country skiing), Florida (Norton goes to a spring-training baseball game and becomes a huge fan of Andres "El Grand Gato" Galarraga. He also falls through the roof of a hotel restaurant, scaring two old ladies to death). There's much time spent in Paris (Norton greets Harrison Ford with a . . . um . . . *petit morceau de la merde dans la baignoire*. He also scares away a luscious Danish model and goes clubbing with Roman Polanski), and a sojourn in Amsterdam

(Norton goes to the taping of a topless Dutch TV quiz show—see, now aren't you sorry you didn't read the first book?!). Peter takes up with Janis, with Norton starring in the crucial matchmaking role of Dolly Levi. Peter buys Norton a house in Sag Harbor. Peter deals with the death of his father. Peter, thanks to you-know-who, finally understands what love is.

And then Peter writes a book called *The Cat Who Went to Paris*, which is about all of the above, and Norton becomes the Tom Cruise of cats. Also the William Styron of cats, since most true fans of the book are convinced he dictated the whole thing to Peter, who merely used his opposable thumbs to get himself a book contract.

Thanks to Tom . . . uh, Norton . . . Peter gets to spend a year in Provence, observing and chronicling the further adventures of his gray, folded-eared friend. In France, a chef at a three-star restaurant creates a marzipan mouse for Norton's pleasure. The sweetest cat in the world almost starts World War III in Italy over an uneaten sardine. In addition, Norton also rides a camel (don't ask), goes to Spain, suns himself in Sicily, tours the cathedrals of the Loire valley, skis in the French Alps, visits Anne Frank's house in Amsterdam and, back in southern France, charms the most charming village in the Luberon Valley.

Then it's back home. Which means New York City and Sag Harbor, Long Island.

Peter writes *A Cat Abroad*. It wins the Nobel Prize, the Pulitzer Prize, and is on the *New York Times* bestseller list for over four years (I just wanted to see if you were paying attention. The first sentence in this paragraph is true. The rest is a slight exaggeration).

In the first book, Peter learned about love from

Norton. In the second book, Peter learned about life. Peter decides there will be no third book because he thinks he has nothing left to learn from his cat . . .

We're up to Norton's tenth birthday, which is a little over eight years ago.

Which is where I left off.

And which is where I'll begin now. And the reason there is a Book #3 is because several years ago, I learned there was indeed one more very important thing I had to learn from my beloved little cat.

Maybe the most important thing of all . . .

CHAPTER 3

AN
AMERICAN CAT

Both cat and human had to make a fairly big adjustment to life upon returning to America from a year in the south of France. Norton had to readjust to chowing down on regular cat food (no combo cans of *lapin et foie*, his very favorite). His dad had to get used to working like a real person again. I also had to realize that I could no longer mutter any snide thing I wanted to in public, since now people could actually understand English.

In other words, we both had to prepare ourselves for being *normal* again, which was not my favorite situation to be in. Luckily for me, Norton made it very difficult to be absolutely normal.

When I first realized that life was truly going to be different on a permanent basis was when we went on our publicity tour for *A Cat Abroad*. I had been pretty amazed at the love and affection that had been showered upon my cat when Norton and I traveled together to promote *The Cat Who Went to Paris*—but that was nothing like this.

One of the first stops was Knoxville, Tennessee. At a Davis-Kidd bookstore, I gave my usual semi-witty speech and reading while Norton calmly sat by my side, in his favorite Sphinx-like pose, looking for all the world like he was my translator. When I was done talking, people lined up, ostensibly to have me sign their books but I'm sorry to say they didn't really care about my signature (or anything else about me). Oh, they were mostly polite, but they were all there to pet and talk to Norton. One man was so jazzed by the experience, he offered me a ticket to the city's biggest yearly event, the University of Tennessee–University of Florida football game, which was taking place the next day. When I thanked him but said, kiddingly, that I couldn't possibly go without my pal because he was a huge Tennessee fan, the man looked at Norton and said, "Hell, I'll get him a ticket, too." I have to say, it was tempting but I finally decided it was better that I stick to the tour schedule than take Norton to drink beer and eat hot dogs and root for UT.

One extremely nice, middle-aged woman came shyly forward when the crowd began to thin. She glanced at me, stared lovingly at you-know-who and said, "I drove over four hundred miles to see him." Her tone was even more reverential than her words. It was a lot like she was viewing the front of one of those refrigerators in someone's RV where the grease has coagulated into a vision of the Virgin Mary. It was so touching to see the attachment she had for my cat, I let her spend a few minutes alone with the star of the evening, who was extremely nice, purring contentedly during their chat. I don't know what they chatted about—and I don't think I want to know—but I can say with certainty that she was not at all disappointed. Afterward she thanked him, was thoughtful enough to thank me, too, then presumably drove another four hundred miles back home.

I happened to have good friends living in Knoxville then, Lee and Linda Eisenberg. Linda is an attractive, sweet, lovely woman and *everyone* adores her. Lee is a tad more cynical. And neurotic. And weird. And . . . well, let's just say that not counting his immediate family, about *three* people adore Lee. Luckily, I'm one of them. They are both transplanted New Yorkers and thus pretty much think they've seen it all. But even they were startled by what they witnessed and heard that night. Lee, who had spent much time with Norton before feline fame had set in, was a little taken aback by the fervor of his fans. He'd socialized with Norton in New York and also in Florida (on our annual spring training baseball trips) and I have a hunch he felt a little bit like he'd been dating Norma Jean Baker before she became Marilyn Monroe—it had been fine but who knew it was *so* fine? After the event, we went back to their Xanadu-like house where Linda made dinner. I think she was a bit surprised that, after all the adulation Norton had soaked up from his adoring public, he decided to revert to being a normal cat and, instead of joining us at the table, ate off a bowl on the floor. I have to admit, I was a little surprised myself.

The evening ended, after the delicious dinner, when Lee took me and Norton back to our hotel. We were dropped off—Lee still shaking his head and looking at

Norton as if he'd never seen him before—and headed up to the room. As we passed the check-in desk, the woman clerk behind the counter hesitated and then called out, "Mr. Norton?" I immediately assumed that this was yet another nightmare to confront in my attempt to keep any of my own ego intact—someone actually calling me by my cat's name—but the fact is, she wasn't talking to me. She was directly addressing the one of us with folded ears, which I realized when I went over to her, started to say, "Well, actually, my name's Gethers," and saw that she wasn't even looking at me. She reached out to pet Norton in his bag and said, looking into his eyes, "I'm a big fan. I just wanted to let you know I'm sorry I couldn't go to your reading. I had to work." I waited—as always, half-expecting Norton to answer and say, "Oh, that's all right, my dear. Care to join me in my shoulder bag for a bit of dry food?"—but all he did was look up and give a solid purr as her hand brushed across his soft fur. That seemed to be enough for the woman desk clerk, however, who had an expression on her face that I personally have never been able to induce in any woman without saying the words "tickets to the Caribbean."

While in Tennessee, we made a second stop—Memphis. It was partly for the book tour and partly because a newspaper, the *New York Daily News*, had asked me to write an article about traveling with Norton. Naturally, when the editor called she asked if *Norton* could write an article for the paper. When I determined that she wasn't joking, I explained to her about the whole opposable thumb thing and finally she said, "Well, we'll let you do it but we really want *his* point of view." So in addition to letting his fans adore him, my assignment was to get Norton's reactions to the sights and sounds of Memphis.

Longtime and much loved girlfriend, Janis, grew up in Memphis, so she agreed to come down and meet me there. The three of us stayed at the Peabody Hotel, which is famous for its beauty, stateliness and ducks. Yes, you read that correctly. Every morning, at 9 A.M., the elevator doors open and a hotel employee leads a line of ducks out into the lobby where they waddle across the floor until they reach a large marble fountain. The ducks then step into the water, where they float around for the day in as dignified a manner as possible. At 6 P.M., they all hop out of their pool, reverse their path across the lobby and disappear back into the elevator. I don't know where they go from there, although I prefer to believe it's to their own suite rather than to some cage on the roof. What I do know is that Norton was absolutely fascinated by this daily ritual. We stayed there for two days and each morning he'd be on my shoulder, staring at the quackers as they paraded by. One afternoon, we were having a drink in the lobby—Norton loved the big comfortable seats—and he strolled over to the edge of the fountain and hopped up onto the little ledge. I suppose that a normal cat, staring at all those fowl, might have been thinking about an early supper. Norton did not have that lip-smacking look about him, however. He was mostly curious. I like to think that what he was pondering was how these ducks had somehow managed to get an even better gig than he'd gotten.

It was early summer when we were in Memphis, which meant that the temperature was only about three hundred degrees Fahrenheit. Janis had warned me about the heat down there and I had blown her off, explaining that I liked and thrived in all extreme temperatures. Which, for the most part, I do. Being in Memphis, though, was not a normal extreme. The only way I can describe walking out of the air-conditioned hotel lobby and into the Tennessee summer air is that it must be a lot like stepping directly into the bowels of hell. But step we did, because I wanted Norton to see Graceland, home of The King.

Elvis was a little before Norton's time—he was much more of an REM and Tom Petty fan—but I thought it would do him good to get a little rock and roll history. Unfortunately, we ran into a direct violation of the FRA—Feline Rights Amendment—and a blatant example of catism, when we were turned away at the door, told that cats were not allowed inside. It was a perfect example of how removed from reality we both were. Since he had dined in some of the best restaurants in the world and been welcomed in cathedrals and museums all over Europe, both Norton and I were astonished that he was barred from any public place, particularly one displaying more suede and velvet capes than any building east of the Liberace Museum. But, after a brief argument, we accepted our fate and turned bravely back into the blazing wall of heat that some people referred to as Memphis.

To make it up to my cat, whose feelings were clearly wounded, Janis's father, Marv, took us all to one of the great barbeque places in the world, Corky's (its only flaw is that, unlike some of the smaller, less commercial barbeque places in Memphis, they don't serve barbequed baloney). There, we escaped the shadow of Colonel Parker while Norton sat in his own chair, munched on some delicious pulled pork and took solace in the astonished murmurings of the waitress, who kept repeating, in her thick southern accent, "Ah nevah saw a cat eat bah-bee-cue befaw."

We more or less toured the country over the course of a couple of weeks. By this time, I had the routine down pat.

Publishers hire "escorts" to drive authors around in each city. These escorts not only make sure we arrive where we're supposed to—and arrive on time—they usually know all the key people at the newspaper offices and radio and TV stations, so they're familiar with the layouts and routines and generally are able to make everyone's life easier. Norton's life was made a lot easier by his escorts. We would leave Boston (or whatever city we were in) and fly to Dayton (or whatever city we were flying to). Driving *to* the airport, the escort would have a ready-to-use litter box in the back seat of the car, so Norton could . . . um . . . take advantage of it . . . up until the last possible moment before having to board the plane. When we arrived, we'd be picked up at the gate—I'd be easy to recognize; I was the one with a cat on his shoulder—then, driving *from* the airport, the new escort would also have a litter box all set up so Norton wouldn't have to miss a beat. I left several needed shirts back home, instead packing in my bag plenty of folding, portable litter boxes and a five- or ten-pound bag of litter, which I'd then set up in the hotel room the moment we arrived. No matter how good the traveler, traveling is hard on a cat, so I was determined to make my guy's life as cushy as possible during the ordeal. I was well aware of the favor he was doing for me, so I swore I'd put him to work only if he were exactly as comfortable as he'd be at home.

Norton's airplane rides were always a little easier than the norm because by this time word was out on the flight attendant circuit. He was often recognized and given VIP treatment. While other pets were usually stuffed under the seats in their carry-on bags, most of the time Norton was allowed to sit on my lap or on the seat next to me if it was empty. He was usually given some food and was always fussed over and petted. The only trade-off was that I had to hear many woeful—and long—tales from stewardesses about how much they missed their own cats. It was well worth it, however, and I know Norton appreciated my stoicism.

Since we lived in New York, it was simple to do publicity whenever we were there. One of Norton's easiest appearances was on a TV show called "The Pet Department" on the FX cable network. The taping went fine (Norton was a seasoned TV pro by this time; he seemed to know exactly when to listen and stay calm and exactly when to upstage me by being cute). The only notable oddity was in the itinerary that was given to me before the appearance. The publicist faxed over a piece of paper telling us where to go, when to arrive, how long the taping would take and who to ask for when I got there. And then at the bottom it said, "HOSTS: Steve Walker & Jack the dog."

Sure enough, when we showed up at the studio, some guy came up to me, said that his name was Steve and that he'd be doing the interview. And by his side, some fairly large dog walked up to Norton, sniffed around, then sat with us when the cameras were turned on and we chatted for the national audience. I must admit, I kept waiting for

Jack the dog to ask Norton about the pleasures of the Washington Square Park dog run, but both animals remained silent and let the humans talk.

I got a lot of similar publicity itineraries during this period. Almost all of them said, at the bottom: "Your escort is so-and-so. She will meet your flight and she will have a five-pound bag of cat litter in the car for you." Not exactly the stretch limo and Dom Perignon treatment, but it worked for me.

For Milwaukee, the publicist's instructions were typical of the way we were greeted. It was for a radio show hosted by Marilyn Mee. On the piece of paper it said: "Marilyn is a HUGE fan. She would like to take lots of pictures of Norton in the studio. She is the one who called to ask if she could conduct an interview with Norton Gethers."

It's the story of my postcat life, trust me.

At the book-signing event in Milwaukee, they had a Norton look-alike contest. Luckily for everyone, the contest wasn't actually held live while we were there; cat owners had submitted photos and Norton and I were supposed to pick the winner. The lucky look-alike won a gift certificate to the bookstore and a can of Pounce.

At all the book signing events, there was always a question and answer session at the end of my spiel. In general, I could anticipate what questions would be asked. There was always someone who wanted to know more about the whole portable litter box situation. Someone usually asked for Norton's key statistics: how old he was, how much he weighed, etc. There was often one person who would reprimand me for letting Norton explore the rooftops of Paris on his own, insisting that I was putting his life in danger. And there was, count on it, one person who would stand up, tell a very long story about his or her own cat, then sit down without asking any question at all. And then . . .

Well . . . there were always a few oddities.

In Seattle, someone asked for Norton's specific measurements. I mean, we're talking sleeve size. I had to admit that was one of the few things I didn't know about my cat, but I guess she was able to eyeball him sufficiently in person because a few weeks later I received a hand-knitted coat in the mail. Size extra-extra-extra-small.

In Boca Raton, a woman asked if I knew Norton's birth date and exact time of birth. The fact is, I did (well, not exact, but close enough), but I wanted to know why she was asking before I responded. She finally admitted that she wanted to do Norton's astrological chart and send it to him as a present. As gently as possible, I broke it to her that Norton did not believe in astrology and that she should skip the chart. I wouldn't have minded seeing her try to read his tarot cards, but I decided not to bring it up.

In San Francisco, the SPCA established a yearly "Norton Award" which stood for service dedicated to improving the lives of animals. I'm still not a hundred percent clear if the award is supposed to be given to humans or to animals but we decided not to ask and just be humble and gracious when the SPCA handed its certificate of merit to the only Scottish Fold cat in attendance at the ceremony.

Norton was very big in Ohio for some reason, so we went to various cities there—Dayton, Columbus and Cincinnati. One group of bookstore workers took him to an excellent pub in downtown Cincinnati to celebrate the occasion. In Columbus, where there are an incredible number of good bookstores, the escort took us around from store to store so clerks and salespeople could meet the famous cat. We were headed to the escort's car in the parking lot of one of the mall stores when two elderly women saw Norton perched in his shoulder bag. One woman came running—well, running may not be the right term, let's say inching—up to him. She began stroking his head and asked me if he was a Scottish Fold. When I said that he was, she got extremely excited and started saying to her friend, "Remember that book I was telling you about? Well this is the same kind of cat as the one who went to Paris." Then she turned to me and said, "He's exactly like the cat who went to Paris." I got the same thrilling rush as if someone had come up to me and asked how to get to Carnegie Hall. I got to smile and say to her, "Well, actually, he's not *like* the cat who went to Paris. He *is* the cat who went to Paris." She screeched and then took her hand away from his head, as if now too awed to touch him.

In Norfolk, Virginia, a bookseller had a good gimmick to help sales and keep her best customers loyal. Whoever bought the most books over a period of six months would get some kind of special reward or gift. Her gift this particular six-month period was a dinner with Norton. So when she picked us up at the airport, we checked in to our hotel, set up this night's litter box, then were whisked right out and taken to the best restaurant in town. There we dined with four of her best customers. The only catch was that each customer wanted to spend some individual time with Norton. Which meant that every twenty minutes or so, we had to move around the table so everyone had a chance to sit next to him. I happened to have an aunt, SaraLee, who was living in Norfolk with her new husband, Micky. I had asked if they could be invited to dinner and the bookstore owner was gracious enough to include them.

SaraLee had never met my cat and she was a little incredulous at the excitement he was stirring up at the dinner table. At the beginning, she announced that there was no need for her to move around to dine next to Norton, since she was really there to visit with her beloved nephew. However, after an hour of seeing the ecstatic expressions on everyone's face, when it came around to her, she looked at me apologetically and said, "I don't think I can pass this up." After dinner, when we said goodnight, she asked, "Does this happen to you all the time?" When I said that it did, she shook her head in wonder. But at least she finally understood what all the fuss was about.

Los Angeles was always a pleasure for Norton. The Four Seasons Hotel was like a home away from home for him. Whenever we drove up to the front, the parking guys would grab the luggage and say, "Nice to have you back, Norton." Walking inside was a little bit like what I always imagined would happen in the court of Louis XIV. No one exactly strewed flowers in Norton's path, but everyone from the concierge to the bellmen to the desk clerks would greet him by name and give him a rousing welcome. He was even allowed to use the pool on the fourth floor of the hotel (well, let's say he used the pool area; swimming was not one of my cat's preferred sports). One of my top ten favorite images of Norton is picturing him sitting out by that pool, relaxing on his own chaise lounge while a waiter would bring him over a small bowl of ice water.

Dining out in America was always a little tricky. It's against the health laws for non-seeing-eye animals to be inside a restaurant, so usually the restaurant owner has to give special permission (as happened in Norfolk) and be willing to risk the wrath of any government inspectors who might happen to wander in. In L.A., Norton was always welcome at the city's most popular restaurant, Spago. The owner, Wolfgang Puck, was a friend (and my mother writes his cookbooks; there's no question that she would like me better than she already does if I spoke with a hint of an Austrian accent and could cook squab the way Wolf does. Now that I think about it, Janis would also like me a lot better if I could cook *anything* the way Wolf does). Plus, Wolf's wife, Barbara, is the biggest animal nut around. She has a llama in her backyard, to illustrate my point, as well as the usual assortment of dogs and cats and God knows what else. When *The Cat Who Went to Paris* was published, we had the launch party at Spago and Wolf made Norton his own special pizza, covered with cat treats. I think they could get away with letting Norton eat in public because Spago is so hot—and tables there are in such demand—that Wolf probably has more clout than the mayor or governor. I mean, I'd hate to be a public official trying to get a table for four at 8 P.M. on a Saturday if that official was the person responsible for Norton's banishment.

This particular trip, there was a special request for dinner. In town at the same time was a very close friend, William Goldman, who is not only a writing idol of mine, he is a serious foodie. He wanted to take two women friends of his, Suzanne Goodson and Helen Bransford, to Spago and I agreed to make the reservation. Helen, who's also an animal nut—in case you think *I'm* weird, *she* often travels with her pet pig!—had heard that Norton was in town, so she got Bill to call me and ask if Norton could join them for their evening meal. As usual, I explained that if the cat came I had to come, too. Bill hesitated but said he supposed that would be fine (he didn't even check with Helen—he just took that heavy responsibility right on his own shoulders).

When we all sat down for dinner—Norton in his own chair, of course—the first thing that happened was that our waiter came over and said, "I don't know if you remember me, but I waited on you for Norton's book party. I had just started and that was my first celebrity event." He then looked down at Norton and said, "It's a pleasure to have you back."

During dinner, we all ordered various delicacies off the menu and, without even asking, the waiter brought over a plate of grilled chicken for Norton. Everything was absolutely delicious, but it was soon clear that Suzanne was not a happy camper. She kept looking over at Norton—I thought that perhaps she was allergic or disturbed by eating in such proximity to a four-legged furry guy. But no. What disturbed Suzanne, which she later confessed to Bill, was that Norton's food looked better than hers. All she had wanted to eat was grilled chicken—but it wasn't on the menu. And clearly Norton was the only one of us with enough clout to get a specially prepared meal.

After L.A., my little buddy and I drove down to San Diego. He was much beloved at Warwick's bookstore and we had a reading there. The appearance went as usual—

people tolerated and chuckled at my shtick then mobbed Norton in adulation. Afterward, we went to dinner at a friend's house, a literary agent named Margaret McBride. Margaret is quite successful and extremely popular, and she and her husband are the perfect hosts. That night, to celebrate Norton's appearance she had a particularly eclectic group of notable San Diegoans (San Diegites? San Dieg-people?). One of them was Audrey Geisel, a.k.a. Mrs. Dr. Seuss. Audrey was very taken with Norton and was rather shocked at how well behaved he was, which isn't so surprising, I guess, since her husband's most famous work was all about an anarchic cat who does his best to physically destroy house and home. I did feel some kind of psychic link, I must admit, between my fairly famous real cat and the wife of the creator of the world's most famous fictional feline. Showing my amazing maturity, I totally refrained from speaking in rhyme during the party or, when hors d'oeuvres were passed, from saying things like, "Gee, do you by any chance have any green eggs and ham?" I'm sure that Margaret was grateful for my restraint. I *know* that Norton was. There would be nothing worse for a cat than being embarrassed in front of the Seuss family.

The other guest of distinction that night was Alexander Butterfield. When I heard the name, it rang a bell but I couldn't quite place it. Then, as he began recounting a few anecdotes—mentioning several famous names, discussing a few historical events—it suddenly came to me. My amazing maturity and restraint immediately deserted me and I blurted out, "You're the guy who blew the whistle on Nixon!"

He was indeed the man who, when called before the

Watergate committee, had revealed one of the great secrets in history up to that point—that Richard Nixon, while president, taped every conversation he had in the oval office. It was, of course, those tapes that led to Nixon's downfall and if the man who was now busily fussing over my cat hadn't brought this to the public's attention, who knows how history would have been altered. Although Butterfield was a Nixon supporter and a devoted Republican, after the revelation he was not viewed kindly by those in the Nixon camp or by his fellow party members. He was vilified or revered, depending on your point of view, which is not always the most pleasant situation to be in. But to me the strangest thing is that he was famous only because he'd done something that everyone is supposed to do on a daily, regular basis—he told the truth, impartially and with no agenda. Just because it was the right thing to do. During dinner, he was extremely pleasant and entertaining. There was something inherently if quietly honorable about him, although at the same time also a touch sad. When we got back to our hotel room, I thought about explaining to Norton the vagaries of fame—the pitfalls and the dangers, the highs and lows—but by then he was already deeply asleep on the most comfortable chair in the room. I realized that, as with most other things, cats do not have to worry about human-style ups and downs. Cats are guileless. They do not need to tape their private conversations and they do not ostracize others of their species for speaking the truth. Cats are, by nature, truthful animals. In fact, cats do not know *how* to lie, which I'm sure is one of the reasons they are able to walk into hotel rooms and immediately fall asleep on the most comfortable chair.

That night, which was near the end of our tour, I decided I would not be audacious enough to explain to Norton about the fickle finger of fame. Instead I concluded that maybe I'd just pay closer attention, see how he coped with life, and do my best to learn from the master.

CHAPTER 4

A CAT
IN THE SPRING

When the book tour was over, I decided that it was time for one of us to retire. Since I could earn money without Norton but Norton was fairly dependent on me for his daily cans of food, the decision was an easy one. It only made sense that I be the one to remain, if you'll excuse a cat's most hated expression, in the rat race. This was not just a financial decision, though. Norton was getting on in years—he was ten at this point—and I very much wanted him to spend the rest of his life in comfort and ease. So, *voilà*, just like that, his life as a literary lion (okay, not exactly a lion, but you'll have to excuse the feline exaggeration; it sounded too good to pass up) was over.

That didn't mean it was the end of his traveling days, however. Those were, by no means, over.

What I'm about to launch into right now might sound like a digression, but trust me, it's a relevant if circuitous way to get back to Norton's traveling. It's also as good an explanation as I can come up with as to why I value the time spent with him so very much.

I'm not in any way, shape or form a religious person. Some readers have already figured this out for themselves because over the years, while I've received thousands of enthusiastic and warm-hearted letters from people who have grown to love Norton, I've also received a much smaller if more vociferous share of really negative, sometimes downright nasty letters. And I'm sorry to say that every one of the latter has been the result of my fairly benign comments about religion.

I've gotten several notes telling me that because of my flippancy and irreverency, Norton was surely going to heaven and I was just as surely going in the far opposite direction (most of these letters actually use phrases like "the far opposite direction"; they're too frightened to even write the word "hell"). Several people skipped over the promise of heaven for my cat and wrote just for the pleasure of letting me know that I was damned and doomed. I've received quite a few pages of scripture from people hoping to educate me or change my thinking (and for anyone who's considering sending more, I should probably let you know that I don't read these pages; as long as I'm going to be roasting on a spit for eternity anyway, I figure it won't really hurt me any further to crumple them up and toss them away. Sometimes, just to tempt fate, I also think impure thoughts while I'm doing that). I've gotten several letters telling me that the writers enjoyed my books immensely until they got to a joke or what they perceived as a snide comment about God, at which point those same books wound up in the trash (For the public record, they were right, those comments *were* snide. If any of those people who were offended went out and bought this book anyway, I guess this is as good a time to break it to you that I meant what I said then and I mean it now. So go back to the bookstore and get your money back before you read any further and work yourself up into another hysterical frenzy). I got one letter from a couple who read *A Cat Abroad* aloud to each other in the car every day while they commuted from home to work. That reading stopped, however, when they reached some paganlike observation and almost drove the car off the side of the road. Quite recently I received a note from a woman who blamed me for corrupting America's youth. Her accusation came about because she was horrified to read that Janis and I slept in the same bed without being married. I certainly don't want to give Janis a swelled head, but I've got to say, again for the record, that horrified woman doesn't know what she's missing! And I have additional bad news for this woman: Norton and I *also* spent many years in the same bed without being married. Not only that, he licked me quite a bit. Sometimes right on the lips!

For anyone who's still with me, what I object to most about religion is not the actual faith or belief in a supreme being or guiding force. That's just fine with me. It's the bigotry and hypocrisy that too often ensue from such blind faith. As always, let us learn from cats, those most unhypocritical of creatures, who, as far as we know, do not attend church or temple or any other restrictive place of worship that doesn't have a food dish readily available. To take the analogy one step further, it's also fairly difficult to imagine a cat agreeing to slay, persecute, maim, torture, hate or ridicule millions of its own species throughout history because they refuse to acknowledge the presence of some sort of invisible, all-knowing tiger who supposedly lives up in the sky.

Cats never let symbols assume importance over reality, which is what happens when religion or just about anything else becomes institutionalized. And I'm fairly certain that any self-respecting feline would agree with my dislike of anything that relieves us from responsibility for our own actions or that exists only to help us escape into an unreal sense of safety. I also do not believe, as many of my two-legged, nonfurry friends do when explaining their attendance of religious ceremonies, in using the excuse that religion provides a sense of community. Thanks, but no thanks. I much prefer choosing my own community, based on real ties and legitimate connections.

What I *do* understand—don't worry, I'm not a total iconoclastic moron—is the concept of rituals. I've got plenty of them that I adhere to and love. But—and this is a big but; feel free to call me a kook—I prefer to create my own rituals and to do them with friends rather than strangers who happen to have some distant relatives who once worshiped the same human, goat or big, hairy guy with a scythe who drinks nectar all day up on Mount Olympus. Rather than fasting on a randomly chosen day or confessing once a week to expunge my sins, I prefer to ritualize things that I enjoy, that have a personal meaning and provide genuine pleasure—spiritual, intellectual or physical. That includes things like having Thanksgiving dinner with the same group of close friends every year, and an annual New Year's Day hike in Provence with a different but

equally close group of friends, and a regular Final Four trip
to Las Vegas with a bunch of guys who like to gamble and
talk like the Rat Pack for forty-eight hours straight.

Do you see where this is leading?

No, probably not.

Well, the point is that every April, Janis and I indulge
in one of my favorite rituals, which is to go on a spring trip
with a group of ten or twelve close friends. We pick a spot,
usually in America, where few of us have been, and we go
there for a long weekend to do some sightseeing, some fine
dining and drinking, and enjoy each other's company. Now
that's my idea of a meaningful ritual.

Especially when accompanied by my very favorite
traveling companion.

The first Spring Trip was down to New Orleans. We
did not know the whole group excursion was going to become a ritual then; it was meant to be a one-shot. Janis and
I arranged almost everything that year because the idea was
to celebrate my birthday (since then, a different person is
responsible for the grunt work for each trip). We rented
out the LaMothe House, a small shabbily elegant hotel in
the French Quarter. And, a week or so before we left, I established another yearly ritual by having a lengthy phone
conversation with the hotel manager, trying to convince
her to allow a cat to stay there as one of their guests. In the
years to come, the hotel employee on the other end of the
phone would occasionally say, "Oh sure, we love cats. No
problem." More often, it was an, "Absolutely not. We do
not allow pets and it's out of the question." I would then assure the place that I would pay for any possible damages or
cleaning bills (although there never were any of either;
Norton was both tidy and considerate of other people's

property). I would also offer to pay extra for the additional guest (even though Norton didn't require his own room, bed, towels or food; at most, he needed two small bowls, one for water, one for nourishment, that could be kept in the bathroom). If none of that worked, I'd pull out the big gun: I'd mention Norton's name. Ninety-nine percent of the time that would do the trick and I'd hear the voice on the other end of the phone say, "Oh, Norton—well, Norton's *different*."

In New Orleans, that first trip, the hotel grudgingly allowed my cat to come, although they made it very clear they didn't approve. But after only one weekend in his presence, they changed their tune—big time. It changed so much that a couple of years later, when Janis and I were planning to go back to New Orleans and called to make a reservation at the same hotel, the manager begged me to bring Norton along. "We're still talking about him," she said. "And we'd be *very* pleased if he'd grace us with his presence."

Everyone who went with us to New Orleans felt that way about Norton. The weekend was extraordinarily fun, made more so by the fact that almost everywhere we went, so did my purring pal. Because we all had such a good time eating like pigs (particularly at Emeril's, where I thought Norton might pass out from the ecstasy of eating the salmon cheesecake), going to antebellum plantations, sipping chicory-flavored coffee and visiting the Voodoo Museum, we decided to repeat the experience the following spring and try traveling to Charleston, South Carolina.

Before departing, I had another long discussion with someone at the small hotel we wanted to stay at. This person was even more adamant that Norton should not come a callin'. Eventually, I wore him down but when we showed up the people at the hotel were so wary and disapproving that they made sure, when we checked in, to include a stern lecture about making Norton stay in his room at all times. Well, all I can say is that we all loved the city of Charleston—we went on garden and house tours, ate well, just enjoyed walking around one of the truly charming cities in the world—but by far the best part was watching what happened at the hotel. At our first breakfast there, Norton snuck downstairs and tried to join us for the morning meal. The manager came in to shoo him out, saw him sitting calmly in his chair and wound up petting him and deciding he was a perfectly fine breakfast guest. Before we went out to dinner that night, all the travelers—including the one feline—met for a drink in the lobby. When it was time to leave for the restaurant, I went to take Norton back up to our room (he was bushed and the restaurant wasn't thrilled about experiencing the pleasures of indoor cat dining). Before I got to the first step, the man at the front desk stopped me and, hemming and hawing, finally said that if I wanted to leave my cat downstairs, he'd be more than happy to keep him company for a little while. That little while turned into the entire evening. When we came back from dinner, there was Norton sitting on the front desk, being petted by the clerk, as well as a few other hotel workers and guests. The clerk explained that Norton was such good company it had seemed a shame to lock him in upstairs, so the staff agreed that they should just let him stick around until we returned. The third and final day we were there, Norton didn't come touring with us at all. He spent the day at the front desk, welcoming new guests and keeping the hotel staff company. I suspect that more than a few tears were shed when we packed our bags and headed back up north.

Over the next few years, the same group, with a few additions and subtractions—some people dropped out, some got married and fell out of the group, some just didn't have room for another ritual in their lives—ventured to San Francisco and the Napa wine country, the Brandywine country in Pennsylvania, the eastern shore of Maryland, Savannah, Georgia and Key West. Norton went almost everywhere with us and, in each place, not only made the trip much more enjoyable for us all, he spread that pleasure to the people we met and came to know along the way.

One of the best weekends—for people and cat—was at a wonderful farmhouse bed-and-breakfast called Sweetwater Farm in the Brandywine country of Pennsylvania.

Janis and I decided to drive there, since the B&B was only an hour and a half or so from New York. There were five of us in the car: me, Janis, my mom and her older sister, Belle (both of whom came to New Orleans for my birthday and had become very popular regulars for these trips), and Norton.

Belle, who was then eighty years old, was an interesting and exceptional person, smart, funny, wickedly acerbic, extraordinary generous, very, very tough, and startlingly truthful. (We were once discussing an acquaintance of my mother's and, trying to be pleasant, I said that she was a nice person. Belle said, "Yeah, if you happen to like stupid, lazy and ugly." I stared at her, somewhat aghast, although her description was 100 percent accurate, and she followed it with, "I'm too old to beat around the bush.") She smoked a ton and had that deep, throaty, smoker's voice that sounded like she had a ton of gravel in her throat, and because she couldn't ever remember anyone's name she used to greet everyone with a raspy, "Hiya, darling." I think I'm making her sound a little bit like William Demarest with a wig on and, now that I think of it, that description's not too far off base. That first year in New Orleans, at our Saturday night dinner at Emeril's, a cloth napkin was passed around the table and everyone signed it with some kind of witty birthday greeting. Belle wrote: "Happy to be here. At my age, happy to be *anywhere*." That instantly became the slogan for that and all future trips. We even printed up buttons for the next year's excursion with Belle's picture and that phrase printed on them.

When the New Orleans weekend was over, my mother went back home to her house in Los Angeles. Belle lived in New York but went with her, a continuation of her vacation. I called my mom a day or two after their return to report that all of my friends—most of whom met Belle for the first time down south—were thrilled that they both had come. They were all particularly impressed that Belle had stayed up as late as we had, walked everywhere we walked, done everything we did and, most impressive of all, drunk everything we drank (Belle, who lived for her daily afternoon glass—or glasses, as the case may be—of scotch, could drink all of us under the table, and pretty much did all weekend. The big drink in New Orleans is something called a Hurricane, a lethal mixture of fruit juices and rum and God knows what else. At one bar, Belle decided that this was something she had to try, but she asked the bartender if he could make a "scotch Hurricane." The bartender had his doubts, it was clear, but did as he was told. Belle proclaimed the concoction delicious—and had two). My mother turned to her sister to repeat the accolades from the East Coast and, in the background, I could hear Belle, indignant rather than pleased at the compliments, say, "What's the big deal? What do they think I am—*ninety*?!"

Belle was the person closest to my mother in their family. Even though my mom was then nearly seventy, she was still the little sister and Belle was quite protective. Belle was the protector of the whole family, in fact, the glue that held them all together. Part of it was due to her background. She was a Depression child, the fourth of six children, and the one who consistently got the worst deal. There was an older brother, who got better treatment simply because he was a boy. There were two older sisters. One was absolutely stunning looking, so she got away with murder. One was smart, so a lot of good things came her way. Then came Belle who, thanks to the onrush of the Depression, was the only child who didn't get to go to college and was forced to work early and continuously. By the time my mother and her younger brother were around, after a gap of quite a few years, the country's hard times were ending and normal life was resumed, so the two "babies" of the family also escaped most of the hardships that Belle had to endure. As a result of timing and the era and certain choices Belle made throughout her life, by the time she was eighty she was tough, independent, deeply cynical and mostly fearless.

I say "mostly" because she was absolutely terrified of one thing and one thing only.

You got that right . . .

Cats.

Which meant that she was horrified when she realized that she didn't only have to drive to Sweetwater Farm with a litter box by her feet, she had to drive with a cat perched mere inches away. She had spent time with Norton before, but always at a distance. Never in such proximity.

We started with Belle and my mother in the back seat. I drove. Janis sat in the passenger seat with Norton on her lap. Normally, Norton would have been happy as could be sitting up front (He was usually not allowed; that was Janis's law—she thought it was too dangerous. I, of course, always wanted him as close as possible. Norton knew that, so when it was just the three of us, he'd wait until Janis fell asleep, then he'd instantly sneak into the front seat and sit on my lap or, his preferred choice of seating, my shoulder). This trip, however, Norton sensed hostility from somewhere in the car. It was a challenge he could never resist. So he kept trying to move to the back seat where he could settle onto the ledge by the back windshield and try to convert Belle from foe to friend. The first half hour or so was mostly spent with Norton waiting until Janis would relax her hold. Then he would quickly sneak into the back. Belle would panic. My mom would grab him. And he'd wind up back up front with Janis trying to convince him to stay put.

The second half hour was spent with Norton nestled on the ledge in the back seat. Belle saw how determined he was to get close to her so she agreed to let him sit nearby— as long as she didn't have to touch him. My mother kept a close eye on the cat, letting him get close but not *too* close.

An hour into the trip, we stopped for lunch at the Black Bass Inn in Bucks County, one of the great spots on the East Coast. It dates back to the 1700s and, except for the modernization of the dining room—picture windows that are both huge and a huge design error—the place still has the feel of a Revolutionary War tavern. It's right on the canal and, in the winter, scarf-wrapped kids skate by it on their way to another town, making you feel like you're about to bump into Loretta Young, Jimmy Gleason and Cary Grant as Dudley the angel in *The Bishop's Wife*. The five of us went in to eat. I noticed that things might be taking a turn for the better when Belle said that Norton could sit in the chair next to her. She gave an embarrassed little cough—in no way did she want to be seen as backing down—and muttered that he was so well behaved, what difference did it make where he sat.

Lunch was fairly uneventful—other than the fact that, somewhere toward the end of her meal, we all saw Belle sneak Norton a little piece of her chicken breast.

The last half hour of our car ride found Norton snuggled up next to Belle, taking up a third of the back seat. I'm sure my mother was a tad cramped back there, but I guess she knew that it was useless to complain.

The weekend we spent at Sweetwater Farm, in the town of Glen Mills, Pennsylvania, was absolutely spectacular. It was run by a couple named Rick and Grace. They had bought the spread, which included a gorgeous 1734 farmhouse and various outbuildings which they'd converted to extra rooms or suites. Rick was this handsome guy who seemed equally at home hunting or playing polo or making world-class breakfasts for the guests (a slightly intimidating combination, I must admit). Grace was the perfect hostess, quite warm and friendly, not to mention pretty. As a matter of fact, she looked a little like Grace Kelly, and there turned out to be a reason for that. The first night we were there, several of us—yes, including Norton—wandered into the den of the main house, where there were a pool table and bottles of brandy. My friend Ziggy (who, along with his wife, Nancy, were two of the regulars on the spring trips; one of the rules on these trips was "No Kids," so their son Charlie was left behind to fend for himself) decided we owed it to ourselves to sip and shoot, so we did, while Norton relaxed in a big, comfortable chair by the fireplace. In between shots, I couldn't help but notice that scattered all over the room were silver-framed photos of Grace Kelly—personal shots, not film stills. The next morning, I asked Rick what was up with that and he said that Grace Kelly was his wife Grace's aunt. This gave us an extra bond, since I'd always thought that I would have made a superb Prince of Monaco.

Norton, who would have made a superb Cat of Monaco, had come into contact with a variety of animals over the years—other cats, all shapes and sizes of dogs, a Vietnamese pig, a camel, even a wild boar. But he met his first goat and his first horse on this trip. The intro to the horse was relatively uneventful. Norton did some sniffing and then darted away, deciding there were far better ways of spending his time than hanging around with something a hundred times his size and one-tenth his intelligence. The meeting with the goat had a little more drama to it.

It turned out that Belle was not just afraid of cats. She was not thrilled with animals in general. So when she was strolling across the property, she did her best to ignore the shaggy-haired, white-gray goat that seemed intent on getting to know her. Being eighty, outrunning the beast was out of the question, so when the goat approached and nuzzled up to her, Belle did the natural thing. She held her hands out to keep him at bay. By the time I heard Belle's voice, calm but firm, saying, "Could someone come out here, please! Now!" what was happening was that the goat had his head down, Belle had her hands straight out in front of her, resting on the top of the goat's head, and the goat was slowly but surely pushing a little old lady across the lawn. You know how it looks when you run out of gas and you shift into neutral, have to put your shoulder down and try to push your car down the street? That's exactly what this reminded me of. Except in this instance, Belle was the car.

It wasn't all that difficult to disentangle her from her predicament, but I do have to say that the first person—well, the first, um, animal—on the scene was none other than Norton (this was several years ago and I was younger, but even then I did not possess catlike speed). Now, I will not go so far as to say that Norton was racing to rescue my aunt. Brilliant, yes, that I'd say about my cat. Fearless? Absolutely, certainly by normal cat standards. But having the instincts of a fireman, rushing off to save people at the drop of a hat? Uh-uh. I think, rather, he was simply fascinated by the sight (as were we all; there was a little difficulty on everyone's part trying not to laugh out loud as Belle was goat-skiing across the grass). When the goat saw Norton, he did turn his head, which gave Belle some breathing room. It's beyond my capabilities to imagine what the goat thought when he saw a cat running straight at him across the farmland. Nor can I picture the thought balloons above my Scottish Fold's head as he took in the image of his elderly traveling companion and the goat. I do know, however, that the standoff ended the crisis. A couple of us were able to push the goat toward some other distraction while Belle moved as quickly as it was possible for her to move back to her room and take a belt from the bottle of scotch secreted in her overnight bag. I also know that there were many other activities over those couple of days: a visit to the Hagley Museum in Wilmington, right across the river (the site of the original Du Pont mills, estate and gardens); Winterthur (one of those must-visit places in America; another Du Pont creation—majestic galleries of decorative art and early American furniture and a spectacular naturalistic garden); Longwood Gardens (Janis can never get enough garden-viewing into her life); and the ever-popular Mushroom Museum (Okay, this probably is not a must-visit place; take it up with Nancy Alderman, who on various trips with us has insisted we visit the Pencil Museum, the Coffee and Tea Museum and now, in Kennett Square, Pennsylvania, a place that revealed the fascinating history of fungi. In their brochure, they announce that you can "See the growing mushrooms in all stages of development" while you "discover the enchanting world of the Shiitake, Portabella, Crimini, and Oyster Mushrooms." There is also an "amazing array of distinctive gift ideas . . . all with mushroom motif." In case you doubt me, ask yourself this: Could he possibly make this stuff up?). But, by far, the best sight of all came in the car ride back to New York City. After spending a weekend with Norton—and surviving the harrowing run-in with the goat—Belle was more than happy to let my cat spend the ride sitting comfortably and purring away on her lap.

Living proof that it is never too late for an old dog— or human or cat—to learn new tricks.

In the wine country of Northern California, our friends Paul and Laurie Eagle "volunteered" to handle all the arrangements for the trip. And they did a superlative job, particularly in renting out three magnificent stone cottages on property belonging to one of the area's best wineries. It felt like we were sleeping in the middle of a vineyard in Tuscany. But as beautiful and as fun as this trip was, Norton was left behind (yes, he would have loved the vineyard accommodations; no, he would not have loved the Sarasota mud baths). I had one strict rule, which I always tried to adhere to when it came to Norton's travels. Flying is hard on a cat. Cross-country flying is harder (you try spending up to eight or ten hours—counting cab time to and from the airport—without your litter box). So unless I was going to be in California for at least a week, Norton would remain on his home coast. If he had seven days to relax and recuperate, I didn't mind dragging him along before putting him back on a plane. But even for the pleasure of his company, it wasn't fair to make him fly three thousand miles if it was only a two- or three-day trek.

Usually when I'd go away for under a week, it was for business, which meant that Janis would also be left behind and could take care of her step-cat. As is well documented, Norton was quite fond of Janis and nobody took better care of him. But as much as I hated being away from him, that's how much he did not like being separated from me. He was comfortable in Janis's apartment and got plenty of petting and friendly conversation as well as very acceptable sleeping arrangements (i.e., my side of the bed—or, in case that woman who wrote me the letter accusing me of moral degeneracy is actually reading this book, on the couch in the living room, where all male overnight visitors slept).

But when I'd call in from the road, here's the report I'd usually get:

Day One: Janis would report that all was fine. Norton slept next to her, tried to wake her up early so he could be fed (something he never did with me; but with Janis he would put his paw on her face and, at 6 A.M., he'd try to gently pry open her eyelids), and spent a peaceful day, moving around from room to room in her floor-through apartment.

Day Two: All was still fine, but Norton didn't do as much moving. He mostly napped in the foyer.

Day Three: Norton wouldn't look at Janis, clearly blaming her for my absence. He didn't sleep with her, either (too intimate, I guess, to sleep with such a traitor). Also, he was no longer relaxed and content. He was morose, hardly moving from the middle of the foyer. She did everything she could to coax him into her room but it was no go.

Day Four: Norton did nothing but sulk. Janis would use words like "clinical depression."

Day Five: He'd had it. Now furious that I was obviously having a good time without him, Norton would go into Janis's bedroom when she was away at her office and leave her a nasty little present. Right in the middle of her bed. Right on top of her antique linens and quilt. When Janis would return home, she'd call me, angry, sure, but also frustrated. "I treat him so well," she'd say. "I don't think it's right that he feels he has to shit in my bed."

I'd assure her that it wasn't personal and that I'd strongly reprimand my cat when I returned. But deep down, I was kind of glad. I certainly didn't wish a soiled quilt on anyone, particularly the love of my life. But if *I* was going to be depressed about being separated from my cat, it was comforting to know that he was just as neurotic as I was.

That San Francisco trip, he didn't stay with Janis, obviously, since she was there along with the rest of the usual group. For the three days we were gone, he stayed with a woman named Ann King. Weirdly enough, I hardly knew Ann. She was a close friend of a friend—and had gotten word to me that she was a huge fan of Norton's. The message was passed along that if the occasion ever arose, she'd love to take care of him (just so you know, *I* never get messages saying, "If you ever need someone to take care of you, just give me a call"). Since the occasion had arisen, I called her, asked if she'd like a cat for a long weekend and she jumped at the opportunity. When I dropped Norton off at her Chelsea apartment, he got his usual visiting-royalty treatment. Ann had special bowls all set up for his food and, while I stood by semi-invisibly, she showed her guest the entire apartment. By the time I left, Norton was happily exploring every nook and cranny. And when I returned to pick him up after the weekend, I got the full report: no depression, no morose sulking, no unpleasant surprises on the duvet cover. On both coasts, it was as successful a trip as it could have possibly been—except for Janis, who, deep down, was hoping that someone else would finally understand what she had to put up with.

The next spring, the destination was the Eastern Shore of Maryland. There was no cross-country traveling involved, so Norton was welcomed with open arms back into the group (Come on, admit it. Don't you think it's impressive that even after all these years I don't overdo the cute stuff and say things like "welcomed with open paws" in almost every paragraph?). I don't ever mean to make these books read like travelogues, but sometimes geographical description is truly in order. I'm also the kind of person who, when I like something a lot, I want everyone to like it as much as I do, so I generally do a lot of ranting and raving. And both Norton and I loved this part of Maryland.

First of all, what needs to be understood is that in Maryland, in the springtime, it is actually possible to eat all the hardshell crabs your little heart desires. And my heart desires a lot of those suckers. If you have never been fortunate enough to scarf some of these big boys down, what you do is go to a semi-divey-looking place with long wooden tables. The tables are usually covered with sheets of thick brown paper. As you sit and drink several pitchers of cold beer or, if you're the more delicate type, white wine, the servers bring out trays of hardshell crabs. Along with the crabs, you're given small wooden mallets (forks and knives are not just unnecessary, they're totally useless). These crabs are covered in the spiciest seasoning imaginable, red and peppery and so hot that I take pity on anyone who has a scratch on his fingers or who bites his cuticles because any exposed cut or wound will feel as if it's on fire. Before even trying to dig in, you get an explanation of how to eat them. Without this explanation, you're doomed to failure and frustration, because you'll wind up spending much money and getting about half an ounce of crab into you. If you follow directions—which involve expertly twisting various parts of the crab, delicately breaking parts in half, gently separating some parts from others, and then smashing down on everything as hard as you can with the mallet so you can get to the sweet, sweet meat—you will be rewarded with the perfect dinner. Most of the crab places I've been to down in those parts disdain vegetables as a side dish (another reason to love Maryland). And a lot of them serve brownies and ice cream with hot fudge for dessert. It's fairly heavenly, particularly if you're a cat. At the restaurant we went to, which was right on the water and glorious in its diveyness, Norton did not handle the mallet very well, but he was hell on wheels when it came to slurping up the crab I'd hand feed him (and if you're thinking of trying this at home, please do what I do: wipe off a lot of the hot stuff and get rid of the tiniest of bones before letting your cat attack it).

The town we decided to stay in was Chestertown and there are very few places like it left in America. It has a population of a little over three thousand and when you walk the streets it's like stepping back in time to the '70s. And not like stepping back to the 1970s. There are no platform shoes and discos here. I'm talking 1770s. The village is dominated by colonial and Victorian influences. If you go late at night or very early in the morning, when there are no cars driving around, stand in the middle of the bridge crossing the Chester River and turn back to Chestertown, you see absolutely no semblance of the modern world. It is not difficult to imagine Thomas Jefferson (or, if you're Norton, Thomas Jefferson's cat) strolling down High Street on his way to a town meeting (or prowling around looking for Betsy Ross's cat).

We stayed at a charming little hotel, which isn't difficult because everything in Chestertown is charming and little. Norton once again won the hotel workers over and spent much time lounging at the front desk. Our one big excursion was into Annapolis, which is the perfect southern seaport town—beautiful row houses, monied enough to be preserved but blue collar enough to be real. And it's got one of the great universities in the country, St. John's, which has one of the most interesting curriculums imagin-·

able. Here's what you do in your four years at St. John's: You read and study the hundred greatest books ever written. You get your basic Plutarch and Aristotle and Archimedes and work your way forward to the twentieth century. The brilliant idea behind it is that at the end of your reading and discussions, you should have a decent overview of what's made the world exactly what it is.

Sometimes—in fact, most of the time; more and more of the time as I get older—I think that cats have a much better idea than we do of exactly what the world really is. They eat, they sleep, they choose who they love and bond loyally. That's not a bad start. Add to it: They're not afraid of being vulnerable, they are willing to please and to accept pleasure with no questions asked. They are remarkably self-sufficient, they are not obsessed with being liked, but they will rarely, if ever, go out of their way to cause any sort of pain or trauma. They are confident, with no need to show it off, and they are kind, with little need of reward other than to have that kindness returned.

I often wonder how different the world would be if Plutarch and Aristotle and Archimedes had had cats.

A lot different, I think.

And I think this, too: a lot better.

CHAPTER 5

THE CAT WHO
WENT BACK
TO PARIS

orton's travels were not confined to
American shores. Whenever I was lucky enough
to go to Europe, there was no question that he'd
be lucky enough to accompany me. And just because he might not happen to speak the language of
whichever country we were visiting, didn't mean that he
couldn't change people's lives.

In Sicily, he totally and permanently transformed the
lives of one of the most interesting and delightful families
I've ever met.

Janis and I went to Sicily with Norton for the first time
in 1991. Before we left—it was when we were living in
Goult, that most heavenly of Provençal towns—our friend
Nancy Alderman faxed us a small story about a restaurant
called Gangivecchio, in the Madonie Mountains. It had my

name all over it: it had originally been an abbey in the fourteenth century, it was in the middle of nowhere and impossible to find, and it supposedly had the best food in Sicily. Put all those things together and you've got this: Pete's goin' there to eat.

We started our Sicilian stay in the touristy but spectacular town Taormina (where Norton's adventures, particularly his tendency to scurry out on a ledge many hundreds of feet high, nearly giving his loving father a stroke, have been well chronicled). Our second day there, I insisted on trying to find the magical restaurant we'd read about, so we drove across a good chunk of the island to Gangivecchio. Or, rather, we *tried* to drive there. It was not as easy as it sounded (and it didn't sound all that easy to begin with). What should have taken two or two and a half hours, took four. Sicilian roads are small and if you're not inclined to blindly pass a slow-moving truck on a winding mountain road, you stand a good chance of driving along forever at twenty miles an hour. We didn't get stuck behind a truck— we got stuck behind *four* trucks. So we were not exactly speeding. And then we got lost (I'm not usually one to make excuses for my embarrassing and horrendous sense of direction—the only person I've ever met who can get more lost than I can is Janis—but the endgame of the directions included things like "When you come to a tree that branches off into a Y, across from a church, make a left"). Eventually we did find the place and it was magical indeed. Four hours of driving, squabbling and meowing were immediately forgotten.

A brief foray into seven hundred years of Gangivecchian history, because I think it's important to put Norton's influence into some kind of historical perspective:

In 1363, Benedictine monks were given a gift of 1,600 acres and began to build a priory on the spot of a village, Gangi, that no longer existed because it had been completely destroyed in a battle in the year 1299. The priory eventually became its own little village and I guess these monks knew what they were doing because at some point the priory had its designation elevated to "abbey."

Many fascinating things happened between that elevation in 1413 and the next 450 years—wars, invasions, religious upheaval, the usual sort of stuff—but the only real relevant item for our purposes is that in 1856, someone named Vincenzo Tornabene bought what was by then the *former* abbey (And just in case you don't think this book is educational, for all you historical dolts out there, 1856 was just five years before Sicily decided to unite with Italy. Tell the truth, you thought Sicily was *always* part of Italy, didn't you?). Various Tornabenes inherited the property over the next hundred years until Wanda Tornabene married the grandson of Vincenzo (whose name was also Vincenzo; trust me, I've spared you a *lot* of Tornabenes who all had the same name). Like many wealthy, land-owning Sicilians, Wanda's Vincenzo, who was called Enzo (I guess the Tornabene ancestors had the same problem I do telling everyone with the same name apart) found hard times after World War II. By the late 1970s, most of his money was gone, as were about 1,450 of the ex-abbey's acres and much of the magnificent furniture. That's when Wanda took over. They needed money, she had one great skill—cooking—so the abbey was now a restaurant. Life was not easy, but they survived—and managed to keep up the magnificent building and remaining property. By 1980, Wanda's cooking lured enough Sicilians so they had to expand the restaurant area and enclose an enormous second-floor terrace so it could function as a dining room. In 1984, Enzo died suddenly, but still the restaurant kept going, run by Wanda and her daughter, Giovanna.

And now we're in 1991. Enter three weary travelers: two humans and a cat.

Quite simply, after we finally arrived, we had the best lunch we'd ever had in our lives. If you want the actual details, we sat in the long room that had once been a terrace on the west wing of the abbey, looked out over the many acres of glorious wild red poppies, watched as various animals strolled nearby (including a pet wild boar) and ate the most amazing pasta with pesto sauce ever devised (one of several key secrets is the addition of five different kinds of crushed nuts: almonds, hazelnuts, walnuts, pistachios and pine nuts), veal rolls stuffed with ham (*"involtini"* is what you ask for, if you're ever lucky enough to make it there for lunch), *cannolis* that were not to be believed, and then something called *sofficini*, which you don't even want to know about because you might give up your life savings and your first born child in order to fly there and wrap your mouths around these things (Okay, I guess you *do* want to know about them, but don't say I didn't warn you: they're fried dough stuffed with warm lemon pastry cream. I guess I should mention that what adds to the taste, as well as the cholesterol level, is that they're not just fried, they're fried in lard. My fairly demanding friend and literary agent, Esther, has actually threatened to withhold payment of my next check that comes in from the publisher unless I learn to make these things and bring her some).

The restaurant was full that day—there were a hundred German bikers on a tour, which meant that every single person in the restaurant other than me and Janis was speaking German and wearing spandex—so we didn't get to talk very much to the two Tornabene women. The only reason they spoke to us at all was because Norton was fascinated with the place and, while we ate, he wandered the ancient abbey, exploring. At some point Wanda, the head of the family, came rushing over to us, muttering in Italian. My Italian basically consists of the following words (most of which I've already used in this chapter): *cannoli, pesto*, and *ciao bambino*. So I didn't really understand much of what Wanda was saying until Giovanna, who speaks lovely, charming, poetic English, also came over and said, "Mama is worried about your little cat." I told them both not to worry, searched for a minute, found Norton dozing on top of a table in some back room of this walled stone fortress, and convinced him that it was time to leave.

The next few days were spent touring the isle. I have absolutely nothing bad to say about Sicily. It's one of my favorite places on earth for many reasons—its beauty, its culture, its food, its relative wildness (as compared to, say, Tuscany, which Sicilians have mockingly labeled "Chiantishire" because it's been so Anglicized, or even to my beloved Provence which has been Peter Mayled to the point where it's almost easier to hear English spoken than French)—but the next few days were pure torture for me. I got crankier and crankier, and more and more impossible to be around, until Janis finally turned to me, while we were in front of the magnificent Greek temples of Agricento, one of the real wonders of the world, and said, "Why are you acting like a total asshole?!" Being the cultured guy that I am, I graciously answered, "Because I don't want to see any more temples, I don't want to go to any more museums, and I don't want to spend one more day being a damn tourist!" She calmly asked, as if talking to a petulant (if not very bright) sixth grader, "Well, then what *do* you want to do?" and I said, "I want to go back to Gangivecchio and eat!"

So the three of us got back in our rented car and drove three hours back to the abbey. Every so often we'd stop and try to call them, to make sure they were open, and we'd get some guy who answered the phone and said, "Pronto!" I'd then say, "Uh . . . openo for luncho?" and he'd hang up. Twenty minutes later, we'd call again, hoping to get Giovanna, the English speaker, but no, we'd get the same guy (we later learned his name was Pepe) who'd say, "Pronto!" I'd then say, "Uh . . . Giovanna?" And he'd say, "Si!" and still hang up. I called five times before we arrived, never managing to make Pepe understand a word I was saying, and when we finally showed up there wasn't a soul eating in the place. But Wanda and Giovanna let us in, served us an even more amazing lunch than we'd had five days earlier, and this time they both sat and chatted with us for several hours, Giovanna doing the translating all around. Norton sat with us for part of the time and spent the rest of the meal wandering around as if he'd spent his entire life there. Wanda, possibly the greatest animal lover I've ever met, was enthralled with my little guy and insisted on walking around with him and talking to him and feeding him.

At the end of the meal and quite a lot of conversation, when we realized we actually couldn't come up with an excuse to stick around one more moment, I said to Giovanna, "Would you like to do a cookbook? Because, if you would, I'll sign you up on the spot." (I worked then and still do work as an editor for various imprints within the humongous Random House Inc. complex, so I can do that sort of thing from time to time). They smiled, clearly thought I was trying to get a free meal out of them and said, "*Ciao.*" I, however, wouldn't give up. When I got back to New York a couple of months later (remember, we were still living in France), I sent them a contract, found them a writer (a woman named Michele Evans, who'd written her own superb cookbooks and who heroically learned Italian for this job!) and we had a deal . . .

Sort of.

We didn't really have a deal because we'd hit one big snag. Wanda—the matriarch of the family and the one with all the recipes—didn't want to do it.

Two reasons. One: she didn't want her neighbors to be able to get their hands on her long-secret, much-valued family recipes. And two: she didn't know me from Adam and, being Sicilian, didn't exactly trust my motives. Why was I doing this? Why would I want to help them? What was I getting out of all this? etc., etc., etc.

Giovanna took care of Issue #1. She worked on her mother for weeks on end and Wanda began to weaken. I was able to push her over the edge by assuring her that the book would be published in English and none of her neighbors spoke anything but Italian, so her secrets would be safe.

Issue #2 was a little harder. What was there that could get her to trust me?

Well . . . there was one thing . . .

Norton.

After thinking and thinking, Wanda decided that anyone who traveled with his cat—and who loved his cat as much as I clearly did—had to be honorable. And anyone who had such a wonderful, brilliant, well-behaved cat, had to be a good person. Because she was so impressed with Norton, she thought there was a chance I just might be on the up and up. So she agreed to do the book. But she made it clear she was only doing it for Norton.

And thanks to Norton, here's what happened: The book was published in 1996. Giovanna and Wanda (who still didn't speak a word of English) went on a nationwide publicity tour in America and took the cooking world by storm. They went on television shows, including "Good Morning America"; cooked a magnificent lunch at the James Beard Foundation in Manhattan; were written about (gushed over is more like it) in just about every newspaper and magazine imaginable; and prepared special dinners at such famous restaurants as Alice Waters's Chez Panise in Berkeley and Mark Peel's and Nancy Silverton's Campanile in Los Angeles. As a result of all the publicity, the restaurant at the abbey in Gangivecchio was soon booked solid. Wanda's son Paolo, an architect, built a nine-room inn on the property (converting the old stables into lovely rooms and a separate dining room, for which he is now the chef). That inn is now always full. They also converted a two-hundred-year-old stone cottage into a luxurious two-room suite with an enormous stone fireplace in each room. To top it all off, their book won the James Beard Award as 1997's Best Italian Cookbook. Wanda and Giovanna Tornabene were officially stars. By the time you're reading this book in your hands, their second book will have been out for several months and will, I'm sure, be at least as successful as their first (and I do know that Wanda is now so proud of the first book, she even shows it off to her neighbors, recipe stealing be damned!).

It all makes for one of my favorite publishing stories. Lives were changed and totally for the better. And none of it would have happened if not for Norton.

Janis and Norton and I did go back to Gangivecchio a couple of years after the first book was published. We stayed at the inn this time and had a wonderful few days strolling the property and, of course, stuffing our faces (Wanda and Giovanna also took us shopping at the open-air food market in Palermo, a major treat). Norton had quite a good time, too. Not only was he fed well, he had 150 acres to stroll and many olive trees to climb and scratch. There were also a ton of animals on the property to keep him company. Paolo had a dog (a lunatic dog, but a dog), Wanda had her house dog, Puffo, and several indoor cats. Giovanna had her own dog, separate from Puffo, who was allowed indoors. And then there were quite a few outdoor dogs, whose favorite activity was to run up to us, barking as loud as they could, then stop short as soon as they saw an unfazed cat sitting on my shoulder and staring down at them. There was also that wild boar, who had his own penned-in area, but Norton, other than an occasional quick peek out of curiosity, tended to stay away from her.

When it was time to leave for the airport and return home, Norton was nowhere to be found. This was very unlike him. The door to our room had been left open, so I thought he was out strolling the property. I walked around calling his name, but got no response. This was now totally unlike him. My imagination ran somewhat wild. I had images of him being munched on by Wanda's boar. I had a vision of his being kidnapped by Sicilian bandits. I even thought that maybe Paolo had sent him to drive the car up to the house and boom!—blown to bits—but then I realized I'd just seen *Godfather II way* too many times. Finally, while standing in our room in the inn, wondering if I'd have to spend the rest of my life in Sicily searching for my cat, I heard a very familiar sound—purring. I searched everywhere and the purring got louder, but no Norton. Eventually, I put my ear to the bed and the purring got even louder. It turned out that Norton had crawled into and under the mattress cover. It was one of the very few times in his life he had tried hiding from me. I had to say, after two days of eating those lemon-filled *sofficini*, I couldn't blame him. But I picked him up (he'd gained a few pounds, just as his parents had), told him I didn't appreciate the anxiety he'd put me through, and did my best to convey the simple truism that all good things have to come to an end.

I don't know if I really convinced him, but he did let me place him in his travel Sherpa bag and we were finally able to return home.

To be honest, I don't think I really did convince him. That whole idea of good things ending was a concept Norton didn't fully understand and I can't say I blamed him. The truth is, I did my best to keep the good times rolling.

Some of the consistently best times were when we returned to France, particularly to Goult, which we tried to do once a year. We'd usually make an arrangement to rent the same house, because we loved it so much, then we'd go for Christmas and stay through New Year's Day, when all our Goultoise friends would have their traditional hike-into-the-hills-to-an-ancient-deserted-village-then-cook-homemade-sausages-over-an-open-fire-drink-wine-sing-songs-show-everyone-that-it's-much-better-to-be-French-than-anything-else celebration.

We actually mingled with two different crowds of people in Provence. There was the Goult crowd, mostly French with one Swede thrown in for good measure, and the ex-patriot crowd, mostly British with one or two Americans and Canadians. There was one Christmas party that was particularly memorable spent amongst the ex-pats. Our friends Margit and Georges decided to have a scavenger hunt. Well, Margit did. Georges, who's a bit more of the subtle, dry, academic type, went along with it. Margit, who's a bit more of the skin-tight pants, tight sweater, flamboyant, va-va-voom type, did all the planning and all the work. In addition to the va-va-voom, she's also been the CEO and CFO of various large companies, so it's not like this was a simple take-two-steps-due-east-of-the-well-until-you-find-a-tree-trunk kind of scavenger hunt. This was a major deal. After a wonderful lunch (did I mention that Margit is a serious cook, too?), we were divided into five different cars with four people—and in our case, one cat—in each car. Couples were split up, to make the whole thing more competitive. Margit didn't have to worry about the teams' competitive spirit, it turned out. By the end of the hunt, people were doing everything but letting the air out of enemy team car tires. Janis, at one point, threw herself down in the middle of the road so my team couldn't move our car—and thus get the jump on her team—without actually flattening her into a pancake. Or *crêpe*, as the case may be. What Margit did was give each team a set of extremely clever poems, some in French, some in English. The poems were complicated clues, each one leading us to find one element of the hunt. But you had to know this area well to figure things out. For instance, one particularly complicated segment of the poem wound up directing us toward the best bread baker in the region. Which meant we actually had to know who the best bread baker was. Whoever was smart enough to work it out, then had to buy one loaf of his particular specialty to prove that we'd concluded that segment of the hunt. My team figured it out, got to this *boulanger* first, but, being France, we got there during lunchtime when he was taking his nap. I was the one with the nerve to go wake him, and I also was the one with the nerve to suggest that he let me buy every single loaf of his special bread so no one else could possibly win. But this baker had too much integrity—or else he didn't understand my horrendous French—and he would sell me one loaf and one loaf only.

We spent the day racing all over what I think is the most beautiful region in the whole wide world. One clue led us up to the very top of the ancient village of Oppede-le-Vieux, where we had to find some hidden marbles. Another clue took us to an eighteenth-century fountain where we had to bring back a small container of water. We needed a handful of red clay from the magnificent village of Roussillon, too. I will admit that Norton was not a lot of help this particular day, although by his excited meowing, I do believe he got into the competitive spirit. Once all the clues were solved and the items collected, the final segment of the poem led us to one of my favorite places in the Luberon, the home of Gianni the Sardinian goatherd (who, as described in *A Cat Abroad*, had the unique arrangement of living with both his wife and his mistress). Gianni *et ses petites amies* lived on top of a mountain with hundreds of goats, some of whom were consumed nightly in the superb if extremely rustic restaurant Gianni had opened. So at the end of the big competition, the twenty or so humans and the one feline all wound up munching on roasted goat and delicious potatoes and drinking an obscene amount of Gianni's homemade (and devastating) *eau de vie*, all relishing our friendship and Margit's eccentric genius and the fact that a cat would actually spend the day helping to hunt for a perfect loaf of bread.

One year, I was lucky enough to stick around after the holidays. Norton and I spent two and a half months alone, ensconced in our house in Goult while I was working on a book. It was ten weeks of wine, cat and song, and just thinking of being able to live there makes me teary-eyed. I'd work all day, with a break or two to go grocery shopping at the mystical Madame Maurel's *épicerie*, where there was almost nothing on earth you wanted that you couldn't find. Norton would stroll down the cobblestone path, accompanying me daily to Joelle Maurel's store. He also liked to hike with me to the butcher shop. (Have you ever seen a cat lick his lips? I used to see it every day.) And to the *boulangerie*, where I'd get my daily bread. For those of you who have read the earlier books, you'll remember my good friend Norm Stiles, he of "Sesame Street" fame. (To refresh your memory, I wrote about how he used to lure babes over to the house we shared in Fire Island, shamelessly using any means possible, but I promised him I wouldn't bring that up anymore since he's now married. And you know me, I'm a man of my word.) Norm came to Goult several times and, in one sense, ruined my life. He used to do an impersonation of French people going through their daily lives and panicking when they realized they didn't have a loaf of bread under their arms. I used to go buy a baguette every single day in Goult and not once did I return to the house without laughing the entire way back, thinking of Norm going, in his horrendous French accent, "Ooh-la-la, I have no bread! If I don't get ze bread to tuck under my arm weezin fifteen minutes, I will be dead! Or worse, arrested by ze bread police!"

I never did figure out a way for Norton to carry his own baguette, which is one of the few regrets I have of time spent there. Other than that, the only word I can think of for Goult and its people and its shops is "perfect." There are many places in the world that I'm happy I've been to, and been able to take Norton to, but none quite so much as this Brigadoon-like town.

Janis and I felt extremely lucky that we were accepted so readily into this tight-knit Provençal society. And it was quite sweet to see the way Norton was accepted, too, just as if he were a full-fledged member of the family (which, of course, he was—but it was *très française* for the entire town to accept that fact so immediately and absolutely). Goult is tiny; there are perhaps a thousand people living there and we got to know many of them. One of the best and most interesting aspects of returning to the same place every year was that we could connect with our friends so strongly, even though we saw them but every twelve months or so. In a strange way, that separation added to the bond; it made our get-togethers more meaningful. And because we felt so close to them but were, in fact, so geographically distant, when we did reenter their lives we were able to clearly see how they and their surroundings had changed. Some changes were for the better, some weren't. I'm not big on change, in general. My succinct philosophy of life, stealing a line once written by Joseph Heller in his book *Good as Gold,* tends to be "All change is for the worse." But I will say that the changes in Goult were always fascinating.

We watched children grow up over the last decade and suddenly preteenagers who had once been shy around the American strangers were now our adult friends. We watched several women break up unhappy relationships with their husbands or male lovers and watched one of them, in quite a surprise move, take on a woman lover—and suddenly, for the first time in her life, have a genuinely good, mature relationship. She wrote to us before we arrived a few years ago, to try to prepare us for this change. Janis's French is better than mine, but neither of us are fluent. It's quite an experience trying to piece together a letter in French in which a friend is explaining that she's become a lesbian. After about seven or eight readings, we were pretty sure we'd narrowed things down. Either our good pal was now happily living with a woman and together they had a new dog called Yum-Yum. *Or* our friend was happily living with a gay dog who thought some woman was so delicious the dog was always saying yum-yum. (I made the case that, for all we knew, "yum-yum" was the French equivalent of "arf arf"). Or—this one was my interpretation—our friend was now convinced that she was a dog named Yum-Yum and she was living with another dog named Lesbian. We finally had to call another friend over there and gingerly ask, "*Qu'est-ce que c'est nouvelle avec notre amie?*" Our first interpretation was immediately confirmed, which, considering the possibilities, was quite a relief.

Over a decade of repeated visits, Janis, Norton and I

had witnessed close-up the ebb and flow of village life. One dear friend got so sick she almost died. Another was dying but made a miraculous recovery. One friend, a musician, moved to Paris and fell in love. Another returned from Paris to live in Goult full-time. Some of the Goultoise learned English since we'd first appeared. Some who spoke English forgot it. One woman sold her house and moved into the most beautiful eighteenth-century house imaginable. Another woman tried to sell her house but couldn't. Other friends built their dream house in the field right below the town.

And that was just on the human level. Norton experienced plenty of change, too. He found that some of his cat pals were no longer around—dead or just run away, no telling—but others replaced them, and as soon as he was back skulking in the lavender garden that comprised part of our backyard, many of the local *chats* would appear to play, hiss or scrounge food, depending on their moods. His bulldog pal, Archie, one of his favorite playmates, disappeared one year. No one in the town seemed to know what happened to him and I know that Norton missed him—he liked to explore the streets of Goult with Archie more than any of his other animal pals. But Norton definitely had a touch of French existentialism to him and he coped with Archie's absence quite well. One year here, the next year gone? *C'est la vie.* Time to move on . . .

No matter what the dramas or traumas, when we returned each year, everyone kissed us on the cheek—not just twice, three times is the rule in Provence—and we exchanged simple gifts and every single one of us thought how lucky we were to be together in such a magical and magnificent town.

My favorite change was pointed out to us one Christmas a couple of years ago. The three of us arrived late at night that year, driving up from the Marseille airport. One of the most startling things about Goult is how absolutely silent it is, especially when flying in from New York City, where silence is something that exists only in one's wildest imagination. Goult at 11 P.M. isn't just silent. It's as if you've suddenly gone deaf. There's not a noise to be heard. We parked toward the top of the village, behind the medieval castle, and walked down the hill, past the house that kept an outdoor canary cage, whose feathered inhabitants for some unknown reason never failed to terrify my heroic feline. Heading toward our house, our footsteps sounded to both of us like claps of thunder. We got the front door open and immediately felt a wave of pleasure sweep over us. The house, owned by a woman named Elisabeth Hopkins, is a special place both in reality and in our hearts, so we slowly and delightedly took it in, as we did every year. We looked to see which books on the shelves were new, if the furniture had been rearranged, if there were any new cooking utensils or sheets or decorations. Norton did what he always did, which never failed to amaze me: he went right for the exact spot where I put his food and water dishes every year and he just sat down, looking up at me expectantly. In case people ever say to you that cats don't have a real memory, ask them to explain how my cat could live in a house for a year, then return every twelve months for one week only, and remember, to the inch, exactly where he had to go for food.

Anyway, to finish off this little anecdote: After putting some French cat food right on Norton's marker, we unpacked, went into our cozy bedroom that had a window overlooking much of the glorious Luberon, and fell deep asleep. When we woke up the next morning, we strolled around town—which takes all of fifteen minutes—to see if we could ascertain what was new. The ruin at the very top of the town had been rebuilt and turned into a windmill, which it had apparently been many hundreds of years ago. There seemed to be a tiny new store that opened up (and when I say tiny, I mean *tiny*; the whole place couldn't have been any bigger than two subway token booths put together) although, since it was closed and all we could do was press our faces up against the window, we couldn't quite make out what it was they were selling. That seemed to be it. Everything else was pretty much the same.

So we thought.

At a respectable hour, we knocked on our friends Anne and Hannah's house (the nice thing about Goult is that no one lives more than about a hundred feet away from anyone else: Anne's house backed up onto our yard, Sylvie's house was ten feet away from Anne's on the other side of the street, Danie's house was fifteen feet away from our front door). Anne and Hannah let us in, made us some tea, put a bowl of water down for Norton, and then Anne went into a rant about how much Goult had changed.

"What's so different?" I asked, a bit bewildered by the tirade.

I was almost sorry I asked. There used to be *two* restaurants in town—now there were *three* (when we started going there, there was only one restaurant, but we didn't want to remind her of that)! Patrick, the owner of the first restaurant, Le Tonneau, had opened a bed-and-breakfast above his bistro! And worst of all, the new store we'd seen in the middle of town, well it wasn't a new store, it was a small tourist agency. Tourists could go there and send faxes or ask about tour guides or . . . or . . . or . . . Anne could barely finish she was so upset.

"Goult, eet ees just like Shee-cago!" she said despairingly.

We tried to explain to her that three tourists showing up there so they could buy a map wasn't exactly like Chicago, but it was no go. She could not be convinced.

"Perspective," I said to Norton when we got home. He was sitting on the tiled roof of the house, outside our living room window, his favorite perch. "Don't ever lose it," I told him.

Watching him lolling in the Provençal sun, staring out at the hills of the Luberon, I had the comforting feeling that Norton's perspective was one thing I didn't have to worry about changing.

Most of the time, when we returned to Goult at Christmastime, we tried to spend a day or two in Paris. Janis and I love Paris, and always have had a perfect time there, but nobody has ever liked it as much as Norton.

When we'd hit the City of Lights, he went everywhere with us: to breakfast, to lunch, to dinner, out wandering the streets. People often stopped to chat with him and he was even recognized a few times. In restaurants he'd be wined and dined (or, to be more accurate, milked and dined), and he was always ready to make himself at home in any of the perfectly groomed parks or pet-friendly cafes.

Once, Janis and I went to do some shopping along *rue Jacob* and up and down all the little streets in the sixth *ar-*

rondissement that are littered with antique shops, and we decided to split up (cleverly hoping to find last-minute Christmas gifts for each other). Naturally, Norton went with me, comfortably ensconced in his shoulder bag. We popped in and out of a few stores, then came to one that I particularly liked and had frequented over the years. Cat and I stepped inside, not only because this woman had beautiful things but because she was very friendly and, over the years, whenever she would see me she would speak French slowly enough so we could have a semireal conversation. I liked nothing better than pretending I actually spoke French and she was nice enough to encourage my fantasy. I remembered that the last time I'd popped in, I told her that we had lived in Goult and she knew the town well, she'd had relatives who lived nearby. So this time, when she saw me, her eyes lit up. (While I do harbor fantasies about speaking the language, I don't harbor fantasies about why she remembered me; I was clearly the only person who regularly shopped in her boutique with a cat on his shoulder.) She got all excited and told me that she'd gone out and bought the French edition of *The Cat Who Went to Paris* after our last conversation. As excited as she normally was to see Norton, now she was doubly thrilled. We spent a few minutes chatting, while she petted the cat. She asked me if certain things had really happened the way I'd described them in the book (they had) and if Norton had really done some of the things I'd said he'd done (he definitely had) and then she noticed that, even as we carried on our conversation, I was staring off to the side and behind her, at the most beautiful antique desk I'd ever laid eyes on. It was late eighteenth century and I'm absolutely terrible at describing furniture because I wind up saying things like, "Well, you know, the front folded down and it was hand carved and the legs were kind of spindly," and no matter how beautiful the object is, I make it sound like the desk I had in my third-grade class. But this desk was spectacular and I'll leave it at that. It was so spectacular that I decided I'd do almost anything to own it, then realized I'd have to relegate this to another one of my fantasies, because when I checked the price tag, the thing cost about twenty thousand dollars. Instead of buying, I drooled and got the store owner to tell me a little bit about the desk's history, then before long, another man had come into the store because he'd spotted the desk from the street and wanted to get a closer look. The four of us—two men, a woman and a cat—stood before the desk admiringly and talked for about fifteen minutes. It was fairly obvious to me that this man wasn't only fantasizing; I got the distinct impression he could, at any moment, reach into his pocket and pay for this baby in cold, hard francs.

But he was quite nice and, after he'd gotten all the information he wanted about *l'objet ancienne*, he turned his attention to you-know-who.

"That is a very handsome cat," he told me in French ("*Le chat, il est très, très beau*," is how it came out). I nodded and smiled.

Then he said, sizing Norton up, "*Et très sage.*" That means, "And quite well behaved." For years, I thought that "*sage*" meant "wise," so I gloated in *A Cat Abroad* that so many French people understood how brilliant Norton was, how truly existential. About a billion readers immediately wrote to me to explain that when referring to animals, "*sage*" actually means "calm" or "well-behaved." Another illusion shattered—and rather publicly, too—but the way this man said it, it still sounded pretty damn good.

"*Oui*," I said, showing him that even if at one point in my life I didn't know what "*sage*" meant, I could *parlez* a little *français*, and I thanked him again.

Then this man, who I noticed was about sixty or sixty-five and incredibly handsome—he had that air of sophistication, that certain *je ne sais quoi*, as if he could walk for hundreds of miles with his jacket draped casually over his shoulders and never let it fall; I do not have quite that same air, since I can't even get through a meal without spilling most of my food all over my shirt—said, "*Et il est très sophistiqué.*"

"Yes," I said, "he is very sophisticated."

The woman who owned the store proceeded to tell this very charming gentleman all about my cat and his travels and how he was a famous literary cat. The man smiled, duly impressed, asked something more about the desk, said he'd be back, then turned and sauntered out.

I turned to say something to the woman but she had a dreamy, faraway look in her eyes and she sighed, "*Je lui adore*" ("I love him." But it came out more like, "I loooovvve him"). I nodded politely, and when she saw the blank look in my eyes, she said, "Don't you know who that is?"

Okay, I have to interrupt now. I have this fatal flaw. Well, I don't know if it's fatal, but it's definitely embarrassing. My problem is that I don't recognize *anyone*. I mean nobody! If I see someone out of context, I don't have a clue. To show you how bad it is, several years ago I had a meeting with an actor. We spent about forty-five minutes together in my office, hit it off fine, and that was that—except that Janis, who then had an office right near mine, was absolutely livid that I hadn't introduced her (as, by the way, was every woman at the company). Two days after the meeting (and a day after Janis stopped yelling at me) we had to go to L.A. for business. We were staying at The Four Seasons, as usual, and we got in the elevator to go down to the lobby. The elevator stopped a floor below ours and someone stepped in. Janis stared at him for a moment, then said, "Oh, I believe you two know each other." The guy looked at me, smiled, and said, "Peter, what are you doing here?" I looked at him with absolutely no recognition, until he finally realized I didn't have a clue who he was. It turned out he was the actor I'd met with in my office, and he said, "It's me. Mel . . . *Mel Gibson.*"

Needless to say, Janis wanted to murder me. But the truth is, there's actually some part of my brain that just can't recognize people or remember their names. No matter who they are. Part of it, I suppose, is that I tend to concentrate on things other than facial features. I remember once waiting in line for a movie on the Upper East Side and saying to my date that night, "Wow! Do you see that guy with the worst toupee in the world?" I also remember her saying, "Do you mean Sir John Gielgud?"

Anyway . . .

I clearly had one of those mental blocks in Paris because when the store owner stared at me incredulously and said, "Don't you know who that is?" I said, "No," and she shook her head and said, "Marcello Mastroianni!"

What made this so pathetic is that Marcello Mastroianni is in my top ten list of favorite actors of all time. Every eighteen months or so I watch *La Dolce Vita*, which probably gets my vote as the greatest movie ever made, to chart my mental health. If I get overwhelmingly depressed, as is usually the case when the film's over since it's the most devastatingly depressing movie imaginable, I figure I'm pretty much on top of things. So before my favorite shop owner could find me any more pitiful than she already did, I dashed out to the street—Norton swinging wildly on my shoulder—and ran until I could catch up to the guy from the shop. I sped about twenty steps past him, then turned and, trying to be cool, walked back the way I'd come, right by him, staring at his face. Sure enough, it was Fellini's favorite actor. And sure enough, he recognized me, too. How could he not, since I was the same guy he'd seen just seconds before, standing in the store chatting casually with a cat on my shoulder.

I didn't speak to him as we passed, I merely ascertained that he was who he was supposed to be, but I've always wondered what he thought when he saw us. Did he wonder how in hell I'd managed to get there and be heading in the wrong direction so quickly? Or *why* in hell I'd managed to get there and be heading in the wrong direction?

Or did he wonder if there were *two* bearded Americans strolling the streets of Paris with very, very wise, well-behaved and sophisticated cats on their shoulders . . .

CHAPTER 6

A CAT IN
RETIREMENT

I don't spend nearly as much time in Europe as I'd like to, or as I think is necessary to keep a civilized and centered point of view. One of the reasons is that there's a town in Long Island which I think of as my American Goult, and that's the town of Sag Harbor.

Sag Harbor is on the north side of the South Fork of Long Island, one hundred miles and a two-hour drive from New York City, except on Fridays during the summer when, thanks to all the traffic heading out toward the beach, it's about a twelve-hour drive.

I hate to sound like Andy Rooney, but like just about everything else in the world, Sag Harbor isn't what it was twenty years ago (reminds you of my motto, doesn't it: All Change Is for the Worse). There are housing developments and lots of traffic now. It's not as quaint as it used to be, it's not as quiet, many of the small town businesses have been replaced by upscale restaurants and tourist (i.e., expensive) shops, and there are too many Hollywood-type people who come east for the summer and can be seen dining and strolling and just generally being repulsive. What's happened to Sag Harbor is that it has become "Hamptonized" due to its proximity to the more glamorous (i.e., *very* expensive) towns of East Hampton, Bridgehampton and Southhampton. All that said, however, it's still a wonderful and special place and it's still got more charm and quaintness and more of a small town feel than most places within a reasonable drive of Manhattan. Lillian, the woman who runs the fish store, lets me sign for my fresh tuna and lobster and sea bass and bills me whenever she gets around to it; Linda Sylvester, who runs the cleverly named and very hip general store Sylvester's, will often give me a cup of hot coffee on a blustery winter day if I show up looking properly bedraggled; at Christmastime there's always a house tour of some of the two-hundred-year-old houses, where they serve little cups of eggnog with Christmas cookies; and the movie theater on Main Street still serves grape drink out of one of those waterfall-looking clear canisters and looks as if Glenn Ford should still be headlining whatever's playing there. I love Sag Harbor and I will love it forever and that's all there is to it.

Norton is largely responsible for my having moved to Sag Harbor and I'd say that his attachment to the place has been just as profound as mine. In fact, there are many parallels when comparing our two existences in our hometown away from hometown.

Norton is not normally an overly social cat, although he learned to tolerate and even enjoy public life. In private, he is perfectly friendly and rarely gets his hackles up, but he is fairly blasé when it comes to reaching out for affection, both with humans and with animals of the four-legged variety. He can, for the most part, take or leave other cats who have on occasion tried to be friendly; he can take or leave the big dogs who from time to time have come into his life; and he can pretty much leave the tiny, yippy dogs who have hopped and barked around him during his normal naptime. But in Sag Harbor, when Norton was about thirteen years old, this little black female kitten kept coming into our yard looking for a playmate. At first Norton, noted macho poseur, would hiss at her and make it clear that playful, youthful kittens were not a welcome addition to his ever more sentient life. But the kitten would not take no for an answer. After several weeks of repeated visits, the hissing stopped and Norton went through his I'll-tolerate-this-but-I-won't-get-too-involved period. That was fine with the kitten, who would run around while Norton sat and watched. Occasionally this black cat would force Norton to move or wrestle or join in a brief hunt for a butterfly that might be fluttering around. Within another few weeks, Norton did not have to be forced to do anything. The kitten had my elder statesman frolicking like a . . . well . . . like a kitten. His new ebony friend would show up every day (to this day I don't know where she came from) hang out in the yard, run around with Norton, and then nestle up close to him and relax in the sun. I think Norton liked this mentoring process because I'd often spot him licking the kitten (cleaning her, I assume, since any other possible urges had long ago been snipped away) or nudging her into more comfortable napping spots on our brick patio. I quite liked to watch this because if I ever felt guilty about anything that I'd ever done—or not done—with my cat it's that I was too selfish to get a second cat for him to socialize with. I always thought that as Norton got older, slowed down, and spent less time traveling and more time at home, I'd get him a companion. That way, if I left for a few days, he'd have some company he could relate to. And, just possibly, he'd stop relieving himself on Janis's bed come Day Five of my absence (of course, the other, more horrible alternative, would be that Janis would have *two* cats taking a dump on her bed; but I didn't even want to think about that possibility). Over the years, however, I never acted on my initial impulse. If you really want to know, I valued my companionship with Norton so much that I really didn't want anything to interfere with that. Yes, I realize that it sounds slightly crazy to think of being jealous of a second cat, but I would have been. I also believe that Norton felt the same way. I knew I couldn't travel with two cats, and I decided that Norton would prefer being with me than hanging out at the ol' homestead with another feline. Our bond, I decided, was stronger than any transpecies relationships that might be needed. But our little black kitten neighbor took care of all my worries. I didn't have to get another cat and Norton had a regular playmate to do the things I would normally pass on—in particular, mousing, butterfly chasing and tree climbing.

I went through a similar process of finding my own play dates in Sag Harbor.

Ever since we returned from Provence, I've spent the entire summer, from June until the end of September, out at my Long Island hideaway, venturing into the city only when absolutely necessary. I do it for several reasons. One, it's a wonderful place for me to work. My office overlooks our beautiful garden (which Janis is totally responsible for, other than my yearly contribution of whining like crazy then working the back forty—or, in our case, back one-third of an acre—to plant several billion tulip bulbs, usually in the pouring rain) and I very much enjoy spending hour upon hour in there hunched over my computer. Two, I can actually be alone out there, or rather, without *human* companionship, and that's something I greatly value. New York City is a social place and my publishing job is a particularly social one. The good part of that is that I get to take writers and agents and almost anyone I find interesting to excellent restaurants. The bad part is that most writers and agents can be major pains in the ass and most people I expect to be interesting turn out to be fairly boring because they mostly like to talk about themselves. The writing part of my life is also fairly social, at least in the city, because it involves sucking up to studio and television executives or, to be more precise, to New York studio and television executives, who are even lower on the evolutionary scale than their California counterparts because, for the most part, if they were any good at all they'd be in L.A. The bottom line is that, if left to my absolute druthers, I'd basically be a hermit. And Sag Harbor lets me pretend, albeit for just a portion of the year, that I can get away from it all.

The first few years I spent my summer there, this was my routine: wake up, run a mile or two, have a little breakfast, work all day, have dinner (way too often pizza and beer). When the wonderful invention known as DI-RECTTV came along and I added a tiny satellite to our roof, I could add to that list: watch sports or movies all night long. I didn't have to talk, I didn't have to be friendly,

I didn't have to do anything for anybody (except for Thursday nights through Monday mornings, when Janis would appear and then I would willingly enter civilization). I could, when work was done, eat, drink and vegetate. On the occasions when Norton would actually deign to eat pizza, we had become true soulmates.

The longer this went on, the more I liked the routine. And then I found out I was not alone. There were a lot of women who did the same thing I did (except mostly without the beer and pizza). Their husbands would arrive in Long Island Thursday nights or Friday afternoons, spend the weekend, then the wives would drive them to the train station on Monday morning, kiss 'em goodbye, and return to their weekday existence of self-sufficiency (and, rather than taking care of a cat, taking care of a child or two or three). I realized that every Monday morn, there I'd be, waving goodbye to Janis at the Bridgehampton train station, standing among a hundred women waving goodbye to their husbands. When the train took off, I'd look around and I'd see many of those women staring at me. I had a feeling quite a few of them were thinking, *Oh, what a sensitive guy. He must be a househusband, taking care of the kids.* I toyed with the idea of having a placard made explaining that I wasn't really so sensitive and that I was actually a cathusband, but I decided I was better off keeping quiet.

On the weekends, I'd discuss this phenomenon with various friends who had houses out there, particularly those friends who were in my exact same position. There were three couples we saw regularly in the summer months: Nancy and Ziggy, who have already been dissected in previous Norton books (You might remember that Ziggy is also known by various other names at his place of employment. Some people know him as John, some as Jack, quite a few refer to him as Aldy, and now, in his latest Wall Street incarnation, he apparently has become Old John, because his new assistant has become Young John), Ed and Caroline, and Tom and Andi. During those months, Ziggy, Ed and Tom would head back to the city every Monday morn, grumbling about my life of ease, while Nancy, Caroline and Andi would remain behind, wondering what I was actually doing all by myself in my little Victorian house. Over a period of weeks, our conversations progressed much like Norton's sparring with his kitten pal. First we'd talk about how lucky we were to be able to stay in Long Island for such a long time. Then we'd talk about how we valued the time alone (or with cat/children). Then we'd say things like, "You know, why don't we all go to a movie on Wednesday night?" Once we did that, it became, "Why don't we go to a movie *every* Wednesday night," and the next thing I knew I was having a Girls' Night Out once a week. Nancy, Caroline, Andy and I (along with a rotating group of women who would be out in our neck of the woods for this auspicious occasion) would head out to a flick, have dinner and catch up on all the typical gal stuff. I'd hear about their kids' soccer games, they'd hear about the latest blue jay who tried to peck Norton on the head. They'd try to get me to drink white wine, I'd see if I could turn them on to the joys of martinis and surf 'n' turf. They'd listen to a little Mets stuff without squirming too much, I'd do my best to listen to something that had to do with women's bodily functions without passing out. All in all, it became a night out on the town that we all looked forward to.

We looked forward to it so much that GNO—as it came to be called—carried over to the next summer. And the next and the next and so on. It became such a popular event that eventually we all got laminated membership cards, legitimizing the group (and detailing the strict guidelines for inclusion, the key being that you can pay for dinner when needed). It also caused a little jealousy among spouses who, when we were all together, wanted to know why they were never invited to our other get-togethers. We'd try to explain that it was girls only—and then I'd realize that everyone would be staring at me and all I could do was smile and shrug and hope no one would spend too much time thinking about it. Especially Janis.

There were a few awkward moments that arose from time to time, I must admit.

Nancy and Ziggy's son, Charlie, also spent the summer out in Sag Harbor and Charlie is, to say the least, a precocious lad. The little bugger doesn't miss a trick or forget a thing. We're also pretty good pals. Now that he's close to his teenage years, he's got the freedom to ride his bike over to my place, which he will do on occasion so we can talk sports or Adam Sandler movies, two passions we both share. He's also obsessed with wanting to see a movie that has naked women in it, which gives us another common passion. Every so often, particularly when he was younger, around eight or nine, I'd go over to pick up his mom for our dinner and I'd get grilled by the Chuckster. A typical conversation would be:

Charlie: Hey, Pete. What's up?
Me: Big night tonight. Dinner and a movie.
Charlie: Girls' Night Out?

Me: Yup.

Charlie: (with furrowed brow and look of great confusion):
   Can I ask you a question?

Me: Sure.

Charlie: Isn't Girls' Night Out for girls?

Me: You bet.

Charlie (after a long silence and a *lot* more furrowing): Have
   a good time.

Once, in my second or third summer of GNOing, Janis
and I were having dinner with two friends, Oren and Betsy
(I had to be in the city that day, briefly breaking my summer isolation). During the course of dinner, Betsy started
hemming and hawing and finally said, "I was talking to
Andi on the phone a few days ago and she was all excited
because she said she was going to Girls' Night Out that
night. She told me how much she looks forward to it and
she was explaining that all her women pals out there go out
and eat and drink and talk . . ."

She kind of drifted off uncomfortably, then Oren
nudged her so she went on: "Uh . . . I asked her who went
and she said Nancy, Caroline, that night Esther was going . . . and . . . uh . . . you."

I nodded and went on eating. Betsy waited politely for
another few seconds then quietly said, "Um . . . is there
anything you want to tell us?"

When I assured her there wasn't, she and Oren resumed eating—and thinking God only knows what.

My cat's life and mine were comparable, too, in ways
other than establishing stimulating, platonic relationships
with members of the opposite sex out there in summery
Sag Harbor.

I wasn't much for skulking through the high grass of our backyard looking for little critters. But I could regularly be found skulking through the fescue of a nearby golf course looking for lost little white balls.

At the end of a tough day in the sunshine, Norton liked nothing better than to chew on a bit of catnip, collapse on the couch in the den and relax. After a tough day in my upstairs office, I liked nothing better than to gulp down a Pete's Wicked Ale, collapse on the same couch and watch any movie that might be on the satellite system that had Greta Scacchi in it (here's an in-print promise to my now twelve-year-old pal, Charlie: when your mom says you're old enough, you can come over and we can watch *White Mischief* together).

Come the late afternoon, Norton liked to clamber up onto my desk to get his ears and stomach scratched and rubbed for quite a long while.

I found out that one could actually get masseuses to work at one's house, so come the late afternoon I would, on occasion, find myself on a massage table in the backyard, listening to Miles Davis or Chet Baker, getting my ears, stomach and just about every other part of my body rubbed.

But we weren't just slugs, Norton and I. For one thing, we did quite a bit of work.

I wrote books and television shows and the occasional movie.

And, after a few years of having nothing to do with the literary community, Norton wrote his own book.

Well, let me elaborate on that.

I'm very grateful to everyone who reads these Norton books (actually, I'm more grateful to those who buy them, but reading them is okay, too). Clearly, anyone who reads hundreds of pages about the adventures of a nine-pound, four-legged creature with folded ears can be legitimately described as a "cat lunatic." Just as clearly, there is a reason why the phrase "cat lunatic" has the word "lunatic" in it. I speak from experience. Not that long ago, my agent, Esther Newberg, called because she was a little depressed. She had just gotten a gift from a friend—a beautiful frame, and inside it was a photo of Esther's cat, Tate. Esther thought it was a tad weird to realize that, as symbolized by the friend's choice of photographic subject, the closest relationship in her life was with a feline. I had to interrupt her and point out that all she had was one little photo of her cat. I'd spent the last decade of my life writing entire *books* about my relationship with my cat. And going around the world talking about him. "*Weird*?" I said. "Forget just being my best friend, my cat also *supports* me!" She agreed that I topped her in the "weird" category.

The point is, I have pretty good anecdotal proof by this time that just about *every* cat person should have the word "lunatic" attached to his or her name as a permanent appendage. But my fans do seem to take it to new heights. So when my good friend Norm Stiles and I dashed off what we thought was the world's funniest book, *Historical Cats*, and put on the cover that it was written by Norton, I have this sneaking suspicion that way too many of my readers went, "Oh, okay, well he *is* a genius cat, I guess he *could* have written it." You'd be amazed, when Norton and I went back on tour to promote this book, how many people asked, at the readings, "So how much did Norton actually contribute to the book?" I would answer, as seriously as I could manage, that the idea was his, that he did the research and chose which cats to use, and that Norm and I only helped him with the jokes. You'd be more amazed if I told you how many heads would nod after that, the look in their eyes saying, "Yeah, that's pretty much what I thought."

Now, I'm not saying he didn't have *anything* to do with the writing of the book. Of course he did. The premise of *Historical Cats* was that, as all of us lunatics know, behind every great human there is an even greater cat. So we imagined various figures throughout history and came up with what we thought was a realistic portrait of that person's lesser known feline companion (and got a brilliant illustrator, William Bramhall, to bring those portraits to life). For instance, there was that great American patriot, Nathan Hale's cat, who uttered the immortal words, "I regret that I have but nine lives to give for my country." And, of course, there was Marie Antoinette's cat, whose dismissive *bon mot* to the French peasants was, "Let them eat dry food." And, among many, many others, was JFK's cat, whose most inspirational rallying cry was, "Ask not what you can do for your human, ask what your human can do for you." Officially, for the record, Norton did not write these. He did use his discerning taste to help, though. While sitting around Norm's house listening to the two of us making each other laugh, Norton would occasionally close the pages of one of our history books or encyclopedias, basically saying, "Nice try, boys, but come up with something better."

And, so I don't shatter every one of his fan's illusions, he *did* write the introduction to the book, which I will reprint here:

INTRODUCTION
by NORTON, The Cat Who Went to Paris

This was not an easy book to write. Let's face it—no book is easy to write when you don't have opposable thumbs.

Living in semiretirement after my last book tour, I suppose I could have been content to spend the rest of my nine lives in the lap of luxury (and I mean that literally; my human has a very comfortable lap). However, on my many travels throughout the world, I did not merely dine out in fancy restaurants and act cute on airplanes, despite the distortions written about me by my so-called owner in *The Cat Who Went to Paris* and *A Cat Abroad*. In my free time, I didn't just curl up *on* a few books, I curled up *with* a few good books. And what I read really began to make my fur stand on end. Ever since I was a kitten riding around town in my human's pocket, I was a history buff. Now, as I began to leap up onto library shelves in search of feline facts, I found a void. A wasteland. An endless litter box in which the history of an entire species seemed to be buried.

While there are countless numbers of books on Thomas Jefferson, where is the book on Thomas Jefferson's cat? Why are his once magnificent catnip gardens no longer found at Monticello? And where do you think Jefferson got the idea for independence in the first place? While we're on the subject, how is it possible that so little is known about Søren Kierkegaard's cat, who developed the brilliant philosophy that all dogs are merely a figment of the imagination? Why is there no monument to Ernest Hemingway's cat, who wrote the classic *A Farewell to Mice*? Or to Joe DiMaggio's cat, who not only ate chicken in gravy fifty-six days in a row, but was married to Marilyn Monroe's cat? The answer, my friends, is *catism*. But the fact that cats have been at the center of all historical events since the beginning of time—remember Adam and Eve's cat, Ribs?—is a secret that can no longer be kept. *Must* no longer be kept.

Thus this book. My collaborators and I have attempted to right the wrongs of history. We have scoured the world in search of rare manuscripts; we have conducted thousands of interviews and skritched hundreds of bellies in an attempt to get information. I apologize for any omissions, but if there are any errors, I can only claim *meow culpa*. If it is true that behind every great man there is a great woman, then it is even truer that behind every great human there is an even greater cat. I just hope that our research and our passion can, at long last, bring that fact forth to the world at large.

—NORTON
Sag Harbor, New York

I have to say, reading that over these several years later, I'm impressed yet again by how eloquent my cat can be, especially considering that English is not his first language. Of course, I shudder to think what that would have read like if it had *been* in his first language. But I'll leave that to the scholars. Maybe Vladimir Nabokov's cat . . .

Although there was this brief foray back into the working world, Norton and I mostly stayed out of the public eye during this period. Of course, with Norton around it was impossible to stay totally away from the social scene. He was too much in demand.

He not only attended any and all dinner parties that Janis and I threw, he was often invited to come along to some of the parties we were invited to. If we'd stroll down to the Halloween parade in town (featuring just about every kid on the east end of Long Island), Norton would stroll along with us. If we went to a friend's house to swim or have brunch, Norton would happily attend—he didn't swim but he was a good sunbather, and he brunched extremely well. If friends gathered, Norton could usually be found gathering as well, and almost always enjoying it. I say "almost" because I have to include the time when we met up with friends Ed and Caroline and their kids to exchange Christmas gifts. One of their gifts was for Norton—an angel costume. We did put the little halo, as well as the translucent white wings, on my cat to see how he'd look. I suppose I have to say he didn't look too good since it took Ed and Caroline a while to convince me that it wasn't actually a reindeer costume. Norton didn't seem too impressed with this form of dress-up, either. I can honestly report that this was a gathering he was not wild about.

One of our weirdest social engagements started as a result of a Sunday brunch with Nancy and Ziggy. When we were seated and about to dip into our scrambled eggs, Zig announced that he had a little story to relate. He then proceeded to tell us about something that had happened to him the night before. He and Nancy had to go to some fancy business party. You know, one of those go-to-a-billion-aire's-oceanfront-mansion-with-a-huge-tent-that-holds-two-hundred-people-on-the-lawn-and-live-entertain-ment-by-somebody-you've-actually-heard-of-like-Gladys-Knight-type of affairs that we all frequent on a regular basis. They had to go because this particular billionaire was one of Ziggy's clients. While there, Ziggy found that his dinner partner was a woman who absolutely terrified him. He described her as the scariest person on Wall Street: tough, brutal, merciless when it came to making money. Ziggy, who's never intimidated by anything, was totally intimidated by her. But he decided, this Saturday night, with some prompting from Nancy, to speak to this woman and to get over his fear and intimidation.

Okay . . . dinner's served, they sit down. Zig bobs his head up and down several hundred times and smiles, trying to think of something to say that won't make him sound like a total moron. They chat about business things for a while, he manages not to put his foot in his mouth. Then, for some reason, someone at the table says something about dogs. The Bride of Frankenstein perks up a bit and asks Ziggy if he's got a dog. He says no. Then he says, for ab-solutely no reason, "I have a friend with a cat, though." She looks at him like he's lost his mind, which he's beginning to think he has. He wants to say, "Oh, forget I said anything and let's just go back to talking about your money!" but he's stuck with this topic for a while, so he goes about the process of digging himself in deeper and deeper. "My friend really loves his cat," Zig now says, starting to sweat a little bit as the rest of the table stares at him blankly. And then, to finish things off and seal his doom, he mutters, "He even wrote a book about the cat."

At this point, the Scariest Woman in the World jerks her head up, stares right at Ziggy and says, in as excited a tone as if he'd just told her that IBM went up a hundred points, "Is his cat named Norton?"

My buddy Zig almost fell over backward in his chair. And the whole thing got weirder and weirder as the New York winner of the Miss Terrifying contest then began to plead with him, begging him for an introduction to my cat.

At the brunch table, our eggs were now cold. Janis was shaking her head in that I-can't-believe-this-is-happening-again kind of way, and Ziggy finally turned to me and said, "So . . . um . . . do you think Norton could pay a visit to my client?" He went on to explain that it would be a major career boost, that it could really help him in the future, that she was his most important client, etc., etc., etc.

As much as I loved the groveling, I finally told him I didn't see any problem. Scottish Folds are known for always wanting to help out their buddies, I said, so after the dishes were cleared away, Zig called the woman, said that Norton would be thrilled to come a calling later that afternoon, and then he reported back to us that he'd never heard anyone quite so excited in his entire life.

A few hours later, Zig drove by and picked us up. Norton was in his Sunday best—which was actually the same as his Monday through Saturday best, but he did look particularly spiffy—and then we drove into Bridgehampton until we got to a very large, very new, slightly terrifying house on the beach. The whole way over, I kept hearing this warning: "Remember, she's really scary. Don't let her

intimidate you. She's really, really scary. Don't let her intimidate you." By the time I'd put Norton back in his
shoulder bag and we were ringing the woman's front door,
I was practically shaking, expecting a cross between The
Wicked Witch of the West, Mommie Dearest and the
Barbra Streisand who directed *The Prince of Tides* to open
up and let us into her lair (in case you're wondering why I
identified Babs specifically as the one who directed *The
Prince of Tides*, it's because as horrible as I imagine her to be
normally, anyone who directed herself in that movie has to
be particularly frightening).

I got someone a little different from the way I was picturing her.

When the Nightmare on Wall Street opened her door,
she nodded curtly at Zig, basically ignored me totally, went
straight over to the cat hanging off my shoulder, stooped
down so she was at his eye level, and said something in a
high-pitched, babyish voice that was remarkably similar to,
"Kitchy kitchy, little kitty, babykins, so happy to see my little baby, oooohhhhh, sweetums . . ."

I thought Ziggy's eyes would pop out of his head because the next thing we both knew, there we were inside
this incredibly ritzy beach house and Ziggy's stern, unfeeling, hard as steel client was rolling around on the floor,
playing with Norton and cooing at him as if she were a
more saccharine version of Shirley Temple.

We wound up staying there over an hour. The only
words that were addressed to me were, "I've always wanted
to meet him. I'm so honored. Thank you so much." I don't
believe that any words were addressed to Ziggy. The rest of
the time, we watched in astonishment as she hand fed

Norton, petted him until I think even he was satiated, and told him several hundred times that he was the handsomest devil she'd ever seen.

When the hour was up, she shook my hand, said that Norton was welcome to come back any time he wanted, and then she gave him a giant kiss on the head.

Back in the car, Ziggy couldn't even look at me. We drove in silence until I said, "I can see why she scares you. Does she scratch you under the chin and coo like that at the office?"

"Oh, shut up," he said, which were the last words spoken until he pulled up in our driveway, took Norton's paw in his hand and just said, "Thank you."

To me, he said, "No one I know will believe this."

To Zig—and to Norton—I said, "*Everyone* I know will believe this."

There were other encounters with the rich and famous over the years. Probably the most exciting—and inadvertent—came when Janis and I were taking Norton to the town of Watermill, about ten minutes from Sag Harbor, for another social request.

Our friend Susan Burden had called to say that her parents were visitng from out of town and her mother was a huge Norton fan. Was there any way I could bring him over to meet them, she wanted to know.

Of course there was. I was always happy for Norton to meet and greet his true admirers, so I told Susan that the three of us would be there in half an hour.

We left, as promised, about fifteen minutes after Susan

called, but we had forgotten one little detail. President and Mrs. Clinton happened to be in the Hamptons this particular weekend, fund-raising and hobnobbing and Spielberging and Baldwining. As I made a right turn onto Scuttlehole Road, the street that leads from Sag Harbor to Watermill, we got all of one hundred feet before running into a horde of policemen and barriers and cars with flashing lights. As soon as I saw all this, I realized that I'd read in the local paper that today was the day the president was playing a round of golf at the Atlantic Country Club— which happened to be right on the street to which I'd turned, half a mile farther along. One cop waved us over to the side of the road and indicated that that was as far as we were going for the moment. When I tried to argue that all we wanted to do was go one more measly mile, he shook his head in sympathy but told us it was no go. I then asked how long we'd have to wait and he shrugged in such a way that I knew it meant, "However long it takes to finish eighteen holes, pal."

We waited by the side of the road for about half an hour and then we realized the motorcade was heading our way. We got out of the car—all three of us—and I held Norton up so he could get a view of the history that was passing before our eyes. I also figured there was a slim chance that Socks might be with them—hey, maybe I wasn't the only one who traveled with his cat!—and that this could turn out to be a genuinely inspiring feline moment.

Unfortunately, we never saw Socks. I wouldn't swear that we saw the president or his wife, either, since their limousine zipped by fairly quickly. But I *think* I saw Bill Clinton peering out at us—at a well-dressed woman looking kind of bored, a total slob of a guy in jeans and T-shirt looking impatient, and a small, gray cat being held aloft as he peered at the road trying to see what all the fuss was about. And I think I saw a very familiar expression on the president's face. One I'd seen before.

On Marcello Mastroianni . . .

We had a slightly less auspicious celebrity session one summer. Actually, it was a fairly entertaining experience for me and Norton. It was only disappointing for the others present.

ARF is this valuable and well-run organization in Long Island. The acronym stands for Animal Rescue Fund and they do great work with animals of all kinds. They have a big shelter in Long Island for strays. They have workers who come and play with the animals daily, they have a very moving area which is quarantined off for cats who have leukemia—the sick cats are also played with every day— and they provide tons of good homes for lost, discarded and deserted pets. Every summer, they have some sort of fund-raiser. This year, it was a celebrity tennis tournament. The celebrities playing were Eli Wallach, Charlie Rose, Chuck Scarborough (a longtime New York newscaster), Dina Merrill, George Plimpton, Cliff Robertson and various wealthy and well-known restaurateurs and businesspeople.

Oh yeah. And me.

Now, I do understand that the above list is not exactly the "A" list of celebs these days. But even by these meager standards, I do jump out as a nonfamous person. To ARF, however, I was a god. Not *the* God. But *a* god (Note to the

Christian Right: this is just a semihumorous figure of speech. Please don't send any more outraged letters). I had supported many ARF events in the past, had done several book signings, and, of course, Norton was a revered figure throughout the entire organization. So they decided I was enough of a name to play in their fund-raising matches.

The way it worked was that ten or twelve generous, animal-loving moguls opened up their grand South-hampton estates—particularly their grand tennis courts—and anyone who forked over enough money could play a singles and doubles round-robin tournament with one celebrity. Then all the celebs, ARF workers and donors would meet at one of the estates for lunch and mingling.

The house I was assigned to was magnificent. My house would have fit two or three times over into their en-try hall. Even more demoralizing, it wasn't just their guest house that was bigger and nicer than my place—their *tennis house*, the little shack where they stored balls and rackets—was bigger and nicer than my place. The main house had a pool *and* the guest house had a pool. *And* they had a pri-vate beach right on that little body of water I like to call the Atlantic Ocean. Just for the record, several months after this event, Janis and I saw the very same house listed for sale with Sotheby's—the asking price was sixteen million smackers! I don't know what the guy who owned the house did for a living, but I do know he was around sixty years old and his attractive trophy wife had probably not crossed to the far side of thirty. I also know that when I asked the Missus if I could make a quick phone call, she wanted to know if it was a local call. I thought about offering her a quarter—and muttering as strong an obscenity as I could muster—but instead decided I could wait to call until I got home. I guess if you save a quarter here and a quarter there, pretty soon you've got a sixteen-million-dollar house.

My embarrassing moments weren't over yet. The first one came during the game itself. Janis and Norton were there, of course—ARF had made a special request for my cat's attendance. But no one had told me that there would be actual spectators. As in strangers. But there were. Maybe thirty or forty people were sitting in the bleachers (yes, their tennis court did have bleachers!) doing nothing but watching us play.

I did my best to compose myself. Okay, I decided, so people were watching. No big deal. I was a good tennis player. I was a *very* good tennis player. All I needed was some nerve, right? A little bit of ice water in the old veins. Besides, how good could my first opponent be? Not much better than I was, right? So I thought about Joe Montana driving the Niners 90 yards for a winning touchdown with less than a minute left. I thought about Mariano Rivera coming into a game in the bottom of the ninth with the bases loaded and nobody out and blowing away three straight hitters for the win. I thought about Michael Jordan hitting a shot from the top of the key to win a playoff game with no time on the clock. That's what I *thought* of. Unfortunately, I then proceeded to *play* like Bill Buckner in the tenth inning of Game 6 of the '86 World Series. In my defense, the first guy I played in singles was once a satellite touring pro. Beyond *any* defense was the fact that I couldn't even get my racket on the guy's serve. A normal point went pretty much like this: He'd serve, I'd hear a noise—kind of like a rocket zooming by—and then I'd turn around and see that the ball I was supposed to hit was already behind me. When it was my turn to serve, I'd either hit it straight into the net or I'd hit a beauty right on the baseline and then, whoosh, there was that noise again and somehow the ball would be behind me again. After the first set, he looked like Pete Sampras at Wimbledon. I looked like Jerry Lewis on the dance floor in *You're Never Too Young.*

That wasn't the worst part, however (although it definitely was the worst part for Janis and Norton; Janis told me that after watching the first few games from the bleachers, Norton snuck inside his bag and wouldn't come out again—she said he looked pretty embarrassed that I was his representative). The most humiliating moment came at the luncheon after all the games were done. I overcame my tennis shame to sit with my group as we munched on sandwiches. Norton overcame *his* shame and sat with us. At some point, I realized there was some unhappiness among the munchers and finally I heard one woman say, "And for all this money, we didn't even get a celebrity!" At first I thought maybe I'd just slink away and say nothing. But no. I had to open my mouth. I did a little bit of hemming and hawing and finally worked up the nerve to say, "Um . . . I think *I'm* your celebrity." The woman who had spoken up earlier now spoke up again, with words that will forever ring in my ears. After looking me up and down to make sure there was nothing she was missing, she said, "Well who the *hell* are *you*?!" I did my best to explain about my books and my writing and about Norton—I even tried pushing him into the middle of the group so they could see how irresistible he was—but no one cared. They wanted Leonard Nimoy, not some geeky writer with a humiliated-looking cat.

By this time, I was quite good at reading the expressions on Norton's face, and there was no question that what he was thinking was, *Great. Not only did I have to see some young stud wipe up the tennis court with you, now you make me go through* this!

I was also good at reading the expressions on Janis's face and clearly she was thinking along the same lines. By midafternoon, when we could gracefully make our escape, we were all happy to leave the big-bucks world of Southhampton behind and head back to our smaller-than-a-tennis-shack house.

Not that we were intimidated by celebrities. Not at all. Norton had met his fair share over the course of his life. My favorite combination of all time was Norton and Wilt Chamberlain. I was editing and publishing Wilt's book—and, yes, before you ask, I was the person who asked him how many women he'd slept with and made him put it in the book. Wilt came up to my office a couple of times and, of course, Norton almost always came to the office with me. Seeing a seven-foot-one-and-three-quarter-inch-tall black man sitting on a couch next to a one-foot-tall light gray cat made for a very interesting juxtaposition.

There was another Norton-related sports encounter that also left a deep impression. This one started with a phone call from my GNO pal Andi, who announced that she and her hubby Tom had become friendly with Sandy Koufax. Now, you have to understand that not only am I a baseball loon, but I grew up in Los Angeles in the mid-60's *and* I come from hearty Hebraic stock, so Sandy Koufax ranked up with George Washington, Abraham Lincoln and Martin Luther King as an important historical and cultural figure in my life. When Andi asked if I wanted to come to a small dinner party they were having—to which the great-

est living pitcher was also coming—I not only jumped at
the opportunity, I immediately called every sports fanatic I
knew to tell them all what I was doing. I know a lot of
sports writers as well as just plain fans, and each and every
one of them warned me about the same thing: Koufax *hated*
being fawned over. He did not like talking about himself,
he did not like talking about baseball, and he particularly
did not like anyone to say these six horrible words: *I'm a
big fan of yours*. So for the week leading up to the dinner
party, I steeled myself not to fawn. I would picture shaking
hands with Koufax, then I'd look in the mirror to make
sure that my face betrayed not an iota of idolatry. And most
of all I spent hours blanking out the words "I'm a big fan
of yours" from my vocabulary.

Well, the night of the dinner party comes and it's a
small group, eight in all. Koufax and his girlfriend are the
last to arrive. In his absence, I'm still willing myself to look
uninterested when I'm introduced. Finally, he enters. Andi,
knowing how excited I am to meet him, ushers him over
to me. I heard the words, "Peter, this is Sandy Koufax." I
give a blasé half turn, barely nod in his direction, hardly
even acknowledge his existence, then turn back to whatever conversation I was already having. I wasn't just uninterested, I actually managed to treat him as if he were some
dirtball who'd wandered into the wrong house. But I'm
feeling pretty good about it, knowing that my mission was
accomplished and I didn't embarrass the guy. About a
minute passes. Then I feel a slight tap on my shoulder. I
turn. It's Sandy. He smiles at me again and says, "I hate doing this but I just have to tell you . . . *I'm a big fan of yours*."

Yup. Turns out that he had read *The Cat Who Went to*

Paris and had become a Norton nut. He and his ex-wife had even bought a Scottish Fold several years earlier after reading about Norton's adventures. Needless to say, I felt like the world's biggest schmuck. I felt like an even bigger schmuck when, a little later, I found myself telling him about a sore shoulder I had and we were comparing aching arms (in case you don't get where the schmuckdom comes in, my arm was a normal, not very special arm, its most distinguishing characteristic being that it was attached to a hand that could type 80 words a minute; his arm happened to be the greatest single weapon in baseball history and when it finally failed him caused hundreds of thousands of sports fans to weep for untold hours). We did talk about Norton for a good part of the dinner, though, and Sandy—as I call him; well okay, actually I call him Mr. Koufax—was even gracious enough to give me the thrill of a lifetime and talk some baseball with me well into the night.

But our most entertaining encounter with fame came that same summer as the tennis disaster.

It began with a rather odd phone call. It was a hot and perfect Long Island Friday afternoon and I was upstairs in my small office in my small house, pretending to work at my not-so-small computer. What I was really doing was staring out at Janis's backyard garden, trying to figure out how anyone could actually remember the names of different flowers, since the best I've been able to do is come up with "that red one" or "that orange one" or, if I'm really feeling daring, "that kind of reddish orangy one." I was also petting Norton, who was sprawled across the computer keyboard, curled up on his side, looking particularly Muppet-like. He was there partly because he liked being close to me and could always pretty much be counted on to keep me company while I worked, but to be honest, it was mostly because the biggest ray of sunlight was aimed directly on the *d* through *k* keys and he was basking in that warmth. While stroking him, I complimented him on his choice of location. Not only was he able to soak in the sun, he was simultaneously providing me with the perfect excuse not to write.

I lunged at the phone on the first ring (as all writers do when they're pretending to work at their computer) and a woman's voice, with a husky British accent, asked for me by name. In my nonhusky American accent, I told her that it was indeed me she was talking to.

"This is Sybil Christopher," she then said, "and it's *sooo* good to talk to you. Especially because I just discovered, to my horror, that you're not coming to our screening tomorrow night."

A little history now, both to add some local color and so you'll be even more impressed that she was calling me. Sybil Christopher used to be married to Richard Burton (she was the one from whom Elizabeth Taylor stole him during the filming of *Cleopatra*). In the intervening years, she owned and ran a few successful nightclubs, all of them called Arthur, in various chic hot spots around the world, and no doubt did a lot of other interesting things as well. One of the interesting things she was doing now, I knew, was running the small regional theater that had recently opened in Sag Harbor. Because of her contacts and powers of persuasion, the theater had attracted quite a lot of talent, writing as well as acting talent, who wouldn't normally be found exercising their creative muscles on the legitimate stage.

The reason she was calling me, she explained, was because, to raise money for the theater, they were having a special screening, the world premiere of a big new movie. And she'd just found out that I was not on the list of attendees.

I was a little surprised at her horror over this omission, since I'd rarely been invited to anything of this sort, particularly in the Hamptons. On those rare occasions when I *had* been invited, I hadn't gone, since I much prefer staying home and watching sports on TV than going out in public with rich, famous people I don't know. To be perfectly honest, for the most part I'd much prefer being forced to walk over hot coals and having an irate crowd of Fundamentalists poking at my eyes with sticks than going out with rich, famous people I don't know (Okay, cheap gag coming up, but mostly true: the only thing worse is going out with rich, famous people I *do* know). So I began to politely decline her invitation, but she began to—metaphorically—twist my arm. It turns out that she was awfully good at arm twisting, good enough so that pretty soon, much to my surprise, I began to consider showing up. It was a benefit, she told me, and it was totally, *completely* sold out. But she thought she could get *one* more ticket from *somewhere*. Not for free, of course, it *was* a benefit, but it was *only* a hundred dollars a ticket. It was well worth it, I was assured, the movie was wonderful, and *everybody* would be there and it was for *such* a good cause—the theater—and she just felt *so* terrible that she hadn't called earlier . . .

Then she closed the deal very effectively, ending with something I couldn't possibly resist.

"I just can't *believe* you weren't invited," she said. "And neither can *Tony*. He *insists* that you come. He *specifically* asked if you were coming and he'll be *very* disappointed if you're not there."

"He did?" I asked. "And he will?"

"Oh, absolutely," she said. "He'll be *crushed* if you don't come."

"Tony will be *crushed*?"

"No question about it!"

"Oh, well, in that case I guess I'll come," I said, adding, "But you'll have to find two tickets, not one," since I knew that Janis would not be a happy camper if I deserted her on a Saturday night to go off to some fancy movie premiere.

"I'll call you right back," Sybil said, and indeed she did, just a minute or two later, to tell me that, miraculously, she'd found two tickets, that they'd be waiting for me at the box office at the local Sag Harbor movie theater (where the screening was being held) and that I could write a check at my convenience.

I hung up the phone, pondered the fact that I was such a sucker for human contact—if this had been a solicitation by mail, I would definitely have saved myself two hundred bucks and a couple of hours in an old theater that smells like a weird combination of fake butter and liquid cleanser—and went downstairs to tell Janis that we were going to the movies.

When I finished my little explanation, she looked at me, slightly confused, and said, "I didn't know you knew Sybil Christopher."

"I don't," I told her. "Never met her, never spoke to her before."

"And who's *Tony*?" she demanded.

"Absolutely no idea." When she looked even more bewildered, I said, "Clearly, they've made a mistake and they think I'm somebody else. So it'll be fun. Let's go and watch 'em get all confused when whoever they're expecting doesn't show up—and *I do*."

So the next night, a dubious Janis donned her Saturday best—she has an amazing knack for elegance on the spur of the moment—while I put on the ten-year-old ill-fitting sport jacket I keep in Sag Harbor for dress-up emergencies, and we went into town.

First we waited on line to pick up our tickets at the box office. While waiting, I pulled out my checkbook and began writing a check for two hundred smackers. As I was doing so, a rather snotty usher strolled by, saw what I was doing and sniffed, "We don't allow checks."

I could tell he thought this particular check was bouncy enough to play basketball with, and I immediately began to regret my decision to come, but since ushers are, in my mind, on the same intimidating, uniform-wearing authority-figure level as policemen, judges and cable TV repair guys, I started politely explaining how Sybil Christopher said I could write a check and how I only decided to come at the last minute and . . .

"What's your name?" he asked wearily.

"Peter Gethers," I said rather weakly, expecting our evening to end a little earlier than I'd expected.

But weak or not, he practically snapped to attention and said—with a vague tone of reverence, I might add— "Oh, excuse me, Mr. Gethers. You don't even have to wait on line. Just go right inside and tell that usher over there to seat you. And I'm very sorry about the mistake. Of course you can pay by check. Whenever you want."

I raised an eye toward Janis and smiled rather smugly. She shook her head in return. I think she was fairly certain we were on our way to imposter's prison.

The next usher was even more obsequious. "Yes, of course," she practically squealed. "Thank you for coming, Mr. Gethers. You're sitting in the celebrity row, with Tony."

"Good," I said. "I wouldn't want to miss Tony."

Sure enough, she led us to a section right in the middle of the theater with three rows roped off, protected from what I was already beginning to think of as the riff-raff. Sitting in these rows were the usual group of Hamptons celebs: actors, actresses, directors, journalists, owners of media conglomerates, hairdressers, publicists and Dick Cavett (I put Dick Cavett in a separate category because I'm not exactly sure what he is these days; the only thing I do know is that he's at every single gathering of celebrities in the area). The usher lifted the rope and told us which row was ours. We followed instructions perfectly and settled in to watch the rest of the theater start to fill up. Every so often, we'd see a friend or two who'd be off to the side in some crummy seat and who would look surprised to see us smack dab in the middle of Fame Row. When eye contact was made, I'd do something sophisticated and mature like stick my fingers in my ears and wag at them.

Eventually, the place was jammed to the rafters. The only empty seats in the whole theater were the two right next to us. As I was wondering about this fact, I noticed that everyone else was applauding. When I looked around, I realized that the star of the movie and his wife had arrived. Not only that, they were being led to the two empty seats to Janis's right. They sat, nodded cursorily at Janis and waited like everyone else for the lights to dim and the movie to start. This gave us a couple of minutes or so of awkward silence, so Janis leaned over and said to the wife, "Hello, I'm Janis Donnaud."

The wife smiled and said, "I'm Jenny Hopkins. And this is my husband, Tony."

Tony?

As in Anthony?

As in *Anthony Hopkins*? *Sir* Anthony Hopkins? The world's greatest living actor?

Yup.

That's when Janis said, "And this is Peter Gethers."

The sound you're not hearing right now is the longest pause in the world.

Both Mr. and Mrs. Hopkins looked over at me, squinted, stared and said absolutely nothing. And I mean nothing.

"This is where we get sent to the balcony," I whispered to Janis.

But not so fast. Because Anthony Hopkins—Academy Award winner, legend, star of *Silence of the Lambs* and *The Remains of the Day*, which was the movie we were about to watch that night—finally cleared his throat and said to me, in that great, booming Welsh voice of his, "You didn't by any chance bring *Norton*, did you?"

When I tell you that I almost fell off my chair, believe that I'm telling you the truth. At some point, I was able to regain my composure and stutter something along the lines of, "Well, no, actually, I don't usually bring my cat to movie premieres."

And then we started chatting. It turned out that both Hopkins were cat fanatics. Jenny had read *The Cat Who Went to Paris*, fell in love with my little pal, and made Sir Anthony—excuse me, Tony—read it. When Sybil Christopher, an old friend from their days in Wales, invited them to Sag Harbor as a favor to help her theater, they had paced around their flat in London, saying, "Why do we know Sag Harbor? . . . Why do we know Sag Harbor?" Jenny said that, after several days of this, Tony had stopped pacing and suddenly screamed out with eureka-like relief, "That's where Norton lives!" They immediately got on the horn to Sybil, asked if I was coming to the premiere and Sybil, assuming that I must be somebody she should have heard of, got on the horn herself and talked me into forking over the two bills for the tickets.

As the lights in the theater began to dim, Tony leaned across Janis to ask me, "Is there any way we could meet Norton?"

"Sure," I said. And then I realized they were waiting for me to tell them how. "Ummm . . ." I looked at our generation's Olivier and asked, "You wanna come over for breakfast tomorrow?" I immediately began fantasizing about telling my mother how I'd served lox and bagels to Hannibal the Cannibal.

"Oh, we'd love to," Jenny said, "but we have a nine o'clock flight back to London in the morning. We have to leave extremely early."

"You could come for a drink after the movie," I suggested.

"Oh no," Jenny said. "I'm afraid not. There's a little party after the movie and we're sort of the guests of honor."

I was momentarily deflated. Also stumped. Then Tony said, "The party is over at Sybil's theater. Could Norton possibly come to that?"

"I don't see why not," I said. "He's a party animal."

I wasn't at all offended that no one said, "Could *you and Janis* possibly come to that." I was, by this time, quite used to being seen in a subservient role as a companion to my four-legged star. So the minute the movie was over, Janis went over to the theater, accompanied by the Hopkinses, while I drove to my house, pulled out Norton's preferred shoulder bag, and went back to the opening night party—accompanied by my cat.

Now, Norton behaves remarkably well in public situations (often, far better than his dad). But he hadn't actually been to any movie premiere parties. When he's in public, Norton is usually assured of being the biggest celebrity in the joint. That was clearly not going to be the case in this instance. So despite my confident reply to the Hopkinses, I admit to having had a few doubts about the wisdom of this little jaunt.

Once again, I was forced to issue my cat a sincere apology.

Because, of course, he was perfect.

I didn't think that putting him down and letting him wander through the crowd was a great idea (he would have been fine, no question about it, but being a foot tall and walking around on four legs isn't really the ideal situation to be in at a cocktail party; also, I wasn't sure if the bartender knew how to mix a catnip martini and I thought it best to avoid that embarrassing situation). Nor did I think that setting him down on the bar was the best solution (I knew this crowd; standing between them and the alcohol was not a great location if one desired any peace and quiet). Finally, I decided to let him sit in the front row of the theater. I pulled the first aisle seat down, set his bag there and then watched as Norton settled in on top of it and did indeed become the star of the evening. Basically, he sat there calmly, as if attending a play. Or, more accurately, as if he were a member of a royal family receiving visitors. Occasionally, he'd swivel his head to check out his surroundings or if he thought someone was speaking too loudly. The Hopkinses would not leave his side. Jenny, in particular, spent most of the night petting him and telling him what a good boy he was. Gradually, the entire party moved down toward the stage area because that's where Tony and Jenny were—and they were there because that's where Norton was. One by one, everyone came over to congratulate Tony on another brilliant performance and then, one by one, everyone would get asked, "Have you met Norton?" (And yes, you're absolutely right, absolutely no one got asked, "Have you met Peter?")

After a few minutes, I actually relaxed and realized my cat didn't need me hovering around him, so Janis and I drank, ate and mingled with the couple of hundred people who were there to support Sag Harbor's newest cultural attraction. Every so often, I'd make my way back toward the front, check on my Fold who, as near as I could tell, was in heaven in the midst of all this fuss being made over him. At some point, I felt someone tap me on the shoulder, and when I turned around I saw that it was Lauren Bacall.

"Excuse me," she said, smiling graciously. "May I ask you a question?"

With images from *The Big Sleep* and *To Have and Have Not* flashing in front of me, I did my best to look debonair and said, "Of course."

"Well, then, my question's this." Her smile broadened even more graciously as she put her hand on my shoulder and spoke warmly. "I don't know who you are and I don't know why you're here. But if I want to talk to Tony Hopkins, who's an old and dear, dear friend . . . *why do I have to stand in line behind your fucking cat?!*"

I looked toward the front of the theater. There were fifty people or so trying to get in close enough to talk to the Hopkinses. Jenny was holding Norton in her arms and Tony's back was to the crowd while he petted and scratched him. I knew it was impossible in the midst of the din, but I was almost certain I could hear Norton purring above the chatter of the crowd. I turned back to Lauren Bacall.

"It's a long story," I told her. "Believe me. It's a long story."

CHAPTER 7

THE CAT
WHO TURNED
MIDDLE-AGED

t turned out that my cat and I had one more parallel going on in our already entwined lives.

We were both getting a little older.

And feeling it.

My brush with the aches and pains that come with no longer being able to describe oneself by the word "thirty" followed by any known number began with what I can only describe as an excruciating, whimper-inducing pain in my right shoulder. Perhaps you've picked up on the fact that stoicism is not one of the words that leaps to mind when most people try to describe me. Nonetheless, my shoulder hurt like hell and the pain led to various doctor visits, x-rays, MRIs, and ultimately an operation that revealed, among other messy but less serious stuff, degenerative arthritis. The operation was followed by a whole bunch of physical therapy (I was usually in a room with a lot of people who'd had their legs crushed by trucks or their arms ripped out of their sockets by machines I would never actually touch much less operate manually, so I had the double dissatisfaction of being in extreme pain but being way too embarrassed to complain about it). It was also followed by more doctor visits, a discussion of my future prospects with one of those doctors that included the unappealing phrase, "How's your pain tolerance?" and another conversation that ended with this upbeat assessment: "Well, the idea is to keep you as pain free as possible for another fifteen years, then we'll do a shoulder replacement so you can feed yourself and brush your own teeth." I'm leaving out the session where my surgeon explained to me that my body was like a tire that was good for 100,000 miles. When he got to the part pointing out that I'd used up about 50,000 of those miles, I just started making pathetic little noises and begging him to come up with some other analogy. After he told me about the difficulties I was going to have brushing my own teeth I decided that the whole tire thing was fine and told him to stick with that from now on.

All in all, although Janis might disagree if I let her insert her own paragraph at this point, I think I handled the pain and trauma (and acceptance that gradually I was disintegrating and falling apart and would soon be little more than a pile of rotting garbage in this stinking, crummy world) with great maturity and grace. I might even go so far as to use the words "regal nobility." However, when my cat got sick and began showing similar signs of middle-age wear and tear, I totally fell apart.

Janis, Norton and I had made another Christmastime trip to Sicily to visit the Tornabenes in their fourteenth-century abbey, and when we returned, I noticed something strange. The water in Norton's water bowl was disappearing very quickly.

I didn't really think anything of it, other than, after a couple of weeks of this, it occurred to me that my cat didn't usually drink a lot of water. At first I thought that maybe my apartment and my house in Sag Harbor were both overheated and that the water was evaporating. I know, this sounds crazy (as well as pretty dumb) but it just never occurred to me that Norton would be lapping up an entire bowl or two of water a day. Then, the next thing I realized was that not only was the water in his bowl disappearing but Norton was suddenly drinking water out of the toilet. At all hours of the day and night, I'd hear that unmistakable sound of animal tongue taking in water as quickly as possible, head in to the bathroom and find Norton leaning into the bowl and drinking like a . . . well . . . like a commonplace *dog*. For a day or two, I did nothing but mull this over and think it was odd. Now you have to understand that for our entire mutual existence, I treated my cat exactly as I would treat myself (except for those occasions when I treated him better). By that, I mean that I believed in living well and making life as easy as possible for myself—and by extension, I wanted him to live as well as I did and have as easy a life. One of the things I didn't do for myself was to go to the doctor very often. I'm not a hypochondriac and I'm not a very fearful person. I also tend toward fatalism and generally think that things will run their proper course. On the other hand, I'm not a total cretin and I'm not above seeking help when help is needed. So after a few days of puzzling over Norton's behavior, just as I would have done over mine if I'd suddenly started lapping up water out of the toilet bowl, I decided that something had to be wrong and that it was time to take him to the vet.

Since kittenhood, Norton had been a lucky guy. Not only was he rarely ill, he had an absolutely sensational vet in Sag Harbor named Dr. Jonathan Turetsky. Jonathan is not only a caring and loving doctor, he is stunningly thorough. Whenever I'd take Norton in for his annual checkups, I'd come home to Janis and say that I wished *my* doctor was as thorough in his probing and analysis. I loved Turetsky. As did almost all his patients—both paying bipeds and sick quadrupeds.

Unfortunately Norton couldn't stand him.

It drove the good doc crazy. For years, he'd greet Norton warmly, talk to him soothingly, treat him wonderfully, genuinely care about his welfare—and my friendly, charming, perfect cat would act as if he were being examined by one of the flying monkeys in *The Wizard of Oz*. All Turetsky had to do was get near him and Norton would hiss and scratch and do his best impersonation of Charles Bronson in *The Great Escape* trying to get out of the tunnel.

As everyone knows by now, Norton went everywhere, all over the world, not just uncomplainingly but willingly. Put him in a car, he'd be happy. Sitting in my lap on a plane, no problem, only pleasure. Trains, boats, you name it (other than the basket on the front of a bicycle, an unpleasant experiment which is best left unspoken) and Norton was happy and compliant. There was only one consistent exception: if I put him in the car to head over to see his vet. When that happened, the second he'd hit the seat he'd start howling like a banshee. We're talking wolflike baying at the moon. I have no idea how he always knew we were heading down Route 114 to Turetsky's office on Goodfriend Drive—especially since we often drove that route without going to the doctor—but he always did and he always cried every inch of the way. To make matters worse for Turetsky's feelings of self-worth, after several years of treating Norton, he brought a new doctor in to the practice, with the great name of Dr. Pepper. It doesn't sound so bad if you throw in his first name, Andrew, but there's no way I can resist just calling him Dr. Pepper. Well, Norton was absolutely fine with Pepper. No hysteria, no cowering in the corner, no pleading looks at me to fork over his transit papers and get him out of Casablanca. This caused even more head shaking for Doc Turetsky but he seemed to accept this strange response and when it came time for him to do things medicinal that Norton particularly hated—like taking blood; that was Norton's least favorite thing in the whole world—he'd often step (and put his ego) aside and let Dr. Pepper do them. I found it touching that he was so sensitive to a cat's needs and tried to explain to Norton that he was lucky to have such a touchy-pawy guy at his beck and meow. But it was no go. No matter how sensitive the treatment, Turetsky was still the Nazi and Pepper was the allied soldier coming to the rescue.

Which made it all the more strange when, trying to get to the bottom of Norton's sudden and insatiable thirst, he willingly sat on Dr. Turetsky's sterile-looking stainless steel table in the examining room and let the doc poke and stab and stick and mutter and squint and weigh and put his gentle hands wherever he wanted. In addition to the fact that Norton was being so passive, I could tell by the expression on Turetsky's face that something was wrong. But he wouldn't tell me what. Not until they got the results of the blood test back, he said.

When Norton heard the words "blood test," his out-of-character docileness instantly reverted to his normal anti-Turetsky aggression (okay, that's a slight exaggeration, it wasn't when he heard the words; but when Turetsky took out the needle and tried to take blood, Norton fought back like the jungle beast one of his long ago ancestors actually was). As usual, they had to sedate my poor little cat so they could take some blood and I had to leave him there for an hour or so, until he was over the sedation.

After coming back to get him, the blood test complete, I nervously drove Norton the couple of miles back to the house and waited for twenty-four hours until we'd get word.

During that twenty-four-hour period I, of course, feared the worst. Although I didn't have any idea what the worst was. I did know that Norton had lost two pounds, which for a nine-pound cat, is quite a lot. I was kicking myself for not noticing how skinny he'd gotten, guilty that my ignorance had led him to whatever horrible thing it was I was sure he had. I was pacing and nervous and, every few minutes, picking Norton up into my arms, cradling him and kissing him and telling him that everything was going to be fine. Janis kept assuring me that everything actually *would* be fine, but my usually optimistic nature suddenly deserted me. When the doctor called me the next day in the early afternoon and told me to come back, with cat in tow, I was a wreck. I didn't ask Janis to come with us, but she didn't have to be asked. She knew this was unlikely to be my shining hour, so she just headed out with me when I put Norton on my shoulder, and came along to lend support.

By the time we got to Dr. Turetsky's animal clinic—with Norton yowling the entire way, as usual—I was even more of a wreck. Since I'd decided he was now riddled with disease, he looked like a totally different cat to me. Suddenly, I was thinking he'd lost half his body weight and was totally skeleton-like. I was convinced the meow I was listening to wasn't just the usual I-hate-the-vet complaint but had to be filled with pain. I also thought his glare was a bit disdainful since I'd clearly ignored the dire symptoms for a few weeks and let him dehydrate. By the time we stepped into Turetsky's examination room, I was drenched in sweat and felt as if I'd aged ten years.

I put Norton down on the steel table, watched him sneak a suspicious glance at his old enemy, then listened as Dr. Turetsky said, calm as could be, "Don't get too upset when I tell you what I'm about to tell you, because we've caught it very early and it's not a tragedy, but Norton's got the beginning of kidney failure."

I took a deep breath. Then another. I tried to stay calm. I thought, *Well, fine, now I've heard the news and I can deal with it. I'm a mature human being and I can definitely deal with it.*

Who was I kidding? Here's exactly what went through my mind when I got the diagnosis:

Kidney *failure*. Not kidney *disease*. Failure = hopeless. Hopeless = dead. Oh, my God, my cat's dying!

I kept a stoic face but I was sure this was it. I was just as sure that the doc had no idea how shaken I was until I heard the words, "Norton's going to be fine, but I think you'd better sit down so you don't pass out."

Much to my chagrin, I took a seat as Janis reached for my hand to give it a reassuring squeeze. My heart was racing and I realized I was trembling. Norton was still seated on the shiny stainless steel, looking not at all perturbed.

"How long does he have?" I asked, expecting to hear the words, "Two or three days," but Turetsky said, "He's not dying. Honest. This is very common in older cats and it can be contained for quite a while. If it doesn't get any worse, he can live for many years."

I managed to say, "Contained? Does that mean 'cured'?"

"No," Turetsky explained. "Kidney failure is irreversible. We can't fix it but what we can do is try to make sure it doesn't get any worse. We've caught it extremely early, the tests show that certain elements in his blood are higher than normal but there's nothing that's remotely approaching a crisis. And Norton is extremely healthy otherwise. I've seen cats live for four or five years, even longer, with this kind of thing."

Because Turetsky obviously thought he was giving me good news, he immediately went on to explain all sorts of things to me: what the levels of Norton's blood test meant, the type of treatment he'd need, what I should look for in his behavior, and I'm sure all sorts of other things, but I wasn't actually hearing one word. I was staring off into space, trying really hard to keep tears from welling up in my eyes, with my thoughts jumbled and sad and terrible.

I remember thinking, *Four or five years, well, that's a long time, that's fine, he's already thirteen . . .*

And I also remember thinking, *Four or five years?! No, no, that's impossible, that's not long enough, I want him for many, many years more than that . . .*

And then I remember thinking, *I can't believe it. My cat's not going to live forever . . .*

At some point, I'm going to be without Norton . . .

While the concerned vet rambled on, I did my best to nod and look like I had some idea what he was saying. I did hear a few phrases such as, "I know you're very attached to your cat," and, "We all know how special Norton is so we're going to do everything we can," but basically I didn't have a clue what was going on.

Turetsky clearly knew I was shaken because at some point he said, "I think with the proper treatment, Norton's going to be fine. But if it ever comes to that, there's even a new operation that involves kidney transplants for cats."

This perked me up. I knew people who'd had kidney transplants who lived twenty, thirty years, even longer.

"I'd definitely be willing to do that," I said.

Turetsky started to say that it wasn't necessary, that it was way too early to even consider, but Janis interrupted him. "No," she explained to him, "he doesn't mean he'd be willing to let Norton have the operation, he's saying he'd give Norton his kidney."

The doctor nodded appreciatively (although I'm sure he was secretly storing this one away to share over several martinis at the next vet convention) then explained, without coming close to laughing, that it was a very nice offer and it was rare to see that kind of bond between man and cat, but the truth was that my kidney would be a bit *large* for Norton. The way it worked, he said—and I have to admit, even in my sudden state of grief, I thought this was extremely cool—was that when they did a kidney transplant on a cat, they took a healthy but homeless cat, removed one kidney, and gave it to the sick cat. The only stipulation is that the owner of the sick cat then had to adopt the donor cat and give it a good home. I thought this was more than fair and he told me that if it ever reached that stage, most of the transplant research was being done in California and he'd get me more information. Then he looked at Janis, smiling slightly, and said, "How did you know that's what he meant? About the kidney."

"Because I know him," she said. "You have to understand, he'd give up all of his limbs for this cat."

"Yes," he told her. "I've been treating both of them long enough so I think I do know that. And not only that, I think I understand it."

One of the reasons I liked Turetsky so much is that I think he even approved.

So now that we were over the first hurdle and I realized I could keep all my own organs, he started explaining exactly what I was going to have to do.

The first thing he did was show me a foot-long plastic bag filled with a clear liquid. I remember him saying something about Norton needing an injection once a week or once every two weeks, depending on his progress. The purpose was to keep him hydrated and to keep his kidney from becoming overworked. And I definitely remember him saying something along the lines of, "I'll show you how easy it is." Then, while Norton was still sitting on the table, Turetsky hung the bag up on a hook several feet above the cat, connected some sort of tube to the bottom, and picked up a box which I could see was filled with needles. He lifted off a small plastic covering from one of the needles to reveal its sharp edge. Then he inserted the needle into the end of the tube—and stuck it into my little cat.

"It's not like a hypodermic," he said. "You don't have

to find a vein. It's strictly a subcutaneous drip. It just has to break the skin and it can go in anywhere. Then you leave it in until he gets a hundred milliliters of liquid."

My eyes widened as I could see the clear liquid flowing into Norton, gathering in his body toward his back legs. When Turetsky decided he'd had enough, he pulled the needle out and I stared at Norton, who was clearly unfazed but looked like he'd swallowed an orange—whole. He had a big round bulge that was sloshing around under the skin.

"That's the liquid," Turetsky said, touching the squishy bulge. "It's just a saline solution. And it'll take a few hours for it to absorb into his blood system." Then he looked at me, saw that my eyes were bulging almost as far as the mound in Norton's midsection, and asked, "Are you all right?"

"I think so," I said. "Except I do have one question."

"Anything," he said.

"Are you saying I'm supposed to stick that needle in my cat and do what you just did?"

"Yup," Dr. Turetsky said.

And that's when I knew that my life was about to change.

Drastically.

I was a bit more relaxed when I left Dr. Turetsky's office. For one thing, although I was still traumatized at the thought of my cat's frailty and lack of immortality, I pretty much accepted the fact that I was in no immediate danger of having him scamper on up to the Great Kennel in the

Sky. For another thing, Turetsky assured me that if I couldn't/wouldn't/didn't want to be the one to stick the needle into Norton's flesh, someone there would do it for me--for a fee, of course. And that's what I did for the next few weeks. I must admit that I used my bad shoulder as an excuse right off the bat, saying that I couldn't rig the drip-thing up, hold on to Norton and keep the needle in place all at the same time because I didn't have the mobility. But the truth was that it was inconceivable to me that I could stick a sharp object into my beloved cat's body and fill him full of saline solution. I just couldn't do it. I was certain I'd hurt him, which was the worst thing I could imagine in life. And—I hate confessing this to all you cat lunatics who might actually have some respect for me—I was way, way, *way* too squeamish.

There. I admit it. I was a major league wimp.

I remember telling my parents, back in those oh-so-great days of the '60s that they'd never have to worry about me becoming a drug addict because the mere idea of stick-ing a needle into my own arm—or worse, letting some drugged-out, Hot Tuna–loving hippie named Free stick a needle into my arm—was enough to make me vote for Richard Nixon (okay, that's a slight exaggeration, but not *much* of one). I always figured if I got diabetes and had to inject myself with insulin, that'd be it for me. Couldn't do it. Uh-uh. No how, no way.

Worse, it wasn't just my aversion to needles. I knew I simply wasn't a natural caregiver. I didn't know if I was ca-pable of it. I was uncomfortable around disease, even more uncomfortable around someone else's pain. My logic al-ways was, that's why I make money, so I can afford to let somebody else deal with that stuff. The closest I'd come to experiencing all of that was when my father had cancer. But even then, while I certainly went through the emotional agony that comes with a father's decline and death, I was three thousand miles away for the worst of it and wasn't really present until the dirty stuff was over with—and only the sad stuff remained.

Sad, I could deal with.

The rest of it . . . well . . . I really didn't think so.

Nonetheless, when it came to Norton, I tried. I really did. But this against-my-nature effort was one of the great fiascos of my life, cat-related or anything-else-related.

We were in the city and I was thinking about the drip bag and the whole IV thing and I decided I could do it. I decided I *had* to do it. Turetsky had shown me how and so had one of the women who worked in his clinic. They made it look easy. Norton didn't seem to mind being stuck. And they even gave me a valuable tip: they said that sometimes the liquid was too cold and it shocked the cat when it hit his system, so they told me to put the bag in a sink with hot water for a few minutes to warm it up and make the process more palatable.

So once I made the decision that it was full steam—or saline solution—ahead, that's what I did first. I ran hot water in my bathroom sink, put the bag in for five minutes, then pulled it out. I touched the outside of the plastic and it felt too hot to me. I took a difficult breath and grappled with the following worry: what if I scald the inside of my cat?

I almost gave it up then and there but decided no, I was doing this. So I let the bag lie out of the water for a couple of minutes, then touched it again. Now it felt too cold. I put it back under the hot water, standing there, touching it every fifteen seconds or so, until it felt close to a comfortable temperature. Then I dried it off in a towel and realized that I hadn't even started yet and I was already ready for a nap.

Try to picture this now. I go to my dining room table which, for some unknown reason, struck me as the right place to attempt this procedure. I laid Norton's shoulder bag on the table, because I knew he found the bag comforting, and then I put Norton on top of the bag. He seemed curious but not adverse to staying there. In fact, he relaxed, stretched his back feet out behind him and his front paws out in front of him, which was his distinct, Sphinx-like and very odd way of getting comfortable. So far so good. Although I have to admit, I was not just exhausted from the whole procedure already, I was already sweating.

Next: I've got this foot-long plastic bag filled with liquid. With slightly warm liquid. I know I've got to hang it up on something, so it can function as an IV and the liquid will drip down into my cat. I've got a chandelier above my dining table—ah ha! That must have been the reason I thought this was a good location—so I hook the bag up to the chandelier. Step Two is done (Really Step Three, if you count putting Norton on the table, which I definitely do) and, although my hands are now trembling, I'm feeling pretty good. I notice that Janis is watching me from a couch in the living room. I tell her that everything's going great so far. I really feel like I'm on top of it, I say. Supportive as always, she mentions that it's just taken me fifteen minutes to put the cat on the table and hang up the drip bag. When Turetsky did this procedure, the whole *thing* took *five* minutes.

Ignoring her dig, I decided I was ready for the tough stuff.

First was a little mechanical maneuver. I had to attach a plastic tube to the drip bag. This couldn't be simpler. All that's involved is pulling a small tab off a little white piece of plastic that's on the bottom of the bag, then punch some weird pointed thing that's at one end of the tube right through it. Easy. Except I'm not the most mechanical person in the world. I remember being in high school once and taking one of those tests to show you what kinds of skills you have that might be useful in later life. I thought the test was fairly easy for the first half hour or so, then I got to the part that tested you on spatial relations and mechanical ability. I got to one diagram that showed two gears touching each other. The question below it said, "If gear *A* spins one way, connects to gear *B* at this point, which way will gear *B* spin?" I spent the rest of the allotted two hours staring blankly and hopelessly at the two gears, realizing that if they left me in the room for a million years I would not be able to answer the question. So even though this little plastic doohickey on the drip bag seemed idiot-proof, I hesitated. When I was sure I had the right end of the tube and the right piece of plastic, I did my thing.

It worked!

The tube was in. All systems were go. Houston, we have *no* problem!

Except now Norton wasn't on the table. He was over on the couch sitting next to Janis, watching me much the same way she was. Which was dubiously.

I sauntered over, very confident now, picked him up and put him back on the table.

And he hopped right off again.

We went through this routine about ten times until finally I got him to stay. I kept saying to Janis, "See? This is a good sign. He's feeling so good he doesn't even *want* his drip. And look at the way he's running around. This is very, very good." And she kept saying back to me, "Okay, it's good. But it would be even better if you could do this sometime in the next twenty-four hours so we can get on with our lives."

Now I was ready. Norton was on the table, relaxed, if still looking a bit dubious. The bag was all hooked up (it did occur to me that the liquid had probably cooled down by now, but I decided Norton and I could both live with that for this first time), and all that was needed was the needle.

I had a Baggie full of needles. I liked this part. It made me feel like I should be hanging out with the guys from Stone Temple Pilots. The woman in Turetsky's office had given me some needles that were covered with protective green caps and other needles that were covered with pink caps. The green needles were big, the pink ones were little. They told me to try the pink first, they would be easier. It would take longer for the liquid to drip, but the insertion process would be simpler. So I rummaged in the Baggie and pulled out a pink capped needle. I inserted it into the end of the tube, exactly as Turetsky had shown me, twisted the protective pink cap to remove it and *voilà!* I was all set up. The bag was in place, the needle was exposed and in my hand and ready for insertion. All I had to do was . . . do it. Get the needle in, slide the switch on the tube that started and stopped the flow of liquid, get the needle out, pet the cat, drink an entire bottle of wine as quickly as possible (that last was my own addition to Turetsky's litany of instructions; by that point, I definitely needed it).

I did my best to gather up a little mound of Norton's skin in the fingers of one hand, as they had shown me. With the other hand, I slowly brought the needle closer to him. I realized that I could barely swallow, my throat was so dry. All I could think about was, *What if I hurt him?* My basic premise in dealing with Norton was that I'd rather die than hurt him. But they told me it *wouldn't* hurt. It sure didn't seem to hurt when Turetsky did it. In fact, Norton looked kind of bored with the entire process. So if Turetsky could do it, so could I. Right?

Sure.

I stuck my cat with the needle, knowing everything would now go smoothly. Except the second I touched him, he flinched.

The second he flinched, I drew back, terrified that I'd done something bad. And the second I drew back, he leapt off the table.

There I was holding the needle, with no cat, and somehow the liquid in the drip bag was now spurting out all over my dining table. I looked like a fireman putting out a blaze more than I looked like a concerned pet owner trying to perform the simplest maneuver possible on an under-the-weather cat.

I flicked the little switch on the tube—which somehow I had touched when I flinched—and managed to stop the gushing liquid. Then I got up from the table and went and got my cat. Again, I put him on the table and again he lay down—although he was definitely not as relaxed as he'd been. Of course, neither was I. In fact, my heart was pounding so hard, I was reasonably sure I was in the midst of a heart attack. I could hear Janis do her best not to snicker, and I decided, okay, this is it, I'm definitely doing this . . .

The needle went in.

Then out.

And the next thing I knew, there was blood everywhere. I tried repeatedly to get the thing into my cat, absolutely couldn't do it, and by the time he jumped off the table and scampered into a closet, I was fairly sure I'd killed him because I had never *seen* so much blood.

"Get the cat!" I started screaming at Janis. "I think I hurt him really bad!"

I couldn't understand why she was laughing.

"I'm not kidding!" I yelled. "I think I stabbed my cat to death!"

"I don't think you touched your cat," Janis said calmly. Well, not so calmly. It's hard to be calm when you're laughing that hard.

"*What* are you laughing at?" I asked, infuriated that she wasn't taking me seriously. And even angrier that she didn't seem to care that I was going to be imprisoned for cruelty to the feline species. And then I realized what was amusing to her. She was right—I hadn't even come close to getting the needle into my cat's skin. What I'd done with that razor sharp little fucker was stab myself—in my fingers, in my arm, in my thigh, in almost every part of my body—about 140 times. Every time I moved, I managed to stick it into some other place where skin was exposed. The blood was all mine.

I gave a huge sigh of relief now that I knew I'd done no harm to my trusting Fold. The relief didn't last too long, though. It disappeared when I realized I might actually pass out at the sight of all my blood.

"I think it's back to Turetsky," Janis said.

"Yeah," I agreed. "But first call an ambulance, okay?"

That was enough to convince me that I was not cut out for this. So for the next three weeks in a row, Janis, Norton and I headed out to Sag Harbor for the weekend and on Friday or Saturday, I'd take Norton in to Turetsky's office, one of the aides would fill him up with fluid, I'd fork over twenty bucks, and then we'd go on our merry way. With all my blood *inside* my body, where it belonged.

For those three weeks, life was good. Then my relaxed state ended because I was suddenly convinced that Norton was on his last legs after all.

This relapse turned out to be another false alarm, but I didn't accept this until I had my first up close and personal experience with Dr. Marty Goldstein.

I had, not long before Norton's kidney diagnosis, come in contact with Dr. Marty (as he's often called by the pet owners who swear by him) in my professional capacity. An agent had called me, said she'd discovered the most amazing vet in the world, a *holistic* vet, and she thought there was a big book in it. I agreed to drive with the agent up to Marty's veterinary office in South Salem, about an hour and a half away in upstate New York, to see what all the fuss was.

The fuss was, in fact, fairly amazing.

The first thing one notices about Marty Goldstein is that he's your basic goofball. He wears ties with stupid-looking dogs on them and has weird cartoons of animals all over his office and I'm pretty sure that at our first meeting he was wearing one of those hats with big, floppy dog ears on it hanging down from each side. He has *Far Side* cartoons on his walls, he cracks wise constantly, is generally pretty silly, and he's more reminiscent of Pee Wee Herman than, say, George Clooney in "ER."

And then one notices something else about Dr. Marty: he's a little bit of a miracle worker.

I can't remember being so jazzed as I was by the end of our first meeting. We got a little lecture which explained the meaning of and philosophy behind holistic and naturopathic animal healing, then we were treated to a series of illustrated case studies. In many of these cases, animals—mostly cats and dogs with some form of cancer—were brought to Marty by owners who reported that other vets had said it was time for euthanasia. In an astounding number of instances, Marty didn't just prolong the lives of these animals, he cured them. We looked at photo after photo of disease-ridden pets who looked to be on death's door, and then saw follow-up photos, some of them taken years later, of these same animals looking happy and, more important, healthy.

Over dinner that night, Marty further expounded on his beliefs and why he thought they were not just right but genuinely important. He explained that veterinary medicine, much like the medical system for humans, was dominated by greed, which often led to easy and false diagnoses. He talked about how important diet was for animal health—same as it was for humans—and how misguided conventional medicinal treatments often were because they were geared toward stifling the symptoms of disease rather than dealing with the disease itself. He also talked about how crucial it was to maintain an animal's health when he was in a state of remission rather than to simply treat and try to cure an animal when he was already ill. It made an awful lot of sense. And what I liked best about Marty is that he wasn't a total New-Age nut. Sure, he was a proselytizer, because he believed passionately in his cause. But he was also someone who had graduated from the Cornell University College of Veterinary Medicine and who had once been a conservative, by-the-book vet. When he began his practice, he said he used 5 percent holistic treatments and 95 percent standard Western veterinary treatments. Over the next fifteen years or so, as he saw standard treatments fail to address the needs of his patients, that ratio had become reversed. Nonetheless, there were cases where he still definitely urged the use of antibiotics and other conventional medicines, and he certainly believed in operations when they were necessary.

I came away convinced—and signed Marty up to write a book for Alfred A. Knopf, one of the country's most prestigious publishing houses and one of the houses for which I work.

Of course, like many people, I was theoretically convinced—but I didn't apply my convictions to my own life.

Until, that is, a month or so after Norton's first injection in Dr. Turetsky's office, when he became very, very lethargic. One day, I noticed he seemed sluggish. Then, for the next two or three days, he didn't eat and he hardly moved. I did what I always did in such situations with my cat—I panicked. I took him to Turetsky, who, after finding out Norton had lost yet another pound—he'd now lost about a third of his total body weight—put him on antibiotics. Another week passed and Norton didn't seem any better. I was worrying more than ever. Even I could see that he was looking bad. And he hardly ever left his spot on the floor. He was beginning to resemble a furry rug more than an actual living, breathing cat.

It was Janis, naturally, who told me to call Marty Goldstein.

"You thought he made so much sense," she said, "why don't you see what he has to say?"

So I called Marty, told him about Norton's diagnosis and his current lethargy and loss of weight, and waited for him to say, "Sorry, there's nothing I can do, your cat's got about an hour to live." Instead, here's what he said: "Oh, sure, no problem. I can fix this in a day."

"You can?" I said, stupefied.

"Don't worry about it. Call your vet and ask him to fax me a copy of the blood test. Then I'll overnight you a few supplements and herbs for Norton. Follow the instructions, they're not complicated, and he'll be fine."

"That's it?" I asked. "And he will?"

"After you give him the stuff, call me the next day and let me know what you think."

So I called over to Turetsky's office, asked them to fax the test, which they did, and the next day I received a package containing four or five different supplements and herbs, which I was to give Norton by dropper.

I was quite skeptical but did as I was told. The bottles all had words like "renal" and "hepaticol" and "glandular" printed on them, words which at the time meant nothing to me, but I followed orders and Norton accepted his medicine as docilely as he'd accepted everything else the past week.

As Janis is my witness—and she is—I woke up the next morning to find Norton meowing his head off, waiting in the kitchen to be fed. I started to feed him, as usual, then suddenly stopped myself. I looked over at my cat with wonder. He was not only waiting to be fed, he was clearly ravenous. And he not only gobbled down every last bit of food, when he was done he began running around the living room of the Sag Harbor house as if he were a kitten.

A *little* kitten.

A little, *healthy* kitten.

I have to say, I ran up the stairs, shook Janis awake and said that Norton was not only moving, he was moving in a way he hadn't moved in years. She started to go downstairs to check it out for herself but she didn't have to, because you-know-who had already bounded upstairs and had jumped on the bed, looking pretty damn happy about it, too. I immediately went to the phone and called Dr. Marty.

"I guess you know what you're doing," I told him.

"We still have more work to do," he said. "Make an appointment and bring Norton in to see me."

I responded with the only thing I felt to be appropriate under the circumstances: "Yes, sir," I said. "Whatever you want."

I took Norton up to South Salem to see the holistic vet a few days later.

We went into Marty's examining room and he came in wearing his usual nutjob outfit (I think this one included a vest with dumb-looking jungle animals all over it). Norton was, by this time, his usual self—confident, unafraid and curious. In fact, while we were waiting for Marty to join us in the room, my cat was climbing all over everything, checking the place out. When Marty came in, he picked

Norton up and cradled him, talking to him like they were old pals. He went on like that for a few minutes—I could see that Norton had taken an instant shine to him and was relaxed—and then Marty set the cat down and spoke to me. And what he spoke about was kidney failure. His words didn't make me nervous or depressed. He dealt with the disease as if it were an absolutely natural and normal part of life—which, of course, it is—and he spoke about it as if there was nothing to fear. He assured me that Norton was indeed in the beginning stage of kidney failure, but he also said that other than that, he was healthy. And then he did something wonderful: he explained to me the various stages of what Norton would go through if the disease went on to its natural end. He said that—and he stressed that this was way, way in the future—eventually what would happen is that when the kidney went into serious failure, Norton would get logy and then even logier, he would lose much of his energy and would start napping more. Eventually, he would fade away into this drowsy state, go into a coma and die. Marty looked at me and said, "When the time comes, it's absolutely painless and easy. Believe me, if you could choose a way to die, it would be kidney failure." He took a breath, then said, "Anyway . . . I just want you to know what it is we've got here. I think the more you know, the better off you are. And the less fear you'll have."

Even though he was dealing with the subject of death—granted, not mine, but still, the next closest thing as far as I was concerned—his words made me feel better. More relaxed and more accepting of what I would eventually be forced to accept. It reminded me a lot of when my father died. He wanted to die at home—he had cancer—

and we were more than happy to oblige. The last few days of his life he was set up in a hospital bed in his bedroom and we had a wonderful nurse from a hospice who stayed with him most of the time. A few days before his death, she spoke to me, my brother and my mother and told us what was going to happen. She described the process we would witness—the process of dying—and she explained exactly what was going to happen physically. She told us that, when the time came, we would see him relax, actually see a certain pleasure on his face and in his eyes. She said that's what people meant when they talked about a glow or a light that seemed to surround dying people. She urged us to touch him, both when he was alive and after he died, so we would know that death was nothing to fear. It was quite a comforting speech, mostly because it rang true. When that time did finally come, I wasn't there to witness it. Janis and I were out buying groceries and when we pulled the car into the garage, my brother and my mom both came out to say that my dad was dead.

To be truthful, there was a part of me that was secretly glad I had missed the final moment. I felt bad that I wasn't with my family but there was no denying that death also frightened me. I didn't really want to be quite so close to it and there was a large part of me that felt that by not confronting it head on, I didn't fully have to accept its existence. Oh, I knew it existed, it's not like I was in a total state of denial. I just didn't particularly feel like touching it.

So, my new veterinary advisor made me feel better and I thought his words rang true. But now it was time for action and I wanted to see what he was going to do for Norton.

Marty told me that he wanted to run his own blood test

on Norton. He asked the lab for different and deeper analyses on certain things, he said. I told him that was fine, but that Norton would absolutely refuse to let his blood be taken unless he was sedated. I hurriedly explained that my cat was perfect—except in this one instance. Marty told me that he wouldn't have a problem and I said, "No, really, I know my cat extremely well. He's the most gentle animal on earth, honest, but he's never, ever, *ever* let a vet take his blood without things looking a lot like the fourteenth round of Ali-Frazier III."

Marty nodded, totally dismissing my warning, and picked Norton back up into his arms. He spoke very gently to the cat. Not in cat language or anything, don't worry, this isn't one of those "ma" and "fa" moments from *Day of the Dolphin*, but he stroked him gently, whispered to him, and within a few seconds he told the nurse, who had suddenly appeared, to prepare the hypodermic. I shook my head, expecting the worst. Marty took the syringe, whispered something else to Norton, looked him straight in the eye and jabbed the needle in. Norton didn't even blink. Not so much as a whimper or an attempted scratch. He just looked right back at Marty, gave him that okay-I-trust-you look, and let the guy take his blood.

I couldn't believe it. It crossed my mind that maybe it was one of those fake syringes, the kind buy for Halloween, and that I was dealing with a total loon, but then I saw the blood rise up into the small vial and I knew I was on to something special here (this scene was repeated, about a year later, with my friend Paul. Marty didn't take Paul's blood, but he did take the blood of Paul's idiot golden retriever dog, Buddy. Buddy, a neurotic mess of a canine who has a nasty habit of barking at rocks all day long, made

Norton's blood-taking phobia look mild. When Marty went forward with the needle, Paul warned him that there was a fifty-fifty chance that Buddy would actually bite his fool head off. Marty just waved him away, looked Buddy right in the eye and did what he had to do. According to Paul, when it was all over, Buddy was so entranced, he did everything but shine Marty's shoes and tip him twenty bucks).

When Marty had finished examining Norton, he told me that as soon as he got the results, he'd send me a whole bunch of new supplements and herbs, geared for the deficiencies he discovered in the report. He also told me to immediately change Norton's diet, that this was the single most important thing I could do. I said that I would, asked him what he recommended, and he told me. And this is something I've got to do a little proselytizing about on my own now.

I became a big believer in this holistic, naturopathic stuff, came to comprehend the logic behind it, but I understand if people dismiss it as voodoo. I never—and would never—give myself over to it 100 percent. I never did anything for Norton without getting a second, more traditional opinion and then weighing the consequences if the two opinions differed drastically. But the one thing I'm absolutely convinced of is that cats (and dogs, for that matter, there's no need to exclude them from this) deserve better food than what we give them. The way Marty convinced me that I'd been doing my cat wrong all these years was he pulled out a food chart. At the top was what cats eat in their natural habitat—in other words, what their systems naturally go for without human interference. At the bottom was what was actually inside a can of Ken-L Ration and the most common commercial brands. In-between were various other forms of cat food, the so-called health food brands like Science Diet. In their natural habitat, cats ate grains and meat and poultry. Thanks to us humans, what cats mostly eat now are plastic, bone, corn syrup and things I can't even bring myself to mention. Marty's food lecture was a lot like watching the movie *Scream*: I wanted to cover my eyes because it was so scary but I had to see who was going to get slaughtered next.

That afternoon, as soon as I got home, I threw out all my cans of normal cat food and went to a pet health food store to buy cases of the good stuff (in case you're interested, the healthy brands of commercial cat food include Solid Gold, Natural Life, Wysongs, Cornucopia, Preside, PetGuard and Abady; they all use chunks of real meat, whole rather than processed grains, essential vitamins and minerals, and no preservatives). But even as I bought them, I knew I'd only be using them as backups. Because the one thing that Marty convinced me of was that I should be cooking for my cat.

Please. Do me a favor. I'm sure there are some of you who are nodding your heads as you read this, thinking, *Of course we should cook for our pets, they deserve it.* But I'm also sure that most of you are going, *Uh-oh, he's officially lost his mind. That's just what I want to do—come home from a hard day's work and cook a three-course meal for my little Puff-Puff. That's why I didn't even have kids, because I don't want to do stuff like that!* I understand, believe me. Just hear me out, then I'll change the subject.

Marty's main point is that our animals should eat . . . hold on to your hats . . . *food*. Not plastic. Not ground-up bone. Not fecal matter or poisonous chemicals. Come on, if you're a cat lunatic, as we all are, that's hard to argue with. The right canned food is fine, and I definitely gave it to Norton from that point forward, but my attitude was that my cat was sick and why shouldn't I do *everything* I could to get and keep him healthy.

The answer was "no reason."

So I began cooking Norton's food.

Using Marty's formula, I whipped up concoctions that were about one-half meat or poultry and one-half grain and vegetable. I'd like to say that Norton gobbled it all down the second I placed it in his bowl, but that would be a total lie. What he did was sniff it suspiciously, much the way I would a steamed vegetable and brown rice platter at a health food restaurant, and then walk disdainfully away. But if my cat was the champion of stubborn, this was one instance when I was not going to give in to him. This was good for him and I was going to make sure he got healthy. It reminded me of the times my mother used to put my father on various diets, casually mentioning that he shouldn't be taking that second helping of potatoes, except that I couldn't make Norton feel guilty about his eating habits and I couldn't shove him in front of a full-length mirror so he could see that he was starting to resemble Jackie Gleason. He looked as dashing as ever and he seemed to feel fine, so he couldn't understand why his Twinkies were being withheld and being replaced by the equivalent of carrot juice. It was a battle of wills—but for the one and only time, it was a battle I was going to win. And I did. At first, Norton would pick out the good tidbits—the chicken or the meat—and leave the vegetables and grain (he was his father's son, after all; in a sick kind of way, I was proud of him for his tenacity). Then, after a few days, I noticed that some of the rice or pasta was gone. Just a little bit. And then, a few days later, more and more of it was consumed. Finally, miracle of miracles, the zucchini or the broccoli rape (Marty swore to me that his cats loved broccoli rape) were also gone. Pretty soon, Norton was licking his bowl clean. When he'd get canned food, on those occasions when I didn't have time to be the Emeril of cats, he did seem to eat with a little more gusto, but he definitely ate and got to like his homemade meals. While I'm on the subject, I should point out that these concoctions were definitely fit for human consumption (yes, I'll admit it right here and now—especially if I added a generous amount of garlic, I'd be unable to resist and would often share the exact same meal as my cat). It was also approximately the same level of difficulty as opening up a can. Once I knew Norton would consume the stuff, I'd make a big batch, enough to last a week, freeze some of it, and presto—instant healthy meals. The only bad moment I remember was when Janis came over one night and saw me chowing down on Chinese food that I'd ordered in. She shook her head—something she does a lot at my behavior, now that I think about it—and observed, "You're cooking for your cat but getting take-out for yourself? Don't you think there's something wrong here?"

The thing is, of course, I didn't think that. Eating my greasy shrimp with hot chili sauce and watching my cat scarf down his perfectly prepared chicken, rice and zucchini, I thought everything was exactly where it should be.

Now that Norton's health was stable and the food situation was taken care of, the next thing I needed to do was find another vet.

Yes, I know, I already had two—Turetsky and Marty; three if you count Dr. Pepper, which I certainly did—but I was only in Turetsky territory (Sag Harbor) on weekends during the nonsummer months, and not every weekend at that. And not only was Marty more of an advisor than my regular vet, he was a long drive away; it wasn't practical to consider using him on a regular basis or in case of emergency. So I began a Manhattan search.

Norton had actually been going to a vet in the city for quite a few years, but I didn't really think the guy was great. I'd stayed with him mostly because Norton had been healthy and this doctor did very little but give my traveling companion the occasional shot that was necessary for his overseas excursions. With all this going on, I decided I needed someone new. What pushed me over the edge was that I twice tried taking Norton in for his weekly dose of saline solution and both times we were kept waiting for two hours. There was no emergency, he'd just over-booked—much like a human doctor—and I thought this was not very considerate of either me or my cat. We began to look elsewhere.

People get very personally involved with their vets. If they're happy with their pet's treatment, they want every pet to have the same treatment. I noticed this when I was having a business lunch and, as most people did, at some point the woman asked me about Norton. I told her I was looking for a new vet in the city and she began raving about hers. He was the greatest, she said. He was fabulous, he was a genius. He was this, he was that . . . He was the first one I'd heard about, so I said I'd give him a try.

He was situated on the Upper East Side, which was totally inconvenient for me—especially if I had to go see him once a week for Norton's drip treatment—but inconvenience was not a deterrent when it came to caring for my cat. If I thought he was good and he was in Alaska, I would have taken Norton there. What *was* a deterrence was the fact that I *hated* this guy.

The first thing he did was tell me that Turetsky's treatment was all wrong. I didn't want to give the cat a big chunk of saline solution once a week, he said, I wanted to give him smaller portions three times a week. I explained that not only did I totally trust my Sag Harbor vet, I'd already had a second opinion, which totally matched Turetsky's, and this vet went into a total funk, as if I'd insulted him. When he asked me a few questions about Norton's health—and he didn't ask a lot of questions, he mainly gave me brusque answers, using a superior tone, letting me know how smart he was—I told him that I'd also been giving him supplements and herbs under the care of a holistic vet. He immediately sneered and said, "I don't believe in holistic medicine. It's a total sham." I told him that, while I wasn't totally sold, I thought it was doing the cat a lot of good. He told me I was completely wrong, that it was doing no good whatsoever. By comparison, when I told Turetsky and Dr. Pepper that I was seeing Marty, they were interested. They both had heard of him and what they each said was pretty much what I felt: that while there might not be enough empirical evidence to show that his methodology was completely sound, there was a hell of a lot of anecdotal evidence. They both asked about the supplements, jotted down the names so they could check them out on their own, and basically said, "Hey, it can't hurt. And if it helps, we're happy."

I was quickly losing patience with the East Side guy, but what really did it was when he began to examine Norton. He wasn't gentle.

I'd never been to a vet who didn't treat my cat as if he were something delicate and wonderful. Something special. This East Side vet handled Norton as if he were some kind of inanimate lump, twisting and turning parts of his body with no regard to the fact that Norton looked as unhappy as a cat can look. It reminded me of writing a script for a movie studio: you come up with a concept that might make a good film, do the best you can to create characters that people could conceivably care about and situations that seem real but can work on screen, and then some executive comes in and, without rhyme or reason, dumps all over it, ripping it to shreds. And worse, demanding rewrites that not only won't make it better but will, in fact, ruin it. Why? Because movie studio executives hate talent. They'd like to make films without the writers, directors or actors. Those films wouldn't be any good, but they'd sure be a lot easier for the executive and give him a lot fewer headaches. It's like a coach who insists that the athletes on his team conform to his system, rather than creating a system that works for the athletes' abilities. Same as the studio exec, that kind of coach hates talent. They want to be the star. They want the glory. At the very least, they want the credit.

I got the distinct feeling that this vet would have done very well in Hollywood or coaching the Knicks: he just plain didn't like his patients. He wanted their illnesses to fit his diagnoses. And he wanted their recoveries to match his treatments. If they didn't, well, screw 'em, he'd treat them the way he wanted to treat them anyway.

When he started rattling off a list of things I was going to do and not do for Norton, I interrupted him and said, "Excuse me, I don't think I'm going to do *any* of that. What I'm going to do is get the hell out of here." And that's exactly what we did. I apologized to my cat the entire way downtown and assured him I would do better. The only encouraging thing is the way Norton mewed at me from inside his shoulder bag—I knew he believed me.

I checked out a couple of other vets, and none seemed great, but then two sources converged and led me straight to the yellow brick road. Norton was in Turetsky's office for his weekly drip and I asked the aide there if she knew a good vet in the city. She told me that she'd worked for a wonderful woman, two wonderful women, in fact, at a place called the Washington Square Animal Hospital. I liked the name, since it meant it was close to my apartment in the Village. The idea of not having to take Norton seventy blocks in a taxi once a week was more than a little appealing. When I went back to the city, I called Ann King, Norton's fan who took such good care of him that one weekend Janis and I were away, to ask if she knew a good vet and she said, "Don't you know about the Washington Square Animal Hospital?" Seemed like fate. So I immediately made an appointment for the next day.

I didn't like Dr. Dianne DeLorenzo, the vet Norton and I met with at the clinic.

I *loved* her.

And so did Norton.

She immediately saw and understood the, as she called it, "stronger than usual" bond that existed between man and cat, and she seemed to get quite a kick out of it. She also picked up on the fact that Norton was different and unique (but remember our earlier lesson, class: not *very* unique), and best of all, when she examined him it was like watching someone treat royalty. There was none of that rough East Side jerk of a vet manner. This was someone who loved what she was doing and who cared immensely for her patients. She kept telling Norton how handsome he was, which, of course, made him extremely happy. And she even seemed pretty good with people. She didn't tell me how handsome I was, but she did manage to keep me calm and nonhysterical.

I confessed about my inability to give Norton his IV and she said she understood, then assured me that I could bring him in for that treatment whenever I wanted. I watched her give it to him herself that first session, and she was the perfect combination of gentle and firm. Norton didn't flinch when the needle went in and she let me hold him in my arms while he absorbed the fluid—her expertise and my loving stroke: the perfect combination for my cat. She also recommended someone named Yvette, a woman who used to work at the clinic, who would come to the apartment to do it if I ever needed that. What totally won me over was when I told Dianne I was also taking Norton for some holistic treatments. Her eyes lit up and she said that she was not trained in that area, knew very little about it, knew that a lot of people swore by it, and she was quite interested in learning more about it. She asked for Marty's phone number so they could speak and she could find out what, specifically, he was doing for Norton. Her attitude was "Maybe I'll learn something that will help me treat my patients better."

By the time I left her office, Norton not only had a new Manhattan vet, I was thinking of proposing marriage. What could be better for my catcentric life than being married to Norton's doctor? My fantasy was short-lived, maybe a minute or two—long enough for me to create a mental picture of my coming home to our snow-bound cabin in the woods to find Norton eating a hearty bowl of stew by the roaring fire and my new wife being serenaded by hundreds of happy, singing cats and dogs—since it turned out that Dianne was already happily married. Of course, for all intents and purposes, so was I, so that whole cabin–Dr. and Mrs. Schweitzer thing—or, rather, Dr. and *Mr.* Schweitzer thing—didn't really pan out. But the vet part turned out perfectly.

When Norton and I strolled out of the clinic and found ourselves on Ninth Street, we were both feeling pretty chipper. Once again, life was good. Everyone assured me that Norton was doing fine. Now it was time to wait and see what life brought us.

Of course, what life brought us was what life always brings.

Plenty of surprises.

CHAPTER 8

THE CAT WHO
STAYED HOME

B asically, things were normal. I was
working away and Norton's kidney problem didn't
seem to be slowing him down one iota. He was eating healthily and putting back on all the weight he'd
lost, going in for his weekly shot (soon after our visit to Dr.
DeLorenzo, everyone decided it was time for the shot to
become twice weekly, so that's what we did), and finding
new fans almost every day.

One of his big fans turned out to be a woman named
Mary Bielaska, who was producing—along with her cat
Zana, she announced—a CD of classical music she was calling *Classical Cats*. The idea, she said when she called to discuss it, was to pick songs that she felt were particularly
catlike and that people could listen to with their feline pets
at their side. She would also rename the familiar titles to

make them more cat-friendly. One of the cuts, for instance, would be "The Sorcerer's Apprentice" by Paul Dukas, which, for the CD, would be retitled "Stalking Grasshoppers." Another would be Johann Strauss's "The Beautiful Blue Danube Waltzes," renamed, for cat purposes, "A Feline's Fabulous Fantasy." I listened politely as Ms. Bielaska (the first time she called, I have to say I thought her name was Baked Alaska, which is why I was so willing to talk to her) described her scheme. While listening, I wondered why she was bothering to describe it to *me*. There was a reason, of course. And, as usual, it had nothing to do with me.

She wanted Norton to write the liner notes.

After some minor haggling—Norton was retired, after all—my cat and I came aboard (with me very much in the background).

For all his fans who have not had the pleasure of listening to *Classical Cats: Music for Your Cat*, I now reproduce Norton's first and only literary dip into the record world (what you're missing out on, as well as the music, is that each CD came packaged with a small bag of catnip).

CLASSICAL CATS
Fe-liner Notes by NORTON

I was sitting in a cafe in Paris, oh, about a year ago now, sipping my usual *lait froid*—and a particularly delightful vintage it was. It was a lazy evening on the Left Bank. My human was occupied, paying scant attention to me, barely remembering to tell the waiter that I liked my *poulet roti* off the bone. Minding my own business, doing my best to ignore the rather large dog who, rudely and crudely, insisted on sniffing under my seat all through dinner, I couldn't help but notice a rather dashing feline sitting several tables to my left. He, too, seemed to be enjoying his *verre du lait*, so eventually we struck up a conversation.

We had quite a bit in common—we were both well traveled, we both thought the lamb at L'ami Louis to be the best on any continent, we were both quite a bit smarter than our owners—and we quickly became good and close friends. So I was not surprised when Zana—for that was my new friend's name—recently gave me a quick meow to tell me about his wonderful new idea for a CD. It was to be called "Classical Cats" and would be a compilation of classical gems that cats have long preferred. The genius of Zana's concept—aside from hiring that brilliant long-hair conductor Micetro Leopold Catscanini—is that he felt by putting all these classics in one collection, he could get human beings to upgrade their usual base taste and spend some time listening, learning and appreciating along with their feline companions. Zana, knowing my predilection for anything by Strauss and Debussy—known in my circles as Depussy— asked me to jot down a few words by way of introduction. Always one to favor the advancement of culture (After all, I'm the one who insisted my human finally stop writing those stupid books about how he tagged around with me all over the world!), I immediately agreed. *Et voilà.*

While Zana, for marketing purposes, had to include the human names for each composition (i.e., Offenbach's "Barcarolle" from *The Tales of Hoffman*), he quite properly has listed each masterpiece under its more appropriate and, I'm certain, original feline name. Thus that same "Barcarolle" becomes "The Butterfly Who Got Away," which, as all cats know, is what that particular orchestration is really about.

I can't quarrel with any of the selections herein (although I would have liked to see something included from Mozart's *Catting Around*, or as it's known to humans, *Don Giovanni*) nor with their well-thought-out order. Grieg's "Stretch and Yawn" is a gentle introduction to any cat's morning. I can't ever listen to these peaceful strains without envisioning myself on my human's pillow at 6 A.M., listening to him snore away, as—since it's clearly time he wake up to feed me—I cleverly stick my coldish nose in his eye and push it open. I also defy any self-respecting cat to listen to the next three selections without conjuring up that trio of life's great natural pleasures—running through and chewing upon a park's lush, green grass; bounding and leaping around a backyard in pursuit of a spindly grasshopper; and creeping up on a garden, thick with colorful, fragrant flowers, and doing one's best to pounce upon a butterfly fluttering just inches out of claw's reach.

Thrill to the heart-pounding excitement of Strauss's "The Dog Chase," then relax to the calming strains of Debussy's "To Purr With Love." Rev up again with the pulsating rhythms of "The Great Mouse Hunt"—can't you see yourself creeping across a sun-warmed linoleum floor, closer and closer yet to some delicious and unsuspecting furry little rodent?—and then luxuriate in the frivolity of Bizet's "To Chase a Tail." Surely, this genius must have had a tail of his own, carefully hidden from human view within the confines of his formal wear. How else could he see so clearly into our minds?

End this delightful concoction by wallowing in the sensuality of Strauss's waltz, then curl up by the fire—or just about anywhere else—and let your glowing eyes slowly close to Debussy's sweet-as-Pounce "Time for a Cat Nap." I myself like to play this one seventeen or eighteen times a day.

I could go on forever but Zana's only paying me three cans of Sheba and a personalized litter box, and even we Scottish Folds have to make a living. So, in closing, let me wish all you classical cats out there your own ball of string, a human to scratch you under the chin, a nice desk lamp to sunbathe under, and an evening listening to Zana's wonderful collection. Happy purring.

The *Classical Cats* experience was unique, in that most of Norton's fans—who kept in steady touch with him over the years—did not want him to do anything for them. They wanted to do things for him.

Gifts never stopped arriving. And I don't mean little cans of Pounce. I mean *gifts*.

One woman knew that Norton liked to zip around town in a shoulder bag (the weird thing is, when people either called or wrote to tell me stuff like this, they never said, "I read that Norton likes to zip around in his shoulder bag," they always said things like, "I know that Norton likes . . ." or, "I heard that Norton likes . . ." as if he told them himself. I never pursued this with them, I guess because I always thought it was possible that somehow he *had* told them, and I decided ignorance was bliss). So this woman sent a very colorful and comfortable shoulder bag—one that she'd hand knitted herself.

Clothing came fairly regularly. Sweaters, shirts, and for some reason, caps. I even got a tie, which I assume was for me because it was longer than Norton. It came from someone in Germany and it had big images of Norton painted all over it—one of him in front of the Eiffel Tower, one of him carrying a suitcase, one of him looking at what appears to be a menu—and on the back of the tie were printed the words "Norton is everywhere!" Luckily, we didn't receive any more angel outfits. One was enough. I used to have weird fantasies about some of this cat clothing. Outside of a church in Sag Harbor, there's a bin which the church uses to collect clothing that they disperse to people who need it. I regularly give them my old clothes, knowing they'll get to people who can really use them, but I was always tempted to toss in one of Norton's handmade sweaters. I just liked the idea of some woman sorting through the piles and coming upon a perfectly made, crocheted sweater that was one foot long and had four holes for arms.

Norton also received a lot of photos during his retirement years. People would send pictures of themselves, their cats, their cats' urns—yes, I swear—their houses, their cars (honest, one woman sent a photo of her car so Norton could see what he'd be chauffeured around in if he decided to come pay her a visit). He also was mailed a lot of poems (usually about cats and cat-related obsessions, but I have to say not always; some people just thought he'd enjoy regular poetry), books (occasionally published by a mainstream publisher, more often self-published, sometimes compiled just for Norton and hand bound), and then many useful items such as food (an English fan periodically sent him rabbit-flavored cat treats) and water bowls, beds, blankets, cat passports, and a wide variety of toys.

A lot of people tried to meet him, too.

For the most part, I'm pretty friendly to Nortonphiles. After all, I'm partly responsible for making people like my cat, so when they do indeed want to express their admiration for him, who am I to blow them off? I respond to almost every letter (except the ones telling me I'm speeding on my way to rot in hell for eternity) and I'm even usually polite on the phone when strangers call me up to talk cat stuff (Although, I must say, I don't like that too much; it's a bit audacious to call someone at home, in my opinion. It's why only my office number is listed now, not my home phone). But one time Norton, Janis and I were in Sag Harbor, relaxing on a sunny summer Sunday, when we got a phone call from someone and the conversation went exactly like this:

Man on Phone: Hello, is this Peter Gethers?

Me (suspicious; immediately recognizing that familiar cat-nut tone to the voice): Who's calling, please?

Man on Phone: My name's Bob Flayman (name changed to protect the cat insane). My wife and I are big fans of Norton's and we're trying to reach the same Peter Gethers who wrote those wonderful books.

Me (still suspicious, but warming to the words "wonderful books"): Yes, this is Peter.

Man on Phone: Oh great. I'm sitting in the car with my wife, we're just a couple of blocks away from you and we wanted to come over and meet Norton.

Me: What?

Man on Phone: We're in Sag Harbor and we're very close by, so we thought we'd come say hello.

Me: What?!

Man on Phone: We're big, big fans and—

Me: How do you know where I live?

Man on Phone: Well, you write about Sag Harbor, so we asked a few people and someone told us the name of the street, but we can't find—

I think I'll end the conversation here because I'm afraid, from this point on, I wasn't very polite to this guy and his wife. I explained that it was a Sunday and we were taking it easy and the idea of total strangers stalking my cat and paying a visit was a nightmare right out of "The X-Files" as far as I was concerned. I think I terrified the poor guy. When I hung up, I felt a little guilty and asked Janis if I'd overreacted. She agreed with my basic premise—stalking strangers are bad—but thought I could have been a little subtler. I felt particularly guilty because a few months later, Norton and I actually met these people. We were making a bookstore appearance in Manhattan and a really nice couple came up to us and said that they were the "nuts" who'd called us in Sag Harbor. They couldn't have been more pleasant, and clearly weren't stalkers *or* nuts, they were just two people who were touched and moved and entertained by the things they'd heard about my cat and wanted to see him for themselves. Hard to argue with, really. So I gave them some time with their favorite Fold and, judging by his purring and contented look, Norton gave them a favorable report.

But my favorite thing of all was when I got word in the early part of 1999 that Norton was being inducted into the Feline Hall of Fame. I got a letter asking me if I had any objection to Norton receiving such a prestigious honor, I wrote back and said no, of course not, then the next thing I knew, a fake scroll came in the mail—in case you're wondering what a fake scroll is, it's a piece of cardboard that has a scroll printed on it so the whole thing seems a lot fancier than it is—that said:

HALL OF FAME
Congratulations

NORTON—
The Cat Who Went To Paris

has been inducted
into this year's Hall of Fame
at the Diamond Level
by

Int'l Scottish Fold Association
This is in honor or memory of
CFA cats and catteries who
have enriched our lives.

They invited us to come to the induction ceremony (I think it was taking place in Florida) but I politely declined.

For one thing, it was a long trip to make and I figured that if they didn't even pop for a real scroll, they were hardly going to spring for the airfare. For another, I couldn't escape certain images that kept popping into my brain about who'd actually be attending a ceremony at the Feline Hall of Fame. I had visions of people dressed up in Garfield suits. And humans who'd had plastic surgery to fold their ears so they'd match their cats. When I started dreaming of the big Saturday night banquet—a long table, no utensils, bowls that had our first names stenciled on them and all the dry food we could eat—I knew it was best to stay away.

All in all, Norton took this sort of fanfare in stride. He was happy to be left alone—or, more accurately, to be left alone with me—but he was pleased, too, when people would fawn all over him. None of that changed during this period. The only thing that really did change after we got word of his kidney disease, is that he stopped traveling the way he used to (the most important reason why he missed his Hall of Fame induction).

The thing about kidney failure is that Norton didn't just drink a lot more, and he didn't just need to get his IV drip on a regular basis, he also urinated a lot more than he ever had before. You don't need to know the details—I'll let him keep his dignity, just as I hope no one ever talks about how many times I have to pee if *my* kidneys ever start to go, or any other time in my life now that I think about it—but he was using that litter box as it had never been used before. So I didn't think it was fair or healthy for him to go for long plane rides where no litter box was available. He'd had a great ride—literally—and all I cared about now was making his middle and old age as easy as possible for him.

This certainly made me revise my thinking when it came to my own travel, no question about it. For years, I could just pick up and go wherever and whenever I wanted, knowing that I could always take my best bud along with me. Now, I thought twice about leaving home by plane (driving was no problem—as far as Norton was concerned, a litter box on the floor of the back seat of the car was just as good as being at our apartment). For one thing, I had to make sure that Norton got his drip twice a week. This was crucial and it was a lot easier for me to be with him to make sure it got done. If I had to be away for business, Janis either took him to the vet or the woman Dianne DeLorenzo recommended, Yvette, would show up on the appointed morn and do what needed to be done in Janis's apartment. Mostly, I stayed close to Norton, though. I never said it out loud, since I thought it did sound just the tiniest bit weird, but I preferred being with him so I could make sure he was well taken care of. The curtailing of the travel didn't really bother me. It mostly meant Christmasing in Sag Harbor instead of Goult, which was hardly the end of the world.

It was a small sacrifice to make. And the fact is, I didn't consider it a sacrifice. If it meant spending time with him, I was more than happy to accommodate my cat's new schedule.

In addition to feline-related matters, quite a few things were happening in the human world, too, during this period.

Janis started her own successful business. She became,

and is now, a literary agent. It was a gutsy thing to do—striking out on one's own without a safety net is always somewhat terrifying—but it worked out well. Recently, she even sold a big novel about a guy's relationship with a cat. Several publishers were convinced I had written it under a pseudonym, but it wasn't me, I swear. In fact, one of the reasons this writer picked Janis is that when he first met her he said, properly cowed, "You're Norton's mother, aren't you?"

My mom also did a gutsy thing: she moved back to New York City after over thirty years in Los Angeles. She'd had it with the earthquakes and the driving. Plus, most of her family—her brother and three sisters and many nieces and nephews—were there, and, at age seventy-five, she was just plain in the mood for an adventure. My mother is big on adventure. A year or so earlier, she'd been on safari in Africa and had a stroke. In her tent, in the middle of the night, in the middle of the jungle. She had to walk a mile or two, hop on a raft and get towed across a river, get in a small plane, fly to London where she spent the night, then fly on to New York. When she arrived, she called me and said that she must have picked up a virus because the right side of her body was paralyzed. I called Janis and said, "Does this sound like a virus to you?" and Janis said, "Get her to the hospital, she's had a stroke!" Sure enough, that's what it was. She totally recovered, I'm happy to say, and, while I'm sure she would disagree, I thought the whole experience was almost worth it just to see the expressions on the various nurses' faces when they heard the part about walking two miles through the jungle.

One of the appealing things about my mom returning to the city of her birth (don't worry, Mom, one of the *many* appealing things) was that we now had a baby-sitter—excuse me, cat-sitter—for Norton when needed. It meant that, when necessary, Janis and I actually could go away for a couple of days and know that Norton was in good hands. And we did take advantage of this grandmotherly convenience from time to time. Norton quite enjoyed visiting with my mother. He ate well, there were some excellent nooks and crannies to prowl in her East Side apartment, and she had some pretty interesting dinner parties, which, of course, he attended. One of the appealing things for my mom about returning to New York—other than the mere fact that it wasn't the jungle—was getting to spend more time with her sister Belle, she of the scotch Hurricane fame. Unfortunately, that appeal didn't last very long because three months after my mother moved here, Belle died from a brain tumor.

She was eighty-three years old, which ain't too shabby, but it still felt like it was way too young because she was so vital and funny, so interested in the things around her and so very entertaining to be around. I was asked to deliver one of the eulogies at Belle's funeral. I agreed to do it and spoke about how, truth be told, Belle was kind of ordinary. She didn't discover the polio vaccine or reinvent the wheel or change the face of the planet. But I went on to talk about how funny she was, and honest, how protective she was of the people she loved, and how I didn't know anyone who was even remotely as generous. I said that I didn't believe that it was actually possible to bring back someone from the dead, but that I was reserving my judgment when it came to Belle, until I went out to dinner with my mother to see whether or not a ghostly vision with thinning hair came down from above to pick up the check.

I talked about how Belle managed something that most people never manage. Most people don't get better as they get older—they just get older. Belle actually managed to grow. She went to new places, tried new things, made new friends, got more sophisticated. I said she was a lot more interesting at eighty than she was at forty. And she was a better person—kinder, more understanding, softer. When you added all that up, I observed, that wasn't so ordinary. It was pretty amazing. I ended by saying that Belle realized that what counted in life was having a sense of humor and a sense of adventure and sharing those two things with the people you loved.

What I remember most about delivering that eulogy is that what should have been a five-minute talk took me about three hours to get through because every sentence or two I had to stop speaking so I could sob and blubber beyond belief. I was mortified that I couldn't keep hold of my emotions for a measly few minutes but there you have it. I couldn't. It's a good thing to remember, so you don't ask me to speak at your funeral. My other main memory came after the whole thing was over, when the entire Spring Trip Group—all of whom came to the service—went out for a drink at the nearest bar. We ordered an extra glass of scotch, put it in the middle of the table, and toasted Belle. Our toast was: "To the youngest person we know." At every one of our Spring Trips since then, we always order a glass of scotch and raise our glasses to my mother's sister.

The reason I'm telling you this sad story is not because I feel compelled to jerk a few tears. It's because what happened after Belle's death is both interesting and relevant.

What happened is that my mother, at age seventy-five, realized that she didn't care all that much for certain members of her family. No, it's not that she didn't care for them—she loved them dearly—they just weren't what she thought they were. For her entire life, they were more symbols than people. There was The Brother Who Was The Head Of The Family After Pop Died. There was The Clever Nephew With The Get-Rich Schemes, The Devoted Son, The Good Kid Who Was Taking Over The Family Business. Those images existed partly because that's the way Belle presented them to us (protecting them, since that was her role, but also I think that she genuinely believed in those images; that was her religion—family). But suddenly Belle wasn't around and my mother had to see beyond the images and what she saw was that they weren't at all what they were supposed to be. They weren't kind or generous or brave or even particularly nice, most of them. There were exceptions, of course (note: this is a good writer's trick; now every one in the family can read this and decide that he or she is obviously one of the exceptions).

What I think happened was that with Belle gone, the glue that held everyone together was also gone. Minus that glue, it ceased to be a family unit, becoming instead a group of individual personalities. And looked upon as individuals rather than as a family, well . . . it wasn't a pretty picture. In fact, if you count some of my cousins' hairpieces, the picture was *really* grotesque. They did what people always seem to do when the strongest among them disappears: they got petty, they got small, they got greedy and, worst of all, they got mean. In a sense, it was horrible for my mom. She lost the one family member she was closest to— her sister Belle—but she also lost most of the others. By choice, yes, when she had her moment of clarity, but they were still lost.

I know someone whose father died several years ago (his mother had died a few months earlier). He was at the hospital with his dad when the final moment came, and he called his sister to tell her the sad news. He told her that he'd have to stay at the hospital for an hour or so, to take care of the paperwork and other details, then he'd go back to the parents' home, which is where he was staying while he was in town. He got back there just in time to see his sister driving away—having taken all the paintings and other valuables that she wanted out of the house. Almost every family I know has stories like that. I've seen and heard dozens of them. Someone important to the family structure dies, others in the family revert to their neurotic (and usually greedy) worst instincts. It's what death often does to families. It breaks them apart.

As my mother saw her long-held image of her family crumble, she could have done one of two things: she could have crumbled herself, which so many people do, or she could have moved on and picked her own "family." Luckily, she did the latter. Even luckier, her new coterie included some *real* family members—me, my brother, my brother's son (I should probably have listed the grandkid, Morgan, first since he's far and away the fave), Janis, Belle's daughter Beth, Lil (another of my mother's sisters), some other nieces and nephews. In addition, there were many close friends who made the cut; people she trusted and loved. Few people are capable of making this sort of transition at any age. At my mom's age, it's particularly admirable. Of course, she's no stranger to admirable life changes. She also started her career when she was in her early fifties. Now she's written eight or nine cookbooks (including a chocolate book that was *Food and Wine Magazine*'s pick for the very best cookbook published in the year 2000) and is still going strong. She's quiet on the outside but inside she's strong enough to not only make choices, she's determined enough to stay the course once those choices are made.

I think choice is preferable in just about any situation, particularly when it comes to who you wind up trusting and loving. It's worked fairly well for me, too. I've had the same best friend since I was eight years old. Most of my other good friends I've held on to for years. Janis you already know all about. And, of course, most of all there was Norton.

Most of my friends are real friends. I feel like they could call me up and ask me to do just about anything and that I could do the same. If you don't feel that way about friends or your chosen family, my attitude is "what's the point?" I tend to push people away at the beginning, but if they get through the radar, once they're in, they usually stay. And that's the reason I wanted to talk about Belle's death. Because thinking about her life, seeing the impact her death had on my mom, giving the eulogy and focusing in on what was important, all served to hammer home the fact that I was pretty happy with the family I'd picked for myself. I felt like I'd made the right choices.

And then, in the year or so after Belle died, a few things happened, as they always do, and a few more choices had to be made.

Some peripheral friends fell by the wayside. A longtime friendship fizzled. There were a couple of divorces and sides eventually were chosen. I wrote a best-selling thriller under a pseudonym, got a chunk of money, spent time with my cat in Washington Square Park and used that money to buy my (and his) dream apartment, right near the dog run.

In the few months it took to fix up the apartment, Norton and I alternated living between Sag Harbor and Janis's apartment. In Sag Harbor, I took him to Turetsky for his twice weekly shots. In the city, that wonderful woman Yvette came to administer his treatments.

Then all the contracting work was done and I was on the verge of moving in. I was absolutely ecstatic. There we were, Norton and I, about to take over a gorgeous apartment, overlooking the park, steps away from his favorite spot in the entire city.

Finally it came: moving day.

Life was perfect.

And then I had to rethink all my choices and all my thoughts on family and what was and wasn't important. I even had to rethink the *concept* of choice.

Because on the day I moved into my dream apartment, I found out that my cat had cancer.

CHAPTER 9

THE CAT WHO
HAD A WILL
TO LIVE

What Norton had developed was a slow-growing, low-grade lymphoma in his liver.

I knew this because after doing so well with his kidney failure for so long, he began to lose weight. Even though he was eating to his heart's content. He'd also begun to throw up more than usual (I know, I know, how can you tell with a cat? But I could tell, believe me). So I took him in to see Dianne DeLorenzo and she looked concerned, ran some tests, then she called me first thing in the morning—while I was standing in my brand new living room—and told me about the cancer.

It was a fairly similar situation to my session with Dr. Turetsky when I heard about the kidney problem. My new vet told me that there were many things that could be done, that we'd caught it very early, that this did not necessarily mean what she was sure I thought it meant. I told her I understood all that and I did, I really did, but when I hung up the phone, I picked Norton up and cradled him in my arms, kissed him on top of the head, told him I loved him about twenty times, and I bawled like a little baby until I absolutely couldn't cry anymore.

When I decided I was composed, I made a few instant decisions.

One was to call Janis and tell her. That's when I found out I wasn't all that composed because I think what I actually said was, "Well, Dr. DeLorenzo called and . . ." And that was it. Then it was another crying jag. Janis waited me out very patiently. When I could finally speak, I tried again, didn't do a whole lot better, but I did manage to convey the gist of the situation. She asked if I wanted her to leave work and come over, but I said no, that I was fine, I just needed to get used to the idea. Truer words were never spoken. I did in fact need to get used to the idea that my beloved cat was not sick now, he was dying.

The second decision was one I couldn't implement for another hour. That was when Yvette came over to give Norton his IV drip.

Yvette was a terrific person, a black woman who had worked for several vets, loved animals, and was incredibly good with Norton. She cooed things like "pretty boy" and "sweet baby" at him and he was a sucker for that. Periodically, when she came, she tried to show me how to do the dastardly thing myself. Even though it would cost her money, she kept telling me that it would be much nicer for my cat if he were receiving the treatment at my hands. Every time she'd tell me this and then show me what to do,

I knew she was right—but I still couldn't bring myself to do it.

Except this was my second decision. My cat was now genuinely ill and, much to my shock, one of the first things that ran through my mind was that I wanted to be the one to take care of him. I didn't want to be distant or disconnected. And I didn't even want things to be nonmessy and safe. I wanted to do whatever needed to be done and I wanted to start doing it immediately.

So when Yvette walked in the door, I told her that Norton had cancer and that I wanted to start giving him the IV. I also told her not to tell anyone—not about my out-of-character decision, about the cancer. I know it might sound silly, but I didn't want people to know. As weird as it seems, I wanted to give Norton a little more privacy. He wasn't like normal cats—people not only asked me about him constantly, people drove hundreds of miles to meet him! When I'd have dinner with friends, they would almost always ask me how Norton was doing, if he'd been anywhere good lately, if he was up to anything special. It was a little like having a teenaged son. A *precocious* teenaged son. People were very curious about almost every detail of his life and I knew that would include his illness. I believed Dianne when she told me that he was in no immediate danger, that he was not going to die right away, so as always, I did for him exactly what I would have done for myself: I kept quiet, so he could go on leading as normal a life as possible and not have people feeling sorry for him.

I paid Yvette but told her I was going to do things myself today. She began to set up the drip so she could show me how to do it. I told her it was unnecessary. She'd shown me plenty of times, I understood exactly what had to be done. I just had to go ahead and do it. She then stepped back and waited but I told her she didn't have to stick around, I wanted to do this by myself. She didn't look thrilled with this decision, but I knew that I'd never be able to do it with someone watching. This was between me and my cat. It was personal.

So Yvette left, shaking her head (Hmmm, do you sense a theme running through my life?) and there I was, alone with Norton and that damn plastic bag.

I'd seen Yvette do this very often, so I followed her example. She always did it in the bathroom. It was a small, confined space, which made it easier for her and, she said, made Norton more comfortable. It was easy to attach the bag so the liquid flowed easily, and one could sit comfortably. Made sense to me. So no more dining room table for the Kid. I put the bag in the bathroom sink, which was filled with hot water, to warm up the liquid. Then I hooked the whole contraption up to the rod that held the shower curtain. So far so good. I still stuck with the pink needles—yes, it would take longer but I wasn't confident that I'd get one of those giant green suckers into my cat without killing him (or me). I hooked up the tube, got the needle ready, put Norton in my lap exactly the way I'd seen Yvette do it. Then I leaned over and whispered for a minute or two in his little folded ear. Not just nonsense babble, either. I said that I really loved him, that I'd never hurt him, and I asked him to please, please, please be good and not to run away while I did this, even if I didn't do it perfectly, because it was really important and I needed his help.

Did I really and truly think he understood me?

Well . . .

Well . . . *yes.*

Okay, damnit, I admit it! *I did.* Honest to god. I was totally, 100 percent convinced he knew exactly what I was saying.

And I still think so.

Because here's what Norton did. I gathered his skin up between the thumb and two forefingers of my left hand, just as I'd been taught, put the needle in (I heard a tiny little pop that let me know I'd done it successfully) flicked the switch so the liquid began flowing through the tube and into his body, and the entire time my cat sat there and purred his little head off.

After about thirty seconds, I relaxed. I didn't realize I'd been quite so tense but I guess I was because it was like coming out of a trance. I realized that I was sitting in my bathroom, a purring cat on my lap, and I'd done what I'd been dreading doing for a year and a half. I began to pet Norton, firmly stroke his side and then his head while the solution flowed into him, and I kept telling him what a wonderful guy he was. I thanked him profusely and when I did—I'm not kidding now—he meowed in response. A soft, gentle meow. Just one, so I knew it was a specific answer. And now I have to tell you that not only am I sure he understood what I'd been saying, I'm positive I understood what *he* was saying.

He was saying: *thanks.*

After that, it was easy as pie. In fact, these sessions weren't just chunks of time I managed to get through, they were blocks of time I genuinely looked forward to. As time progressed, Norton needed the drip more than twice a week. Eventually, he needed it every day. And every single day, they were my favorite ten minutes in that day. We'd go into the bathroom, close the door. Norton would nestle on my lap, purring the moment he was snuggled into the proper position. While he purred, I spoke to him, telling him how great he was, how much I liked him. Then I'd slip the needle in—eventually I even got comfortable using the large green suckers instead of the little pink ones; hey, I was a pro—and he'd purr even louder. We'd sit for five minutes while the soothing liquid flowed into him. While sitting, I'd talk more, he'd purr, occasionally meow in response. Sometimes he'd lick my hand and bury his nose into the crook of my arm. There was never a time I sat there with him when I didn't have the warm feeling that we were both where we wanted to be, doing what we wanted to be doing, which was spending time together and making him feel better.

Here's the other thing I'm absolutely positive of:

Norton was helping me. He knew how nervous I was. He understood how afraid I was of hurting him and screwing up. He understood how worried I was about him. So he helped me. He didn't just stay calm, he went out of his way to be friendly, to show me that what I was doing was okay, that the whole situation was okay. He understood that I was helping him—the daily liquid clearly made him feel healthier and happier; I could see it within seconds of starting the drip process—so he did the same for me. Noncat people might not believe me (although any noncat person who's reading this book has got to be pretty weird, so he or she might believe me at that), but I'll bet when the letters start rolling in after this book is published, I'm going to get a lot of similar stories of cats guiding their owners through difficult situations. And even if I don't, I *know* that Norton took me through the process and showed me how to do it. Showed me that I *could* do it.

I was used to Norton being such a good teacher. He'd imparted valuable life-lessons—forcing them through my thick skull—his entire life.

What I wasn't expecting was just how great a teacher he was.

And what I didn't realize was that the lessons were just beginning.

The next thing I had to deal with was treatment. This went beyond the subcutaneous drip I was finally administering for his kidney failure. This was cancer, after all. This was serious.

I went in to meet with Dianne, who did a good job explaining what was happening to my cat's body. She showed me the results of the blood tests: what was high or low, what was still normal, what was dangerous and had to be closely monitored. She also had done a needle biopsy which confirmed the diagnosis of lymphoma and said that all signs indicated that the cancer had not spread beyond the liver. This was good news. But she also said that I needed to see an animal oncologist. It was the first I knew of such a profession but I said I would willingly make an appointment. Dianne said that it was likely Norton would need chemotherapy.

When Norton and I got home—to get from the Washington Square Animal Hospital to our new apartment we had to walk right through Washington Square Park and past the dog run, so this became our regular routine: going to the vet, Norton in his shoulder bag; stopping on the way back to sit among and check out the frolicking canines—I called Marty Goldstein. I told him about Norton's cancer and, as always, he was not just calm he was extremely comforting. He stressed that what he said might sound odd but that the kidney problem was relatively stable, so other than the cancer Norton was healthy. His appetite was good, everything else was functioning, and the cancer was contained in one small area. "Norton feels good, doesn't he?" Marty asked. I looked at my cat, who was curled up happily next to me on my desk and I said that yes, he felt really good. Marty then told me he was going to talk to Dianne and get her to fax him the results of all the latest tests, then he wanted me to bring Norton up to see him. He'd had extraordinary success treating cancer in animals, as I well knew, and he told me not to worry. He said that the odds were that Norton had a relatively long life ahead of him. There was no need to panic. When I told him about making an oncologist appointment, he told me that was exactly the right thing to do, but he also said that I should talk to him before making any commitment to treatment.

The next day, I took my cat uptown—to the Upper West Side this time—and we went to the cat oncologist.

Remember my unpleasant interlude with the East Side rich cat vet? Well, this was even more unpleasant. I stood by while Norton went through a battery of tests, mostly with nurses, and then the doctor himself came in. He was perfectly nice and recognized both how nervous and upset I was. He gave me some literature to read, pamphlets that explained exactly what cancer was and what the various treatments were, and then he explained to me about the chemotherapy. It was to be administered via shot once a week, as I recall, for six or seven weeks. And before the shots commenced, Norton was to immediately start taking something called prednisone twice a day for two weeks. I tried to ask reasonably intelligent questions but I was in that nether land where nothing seemed quite real. I do remember asking two questions, however. One, would the shots make my cat sick? And two, what would they actually accomplish? In other words, Was I going to be ruining my cat's life just to keep him alive? And if so, for how long would he actually be *kept* alive?

I also remember the doctor's answers very clearly. He explained to me that chemo on cats doesn't cause the same side effects it does on people. He said that Norton would not get ill from these shots. Not at all. And then he said that with the shots, Norton could live as long as nine months. Without them he'd definitely be dead in two months.

Excuse me?

Those were my exact words. It was all I could manage to get out of my mouth.

And he repeated what he said, unemotionally, a throwaway: If I gave him the chemotherapy treatment, my cat had nine months, tops. Without it, it was absolutely certain he couldn't live more than another eight weeks.

I started stammering: "But . . . but . . . but . . . Dr. De-Lorenzo said he could live quite a wh-wh-while." I started to explain that Marty Goldstein even said the cat was fairly healthy other than the cancer but it sounded kind of ridiculous coming out of my mouth.

The oncologist shrugged and said, "It's your choice.

You can do what you want." It was as if he lost interest the second I hinted that I was questioning whether or not I'd go for the chemo. "All I'm saying is that if you don't do it, your cat'll be dead very soon."

That was the end of the consultation. Except that he told me I should make up my mind quickly. If I waited more than a few days, it would be too late.

When I left his office, I felt as if I'd been hit over the head with a sledgehammer. And needless to say, my trip back downtown with Norton was not a happy one.

The second I walked in the door, I called Marty. He calmed me down, talked me out of my hysteria and told me to bring Norton up to his clinic the next morning. Before hanging up, he said, "Hey, I told you not to worry and I meant it. Your cat's going to live quite a while yet."

Not worry?

Oh sure. No problem. Dr. Frankenstein had just told me I had two months left with my favorite creature on earth and I wasn't supposed to worry? Right.

Do I have to bother to say it? I spent the rest of that day and night doing *nothing* but worrying. Then Norton and I got up bright and early the next morning and drove to South Salem.

Marty did his usual gentle poking and probing with Norton, elaborated on a few of the things I'd already heard about his latest tests, x-rays and biopsies, and then said, "It's like I told you. Your little buddy's got cancer—but other than that, he's pretty healthy."

"But the oncologist," I started to moan. "He said—"

And then Marty Goldstein said nine wonderful words: "Doctors are not gods. Sometimes we get things wrong."

I didn't realize you were allowed to say that about doctors. Once the realization sunk in that you were, boy, was I happy.

Marty then went on to elaborate. What he said was that it was certainly a viable option to put Norton on the chemotherapy cycle. He was very reasoned about it and said that it definitely could and probably would help. But he also said that contrary to the oncologist's assertion, there was at least a fifty-fifty chance that the treatment would make Norton sick, to a lesser degree than it would with a person, but sick nonetheless. Marty said that I couldn't make the wrong choice—whichever way I went would be correct. When I asked what he would do, he said that if Norton were young, say five or six, rather than fourteen, he'd give him the chemotherapy. His system could withstand it and it could conceivably knock out or at least slow down the cancer. But at Norton's age, the question was, was I going to go for quality or quantity. He said he could keep Norton healthy and happy for a fairly long time without poisoning him, which is essentially what chemo does. My wonderful, perfect cat wasn't going to live forever, Marty made sure I understood that. But he was not—repeat, *not*—in immediate danger. He was not going to live for just two more months. In fact, Marty doubted very much that the oncologist's nine-month projection was his limit. He said, again, that my pal was happy, felt good and had a genuinely strong will to live. Marty says stuff like that—things like one's cat has a strong will to live—and at first I thought he was pretty much full of it. But he wasn't. And in this instance he was as right as anyone could ever be.

He told me that he wanted to put Norton on an elaborate new system of supplements. He said that I should get blood tests on a regular basis with Dianne DeLorenzo, so we could monitor his progress. If I didn't like the way things were going, I could always go back and opt for the chemo (although Marty would never say this, my interpretation was that the oncologist was full of shit when it came to that, too: there was no reason I had to make my decision overnight). And then Marty said that he wanted to put Norton on a two-day continuous supplement drip to flush out his entire system. I asked how I could keep him on an IV for forty-eight hours and he said that I didn't have to, I was going to leave Norton with him. I started to protest, but he said it was important. He also said he wouldn't leave Norton alone in the clinic overnight—he'd take him home with him.

I took a deep breath, decided I felt a little bit like I was sending my cat off to Mexico to get treated with apricot pits, and said okay. I bit my lower lip to keep from sobbing again, kissed Norton goodbye, got in my car and drove back to the city.

For two days, I paced around my apartment, went to the dog run by myself and felt like an idiot, and worried like crazy. The first night, I called Marty at home to see how Norton was doing. The report came in: Just fine. And he was getting along with Marty's various cats and dogs like gangbusters. In fact, it was going so well, Marty wanted to keep him for one extra day. "Really," he said. "Trust me."

At the end of the seventy-two-hour period (and yes, in case you're wondering, I did call a couple of more times to check on my cat's progress; well, okay, more than a couple—I called about ten times), I headed back upstate and picked Norton up. Naturally, he had totally charmed everyone in the clinic. They were not at all happy to see me, knowing I was there to take him away.

Marty told me the treatment went well. With a big smile, he instructed me to take Norton back to Dianne and, in twenty-four hours, to get another blood test. After that, he said, I should start the new program of supplements and vitamins and get a blood test every three to four weeks.

I said okay, drove back to the city, petting my cat—who, I have to admit, looked particularly healthy and perky—the entire way, and made an appointment at the Washington Square Hospital.

When I got to her office, I told Dianne that I'd made my decision. I was going to see how Marty's treatment went and, for the moment, I was going to pass on the chemo.

I don't think she approved, but she was very understanding. She, too, said I could change my mind at any time. She even said that she could administer the chemo shots, if that would make me more comfortable, as long as the oncologist prepared the proper dosage. I said that it would indeed make me more comfortable, but at the moment I was going to see how this played out without it. I had thought long and hard about this. I really tried to keep it in perspective and I kept telling myself I was talking about a cat, not a world leader or a relative or even just a regular, normal human being. Nonetheless, perspective be damned, I felt as if this were one of the most important decisions I'd ever had to make and I felt very strongly that I had to trust my instincts. And my instincts were, overwhelmingly, to go for quality over quantity. They were to go ahead and do what I'd done so far during all the years I'd spent side by side with my beloved little pal: give him the best possible life he could have, so when it ended there would be no regrets for either one of us.

Once before I'd been faced with a similar situation. When I'd gotten the word that my father was dying, I flew (actually, Norton and I flew together) to be with him. He was still in the hospital then and it looked pretty bad. His doctor pulled me aside and said that when the time came, if I saw my father was in too much pain or had passed the line where we thought his life was no longer worth continuing, he could do something about it. Lowering his voice, he said that he could increase the morphine drip, gradually put my father into a coma and . . . He trailed off but the end of the sentence, the words he didn't and couldn't say were, "and kill him." There was no question in my mind that it was a humane offer. And one I would jump at if it needed to be done. I thanked the doctor—who made it clear that, officially, we had not had the conversation— then I went and explained the situation to my mother and brother. My mom said that she felt it was the right thing to do if the time came when we thought he was suffering too much or if his brain stopped functioning. My dad had made it very clear that he did not want to stick around in any kind of vegetative state. But she also said that she couldn't be the one to do it. My brother was in total agreement but wasn't a hundred percent sure if he could do it, either. I knew that I could and I told them that. So we tacitly agreed that if things got worse, I'd tell the doctor and no one would ever know—including them.

Luckily, it didn't come to that. Just because I *could* do it didn't mean that I *wanted* to. My father perked up slightly, enough to let us know that he wanted to die at home, which is what he did a few days later—naturally, with no artificial acceleration.

I remembered that conversation as if it had happened yesterday and strangely enough, this situation with Norton was a more emotional decision for me. I was weirdly unemotional when talking to my father's doctor. I do know the difference between humans and animals, don't worry. I haven't totally crossed that line yet. But with my dad, it was a question of days, possibly even hours. And it was a question of relieving rather than prolonging the suffering. I didn't even think it was a difficult decision—it struck me as the *only* decision. Now, however, if the oncologist was to be believed, what I was doing was, by my gamble, possibly taking six months to a year from the life of the sweetest, gentlest, most genuinely loving creature I'd ever encountered. I didn't know what kind of suffering would be involved either with or without the treatment. I didn't have a clue. But I tried to think what I would have done for myself—and I realized I'd be doing exactly the same thing. I'd never actually faced up to this question before. Yes, I wanted to live as long as possible. No question about it. But that desire was not as powerful as my longing to live as well as possible. If it were me, I'd try for quality and I'd try for natural.

So that's the decision I made for my cat.

When I realized I'd made the right call was when Dianne called me the day she got the results of Norton's latest blood test.

"I don't quite know what to tell you," she said. I prepared myself for the worst, but that wasn't what she meant at all. "I don't understand it," she went on, "and I don't see how it's possible . . . but after whatever it was that Marty did up there with that drip, the results of Norton's blood test are exactly as if he'd had a very successful chemo therapy treatment."

Thus began my new stage as primary caregiver to a cat.

When we were out in Sag Harbor, I made a special trip over to see Drs. Turetsky and Pepper and I told them about the cancer. They were genuinely sad. I think their sadness stemmed partly from the fact that they were compassionate people and loved animals and they didn't like the idea of any of their patients getting cancer. But I also think there was something more going on, particularly with Turetsky who had treated Norton since he'd been a kitten. They had come to be attached to my cat. They liked him, and I think they recognized that elusive will to live, so part of their sorrow was personal. They didn't want to lose him. While I was there they asked about the treatment he was getting and I described everything that had happened so far. Naturally, they put themselves at Norton's disposal but during the next few months, we were mostly going to be in the city, so their contact would, at best, be on the occasional weekend.

Because we were spending more time in Manhattan, my wonderful new apartment soon took on the air of the emergency room at St. Vincent's Hospital. I had the IV drip bag hanging from my shower curtain at all times. In my pantry were several large Baggies filled with needles. Marty said that Norton needed to receive certain new supplements via hypodermic needle, so I had hypodermics lying around, too—and not only did I use them on my cat, I got pretty good at using them.

Feeding Norton was now nearly a full-time occupation.

When Marty sent me my latest box of supplements, it came with an official-looking sheet that had scribbling all over it and a box that explained the codes used so I could understand the scribbling. There were thirteen supplements, each one listed on the left of the sheet. If a liquid, it would indicate that I was to give two or three drops or a third or a half of a dropper. If it was a pill it would tell me to use the whole pill or half or a third (just for the record, it's really a lot of fun to try to chop tiny little pills into thirds!). If it was a powder, I'd get the dosage in teaspoons: a third, a quarter, a half. On the right of this piece of paper, and corresponding with each individual supplement, there were things written such as OD AM O/F. There were also things like BID and EOD and A/D. Thank God for the key code because, even with it, it took a lot of studying before I eventually figured out that OD meant that Norton was supposed to get that particular supplement once daily. BID was twice daily. TID was three times per day. EOD = Every other day. OCC was once or twice per week. A/D meant alternate days, O/A was orally alone, O/F was orally or with food. F/D told me I was supposed to follow the directions on the bottle and A/N was as needed.

So in addition to cooking his fish, chicken or shrimp with rice or pasta and fresh, green vegetables, my routine was as follows:

Every morning, as soon as we were both awake, I

would head into my pantry, pick out several small bottles, place Norton on top of the butcher block kitchen counter and give him half a dropper of something called Super Glandulars, which was described on the label as high-concentration 1050, liver and B-12 glandular. I also gave him half a dropper of something that Marty concocted that was simply labeled "kidney." I can't say Norton loved taking this stuff but he never complained, rarely even squirmed. I'd pet him, he'd open his mouth and in the stuff would go. Next, every morn, was Hepaticol Drops, four drops' worth. The label described this tasty brew as Homeopathic Endocrine Sarcode Combination HHD. Yum yum yum. Every other day (EOD if we remember our secret code) in the morning, Norton got two or three drops of Milk Thistle Seed. Each evening he was given different drops. His predinner warm-up was small doses of Renal Drops and D.A. Gland Formula 1010. For pills, in various combinations at various times during the day, he got Cod Liver Oil (softgels), some truly weird-sounding thing called Tang-Kuei 18, Lipotrope, Beta-Thyme, Hemaplex and a very foul-smelling Raw Kidney Concentrate which had to be crushed up into a powder. As if this weren't enough, he also got two additional powders mixed in with his meals, Psyllium Husks Powder and Vet-Zimes Formula V5. And I'm not done yet, because Marty gave me some additional pills that basically had many features of the chemotherapy treatment: Natural Cortisone. To top it all off, Norton was quite often nauseous, so Dr. Pepper gave me an antinausea prescription for something called Metoclopram while Marty provided the all-natural version. Both pills were a great help but even with them, for some periods of time Norton would throw up once or twice, even three times a day. This was practically the most heartbreaking thing of all for me, listening to him cough and choke and spit up, knowing there was nothing I could do but hold him and rub him and try to soothe him. Often, in the middle of the night, I'd hear him down on the floor, giving that little cough of his that I came to know so well. It meant he was struggling to get something out of his system. He never did it in bed—he'd always hop down on the floor and try to do it as discreetly as possible—so I'd swing myself out of the covers, find him, and spend five or ten predawn minutes petting him and talking to him to keep his spirits (and mine) up.

The hardest part of all this was getting my stubborn little friend to swallow pills. The drops were no problem, he took those like a champ. He wasn't wild about the various powders that went into his food, but eventually he'd get hungry and have to eat. But the pills. Damn, those were tough! If I cleverly tried to mix them in with his food, I'd come back to check when he was done eating and all the food would be gone—and the pills would be there in the middle of the bowl, licked clean but absolutely whole. If I tried to force them down his throat—and I was terrible at doing this; it's the one thing in which I never got even *close* to vet-level skills—I'd be positive he'd swallowed, go away satisfied, then an hour later I'd see the very same pills lying on the floor in the kitchen, where he'd somehow managed to not only spit them out but leave them in a very visible spot so I'd be sure to know that he'd outsmarted me. Eventually I was able to figure out a way to get them inside him 90 percent of the time. After all, I *was* the one with the larger brain (and if you believe that, I've got a uranium mine in Asbury Park I'd like to sell you). My trick was that I wrapped the pills in a tiny dab of peanut butter, which

Norton loved. It also was pretty amusing to watch him eat, because the stuff was so good but so sticky that he'd be licking his lips for half an hour afterward. Even with the peanut butter (either smooth or crunchy, he wasn't fussy), occasionally he'd still manage to spit the pills out, but not nearly as often.

My duties didn't end there, either. Every so often, I'd dip a syringe into a vial labeled Adrenal Cortical Extract and zap it into my very accepting cat.

If you're getting the urge to refer to me as Dr. Pete, I'll accept the moniker, because I was also becoming quite adept at reading Norton's medical charts. I had many conversations with Drs. DeLorenzo and Goldstein in which I would study the fax that one or the other had just sent me, then call and observe, "The hemoglobin count is a little low, don't you think?" or, "The phosphorus is right in midrange, that's a big improvement," or, "The creatinine level is still high but it's come down drastically from the last count, so I think things are going well. Maybe we should go OD instead of OED on the kidney drop." I started having lengthy conversations about lecithin deficiencies and digestive enzymes and bilirubin counts and many other things I'd never heard of or wanted to hear of a scant few months earlier.

The other thing that was kind of interesting is how Norton's illness was slowly but surely altering my own life and lifestyle.

I saw the effect of Norton's healthy diet on his behavior. I had come to believe that it was helping to keep him alive. It made sense. Take the poison out of his system, replace it with things that were nutritional and replenishing, naturally his body would be better able to fight off disease.

And that's exactly what happened. So I started doing the same thing. I mean, I didn't start inhaling heaping plates of Vet-Zimes Formula V-5 but I cut out a lot of the fake non-food we all consume on a regular basis and tried to think a bit more holistically, without becoming a nut about it. (Let's face it, who wants to live to 120 if we can't eat the occasional bucket of Popeye's fried chicken, garlic, onion and pepperoni pizza or, best of all, the chocolate caramel dessert thing at the Gramercy Tavern restaurant?) But, overall, I followed my cat's example and began to think that a sensible diet might actually be a good thing. As usual, though, I never should have mentioned this to Janis, who actually knows about most things medical. She, too, saw what was happening with Norton and it had the sobering effect on her of trying to save me the way I was trying to save him. As soon as I showed the slightest interest in my own health, I started getting a fax a day from her: newspaper articles talking about how tomatoes can effectively fight cancer, magazine articles detailing what vitamins to take to combat arthritis, lists of carcinogenic foods, essays on what herbs to take to keep one's vision from disintegrating into a blurry blob. Some of the suggestions I took, others I just *told* her I was taking so she'd stop nagging me, but didn't do a thing about. Generally, though, seeing what holistic treatment did for Norton made me accept it as a very viable way for humans to live.

I also had become much less *afraid* of sickness. And of the messy side of life.

If Norton threw up, and spasms racked his little body, I was more than happy to hold him and massage his throat until he was back to normal. I cleaned up after him constantly, sometimes all day long, because slowly and gradually he was becoming incontinent. At least two or three times a week, he didn't seem to make it to his litter box. But I didn't care. So eventually I'd have to get a new carpet (or couch or hell, even a new apartment), what difference did it make; the only thing I wanted was for his life to be enjoyable and pain-free. I liked feeding him all the weird supplements he was taking, I liked holding him when I gave him his shots, I even didn't mind wrestling with him to get those pills down his throat. It was contact, physical and emotional, and I am absolutely convinced that, even as his body was failing, he knew that this contact was bringing us closer and closer together.

I appreciated the time we spent together more than I ever did. We'd go for walks together or sit in the park almost every day. At home, Norton had always been independent. He was not a lap cat. He liked to keep an eye on me, and usually stay in the same room I was in, but he rarely came up and collapsed on my lap when I was reading or watching TV. Now, however, he seemed to want to be as close to me as I did to him. He was *always* by my side. When I was working, he napped on the desk next to my computer, inches from my touch. If I was relaxing on the couch, he'd hop on up and manage to slide in next to me, his body brushing against my thigh. In bed, he was back to sleeping right next to me on the pillow, which he hadn't done on a regular basis since he'd been a small kitten.

It was as if he were saying, *I trust you.* He knew that I understood what he was going through and somehow our roles had become slightly reversed. In all the years past, if I had the flu and felt rotten, Norton would always be there, providing a comforting presence and touch. When I had my shoulder operation and spent a few days in bed, moaning and groaning and not being able to move, he never left my side, purring and pushing his nose into my hand or my face to let me know that he was concerned. Now, he was coming to me for that same comfort and I was only glad that I was able to provide it for him.

If forced to examine the details of my own life, I will admit that I am a selfish person. I have lived my life the way I want to live it, within reason of course (I haven't actually murdered all the people who work for the phone company, which I have often been tempted to do, so I understand that my selfishness and self-absorption have limits). I have defied several conventions and tried to follow my own course as much as possible. I've had a strange career because I opted to do several things instead of focusing on just one. As a result, I've made a lot less money than I could have, but money has never been a motivating factor for me. My own satisfaction is much more of a guide. On a personal level, I have an excellent and long-lasting relationship but have never gotten married (and just to anticipate more letter writers, no, we still don't even live together—I'm too selfish and, luckily, she's got certain saintlike qualities that allow for it). Marriage is another convention and ritual I don't believe in. No one is going to tell me, by saying a few words, giving me a piece of paper and having me exchange rings, that I now have something permanent and valuable. *I'll* decide what's permanent and valuable, that's my attitude. I've never had kids. Always thought I'd want 'em eventually but guess what—I'm in my late forties and "eventually" still isn't here. I've turned down big jobs and chosen most of my relationships with people purely on the basis of friendship rather than usefulness or value to me. And when you add it all up, I think it's fair to say that I'm one of the few people who truly likes the life he's leading, *really* likes it and has few regrets. A very big part of that is because I've been able to live selfishly.

But treating Norton, once he got cancer, taught me the joys of living unselfishly. No, "taught" isn't exactly the right word. It's not something that can *be* taught. It's something that must be experienced. And what I experienced was the feeling—and the ensuing knowledge—that there was practically nothing I wouldn't do for my cat if it allowed me to give him just a little bit of the same pleasure he'd given me for most of my adult life.

As that great philosopher Søren Kierkegaard once said: "Go know."

Okay, that's kind of a paraphrase.

Anyway . . .

I took care of Norton as best I could and he did just fine. He was happy, he seemed healthy, he did stuff, he was in no pain. The two-month deadline given to me by the oncologist came and went. So did the nine-month deadline. A full year passed since the cancer had struck him and then *another* six months passed. Outwardly, Norton showed no signs of really weakening or being in any way un-Norton-like. Except for the still too prevalent throwing up and the occasional accident away from the litter box, he was the same old Scottish Fold wunderkind.

For almost two years.

He had that will to live, I guess.

Then I noticed he was losing weight again.

And he seemed a little wobbly when jumping from bed to floor. Then just walking around . . .

And those damn blood tests kept getting faxed to me

and too many counts were suddenly either too low or too high.

So I went back to Dr. Dianne DeLorenzo to see what was what.

And what it was was the beginning of the end.

CHAPTER 10

THE CAT
WHO WENT BACK
ON THE ROAD

The cancer was spreading.

That was the word from Dianne DeLorenzo and this time I accepted it. I could see it. For the first time since I'd first met my little cat, when he was six weeks old and fresh off a plane from Los Angeles, he looked frail.

The treatments continued, of course, and I took as perfect care of him as always. One of the bonuses, as far as Norton was concerned, was that I basically said, "Fuck it," and decided he could now eat whatever he wanted. I wasn't going back to the horrendous canned cat food—that would have been like saying to a dying man, "Okay, you get to eat nothing but McDonald's the rest of your life"—but I knew that what he particularly liked was shrimp. He liked it much more than chicken, much much more than hamburger meat or even steak. It wasn't the absolutely best thing for him but my cat loved shrimp so at this stage of his life shrimp is what he got. Twice a day if he so desired, although I tried to vary it so he wouldn't get sick of it (although he *never* seemed to get sick of it). I'll even confess that I usually bought this shrimp at the best seafood markets, at places like Balducci's, so it was fresh and perfect. Once, though, I was at my neighborhood supermarket and I was pressed for time, so I bought a packet of shrimp from their fish section. It was perfectly fine, it just wasn't, you know, the best. But as I was heading to the checkout line, an elderly woman, and clearly a woman who lived on a budget, stopped me and told me that the shrimp I was buying looked delicious. Without thinking, I said that it was for my cat. She said, "You must be very well off. I buy that twice a year for myself—as a treat." Horrified at my thoughtless blunder, I tried to stammer my way out of it and said, "Well, I like my cat quite a lot." And she got a wistful, faraway look in her eyes and said, "I'd like to *be* your cat." I told her that a lot of people felt the same way, and I asked if she'd mind if I bought her a little present. She said she wouldn't mind one bit, so I bought and gave her another couple of pounds of shrimp. She was very pleased.

In addition to his daily, and often twice-daily, pleasure when munching on his *crevettes*, Norton still had some major periods of remission where he felt absolutely fine. A couple of these remissions came after Marty prescribed Epogin, which brings the red blood cell count back up and stops the anemia. The more amazing remission came when Marty sent me something called Poly-MVA. Marty had recently seen it work wonders, and even Dianne's partner, another superb doctor named Ann Wayne Lucas, had witnessed something remarkable in a cat who'd taken it. Dr. Lucas had seen a tumor—a lymph cancer on this cat's nose, one that everyone thought was days away from killing the cat—not just shrink but flat out disappear.

So I administered a few doses of Poly-MVA, as instructed (for this one I had to use a hypodermic needle) and sure enough certain things improved and Norton was a lot happier, but by this time it was a stopgap treatment and even I had to admit it. I had to accept, once and for all, that sooner rather than later, I was going to be catless.

I cried a little in Dianne's office as we discussed all this (All right, all right, get off my back—I cried *a lot*! But I'm trying to remain somewhat manly here). She didn't know exactly how long Norton would live. It could be several months still, she said. But it could be weeks. Once this wretched disease starts to spread, it can spread quickly. And it can wreak havoc.

She also brought up something that I had never even considered. No, that's not right. It was something that I had not ever let myself consider. She started to explain to me that, at some point—not *now*, she immediately stressed when she saw the look on my face—but when and if it was necessary, I'd have to make a decision about putting him to sleep. I nodded, as if this was something I could absolutely deal with like a mature adult, then I started to ask a question and burst out sobbing. This went on for a few seconds until I wiped my tears, composed myself, decided I was okay, and started to ask the question all over again. I got maybe the first word out of my mouth, burst back into tears, and had to sit there in her office, chest heaving, feeling like an idiot. Luckily, Dianne had experienced this before—many times before—and she could not only anticipate my questions and finish my sentences for me, she could give me compassionate answers. This was a good thing because, try as I might, I could not speak.

"What about . . . when . . . when . . ." I'd say and then the crying would start again.

"What about when it's time," Dr. DeLorenzo would prompt me and I'd manage to nod. "First of all," she said, "you have a great understanding of your cat and you'll *understand* when it's time. You'll know. I promise you. And you shouldn't do it until you know it's right."

Then I said something like, "And . . . (sob) . . . when it is . . . (sniffle) . . . right . . . (choked back sob) . . . what do . . . ? . . . (torrential tears) . . ."

Dr. DeLorenzo: You can bring him in here.

Me: Will . . . ? . . . (major crying jag)

Dr. DeLorenzo: Yes. I'll do it. You can be with him and even hold him if you want.

Me: (Not even close to getting a real word out, just body-wracking sobs.)

In between my bouts of hysteria, Dianne managed to explain that if I wanted Norton to die at home, there were some doctors who'd come to the apartment to perform the service. But I said no, I wanted her to do it. Well, I didn't actually say it. I gasped and snorted and got a few syllables out that sounded something vaguely like it. I then tried once again to ask a practical question. I wanted to know about cremation. I tried two or three times on this one but never actually got past the hard *c* sound without having to go for the Kleenex. Dianne understood, once again, and told me that she could and would handle the whole thing. It was not something I had to worry about.

Then she said something wonderful, both sad and sweet and totally accurate.

"The only thing wrong with our pets," Dianne DeLorenzo told me, "is that they don't live as long as we do."

I was giving Norton his IV drip every day now and those minutes we spent all alone were minutes I knew we both valued. We were connected as two living creatures rarely are. And because I was so aware of that connection, I had an idea.

I kept it to myself for a little while. Let it percolate to see if it would linger or disappear. It lingered. Particularly when we went out to Sag Harbor in mid-April. Over that weekend, the idea took form—and then took over my thoughts completely.

While in Sag Harbor, Norton was as active as he'd been in weeks and weeks. He insisted on jumping on and off the bed, even though he really couldn't jump very well. At the end of each leap, he'd mostly sprawl and slide along the bedroom floor's wooden planks. I showed him how he could use the antique trunk at the foot of the bed as a midway stopping point—both on the way up and on the way down—but he didn't like that idea. He finally used it to get up on the bed but he refused to acknowledge its existence when he'd hop down. I think he felt it wasn't dignified. A cat was supposed to be able to get down on his own from a bed, so that's what he was determined to do. For these few days, he absolutely refused to give in to the fact that his body was playing such awful tricks on him. When we'd leave him downstairs, even for a few minutes, he'd somehow go up the stairs to join us (this was the first time he had trouble climbing; each step was difficult for him, because it was steep, but that didn't stop him). He ate a ton, more than he had in a long time. All weekend he meowed for food and whenever I'd put some in his bowl, he'd gobble it down.

I have this theory about aging. I think that as people get older, they become more and more like their real selves. If you're cranky as a young person, the older you get the more crotchety you'll be. If you're fearful, old age brings terror. If you're rigid, when you hit a certain time of life you'll be as unbendable as a flagpole. If you're a loner, there will come a time when all you're going to want is to become a hermit. Age brings out one's quirks and allows them to flourish and, I guess, it brings down defenses and restraints so there's no choice but to *let* them flourish. My cat was a perfect example. As Norton aged and got closer to death, he got sweeter. Gentler. And even more courageous. It was quite something to see.

Over the past few weeks, I had finally told people that Norton was sick. It was now obvious, so I didn't think there was any more reason for secrecy. Once the word was out, calls started coming in. I was actually a little stunned. People were calling to see how I was holding up, sure, but really they were concerned for Norton and wanted to show that concern. He was one of *them*—and they wanted to acknowledge that. Susan Burden (she's the one we visited the day Norton saw President Clinton) told me that she called her mother down in Florida to tell her that Norton had cancer and she said her mother burst into tears. Nancy Alderman called to check up on the little guy. After I filled her in, she put her son Charlie on the phone. We chatted and hung up. Nancy called me back a few moments later because she said she'd asked Charlie if he'd asked me about Norton. Charlie—in a hushed tone—said, "Oh no, I didn't *mention* Norton." There was something very sweet about a nine-year-old boy trying to protect me from the pain he knew I was experiencing.

Several writers I worked with called me during this period to see how my guy was doing. My close friend Micheline called every day. Norm Stiles, who now had his own amazingly adorable Scottish Fold named Gozzie, called practically hourly. I had talked to my old friend Roman Polanski, who had shared many experiences with Norton in Paris. Roman was pained to hear about my cat's decline and he called that weekend in Sag Harbor to check up on him. Almost everyone I knew who also knew Norton called to check up on him that weekend. It was overwhelming.

I took him in to see Drs. Turetsky and Pepper, for the first time in months; they were surprised at Norton's fragility. Pepper examined him very, very gently. When I told him that Norton was having trouble going to the bathroom, that it seemed to really pain him each time he got in the litter box, the vet gave him an enema (this was the only thing I felt I just couldn't bring myself to do, although I think we all know by now that if I had to, I would have). Dr. Pepper also weighed Norton. He was down to five pounds (from his normal nine). "He's an amazing little cat," Turetsky said when I was leaving and I knew that was his way of paying respect and saying his farewell to his long-time patient. Which is really why I had brought him there.

I waited until we got back to the city before I finally discussed my big idea with Janis. I expected her to say that I was crazy or, at the very least, a sentimental fool. Instead, she smiled and nodded and told me that she thought it was an excellent idea. When I tried to argue myself out of my own plan, she told me to stop thinking so much and just get on with it. I needed closure, she said. I needed something special that would help me get over what was sure to be a devastating loss. She said that my idea was indeed special. And that it felt right. And then she said what I really wanted to hear: that Norton would love it.

So I went to see Dr. DeLorenzo and told her what I wanted to do. She thought it was a little odd but by now she was used to odd when it came to me and Norton, so she gave me the thumbs-up. She said that I should be prepared for the fact that Norton could fade at any time—and fade quickly—but for the moment he looked to be able to handle the adventure I was proposing. Then she asked the key question: Was *I* able to handle the adventure I was proposing?

I told her I wasn't sure. But I was going to give it a shot.

My idea was a simple one: Norton and I had spent much of our lives together traveling. We'd been all over Europe. We'd flown around most of America. We'd spent a huge portion of our existence together in hotels and motels and fantasy houses in medieval villages, in cars and planes and buses and boats. We'd dined out together in exotic places, sharing meals and unique experiences. We'd gone to major sporting events and nightclubs and offices and sales conferences and we'd met interesting, weird, brilliant, sometimes crazy people. Quite simply, the most fun both of us had had over the past sixteen-plus years was when we were on the road doing what we both liked the best: experiencing new things, taking chances and doing our best to keep life from ever getting dull and predictable.

So here's what I wanted to do: I wanted to go back on the road with Norton.

I wanted to share some of his final moments on earth the way we'd shared so many of the vital moments that had defined both of our lives. Together. Just the two of us. I wanted to do what so many people never got a chance to do.

I wanted one final trip with my cat so I could say goodbye.

I moved quickly, decided that the way to go was to see some new sights, have a few new adventures, but mostly return to some of Norton's favorite places.

I planned this so thoroughly, taking care of every little detail, making sure that I thought of absolutely everything and every possible contingency, that I felt a little bit like I was going off on my honeymoon.

"I think I might have crossed the line and become a total lunatic," I said to Janis the morning we were leaving.

"You *think?*" she said. And as I winced, she gave Norton a gentle and tender pat, gave me a not-so-gentle but equally tender kiss, and told us, "Just go. Just go and the two of you have a very, very good time."

I had packed everything that might be needed: several

litter boxes (one for the floor of the front seat, one for the back, so he would never be more than a step away) several bags of litter, towels (in case Norton didn't make the litter boxes, either in the car or in the places we were staying), drip bags, needles, medicine, bottled water, food (I even brought some fresh-cooked shrimp in a small insulated Styrofoam box, packed in ice, in case I couldn't find something that Norton liked along the way). I had special travel bowls for food and water so Norton could have whatever he wanted while we drove. And I took a whole bunch of catnip (I figured it was like medicinal marijuana. There's nothing my cat liked better, in the whole world, than a little taste of catnip, so I figured why not keep him rolling in the stuff). My little red car looked like a MASH unit by the time it was full.

When I was certain there was absolutely nothing left to take that he could possibly need, I put him in his shoulder bag—he weighed so little now and the impact of that hit me so hard as we were walking to the car that carrying him on my shoulder nearly brought tears to my eyes—and we were off.

I knew I'd made the right decision almost as soon as the drive began.

I have a small, 1989 BMW convertible. My father bought it soon before he died and he loved this car. My mother loved it just as much but when she moved to New York she didn't need or want it anymore. So I was allowed to buy it from her cheap (*very* cheap: one dollar). And I was as crazy about this automobile as both my parents were. But not as crazy as Norton was.

You see, Norton had discovered something about the car the very first winter that I had it. He and I were driving together from Sag Harbor back to the city. Norton was sitting in the passenger seat and when I glanced over at him I thought he seemed particularly happy and content. He was purring away as only the happiest of cats could. At first I was quite touched, thinking he was just pleased to be with me, and so near (Janis wasn't making this drive, so Norton didn't have to stay in the back). But that wasn't it at all. What I realized was that the car had switches in between the two seats: black switches that activated individual seat warmers. Norton was so happy that particular winter two-hour drive not because he was next to me but because he'd accidentally hit the switch and his seat was toasty warm. And so was he.

At least I'd *thought* it was accidental.

Naturally, I had once again underestimated my pal.

Because from then on, every time Norton was in the car and allowed to sit by himself in the front seat, he'd casually reach over, flick the seat warming switch, curl up in a ball and settle in for a perfect ride.

As we were pulling out of the city on our final voyage, I wondered if he was too feeble to bother or if he'd go for the heat.

The answer, of course, was yes, heat all the way. Cancer be damned, he was going to be as comfortable as he could be. Before we'd even gotten a full block away, his paw was stretching in my direction, the button was pressed, and Norton was purring away.

He purred all the way to Washington, D.C., which I'd decided was going to be our first stop. I had not spent much time there and neither had Norton, but it seemed like a fitting place to begin. We checked into the Madison Hotel—nice, not far from the White House, and reasonably cat-friendly. I wasn't sure if he'd be up to any sight-seeing but once we were settled and he'd had a little shrimp, he seemed quite game. So we headed out and Norton saw the Lincoln Memorial for the first time, and the Vietnam War Memorial. We also sat for a bit in the park across from the White House but there was no dog run, so for Norton it was not nearly as interesting as what he was used to. After a while I decided he'd had enough excitement, so we headed back to the Madison.

Because we'd done so much touring, I thought it would be better if we shared a room service meal instead of dining out. Norton was grateful to get his second IV drip of the day—I'd gone to twice a day for the past couple of weeks; he always seemed to feel so much better afterward—then eat a little grilled chicken and get to bed.

The next morning, we were headed for Pennsylvania, but our first stop was Valley Forge. We got out of the car at the very spot where George Washington crossed the Delaware. I felt like there should be some spiritual or, at the very least, symbolic connection. Something that tied it all together—the beginning and the end, the long ago adventure that created something big and great and the modern adventure that was ending something small and great. But I couldn't find anything and neither, I'm sure, could Norton. We just weren't big on symbols. Nonetheless, it was an impressive spot, awe inspiring as only history can be. So we soaked in the atmosphere, got back in the car, and then we drove back to one of Norton's favorite bed-and-breakfasts, Sweetwater Farm.

For those of you who haven't been paying attention, Sweetwater was the site of my aunt Belle's encounter with the goat on one of our Spring Trips. It was a beautiful and extraordinary place. The main house was an old stone building, going back to the 1700s. There were several out-buildings that had been converted into individual rooms or suites, some stone, some wood. There were many acres of lush land, a swimming pool, and near the pool was a lovely mesh tree swing. By the swing, placed under a large oak tree, were wooden chairs and a wooden love seat.

Cherry trees were scattered around the property and, in the few years since we'd been there with our Spring Group, they'd added more horses, and the fenced-in corrals had been greatly improved.

I checked in with Rick and Grace, the husband and wife innkeepers, who were happy to see me and, as always, happier to see Norton. I could see, however, that they were startled at his appearance. Even just poking his head out of the shoulder bag to say hello, they could tell that he wasn't well. Rick gave him a friendly, soft pat on the head and looked at me sadly. I nodded. I had decided that nodding was, in general, my best course of action, because it was difficult to cry if you nodded hard enough.

We got the same room we'd been in when we first stayed there: a suite in one of the small wooden buildings, the Gardener's Cottage, on the property. There was a porch, a sitting room, a bedroom and a bathroom. And I immediately went about setting it up for Norton's comfort. So he didn't have to move if he didn't want to, I put food and water bowls down in both the sitting room and bed-room, did the same with the litter boxes, and rigged the drip bag up in the bathroom. Then I took him outside and we sat in the shade of the oak tree, on the wooden love seat, for most of the afternoon. I did what were to become my two favorite activities on this trip—I read and I cried.

I guess I should warn you that you're going to have to get used to the fact that you're going to hear a lot about me crying for a while, because I don't think I made it through one whole sentence on this trip without having to stop and let a few tears escape. Sitting on the bench, doing both of those things, sometimes one, sometimes the other, sometimes both at once, Norton mostly sat with me, but he also did a little wandering in the high grass. He didn't wander too far, however. Walking was not his best thing by this time. He reminded me a little bit of Terry Malloy, the Brando character, after he'd been beaten up at the end of *On the Waterfront*, walking into the warehouse so he could break the evil union. Norton was unsteady, he lurched and was usually at a tilt—but, like Brando, he never fell. That strong will, you know. It was still working full blast.

From time to time during the day, when he wasn't either keeping me company or exploring, he'd hop off the bench, do his version of walking, find the perfect sunny spot, settle in and doze. When I was neither reading nor crying, I'd watch him. He looked handsome there in the grass. And because he'd gotten so small, to me he looked young and healthy—like a kitten again. It was a nice thing to see: Norton in the grass, butterflies fluttering, birds chirping everywhere. It was as serene a setting as could be imagined. And it was peaceful. Norton wasn't sick. Not now, not outwardly. He wasn't throwing up. He wasn't in pain. He was just quiet, sitting there in the sun.

He was just fading.

Occasionally, he would meow. A sweet mew, not at all cranky. Norton had a distinctive happy meow—it was brisk, trilling, a "brrrrr-brrrr-brrrr" sound, like a putt-putt motor boat with a tiny bit of a Scottish accent—and this was definitely his happy sound. I think those mews were letting me know I'd done the right thing.

We stayed at Sweetwater Farm for a couple of days. At night, we'd go back to the common room in the main house. I shot pool on the red felt table until the early morning hours while Norton sat in the comfortable wing chair, on top of a thick blanket with a picture of a polo player on it, and watched. But, almost hour by hour, all day and all night, I could see him fade just a little bit more.

Despite the twice daily drips he was getting, Norton wasn't going to the bathroom very often now. I'd had so much medical training by this time, I knew what that meant. His whole system was failing. He was not able to expunge the disease—diseases, really—that had overtaken his body. He had lost so much muscle, that's why he was having trouble walking and jumping and now even performing the normal bodily functions. Even the small intestines need muscle to function—and the cancer had eaten most of Norton's muscle away.

It was all happening very quickly. Two or three weeks earlier, my cat did not look sick and did not act sick. Now the disease was in overdrive. It was getting nearer and nearer to the end. I remembered something that Marty Goldstein had told me when I had called him to say that things were getting worse. He compared Norton to the Ukrainian peasants who lived to be a hundred and thirty. They die quickly, he said. We're used to stretching death out—we die for about one-third of our lives. Those peasants are healthy, then, boom, they're gone. That's the way it should be, Marty said. Live a good life, stay healthy as long as possible, then die. That's what was happening to

Norton, he said, and I should be grateful that he was getting to go out this way.

I was. Really. I remembered that a few months before, I was with my mother when she'd called her two oldest friends. It was one of the worst conversations I'd ever heard. First the husband answered—this is someone my mother had known for fifty years. I heard my mom say, "Henry, it's Judy." Then she said it again: "*Judy.*" Then she had to say, "Judy *Gethers*," and then I saw this horrified look on my mother's face as she realized he didn't have a clue who she was. She tried to explain but the more she did the worse it got. She finally asked him to put Vera, his wife, on the phone, but when he complied, my mother started to cry—I guess you can tell we're related—and couldn't talk to her. I had to get on the phone and make a few excuses before hanging up. It was just a terrible thing to be privy to. It was something that shouldn't happen to anyone, that ebbing of one's faculties, that state of living but not really living. So yes, I was glad that wasn't happening to my cat. But it didn't make what *was* happening any easier.

I thought about heading home with him after our stay at Sweetwater, but as Dianne DeLorenzo had said, I understood my cat. I had a very strong sense of what was right or wrong and I decided he was enjoying this. I truly think he understood the whole concept of closure and that he wanted to play this through to the end as much as I did.

So we headed off in our mobile medical unit, a.k.a. The Red Beamer, to go to Charlottesville, Virginia.

This was another town that Norton had loved and when the car cruised in, I drove slowly through the city's downtown streets as Norton sat up, craned his neck, and looked out the window at the sights. We didn't stop for lunch, though. I wanted to get Norton all set up at the hotel, so we went straight to one of the great inns in the country, the Clifton.

It was a thrilling place, for both of us. The manor house was built in 1799 by Thomas Randolph, a governor of the state and the husband of Thomas Jefferson's daughter Martha. There were all sorts of legends about the house concerning the Civil War years, when it was owned by John Singleton Mosby, the "Grey Ghost of the Confederacy," who supposedly used secret hiding places in the mansion to store supplies and provisions, aiding those Johnny Rebs in their fight against the Yankees.

We were put up in a suite which was, years before, part of the original stable on the property. Even by Norton's high standards for comfort, the place was a gem. It was separate from the main house, providing plenty of privacy, and it overlooked the gorgeous gardens as well as Lake Leanna, the property's private lake. The bedroom had a queen-size bed and beautiful wooden floor and there was a sitting room with a rocking chair and a comfortable window seat. And there was my cat's favorite thing in the whole world: a fireplace.

I put Norton in his bag and took him over to the main house so he could check things out (I'm sure you've picked up by this late point that I didn't want my cat to miss out on anything). The people at the hotel went absolutely wild over him. Everyone came out to meet him. The manager had read the two books about him—a friend of his had given them to him long before I'd thought of bringing Norton down there. The executive chef, Rachel, provided a shrimp wrapped in bacon which, needless to say, my pal gobbled down immediately. Linda, the woman at the desk, told me that she raised dogs but had recently become a cat fanatic—and now had five of them. She sensed that Norton was sick—possibly I gave it away when she asked me how old he was and my eyes welled up with tears, I got short of breath and I had to sit down. It was a pretty good hint. He was sitting up in his bag, his upper body out in the open, and she stroked him gently and told him how beautiful he was. Then she said that even if his body was going to die, his spirit would live on. I responded that I wasn't too sure about people's spirits—but I thought that Norton's spirit at least had a decent chance. She immediately decided I was a heathen—I recognize the look by now—but she clearly didn't hold it against my cat because she kept stroking him and talking to him and he was about as happy as he could be.

That night he was invited to dine in the dining room, breaking *all* their hard and fast rules, but I could tell he was cranky and tired, so I took him back to our room. I brought with us some more of the chef's shrimp in bacon, so I knew Norton wouldn't be unhappy dining alone.

I guess I needed a break—it was a little bit like traveling with one's invalid grandfather—because dining alone, I was absolutely ravenous and I felt calmer than I'd felt in a long time. I ate well (the Clifton's restaurant is superb; the meal was highlighted by local fresh vegetables and edible local flowers, including a champagne pansy sauce—no cracks, please—that was poured over the grapefruit sorbet dessert) and drank a bottle of Virginia red wine. I wanted to drink about seven bottles, but I settled for draining every last drop of the one.

By dessert time, though, I couldn't stand it—so I went

and got Norton and brought him back for the final course. He was unobtrusive sitting in the chair opposite me. He meowed once or twice, I gave him a couple of teaspoons of the champagne pansy sauce, which he quite liked, and then we strolled back to the room, both of us content.

The only thing that worried me at the Clifton was the bed. It was beautiful and large—but it was also dangerously high with Norton being so fragile. I didn't want to risk his jumping off and hurting himself but, selfishly, I wanted him with me. So for that night, I slept on my back, cradling him in my arms. Three or four times during the night, he moved, wanting to get down. So I carried him to his food or water or litter box. He did what he wanted to do, then I'd put him back in my arms, get back into bed and go back to sleep—until the next time he wanted down. We both seemed quite happy with the arrangement.

The next day, Norton was doing well so we did a little touring. I took him to Monticello, which I genuinely think is the one place every person in America must visit. What you come away feeling, after a tour of Jefferson's home, is not just a sense of pride, awe and historical perspective. What you mostly leave with is a sense of total and absolute inadequacy.

In case you ever are feeling smug or self-satisfied, consider this: Thomas Jefferson had engraved on his tombstone the three accomplishments of which he was most proud. Being president of the United States wasn't one of them! For the record, he picked writing the Constitution of the United States, writing the Religious Freedom Act of the state of Virginia and founding the University of Virginia. I know that if *I* were ever president of the United States, I'd pretty much *have* to put that as one of my three top accomplishments (And you'll have to trust me here: you don't want to know what the other two are. The only hint I'll give is that one of them involves a former Miss Bermuda).

When you go through Monticello, you find out that Thomas Jefferson brought the first roses to America. He was our country's first and greatest gardener. He grew the first grapes and was America's first vintner. He brought French food to us. He built the first clock that not only kept time but kept track of the days for up to a week. In his study upstairs, he had (because he invented it) the first copying machine. I swear! There was this amazing contraption that he concocted because he knew he was Thomas Jefferson and that people would want records of everything he did. The way this thing worked is that whenever he wrote something, the machine was attached to his arm, a pen was attached to the machine and the whole thing moved along with him in a mirror image, making a duplicate copy of what he was writing. So you walk out of there thinking that Jefferson invented food, wine, government, freedom, the Xerox machine, America and just about everything else you've ever heard of. Just walking to the parking lot with Norton, I was certain that not only had Jefferson invented parking lots, he probably invented the very air we were breathing!

After Monticello, Norton still seemed pretty active, so we went off to the University of Virginia and took a quick tour. We sat on the campus for a little while which, even with no dog run, obviously impressed Norton, and then we hit the almost indescribable Rotunda, the library which

Jefferson designed (I'm sure he was not only our first architect, he probably invented the whole idea of books! You know, he's starting to steam me!).

After this academic tour, it was time to return to the Clifton. We relaxed the rest of the afternoon while I got in my daily quotient of reading and weeping, then we had dinner together in the dining room. Norton was exhausted and dozed through almost the entire meal. He perked up for another teaspoon of the champagne sauce, and even a little bit of the sorbet, but other than that, he slept while I guzzled more Virginia pinot noir.

The next morning, I decided our road trip was over. During the night, I sensed that Norton had taken a turn for the worse. He was logy and suddenly, for the first time, his legs were buckling when he walked. Several times in the middle of the night, I carried him to his food and water dishes as well as to the litter box. I'd done that before because I knew it was easier for him. But now, for the first time, I did it because I didn't think he could walk there himself.

In the car, heading north, I had a lot of time to reflect. I thought about a poem by Gerard Manley Hopkins called "Margaret, Are You Grieving?" I am hardly a poetry expert. Most of the poems and poets I know I read in college. Okay, *all* of the poems and poets I know I read in college, except for the contemporary classics that begin with things like, "There was a young man from Nantucket." Actually, that's not totally true. When Janis and I were first dating, I did read Yeats and Donne and William Carlos Williams aloud to her, but that was so she'd think I was sensitive and would have sex with me, so I'm not positive that really counts. But driving along, the Hopkins poem kept entering my head. It's a brilliant piece of writing, basically about the fact that when we grieve for those who die, what we're really doing is grieving for ourselves. We're really mourning our *own* mortality. Despite what some people might think, I'm not a total nut. I knew—and know—that Norton was a cat, that he wasn't a child or a member of my family. But having perspective doesn't necessarily alleviate the sadness one feels. I tried to think what it was that made me love my cat so much, what it was that was forcing such grief upon me. When my father died, I did exactly what the Hopkins poem said we all do. I knew I was grieving for myself—at what I had lost, at what I would miss by not having my father around, at the wound which would remain with me forever as a result of losing him. With Norton it was different. Yes, of course I was grieving for myself. I was going to miss this little creature who had somehow, over the years, meowed his way into my heart to become my very best friend and my treasured companion. Norton loved me, had since the day we met, and I loved him in return. That love was real and powerful and valuable. So in that sense, I was grieving for what I was losing. We do not—me or anyone else—have such an abundance of love in our lives that we can cavalierly gloss over its disappearance, when it does indeed disappear. But I knew this was more than that.

I believe I was genuinely grieving over my cat himself.

The only way I can possibly explain it is that people are flawed. Even the best people. And even those we deeply love evoke mixed and complicated emotions because along with that love there is always some amount of pain or frustration or compromise, there is always some other complexity in relationships between humans. Norton was *not* flawed. He was, in fact, perfect. He could *be* perfect because he was a simpler creature than most human beings. He gave without demanding anything (other than cat treats and the occasional stomach scratch). He comforted without complaint. He provided companionship and compassion and as I realized all this, I decided my grief was not just valid, it was important, because Norton's death was not going to just be a loss for me, it was going to be a loss for everyone. There is not so much of that perfection thing going around that we can afford to lose it without grieving.

While I drove, and thought these morbid thoughts, Norton sat in his warmed-up seat, although this time I flicked the switch for him since he did not have the strength to do it himself. I talked to him the entire way back to New York. Told him how wonderful he was, told him how much I was going to miss him. He'd meow grumpily—not in pain but in a kind of anger and annoyance. It was as if he were saying, "Why can't I jump up and sit on your shoulder like I used to?" I could tell he was frustrated. He didn't understand what was happening to him. Or why he couldn't jump or walk or even pee the way he should. He was also embarrassed, I think, at his physical condition, and about the fact that I had to see him like this. I kept one hand on him most of the time I drove. And I told him that he shouldn't be angry or embarrassed. That he was as perfect as a thing could be.

I could see how really weak he was now. Occasionally he would force himself up on his haunches so he could look out the window—always one of his favorite activities. But mostly he lay still. Sometimes when he meowed, I could tell he was thirsty. But he didn't have the energy to get to his bowl of water. I kept a bottle of water next to me, so periodically I'd wet my fingers and let him lick the water off. It made me grin because I always loved the feel of his rough tongue on me. Cats don't smile, so I couldn't be positive, but I was pretty sure he enjoyed it, too—the water and the familiar touch and taste of my skin.

By the time we'd gotten halfway to the city, I was a mournful shell of a human being. We actually passed two funeral processions along the way. I'm not kidding. Each time we saw one, I totally lost control. As the second one passed, I tried calling Janis on my cell phone but all I could do was sob. Somehow, she knew it was me (I wonder how?!) and she just said, "It's okay, you don't have to talk. Just call me when you can."

To totally wallow in my melancholy, I played Loudon Wainwright CDs the whole way. He is just about my favorite singer-musician and almost every one of his songs was about someone leaving or growing old or going away or dying. It must have been a strange sight to anyone who happened to glance into my car. For quite a few hours, all they would have seen was a man driving, talking to his cat, and blubbering like a madman.

Back in New York, back in our Washington Square apartment, I did everything I could to make Norton as comfortable as possible. It didn't take long before walking was an impossible feat for him. Soon, almost everything else was just as impossible. His breathing was heavy and forced, his meowing was weak. His appetite was nonexistent. Even his favorite, shrimp, was left untouched in his bowl.

On Friday, May 7, I went to give him his IV drip but

he was so skinny I couldn't find any extra flesh in which to put the needle. Holding him on my lap, I could feel that his skin was now completely dry. It was crinkly, almost like a snake skin, or like Saran Wrap when you touch it. I petted him as gently as I could, but it felt as if under the fur his skin would slide right off his body. When he looked at me sadly, I knew he didn't even want his drip. So I didn't bother. I knew what he wanted. I held him on my lap for quite a while, didn't say anything for a change, just touching him and sometimes kissing him, and made the hardest decision I've ever made in my life.

When Janis came over after work, I told her that I'd tried three times to call the receptionist at Dianne De-Lorenzo's office to make an appointment for the next morning to put Norton to sleep. I also told her that each time I'd called, as soon as the receptionist answered the phone, I had burst into tears and been unable to speak. She asked me if I was sure this was the right thing and the right time and I remembered what Dianne had told me: I'd know. She was absolutely right. I did know. There was no doubt. So I nodded—that nodding trick was still working—and Janis called the Washington Square Animal Hospital, spoke to the receptionist, and made the appointment for nine-thirty the next morning.

That night, I asked Janis if she'd mind not staying at my apartment. I wanted Norton to be as comfortable as possible and I wanted him to sleep with me. I wanted to be next to him for one final time and because his set-up was so elaborate—I had him in my bed, with towels all around him, food and water right next to him—I didn't think there'd be room for all three of us. Janis ain't no dummy—she knew what I really wanted was just to be alone with my cat on his final night on earth—so she kissed us both and went to her own place around nine o'clock at night.

By ten, my cat and I were both in bed. I was exhausted (You know what? Crying all the time is *very* tiring). I had Norton tucked in under the covers, his head on the pillow, the way he liked best to sleep. I was next to him, turned on my side so I could both watch him and touch him whenever I wanted to.

I slept, but not at all soundly. Periodically, I'd get up and wet my fingers with water and then let him lick the tips. His breathing was raspy and heavy.

At one-thirty in the morning, I awoke with a start. I could hear him coughing. Not loudly, more of a quiet choking noise, as if he was clearing his throat. I put my hand on his head, softly and as gently as I was able. His breathing was very slow now. Regular but almost imperceptibly soft. I took him out of the covers, picked him up and cradled him in my arms. As I did, he began purring. We sat that way for about half an hour while I stroked him and kissed him and told him how much I loved him and how much I was going to miss him.

And then Norton showed me how much he loved me, too.

Of every single thing that had happened and that I knew was going to happen, the one thing I was dreading the most was putting him to sleep. I knew I could do it, knew I would even be strong enough to be there in the room, but the idea of it was just as awful as anything I'd ever envisioned. I didn't want my cat to go that way. I didn't want to see it and I didn't want to have to think about it the rest of my life.

So Norton spared me that.

He had done many amazing things during his life, from learning to unlock our bedroom door to keeping me company by walking miles along a crowded beach to operating his own automobile seat warmer. But now he did the most amazing thing he'd ever done.

At two o'clock in the morning, on May 8, 1999, Norton purred right up until he closed his eyes, took one last shallow breath, and died in my arms.

CHAPTER 11

THE CAT WHO'LL
LIVE FOREVER

The aftermath of death is an interesting and strange thing.

The immediate sensation was one of surprising calm and relief.

The moment Norton died my tears stopped.

It's not that I wasn't overcome with loss, it's simply that death itself was so much more peaceful for him than the last two or three days of his life. I was instantly overcome with the realization that he was gone and that all the good things I loved about him were now part of my memory rather than the present. That is always a jarring emotional adjustment, because we all place so much more value on the here and now than we do on memory—but the fact is that he was no longer in pain and, about that, I was glad.

I held him for a fairly long time, maybe fifteen minutes or so, until I was absolutely sure he was dead. I'd never been in this situation before, so while I was as certain as I could be that his breathing had stopped, I didn't want to be mourning him and suddenly have him meow and startle me to my own death. So I sat there and stroked him and finally accepted the fact that yes, he was gone. I remembered what the woman from the hospice had told me about my dad when he was dying, so I kept my hand on his chest, was strangely comforted by the contact and the intimacy. After a while, I kissed him on top of the head, and decided that was my final physical goodbye.

The trauma was over, the crying had ended, and now reality was setting in. I sat there, trying to decide what to do—sleep was out of the question—and decided that it was okay to call Janis, even if it was now two-thirty in the morning. When the phone rang, she knew who it was and why I was calling. I told her that Norton had died, she asked if I wanted her to come over and I said no, that I was okay, really, and this time I was telling the truth.

But when I hung up, I realized that I did have a new problem to deal with.

I've explained that "squeamish" might as well be my middle name, so I was not able to simply shrug off the slightly ghoulish situation facing me. That situation was that, with all the calm and peace and intimacy surrounding me, there was no getting around the fact that I had a non-living cat in my bed.

I called Janis back and said, "What the *hell* am I supposed to do now?"

What I finally did was call Dr. DeLorenzo's office and the night operator gave me a number for Manhattan's twenty-four-hour animal hospital. I called them, told them of my situation, and the woman there asked if I had a bag.

"What kind of bag?" I asked.

"A bag that your cat'll fit into," she said, not as sensitively as she might have.

I said that I probably did and she explained that I should put him in the bag, cover him up with a blanket, and bring him to my regular vet in the morning. I said, "That's it?" and she answered, "Well, what else did you have in mind?" I decided I wouldn't utter exactly what I had in mind for her, simply said, "Okay," hung up and looked over at Norton. The strangest thing about what happened next is how *not* strange it was for me. It wasn't distasteful, it wasn't even unpleasant or sad now. It was as if this were just a normal part of the cycle. I had cried for him when he was alive and, as I've said, there really was this deep sense of peace now. So it didn't seem odd or distasteful to me to pick him up and carry him to the Sherpa bag he normally used when he flew on planes with me. I will say that I did kiss him one last time, knowing that it would be the last time I was able to touch him, then I put him inside, zipped it up, got a towel and draped it over the bag.

When it was all done, I climbed back into bed and suddenly knew that I could, for the first time in days, maybe even weeks, go right to sleep. And not only that, I knew I could finally sleep soundly and deeply, and without the fear of what I'd wake up to find. The time for fear, as for pain, for both me and Norton, was past.

Janis came over first thing in the morning and we took Norton to the Washington Square Animal Hospital. The woman at the desk was expecting us and started to explain that Dr. DeLorenzo wasn't in quite yet but I explained that we'd come early and that we didn't need the doctor, that Norton had died already. I said that I just wanted to leave him there to be cremated.

She came around the desk and took the bag from me. I did have one last crying jag as I watched her carry him into the back. But it was only a brief one, nothing too drastic, and Janis held my hand and patted me lightly and comfortingly on the back, like one would do to a colicky baby, until I dried up. When the receptionist came back with the empty bag, Janis and I went outside into what was already becoming a hot and humid spring day. We went and had a huge breakfast at a diner on Bleecker Street. Tapping our orange juice glasses together, we had a bittersweet—and exhausted—toast to my sixteen and a half superb years of companionship.

I assumed that I'd now make a few calls, send a few e-mails, tell a few people, mourn for a little while, or even a long while, know that a small but valuable piece of me would be missing forever, but that things would go on much as before and that would be the end of it.

Uh-uh.

In death, my sweet, sweet cat continued to astound, possibly even more than he had in life.

The friends I called or e-mailed immediately called or e-mailed other friends, who contacted a whole other circle of people, and the next thing I knew I was getting calls from nearly anyone I'd ever met, talked to or heard about. Every close friend or relative who called sounded almost as sad as I felt. If there was any unanimity of sentiment in all these conversations, it was that all the people who called felt as if they themselves had lost a close friend.

A writer pal of mine, John Feinstein, another serious cat guy (he once flew home to Maryland from Paris, where he was covering the French Open tennis tournament, when one of his cats died suddenly), called and left this message on my phone machine: "I'm sure you're sad, but you shouldn't be *that* sad, because no cat ever had a better life." John's wife, Mary, sent me a wonderful note: "All the Feinsteins have been thinking of you. Yesterday Danny [their young son] asked if Norton could be his [Danny's] grandmother's cat in heaven. We figure anyone as widely traveled as Norton has found his way to the afterlife, and we told Danny a cat so well-loved would be unbeatable as a companion anywhere." Roman Polanski called from Paris to convey his condolences. "We had some great dinners together, Norton and I," he said wistfully. Norm Stiles, who probably knew Norton better than anyone outside of me and Janis, said, "It's amazing, isn't it, how our cats get into every minute aspect of our daily lives." And that's exactly the point that Janis made to me, when I began apologizing for how deeply sad I felt and how seriously I was grieving. "He wasn't just your cat," she had to explain to me. "You were with him practically twenty-fours a day. He was involved in your social life, your day-to-day life *and* your professional life. You didn't have that kind of all-consuming relationship with anyone else."

Young Charlie Alderman called and was his usual comforting self. "He died in a good way," he told me and I had to tell him that I agreed. His mom Nancy let me know a few days later that the Chuckster had been asked to write his autobiography for school. The ten-year-old's opening sentence was, "The first friend I ever had died when he was sixteen years old." He was, of course, referring to Norton, who was indeed one of his very first friends, meeting Charlie when the boy was days old.

Ben Eagle, the slightly-older-than-Charlie son of my best friend Paul, wrote and told me that he was dedicating a part of his own Web page to Norton.

Things started to get out of hand when a reporter

named James Barron from the *New York Times* called. He had heard about Norton's death (I believe from my agent, Esther, who had her own Scottish Fold, Tate, and was taking Norton's demise almost as hard as I was) and he wanted to write an obituary. I was taken aback but I must say, I liked the idea of Norton being the first cat to get an obit in the paper of record and I was positive that he would have loved it, too. Barron did a great job; he totally caught the spirit of my cat and our relationship. Best of all, he made it fun and funny, writing it as if Norton were a person, not a pet (which, of course, is the way I thought about him). I'll reprint it here, below, but I should point out my very favorite line, which comes at the end: "Besides Mr. Gethers, Norton is survived by Mr. Gethers's friend, Janis Donnaud." I think that's just perfect, and I know Norton would have liked that.

Naturally, even in death, Norton had to take center stage. Soon after the obit writer interviewed me, I got a call from a woman at the *Times* who said they would like a photo of Norton to run with the piece. I explained that I'd have to look to see what I had and she said that they were on deadline, they needed it quickly. I told her that if they could send a messenger, I'd have something ready, but she didn't know if they had time for that. She said she'd check and call me right back. Five minutes later, the phone rang again. It was the woman from the *Times*.

"Never mind," she said. "It turns out we have a photo of Norton on file here."

"Um . . ." I managed to say before she hung up again. "Just out of curiosity, do you have a photo of *me* on file there?"

"You don't want to know," was her answer.

NORTON

Recalling a Cat Who Got Around

Norton, a grayish cat with small, folded ears whose far-flung adventures were described in two books, died on Saturday. He was 16, said the person with whom he lived, the author **PETER GETHERS**.

He had kidney trouble and cancer, said Mr. Gethers, an executive at Random House who has also written novels and screenplays.

"He was a gift from an ex-girlfriend," Mr. Gethers said. "I didn't like cats at all. She brought him back from Los Angeles and gave him to me. It was an instant relationship."

Soon they were going everywhere together. One early trip was to a weeklong writers' conference in San Diego, Calif. During one workshop, **LEONA NEVLER**, an editor at Ballantine Books, became concerned that Mr. Gethers had left Norton (unattended and unleashed) by the swimming pool at their hotel.

"She couldn't get over why I wasn't worried," he said. "I went to the last place I had seen him and whistled, and he came out of the bushes."

Later Mr. Gethers told her that Norton had flown on the Concorde, had lived in a hotel with views of the Parisian skyline (as well as open-window access to nearby rooftops) and had attended meetings with the director **ROMAN POLANSKI** and the actor **HARRISON FORD**.

She said, "You should write a book called 'The Cat Who Went to Paris,'" Mr. Gethers recalled yesterday. "I'm supposed to have my finger on the pulse of American culture, but I totally blew it off. I said, 'Right'"

But Ms. Nevler called Mr. Gethers's agent, **ESTHER NEWBERG**, and worked out a deal for the book. That first volume, published in 1991, was followed by "A Cat Abroad" (Crown, 1993).

Eventually, Mr. Gethers's traveling companion became so well known that mail addressed to "Norton, Sag Harbor, N.Y." was delivered — naturally, Norton had a place in the Hamptons. He was recognized throughout Europe. Once, on a walk through Amsterdam — Mr. Gethers was doing the walking; Norton was riding on his shoulders — someone stopped the pair and said, "Excuse me, is that the cat who went to Paris?"

It was. And as Mr. Gethers's readers came to understand, Norton was a cat with a distinct — and distinctive — personality. "He was independent without being standoffish," said Ms. Newberg.

Besides Mr. Gethers, Norton is survived by Mr. Gethers's friend, **JANIS DONNAUD**.

Once the *Times* announced my cat's departure from all things worldly, things got truly wild.

Various other news services picked up on the story, so Norton's death was written about in *USA Today* and, thanks to the Associated Press, printed in hundreds of local papers around the country. *People* magazine not only ran a full-page "Tribute" to my cat in the issue that came out ten days or so after his death, six months later they also included Norton in their special, year-end double-issue in the section "Notable Deaths." In this second story, Norton—depicted in a photo I took of him at Sweetwater Farm during our final trip together—was placed alongside the likes of Mel Tormé, Joe DiMaggio, Raisa Gorbachev, George C. Scott, Wilt Chamberlain, King Hussein, Stanley Kubrick and, I was particularly pleased to see, Señor Wences. My favorite part—this really made me chuckle as I knew it would have pleased my pal greatly—is that they didn't bother to identify him. They didn't say, "star of *The Cat Who Went to Paris*" or anything like that. They simply listed him, under his photo, as "A Literary Adventurer," gave his age as sixteen, and then got Rita Mae Brown to give a wonderful epitaph: "He was born a cat, but died a gentleman. His manners were perfect, and he was a very good traveling companion."

I couldn't have said it better myself.

I got a call from a friend, Linda, whom I hadn't spoken to in several months. She said that she'd heard about Norton's death and wanted to convey how very sorry she was. I asked if she knew about it because she'd read the

Times obit and she said no, she heard it on the radio. My exact response to this was, "*What?*!!!" and she then told me that she'd been driving into the city from her country house, was cruising along the Long Island Expressway listening to WCBS when, on the news, they announced that Norton—describing him as "the legendary Cat Who Went to Paris"—had died. She said she almost drove off the side of the road, but managed to compose herself as the station then went on and did a thirty-second tribute to the world's favorite Scottish Fold.

I called Janis immediately to tell her about this and then I had to shake my head. "You do realize," I told her, "that when *I* die no one's going to do a thirty-second tribute on the radio for *me*."

"Yes," Janis said, as sympathetically as she could muster, "I definitely realize that."

Letters and e-mails started pouring in. I am not exaggerating when I say that I received at least a thousand notes, each expressing sorrow and sympathy at Norton's passing. Writers I worked with, coworkers from the publishing business, more notes from friends. One writer who I published and also played with in the occasional game of poker, Bob Reiss, wrote: "I didn't think of him as your pet. I thought of him as your friend. Condolences in a time of grief." An agent, who I didn't know all that well but who had met Norton at various Random House meetings as well as at a couple of writers conferences, wrote: "He was the embodiment of otherworldly sophistication and his like won't be seen again. I mourn with you." Ann King, who took care of Norton the weekend Janis and I were in San Francisco, sent a note thanking me for letting her have the opportunity to spend those few days with him. I got letters from salespeople into whose stores I had taken Norton while I was shopping. The woman who bought my old apartment, and who had scratched and petted Norton while she was deciding whether she wanted to meet my asking price, sent these words: "Although I only met him twice, Norton left a lasting impression on me. He had an otherworldly quality about him, and I found myself telling everyone I knew about him. He really was a unique cat."

One of my favorite comments came from a dear friend, Becky Okrent, who sent a black and white postcard that was a photo of a cat standing on a young man's shoulder. The printed paragraph on the back of the card explained that the cat was Mrs. Chippy, a male cat who belonged to Henry Mcnish, an adventurer on the ship the *Endurance* during Shackleton's legendary arctic expedition. The man in the photo was not Mcnish but another sailor with Shackleton, Perce Blackbourne. Becky's note read: "Don't ask what happened to Mrs. Chippy when the crew was forced to abandon ship. But I hope he and Norton are sharing a few brews and tales of adventure in cat heaven."

Sharon MacIntosh, a friend and major cat lover, had these wise words to impart in an e-mail: "I think we're only allowed temporary guardianship of cats. Though I don't believe in heaven for people, I've always thought that all our good cats would meet up in cat heaven, where they'd have Fancy Feast, no fleas and MEOW MIX as often as they want. Most of all, I think cats—even more than humans— want to die with love and dignity. You gave Norton both."

When Norton's cancer had reached a fairly advanced stage, two of the few people I'd revealed this to were the women in Sicily, Wanda and Giovanna Tornabene, whose cookbook I'd published. Wanda, the mother, sent me the following fax when she first heard Norton was sick:

Dearest Peter,

Giovanna translated for me your letter and now she doing the same for my letter to you. You know how much I can understand your feeling about Norton. I have the same for my Puffo [her dog]. He is now 14 years and I can't imagine my life without him. So please give me, as often you can, news about Norton's health. Norton is not to me only your beloved cat. He is the mysterious go-between who gods decided to use to change, in some way, my life.

When Norton died, I got what I think are the most moving letters I've ever received, one from Wanda and one from her daughter. I am not changing a word of their English because while it is not technically perfect, it is, in fact, emotionally perfect. Wanda's note read:

Dearest Peter,

For my long experience, nothing can console you for the less of Norton, and nothing, for long time, will fill the empty he left in your heart and in your house. The truth, my dear friend, is that our little beloved animals are the mirror that reflects what we humans might be and often we are not. When they leave us, they bring with them our best part: the tenderness and all that enormous love, sometimes expressed just with a glance, secret words whispered in those little hairy ears, sure to be understood, the happy moments, the pains lived together. Norton had a wonderful life and he made your life wonderful. I am sure he teached you, about yourself, more than a thousand humans. I want to tell a story many years ago, after the death of my little cat, Lilli. I asked to my doctor and friend Vincenzo, "Do you think I am normal if, when I see to die an animal, I suffer more than when a human dies?" And I remember that he answered to me, smiling, "Not, you are not," then he added, "Maybe . . . maybe . . ." and his eyes became sad, surely he remembered his dog, Argo, buried on the top of a mountain in the Madonies, where today, with his ashes, Vincenzo sleeps, too. And often this, my "abnormality" brings me to suffer today, Peter, and your great pain is mine.

Love, Wanda.

Giovanna's note was on the same piece of paper, added to the bottom:

I've just translated my mamma's letter and, believe me, it has been so hard to write, crying, about Norton's death. To me he will be, forever, the ironic, independent creature who walked and danced over our restaurant tables years ago. To me he will be always alive in the Sicilian sun, as alive as will be our friendship.

Dr. Jonathan Turetsky sent me a wonderful note, part of which read, "I truly was saddened to hear of Norton's passing, although I know he was never particularly fond of me. I have learned, over the years, not to take too personally the resentment of some of my patients. I well realize that many don't easily grasp the concept of distasteful things being done 'for your own good,' and I content myself with the knowledge that, nevertheless, I am helping." He also enclosed a moving article which he'd written about the death of his dog several years ago. Marty Goldstein called and talked about Norton's spirit, which he said would never really leave me. And Dianne DeLorenzo's note said that, "In the short time I knew him he touched me deeply . . . Everyone should be so lucky to have a love like Norton in their lives. You both were blessed to have each other." Drs. Turetsky and Pepper and Dr. DeLorenzo and her partner Dr. Lucas sent donations in Norton's name (Turetsky's and Pepper's went to Tuft's University School of Veterinary Medicine; DeLorenzo's and Lucas's went to the University of Pennsylvania School of Veterinary Medicine). Actually, quite a few people made donations to animal hospitals and veterinary schools in Norton's name. I started to feel as if pretty soon I'd be running my own Labor Day telethon.

I got calls and letters from heads of companies and waiters who served Norton in restaurants and normally cynical, hard-bitten media people, all of whom had come into contact with my cat over the years. But, most astonishing, I got tons and tons of mail from total strangers who simply had to share their sadness and the fact that Norton had touched and even changed their lives.

Many of these letters were from people who felt the need to reach out and share my grief or tell me about their own losses. Most were sweet and compassionate and I truly was amazed at the degree to which Norton had entered their lives. I was equally amazed that so many people understood about Norton the way I thought only I understood. People wrote such things to me as "Needless to say, today's obituary in *USA Today* was a great shock to me and I've wept constantly all day," and "Knowing that Norton passed away I find myself with a gnawing sadness," and "Although I never did meet him in person, I felt I knew and loved him through his books" and "GOD!!! I'm still trying to recover from reading about Norton's death, which a friend sent to me over e-mail."

A huge number of the people writing told me about their own cats and the pain they experienced when those cats died. Many of those letters began with, "I had a Norton in my life" and then proceeded to tell me about the joys brought to them by their Mincemeat or Ju-Jube or their Snowball. Many of them also went on to detail tales of woe that included horrid diseases and sudden car accidents and runaway felines. Some of it was pretty morbid—but the intent, I know, was to show that whatever sadness I was feeling, I was not the only one who had experienced this. There was a cat community out there of which I was part—and at the center of which stood Norton.

A lot of people felt the need to simply pay tribute to their favorite feline and tell me they were sorry he was gone. Quite a number of them wrote to assure me that Norton was an "immortal cat" and would live forever not just inside me but in the minds and hearts of his fans. I soon discovered that various cat organizations, notably the Scottish Fold Association—needless to say Norton was a god amongst kittens as far as they were concerned—had posted the news of his death on their websites. Some even sent out special e-mailings to all of their members. These people were all shaken to the core. I got terrifically nice offers from breeders for a free cat if I ever decided to get another one. I got letters thanking me for showing them the way to happiness by introducing them to the Scottish Fold breed (I got so many of the latter that I was beginning to suspect I should do a book called *The Tao of Fold*). And I got plenty of letters similar to the one that just said, "I'm shocked. I don't know what to say. I hope you're doing well."

There was one couple who had written to me on a regular basis over the years. The first time I heard from them, they had told me that their young daughter had some mental and emotional problems. The only thing that consistently got her attention and made her smile was when they would read *The Cat Who Went to Paris* to her. As time passed, they would fill me in on their daughter's progress, which was considerable. The one constant was that she remained very attached to Norton. When he died, they told me how sad the girl was—but they also told me that she had made even more improvement. They absolutely gave credit to Norton for helping her make that improvement.

Several letters arrived—*quite* a few, actually—purportedly written by cats. These typically began, "Dear Mr. Gethers, My name is Gingerbelle and I'm a 4-year Manx owned by Delilah Heffenpheffer. I was very sad to read about Norton's death as he was my idol."

I got one page of cat haikus, which I do have to say, made me laugh. I particularly liked:

Small, brave carnivores
Kill pine cones and mosquitos
Fear vacuum cleaner

and

> The rule for today:
> Touch my tail, I shred your hand.
> New rule tomorrow.

and

> Want to go outside.
> Oh no! Help! I got outside!
> Let me back inside!

But my favorite, no question, was this one:

> The Big Ones snore now.
> Every room is dark and cold.
> Time for Cup Hockey!

I got all sorts of cat cartoons and cat jokes, too, most of which were funny, although all the jokes almost always ended in, "And the dog was happy and the cat didn't give a shit."

Of course, there were a lot of spiritually oriented notes. Most of them were generous and warm and I was grateful for the good wishes they passed along

A lot of them said that they knew or suspected I did not share their beliefs but nonetheless they wanted to send me what they considered an appropriate prayer or poem or comforting thought. (Just for the record, I did get a few that brought up the whole "hell" subject again. The one I remember best was kind of taunting. It said that wasn't I sorry now, because Norton was definitely going to heaven but because I was such a heathen, I was definitely not. Too bad, he said, because if I'd been better I might have seen him again. But now . . . no chance! I thought about writing back to this fellow and asking him if he thought such extraordinary meanness was going to get him a place in good standing Up There, but I did the wise thing instead. I threw the letter away.)

Several people sent me information on pet loss support groups and pet loss counselors, which I also appreciated, but did nothing about. I couldn't imagine standing up in front of a bunch of other crying animal lovers saying, "Hi, I'm Peter. I'm catless."

One person sent me a copy of a page from the *Mayo Clinic Health Letter* which was devoted to pet loss and grief. This page had helpful little hints about what to say to a friend who's lost a pet. I learned that to console someone you do say, "I'm sorry to hear of your loss." You don't say, "You can always get another pet." Good tip, I thought.

That Mayo Clinic flyer also told me that I'd be surprised at the depth of my sorrow (they were right on the nose with that one, I'll give them credit for that), and that there were pet loss support hot lines, pet loss websites and books and videos which could all help me cope.

I had no idea that pet loss was such a big business. I was surprised to receive so many spiritual writings that were bought in stores and sold for just such an occasion. Most of them were not just about death and dying, they were specifically geared to the death of a pet. I got a ton of fancy cards that were engraved in very swirly writing with things like "We're sorry for the loss of your very special cat." Many of them seem to be made by a company called Pet Love (in their logo, the *o* in "love" is heart shaped). They featured a lot of photos of cats sitting in front of windows, with sunlight casting a heavenly glow about them. There were also quite a few peaceful cats lolling on fluffy pillows. The poems that were part of the cards were almost all about how we have to refill the food dish of life and pet the meowing spirit that lives on and let animal footprints dance gently on our heart forever.

I got many, many copies of an inspirational poem or essay—I'm not quite sure what it is—called "Rainbow Bridge." I mean, I probably got fifty of these in the mail. The sentiments are quite nice but whenever I got to the part about the meadows and hills where our special friends are playing, I'd get a little woozy. I always get woozy when I read the phrase "our special friends." Even though I did not believe that Norton had crossed over into heaven on Rainbow Bridge, I was glad to have seen this poem. It made me really confront my own feelings and define my own perspective. It got me to accept the fact that I really did believe that we live and we die and that even though the things in-between aren't always perfect they're what we've got and should be appreciated. End of story. While some people might not agree, that realization did indeed comfort me. I did not have to dream wistfully about joyful reunions in green, grassy fields somewhere up in the sky.

I grieved for my cat and grieve for him still. My comfort comes from the fact that I know and accept that my sadness is real. And heartfelt. I grieve for what I lost at the same time I celebrate what I had. I don't want to make myself feel better by pretending that there's more than there was to my relationship with Norton. Or that more is coming.

I don't need any more.

What we had was strong enough to last forever.

About a week after my cat died, I had to go pick up his ashes from the animal clinic. I can't say I was looking forward to this but when they called and said it was time, I walked over there and got him. The receptionist handed over a small, gray cardboard box that weighed practically nothing and was wrapped with a red ribbon, as if it were a Christmas present. On the label, I saw that this package came courtesy of the Pet Crematory Agency, Inc. And that it contained the "cherished pet of Peter Gethers: beloved Norton." Yes, for a change I did do a little sniffling, then left to take the remains of my cat home.

On the way back, I made a grand and sentimental gesture. I stopped off at the dog run in Washington Square Park. I settled on the bench that Norton and I usually sat on, held the box on my lap and leaned my head back, letting the bright sun hit my face. I stayed there for a decent amount of time then . . . well . . . to be honest, I felt a little silly. I'm not usually one for such gestures and I don't know why I went there. I suppose that partly it was another farewell. For me, sure, but also for Norton.

People had been asking me since his death if I was going to have a memorial service. At first I said no. I've made it more than clear how I feel about forced rituals, but I do have to say that the demand was overwhelming. Janis finally came to me and said that she thought it was a good idea. We had his ashes, she said, we were going to bury them, so let's do what he would have liked and have a little party. I still wasn't sure and told her I had to think about it.

A few days later, we were out in Sag Harbor for the weekend. I took out the cardboard box from the crematorium and opened it. Inside was a small, multicolored tin container. And inside that was what had once been my cat. Janis came up to me, put her hand on my back, and I told her that she should start calling people to invite them to a memorial on Sunday. When she asked what had changed my mind, I told her there were two things. One: I wanted to invite only those people who had actually shared a meal with Norton. I wanted to invite *his* friends. He had a lot of them and they all deserved the chance I'd had to say good-bye. The second thing I told her was that it was a chance to once and for all disprove Ziggy's favorite now-classic quote by my ex-girlfriend: "There are certain times that are inappropriate for humor." What I wanted to do, I said, was share with everyone who came, all the things that had happened since Norton died. I wanted them to feel as good as I did about the impact he'd had on people's lives. I wanted them to laugh the way I had, at so many things that had happened since that awful Saturday morning when he took his last breath.

So on Sunday morning, twenty-five people came over to our backyard. We ate a nice brunch outside, drank a little champagne, and then I delivered a short eulogy.

I've already mentioned how eulogy-readings are not my best thing. I did manage to get through this reasonably well. There were a few stops and starts and a lot of coughing in an attempt to hide my tremors. But except for the very, very end, when Janis had to step in and take over, I did it. I admitted that I felt a little foolish having a funeral service for a cat, said that I didn't know if I'd do it for a person, but I explained why I was doing it. And why they had been the ones invited. I talked about all the stuff that had occurred since May 8—the obits and the letters and weird poems and the amazing outpouring of affection. I got a few laughs and I don't think I was the only person in the yard shedding tears. And then I said I didn't think I could say anymore because I wouldn't just shed tears, I'd turn into that new comic book superhero, The Blubberer. I said that my cat loved this garden, so let's put him in it.

Which is what we did, burying him, scattering his ashes, under his favorite magnolia tree in the middle of his favorite garden.

As I write these final words, over a year and a half has passed since Norton died.

Letters and e-mails and calls are still coming on a regular basis. Some from people who just heard the news and are sending their shocked condolences. Some from people—people I've never met—who get in touch to tell me they're still thinking about me and about Norton and wondering how I am and if I've gotten another cat yet.

My favorite postfuneral letter came from a guy in Northern California who'd written a few fan letters after reading the first two books. When I opened the envelope, a twenty-dollar bill fluttered out. I fished out the letter and it said that this was the three-month anniversary of Norton's death and that I should use this twenty bucks to go out and get drunk.

I sent him back a thank-you note and with it I returned his money. But I did take his advice and had more than a few drinks to commemorate the sad occasion.

I have not gotten another cat yet. I'm not totally sure why. I think it's partly because I'm afraid. Norton was such an amazing animal and we had such an extraordinary bond, I don't know how I'd feel having a cat who wasn't quite so amazing or with whom I didn't have such a strong bond. I'm a little concerned that it would be like the lobster scene in *Annie Hall*. Things would be the same, but a little off. I'd take my new cat on a trip with me, expecting him to travel like Norton, and he'd freak out on the plane and be one of those cats you read about who spends three weeks living in the luggage compartment before being found by a janitor. The other thing that must be said is that it's somewhat free-ing not having a cat. No responsibility. No lugging around portable litter boxes. No rushing home at night so he doesn't worry that I've been eaten by a predator. I'm sure I'll get one one day. When the time's right.

When I'm ready.

What happened to my cat—a long and happy life fol-lowed by a quick and fairly painless death—is not a tragedy. It is something that happens to everybody, in one way or another, sooner or later. Death defines life, and it's natural, and there's nothing we can do about it, but I suppose that I'm still grieving. The thing that eventually strikes you about the death of someone you love is the permanence. When that hits, there is an overpowering sense of loneli-ness and aloneness. Those wounds do not remain raw, not forever, but they do remain.

This past winter, I went back to Gangivecchio, spent a

month with my friends in Sicily writing a new book. It was wonderful but it was strange and sad to be there without Norton. I was fed like a king, met some eccentric Sicilians and heard some major stories. It was a productive, serene and, yes, I'll say it, almost spiritual experience. But every time I opened the door to my cottage, I half-expected my cat to be waiting there, meowing angrily that I'd forgotten to let him in. That kind of thing happens often. Soon after he died, hardly an hour went by that I didn't hear a noise and turn, expecting to find him rubbing up against the bedpost or trying to open the cupboard to get to a cat treat. When I'd sit at my computer to write, I'd automatically clear a space for him. Then I'd realize that he wasn't there to fill that space. I still do that occasionally. Not every time. Too many months have passed. But occasionally.

For a long time after Norton died, his little black friend kept coming over to the yard, looking for her pal. When he didn't come out to play, she would hang out by our back door, sometimes sneaking into the house to see if he was hiding. She still meanders into our yard, but I don't think she's looking for anything anymore. She just comes because it's a nice place for a cat to hang out and, if Janis and I are around, we pet her and tell her that she's looking mighty fine.

About a year ago, I went to stay at The Four Seasons Hotel in Los Angeles, one of Norton's all-time favorite haunts. It was a nightmare. I pulled up in my car and the parking guy gave a big smile and said, "Welcome back, Mr. Gethers. Is Norton with you?" I quietly mumbled no, that I was sorry to say that he'd died. When I got to the door, the doorman said the same thing, "What, no cat?" Again, I shook my head, felt a little self-conscious, and said, "No, no, my cat died." As I walked through the lobby, the concierge called out to me, "Where's Norton?" and so did one of the bellmen who had carried many bags of cat litter up to the room for me. By the time I got to the desk clerk, who did nothing more than smile and say hello, I couldn't stand it, and I screamed out, "He's dead! Okay! He's *dead*!!!!"

I'm not nearly as welcome now at The Four Seasons as I was when Norton stayed there with me.

Several months ago, I had occasion to call Sweetwater Farm. I told Rick, the owner, that Norton had died and he said, just like this, "We had a death around here, too." I expected him to tell me that the goat had passed on, but when I asked who it was he said, "Grace." I said, "Grace, your *wife*?" And he said, yes, that a few months earlier she'd had a stomachache. It went on for three days, got really bad, so she went to see a doctor. She had stomach cancer. And three weeks later she was dead.

The woman who called to tell me she'd heard Norton's obit on WCBS radio, she died recently, too. It doesn't just happen to cats, you know. An old friend of mine died of AIDS. A close friend's brother died in a plane crash.

Things change. People die. But life goes on.

It's different. But it goes on.

And it can be just fine.

The Spring Trip this year was to Cuba, as thrilling a place as I've ever been. We smoked cigars and consumed a lot of aged rum, met kind and brave people, and heard magnificent, sensual salsa music. We didn't just toast Belle at our Saturday night dinner. This year we drank a *mojita* to a small, gray Scottish Fold and we all felt particularly lucky to be where we were and with close friends and to just be having a damn good time.

A few weeks ago, Janis and I went to Paris. Had dinner with Roman Polanski and his wife Emmanuelle, saw their two gorgeous children, stayed at the Tremoille Hotel. We ate the amazing chicken and even more amazing potato pie at L'ami Louis, and it doesn't get any better than that. We shopped, we strolled around all our favorite neighborhoods, we pretended we spoke French. It felt like old times. Except that woman with the antique shop, the one where I saw Marcello Mastroianni? That store's gone now. And except for the fact that several times I came down the steps at the Tremoille and saw a cat sitting in a chair in the lobby and each time I thought: *It's Norton, how did he get out of the room?*

And then I remembered that he didn't get out of the room.

But mostly what I remember about my cat is how much better my life is because he was in it.

Norton, throughout his lifetime, made many things possible for me, and he taught me about many things. About love and about relationships. About adventure. About independence. At the end of his life, he showed me that it's possible to die with dignity and grace. And, to a certain extent, that it's possible to end one's life on one's own terms. Ultimately, what my cat showed me is that it's possible to die with love and without fear, and that's a pretty damn valuable lesson.

It means that even with the sadness that's sure to come, life can never really get too bad.

Several weeks after he died, I ordered a small stone marker for his grave in the garden. Engraved on it is:

NORTON
T.C.W.W.T.P.

So some of you don't have to puzzle over the letters for the next several weeks, they stand for "the cat who went to Paris."

The marker is still there, will remain there as long as I own the house. I don't go out to look at it every day that I'm in Sag Harbor but I do go from time to time. Usually, just for a few seconds. I'll stand or I'll sit on the small wooden bench that's on the grass nearby.

Most of the time, when I see the grave, I have tears in my eyes.

Always, when I see the grave, I smile.

AFTERWORD

You'd think by now I'd have learned. But, being human, of course I haven't. I am still amazed and surprised and startled that several years after his death, my beloved Scottish Fold pal is still teaching me valuable lessons about life, death, and just about everything in between.

The hardcover edition of *The Cat Who'll Live Forever* was published on September 7, 2001. I was quite proud of this book, felt it was the best thing I'd ever written. It was also the *hardest* thing I'd ever written. When I knew I was getting close to the end, I went out to Sag Harbor and spent three weeks by myself, writing day and night to meet my deadline. I not only work better in isolation, in a sense I felt that it would be the last stretch of time I'd ever get to spend alone with Norton. I knew it would be the last thing

I ever wrote about him, at least in any sort of depth, and somehow, without turning into the kind of guy who'd have his own TV show communing with those on the "other side," it felt appropriate to have one final bond with the sweetest of creatures I'd spent sixteen years bonding with. When I finished typing the very last sentence of the book into my computer—and this will come as no surprise, I'm sure, to anyone who has actually read the whole thing rather than skipped ahead to peek at this all-new, extra-added-value section—I sat at my desk, overlooking the garden and Norton's grave, and sobbed for a good twenty minutes. Pulling myself together, forcing myself out of this latest burst of emotional wimpiness, I decided I had things under control, I had moved beyond the stage where the mere thought of Norton would reduce me to tears, and called Janis to tell her that I was finally done. The phone rang, she answered it, I said, "I'm . . ." —and I never even got to say the word "finished," because I started sobbing yet again for another twenty minutes or so. I told her I'd call her back, which I was able to do some three hours later with only a modicum of hysteria.

Over the next several months, various people read the manuscript. My agent, Esther, was the first to take a look (and she actually cried even harder reading the book than I cried writing it. When she finished the final page, she called me, around eleven at night. I heard some strangled gasps and snorts and sniffles, then she muttered, "I hate you," and hung up). The editor and publisher and several marketing and publicity people were the next to go over the pages. Everyone seemed to like it and expectations were fairly high. Early reviews were good and on September 7 I appeared on the *Today* show with Soledad O'Brien (on whom

I developed a major crush). My biggest fear in life was that I'd burst into tears on national TV talking about my cat—thus ending, once and for all, any macho fantasies I had about being cast as the next James Bond after Pierce Brosnan steps down—but I managed to get through the segment with my dignity reasonably intact.

On September 10, a Monday, Stephen Rubin, the publisher of Doubleday/Broadway, called me at home. As a result of my lovefest with Soledad (call me nuts, I think she had a little crush on me, too), *The Cat Who'll Live Forever* was number 20 on the amazon.com bestseller list and the *New York Times* had called to track it for their list. "I don't want to jinx it," Steve said, "but it looks like we've got a breakout bestseller on our hands."

The next day, of course, was 9/11 and for the next many months the world as we knew it basically came to an end. Eventually I found the nerve to tell Steve that he'd not only jinxed my book, he'd jinxed the entire United States.

Now, the reason I'm going into all this is not to whine and complain that terrorists hurt my book sales. There's a little thing I like to call "perspective." I live in downtown Manhattan, reasonably close to the site that was the World Trade Center and, believe me, I am not that selfish or egocentric. On September 12, I was not buried under tons of rubble and I did not lose anyone near and dear to me in the tragedy, thus I knew I had (and have) no reason to complain about *anything*. What I did have to do, however, was go out on a publicity tour. Which I did, two or three weeks later.

At first, I almost requested that the tour be canceled. Forget the fact that the media only wanted to talk about germ warfare and dirty bombs and anthrax and how we were going to strike back at the evildoers. (Well, let's not forget it for just a moment. While we're on the subject: Whatever *happened* to anthrax? How come no one ever mentions that we don't have a *clue* who was responsible for all that and never even came close to finding out who was mailing the stuff out? And how come no one ever brings up the point that we were told the whole reason we invaded Afghanistan was to find bin Laden? The *whole* reason. Then we *didn't* find him. So then we were told it didn't matter if we found him or not, he no longer mattered. And, okay, okay, this isn't going to turn into a political treatise— there are many observers more qualified than I am to comment on these things—but I do tend to mouth off in these books, so I'd also like to find out why we first decided that all terrorists are evil and you're either with us or against us when it comes to the war on terrorism—unless you're against us but you can actually do us some financial good or we need you for some reason, particularly if that reason has something to do with oil or blocs of votes. Then it's just *mildly* bad that you support terrorists or *are* terrorists and we'll simply ignore it and look the other way. I'm just asking, you understand.)

Anyway . . .

Because of the volatility of what was happening around the world, I knew I would be ignored by the media while on tour, but I did have commitments to speak in bookstores in many parts of the country and I didn't think it was particularly fair to stiff them, especially since a lot of other people were stiffing them, because everyone was afraid to fly (or, not to be too cynical about most authors out on tour, afraid to stand in line at the airport check-in counter for two hours and be incredibly inconvenienced). Still, I went back and forth on this issue. I really didn't want to offend or disappoint the bookstore people, but I just wasn't sure that what I was going to talk about—my deeply sick relationship with and love for my deceased cat—was remotely appropriate. It seemed so . . . trivial.

So what I did was do a trial run.

I did a bookstore appearance in Sag Harbor.

I was extremely nervous about this public appearance until just an hour or so before heading to the store, when I was talking to my friend Adrienne Harris (neighbor, psychologist, gardener, baseball fan—what could be bad?). I was telling Adrienne that I was particularly worried because, on top of everything else, my prepared talk—even if ultimately about Norton's death—was meant to be really funny. I said to her, "I don't know if anyone's in the mood for funny these days."

And she said, "Are you kidding? We're all *desperate* to laugh."

It turned out she was right. Not only that night but as I toured the U.S.A. And what surprised me even more was that people weren't just delighted to hear the funny and warm anecdotes, they were anxious to discuss what I'd decided was the point of the whole book: that *The Cat Who'll Live Forever* isn't really about death and loss but about life and how to use its limits so it can be appreciated to the fullest. However trivial the context, it was a message that people could relate to and were extraordinarily anxious to hear. In some ways, because it was so personal and about something so normal as the loss of a pet, the book became something they could relate to far more than they could relate to the overwhelming scope of the tragedy of 9/11.

As always, Norton managed to put things in perspective.

Letters began to pour in after the book was published (cat nuts do tend to like to share their feelings, I've learned over these many cat-writing years). Most of the letters were quite wonderful: supportive and moving and friendly. Many of them shared their own stories of loss and many of them said that the book helped them deal with loss—the two-legged as well as the four-legged kind.

One topic was raised more than any other. More of a question, really: Had I gotten another cat yet?

As of this moment, the answer is still no. And for all the reasons I already explained in the book.

But . . .

I'm finally thinking about it. The fact is, for the first time since Norton's death, I'm more than thinking about it. I *know* I'm going to bring another little critter into my life.

I've been feeling this urge for a while now, but things got cemented a few days ago. I had a conversation with a friend that really disturbed me. The friend was talking about how he wouldn't go on a trip to Europe because of all the disturbing things that were going on in the world—the nightmare in the Middle East, the threats of terrorism, the instability of various governments, for all I know, even the fact that Chevy Chase is being given another TV series. He was afraid to leave home. Afraid to be separated from his wife and children. It really started me thinking. It depressed me that people still haven't learned, after all our years on this earth, that we can't allow ourselves to live in fear. We can't stop living because we're afraid of dying. Or anything else. Once that happens, the bad guys have won. Planes crash—does that mean we must be too afraid to fly? Cars crash—should we never drive again? People get killed while crossing the street—should we stop walking? Terrorists are walking around in some places with dynamite strapped to their chests. People leave their spouses and we find out that endings aren't always happy and that even love sometimes hurts. Giant corporations that are supposed to protect their employees go belly up and the big guys make gazillions and the little guys get screwed. Guess what? In a lot of ways, life sucks. So what do we do? Stop living?

The more I pondered the whole topic, I realized that this doesn't just apply to the big issues—family and death and loss. It applies to the smaller, more trivial portions of life, too. It applies to how we deal with our jobs and whom we vote for and what we stand for. It certainly applies to our daily relationships with people and, dare I say it, with animals.

I loved my sixteen-plus years with Norton. I loved Norton.

Will my next cat be as brilliant or wonderful? Probably not. Will I bond with the next one the way I did with Norton? Probably not. Will my next pal be able to support me in the Nortonesque style to which I've, unfortunately, become accustomed? Probably not. But does that mean I should be scared away from starting another long-term boy/cat relationship?

Definitely not.

It won't be the same, but I'll love the next one, too.

And I'll love however many years I get to spend with the next feline that enters my life.

Of that I'm sure. Which must mean I'm ready to take the leap.

I can picture Norton, particularly when he was a kitten. He was never the greatest jumper in the world but he did like to leap. I remember once, he was sitting on my kitchen counter, which was right next to the front door of the apartment. For some reason the front door was open. I could see Norton eyeing the very top of the door, that little tiny ledge, which was maybe eight feet off the ground. The kitchen counter was perhaps three feet off the ground. Not a bad jump, considering the landing area was, at best, two inches wide. I watched Norton gather his legs up under him and go into that cat-about-to-pounce mode.

I remember I said, aloud, "You're a making a mistake. You're not going to be able to do it."

I also remember my cat looking at me. There's no question what that look said. It said, "Oh *yeah*?!"

And then he jumped.

He teetered and swayed on the top of that door, but he righted himself and there he was. In retrospect, it doesn't really matter whether he made it or not. But the fact is he did.

He took the leap.

And he was pretty damn happy about it.

So I guess that's what I'm going to do. Take the leap and be happy about it. It's what I think we should all do.

The last lesson I guess I'll learn from Norton.

Thanks, pal.